The Life and Diaries of

Field-Marshal

Sir Henry Wilson

Volume II

Marshal Foch and Sir Henry Wilson

The Life and Diaries
of
Field-Marshal
Sir Henry Wilson

Volume II

By C. E. Callwell

Legacy Books Press
Military Classics

Published by Legacy Books Press
RPO Princess, Box 21031
445 Princess Street
Kingston, Ontario, K7L 5P5
Canada

www.legacybookspress.com

The scanning, uploading, and/or distribution of this book via the Internet or any other means without the permission of the publisher is illegal and punishable by law.

This edition first published in 2023 by Legacy Books Press
1

This edition © 2023 Legacy Books Press, all rights reserved.

ISBN: 978-1-927537-81-7

First published as *Field-Marshal Sir Henry Wilson Bart., G. C. B., D. S. O.: His Life and Diaries, Volume II,* by Cassell and Company, Ltd. in 1927.

Printed and bound in the United States of America and the United Kingdom.

This book is typeset in a Times New Roman 11-point font.

Table of Contents

Chapter XIX – 1917: Two Months Unemployed 3

Chapter XX – 1917: The Setting Up of the Supreme War Council 17

Chapter XXI – 1917-18: Two and a Half Months Military Representative on the Supreme War Council 43

Chapter XXII – February and March, 1918: The Great German Offensive 77

Chapter XXIII – 1918: From April to the End of June 102

Chapter XXIV – 1918: July to September. The Turn of the Tide 135

Chapter XXV – 1918: Last Six Weeks of the Great War 157

Chapter XXVI – The Close of the Year 1918 182

Chapter XXVII – 1919: January to March. The Peace Conference in Paris 194

Chapter XXVIII – 1919: April to June. The Peace Conference in Paris 216

Chapter XXIX – 1919: July to December 245

Chapter XXX – 1920: January to June 265

Chapter XXXI – 1920: July to December 295

Chapter XXXII – 1921: January to June
. . . . 330

Chapter XXXIII – 1921-22: The Field-Marshal's Last Eight Months as C.I.G.S. 356

Chapter XXXIV – 1922: In the House of Commons 393

Chapter XXXV – The Death of the Field-Marshal 413

Index 422

About the Author 437

Chapter XIX – 1917: Two Months Unemployed

Wilson attends a meeting of the War Cabinet — Visits Ireland — The Flanders offensive started — Wilson's plan of an Inter-Allied War Committee — He accepts the Eastern Command.

Entries in Sir Henry's diary leave no doubt that when he returned to England he felt somewhat troubled as to the possible issue of the contest. Optimistic though he was by nature, he had been profoundly impressed by well authenticated reports of indiscipline amongst the French troops, and he had lost all faith in the Ribot-Painlevé Government and in French politicians as a body. Then again, he regarded the lack of co-ordination between the responsible military authorities of the Allied Powers, and the absence of a common understanding between their respective Governments, with the gravest concern. There furthermore was the question of the extensive operations in Flanders which the B.E.F. was about to undertake, and in respect to the outcome of these operations he felt misgivings.

He had stayed two nights at Blondecques, Haig's headquarters, on his way to Boulogne, and had come to the conclusion that in their views and their anticipations the Field-Marshal and his C.G.S., Kiggell, were unduly sanguine. A special responsibility had moreover been imposed upon him in connexion with this contemplated offensive on a great scale to be undertaken by the

B.E.F. For he had been informed at G.H.Q. that the War Cabinet were opposed to Sir Douglas's plans, but had been urged to give them his support when he was called before the War Cabinet on arrival in London, and he wrote as follows in his diary after getting home to Eaton Place on June 28:

> I had a long talk with Haig this morning. He told me that the War Committee had only given him authority to go on making his arrangements for an offensive, that Albert Thomas (just back from Russia) was going to report on the state of France in a fortnight, and that the War Committee would then decide whether to let Haig attack or not. The Committee were going to send for me, and very much, if not everything, would depend on what I said, and he wanted to know.
>
> I told him the same as I told Kigg last night, viz: that I did not think the French would be able to make another serious attack this year under Pétain's leadership, but that they would fight all right defensively, and would help all they could by simulating attacks, and that, as one of our main objects now was to keep the French in the field, I was absolutely convinced that we should attack all we could, right up to the time of the mud, and should then be prepared to take over.
>
> I told Haig that if he was successful in his attacks, and he later on got the chance of disengaging Ostend and Zeebrugge, or of disengaging Lille, he was not to hesitate for a moment, but should disengage Lille. Haig told me that in his opinion, if he disengaged Ostend and Zeebrugge he would form such a salient there that the Boches could not remain in front of the French. However, he was satisfied with what I was going to say to the War Cabinet.
>
> He was most nice to me, begged me to do something with my "great brains," and said that there was always a bed and a welcome at his headquarters for me. He told me that there was much "chat" about me at home, as (he reminded me) I had predicted. So I told him that if no employment was found for me I would probably get into mischief, but that it would always be the sort of mischief that had the object of beating the Boches. He said that he knew it well, that he trusted me absolutely, and that I had been invaluable to him and so on. So we parted.

Suggestions had been made to Wilson from various quarters that he ought to go into the House of Commons, and he had further been given to understand that there would be no difficulty about

Two Months Unemployed 5

fihiding him a seat; but, although he had been somewhat attracted by the idea, he would not seem to have regarded it very seriously at this time. Still, this, no doubt, was what was in his mind when he was closeted with Haig, and when he spoke of possibly getting into mischief if unemployed. He saw Carson after arriving in London, and was promised a seat in Ulster if he should care to stand; but Milner on the following day urged him not to do anything of the kind in a hurry, and gave him to understand that the Cabinet had some employment for him in their minds. He was summoned to attend a meeting of the War Cabinet on July 3, and of his experiences in Downing Street on this occasion he wrote in his diary:

> I explained the situation in France and finished by saying that, although not desperate, it undoubtedly was serious. I was struck by the tone of the Committee, except Smuts who seemed rather to revel in the idea that the situation was desperate and impossible. Of course, this is nonsense. After 35 minutes the Committee broke up, no one saying anything to me about myself, and so I walked away.

Sir Henry then went to see Milner at his house, and this appears in the diary:

> He told me that he wanted to see me as C. in C. in the Balkans vice Sarrail. This does not smile much on me, as I told him, because I can't see that there is much to be done there, even now that the Greeks have joined us; and I told Milner I was more inclined to go in for mischief. Milner did not mention my going on to the War Committee.

Wilson would appear to have had the notion that it was something of this kind which the Cabinet had in view for him.[*] On

---

[*] Sir Henry in his diary at this stage constantly speaks of the "War Committee." The arrangement actually was that there was what was called the "War Cabinet" composed of five members of the Cabinet — Mr. Lloyd George, Mr. Bonar Law, Lord Curzon, Lord Milner, and Mr. Henderson. General Smuts joined it shortly afterwards. Henderson held no portfolio, nor did Milner. Wilson could hardly have become a member of this body. He could have attended it in an advisory

his visiting the C.I.G.S. at the War Office later in the afternoon Robertson told him that there was absolutely no way of employing him at home, and Sir Henry noted in his diary:

> So I told him that I should probably get into mischief. It seems a little hard to be shuffled about the board, and, in order to suit other people, to drop from £3,000 a year to £600.
> I had nearly two hours with Smuts at the Savoy. He wants to put Egypt and Salonika under one command. I think that this might be an improvement, but I don't know enough about it. He has vague ideas of bringing in Holland, Denmark and Norway, but he does not yet understand the European questions, though he is learning, I thundered about the Foreign Office; of the absolute necessity for diplomatic action while Russia was still in the field; of the necessity for a real strong, cleancut policy and of obliging the French to conform; of the rottenness of our Foreign Office, and the vital need of the War Committee taking it by the throat. I think that I impressed him.
> He was very anxious to know what I was going to do, and I replied — mischief. Which amused him, but he said that I must be available here,
> I told him that we had all the cards, and if we were beaten we should richly deserve it. We had more men, more guns, more ammunition, more money, and the salt water. How could we be beaten?

While he happened to be with Bonar Law at 11 Downing Stteet during the forenoon of July 7, the great German daylight air raid over London took place, and he viewed it from the garden in company with the Chancellor of the Exchequer. He wrote in the diary:

> Then when Bonar and I came in from watching this show we discussed my affairs. He told me that Robertson and Haig were terrified of Lloyd George. This made me smile. They are terrified of his mad schemes and not of him. Then he told me that all the members of the War Committee were very fond of me and had an intense admiration for me.

---

capacity, just as Robertson did, and as he did himself when he became C.I.G.S. some months later, but he would merely have been in the position of counsellor.

It, however, turned out that Bonar Law could see no post that was suitable for him at the moment, and could only beg him to exercise patience. They then discussed the progress of the war, and Bonar Law expressed himself as opposed to Haig's offensive because of the loss that it would entail, to which Sir Henry rejoined that "the loss of men might have been a good reason for not entering into the war, but a bad reason for not fighting when in the war." Bonar Law entertained hopes of the Irish Convention, then sitting; but of this assemblage and of its labours, Wilson entertained no hopes whatever, and he came away from Downing Street with an impaked confidence in the War Cabinet.

In so far as the daylight air-raid was concerned, his diary serves to show that considerable trouble arose at the War Office in connexion with that unpleasant incident. Two ak squadrons had, as it happened, been removed from England and sent over to France during the very week before the raid took place, this, in spite of a protest from Lord French, which protest had, however, somehow gone astray. The War Cabinet were much incensed in consequence, and Wilson wrote in the diary:

> The whole thing is rather mysterious, and meanwhile the House of Commons has so far lost its head— and so has the Government— that there is to be a secret session to-night at 8.30 p.m., and I hear that a couple of squadrons are to be brought back from France. How the Boches will laugh!

Of a meeting with the Adjutant-General, Sir N. Macready, at the War Office, he wrote on the 9th:

> He says that this Government is worse than Asquith's, that there are 500,000 men available in Government employ and that they can't be got, that in consequence he gets very few recruits; and he showed me his monthly returns for January last, where he got 44,000 men, this number steadily dropped, and last month (June) he only got 25,000 and now he did not expect more than 18,000 in July.
>
> Of course, all this is most scandalous work. The Government is afraid to comb out, and afraid of the north of England, and terrified of Ireland, and so they are losing 1,000,000 men. What a scandalous thing. Macready said that he had written the strongest letter which had

ever emanated from the War Office, so strong that the Army Council would not sign it, but endorsed it and said they agreed with it — the whole theory of the Council being a corporate body! Macready told me that he had made up the forces in France to within 18,000 of estimate by emptying the convalescent homes, etc., which, he said, was a monstrous thing, and I agree.

Macready also told me that he was so disgusted with the Mesopotamia Report,[*] and the evident intention of the Government to "cart" the soldiers and save Hardinge, Meyer & Co., that he had ordered a Court of Inquiry on the soldiers, and had put Rundle on as President. He says that the evidence will damn the civilians and to some extent save the soldiers — or some of them.

Wilson arrived in Ireland on July 12 — his first visit to his own coiintry since before the War — and in the first instance he proceeded to Garvagh, a house on the Currygrane estate where his brother Jemmy was living, as Currygrane House was too large for him. Lord French was over in Ireland on inspection duty, so Sir Henry went on to Galway by arrangement to meet him and he wrote of this visit in his diary:

> I wandered about the town; there were a good many Sinn Fein flags. Amazing. We went to the old fishing village of Cladagh, which is intensely loyal and has all its men either in the Navy or the Army. I had a talk with some old men. We were mobbed by women shouting, "Long live the King; Long live England." A curious experience in Galway.

Lord French held a review in Eyre Square, and from Galway the party proceeded to Belfast, where Wilson found himself warmly welcomed by the Ulster leaders. They were very anxious that he should stand for North Belfast, where a vacancy was expected very shortly, and where, he was told, he would "get in as round as a hoop." He promised to give them an answer soon, and he wrote in the diary:

---

[*] The Report of the Royal Commission on the Mesopotamian Campaign, which had recently appealed.

Two Months Unemployed

I was very much struck by the number of people who knew me; and when Sir Robert Liddell introduced me at the club as "General Sir Henry Wilson" and then added, "our General Wilson," the reception was instantaneous.

He returned to England more convinced than ever that conscription ought to be introduced in Ireland without delay, and this not merely because the men were so urgently wanted for the effective prosecution of the war, but also because he believed that the measure was called for in the interests of law and order in Ireland itself.

Duncannon and others were busy organizing a party in the House of Commons to bring pressure on the War Cabinet, and to oblige that body to adopt Wilson's ideas concerning the plenary tapping of the existing resources of the United Kingdom in manpower, and concerning the vital importance of, by some means or other, eliminating Turkey and Bulgaria from the struggle. Sir Henry had indeed come to the conclusion that, with the honourable exception of Smuts, no member of the War Cabinet believed in the possibility of victory. In frustration of its ineptitude and incapacity, Macready informed him that, whereas the Government departments had in March been commanded to hand over 225,000 men to be recruited as soldiers, the Adjutant-General's representatives had not, up to May 25, secured one single man from this source. Just at this time Sir E. Carson was transferred by Lloyd George from the position of First Lord of the Admitalty to that of Member of the War Cabinet without portfolio. Sir E. Geddes taking his place at the Admiralty; and Wilson was informed that the reason for this change was that Carson had refused to remove certain of his subordinates at the dictation of the Prime Minister.

From two of those present at a recent big conference in Paris — there had been no fewer than 43 representatives at the table — Wilson gathered that its proceedings had been even more than usually inept and unprofitable. There had been a wrangle about sending a division from Salonika to Palestine, and no decision had been come to even about that.* Russians, Rumanians, Greeks, Portuguese, Siamese, and French had given vent to impassioned harangues, but nothing whatever had been settled. The question of replacing Sarrail, as to the expechency of which the War Cabinet and all our military authorities were absolutely at one, had not even been mentioned. This particular fiasco was, however, for the moment forgotten in Cabinet circles owing to a bolt from the blue during the progress of a meeting in 10 Downing Street on July 26. It was the practice at these reunions for a good many people, besides the actual Members of Cabinet and the secretariat, to be present, and by one of these interlopers Wilson was furnished with a spirited account of what had occurred, and this is duly recorded in the pages of the diary:

> There were present Bonar Law, Curzon, Carson, Henderson, Barnes, Bob Cecil. At this meeting Henderson had said that he was going to Paris with four Russian Socialists (of whom two were Boche) and with Ramsay Macdonald, to make arrangements for the Socialist gathering in Stockholm, where he [Henderson] was going to take part.† There was to be a preliminary meeting in England on August 4. Henderson wanted a destroyer to take the party across the Channel the following day.
>
> Bonar Law said, in Lloyd George's absence, that he did not know what to do; Curzon made some pompous observations; Carson said he was a new boy; Barnes did not utter a word; and Bob Cecil asked if he was to issue passports. Henderson said that of course he was to issue passports and to order a destroyer. These things were done, and the party went over yesterday. This is a shocking business.

---

* One British division (the 60th) had been moved from Macedonia to Egypt during the month of June, The dispute here referred to must have been with regard to me move of a second. This (the 10th) proceeded from Salonika to the Nile Delta in September, raising the number of divisions in the Egypt-Palestine theatre to seven.

† Mr. Ramsay Macdonald's pronounced defeatist proclivities, as made manifest during the war, had made him obnoxious to patriotic citizens; and the Sailors and Firemen's Union had placed a ban on his taking ship from the United Kingdom. Mr. Henderson resigned from the War Cabinet in consequence of the strong feeling which his action in this matter had, in spite of his loyal services to the nation's cause, aroused.

Wilson dined with Smuts a night or two after this, and he there heard about the recent abortive Paris Conference. Smuts had been shocked by the experience, pronounced it to have been the most futile exhibition of incompetence that he had ever witnessed, and said that such meetings really must be stopped. He entirely agreed with Wilson's contention that there ought to be a body composed of three soldiers, English, French, and Italian, with suitable staffs and full knowledge, who would be empowered to draw up plans of attack and defence along the whole line from Nieuport to Egypt; Smuts, moreover, declared that Wilson must be the English soldier. He realized that something of this kind was imperatively needed, and that the existing procedure of huge conferences ought to cease, and he was much incensed with Henderson for taking Ramsay Macdonald to Paris. But when Wilson tried to persuade Smuts to take up the question of conscription for Ireland, the South African statesman displayed no inclination to intervene in that particular matter. "He called me the Hindenburg and Ludendorff of this country," Wilson wrote in the diary, "and was altogether friendly."

Sir Henry was enjoying a very interesting conversation with Admiral Hall, the Director of Naval Intelligence, on the following day, and was being made acquainted with much that was very secret concerning German communications with President Wilson, with Mexico, and with the Sinn Feiners, when the First Lord's secretary "came flying in to ask Hall whether he knew if Macdonald had gone over in a destroyer with Henderson, and said there was the devil to pay going on at a War Committee over the way! Good." There is also the further entry in the diary:

> The Lord rang up before dinner to tell me that he had asked Bonar Law about Henderson and Ramsay Macdonald,[*] and there had been no end of a business over it. A Cabinet had sat, and the whole place was rocking. Bonar Law begged the Lord not to ask the question, but he had stuck to it.

Haig started his offensive in Flanders on July 31, and he made a very good beginning; for Gough's Army, and the French on

---

[*] In the House of Commons.

Gough's left, secured all their objectives on a long front to the north-east of Ypres, took 5,000 prisoners, and recovered the whole of the ground which had been lost on the occasion of the first German gas attack at the end of April, 1915. Rain, unfortunately, came on and interfered seriously with further operations, just as wet weather was to Awart this Flanders offensive during practically the whole of its prolonged duration. Foch arrived in London with Ribot and Painlevé on August 6 for another of those recurring civil and notary conferences that were so popular with the politicians, but which never appreciably advanced the cause of the Entente. Foch told Wilson when they met that he was very anxious to make progress with plans for 1918, but that he found it difficult to arouse any interest in the subject on this side of the Channel. He favoured the idea of sending an expedition to Alexandretta so as to cut the railway near there, and he also would like to withdraw some of the British and French troops from the Salonika theatre as soon as a few Greek divisions were ready to take their place.[*] He did not hold with the idea that Salonika should be evacuated altogether, because the result of such a withdrawal would be to lose the services of the Serb forces which were under Sarrail. Foch, moreover, gave Wilson the following account next evening of events since the party from France had arrived in London:

> He told me that Painlevé, on arrival yesterday about 5 o'clock, went straight from Charing Cross to see Lloyd George, who was in the country, and that he lost his way and did not get back to the Ritz till 2.30 a. m.; but he saw Lloyd George. Poor Ribot wandered about all this morning, having no one to talk to, as Painlevé said that he did not wish to be called till 11 a.m.
> The first meeting of the Conference took place at mid-day at Downing Street, with Lloyd George in the chair. Lloyd George was very "*maladroit*";[†] he was tired and peevish, he wanted to send troops

---

[*] Greece had broken off relations with the Central Powers on June 30 and was organizing her forces, with French and British assistance in respect to war material.

[†] "Clumsy".

and guns to Italy *now*, he wanted to wire to Russia to say they were conducting their business badly, he said that we always were late. But he did not approve of Foch's proposals to get ready for the 1918 campaign. Foch thinks Lloyd George is beaten. He said that the Conference was an absolute fiasco, even though it had agreed to another of our divisions being withdrawn from Salonika to be sent to Egypt — the only decision reached. The meeting in the afternoon was even worse than in the morning, and, as there was no agenda, the talking became general. Lloyd George, who was in the chair, did nothing, and the whole thing was deplorable. Smuts was not present either morning or evening.

Sir Henry saw Smuts next day and told him how disappointed Foch had been at the proceedings of this latest conference, whereupon Smuts declared that he entirely agreed as to such gatherings being pure waste of time, and he moreover expressed his intention of attending no more of them. Smuts also told Wilson that Lloyd George was now eager to send ten divisions and 400 heavy guns to Italy at once, and that Milner was rather taken with this idea. Smuts, however, fully realised that there was no time for such a transfer of force to take place before the bad weather might be expected to set in, and that it would entirely dislocate Haig's plans, Wilson wrote in his diary:

> I warned Smuts that the French were getting more and more tired, and that next year they would like to change the theatre and have fighting carried on either in Italy or Turkey rather than in France, and that this was a factor to be considered. He said to me, "You must help us by doing some hard thinking," to which I replied that I was not in possession of the facts and that ''without facts hard thinking was simply waste of time!"

A few days later Sir Henry was sent for by Robertson. He was asked if he would accept a Home Command, and it was settled that he should take up the Eastern Command on September 1. He also heard that Lloyd George and Lord French had between them hit upon a scheme under which Robertson was in future to submit his plans to a military triumvirate composed of French, Wilson and another general; but Sir Henry realized at once that this was a ridiculous and unworkable plan. He said so when he saw French, to whom he unfolded his own plan of a superior Inter-Allied staff, charged with dealing with the whole of the various fronts, a staff which would set to work at once on plans for the year 1918. French thought this an excellent idea, and arrangements were made for Sir Henry to have a talk with Lloyd George on the subject, the meeting taking place on August 23. Of what passed, Wilson wrote in his diary:

> Found Lloyd George and Philip Kerr there. A long talk, and got back here at 7 o'clock. Johnnie was quite good about Haig, who, he said, was all right in fighting and in asking for all that he could get. Lloyd George then asked me for my plan.
>
> I first told him that I thought his plan of Johnnie and me and another soldier to overhaul Robertson's work was a bad plan and unworkable, and unfair to Robertson. I then disclosed my plan of three Prime Ministers and three soldiers, to be over all C.I.G.S.s and to draw up plans for the whole theatre from Nieuport to Baghdad. I told him that I had had this plan in mind for 2½ years, and I made it clear that it was not aimed at Robertson, or Haig, or anybody. I told him that if he was to remove Robertson, *now*, and to place me as C.I.G.S., I would still press for my plan, as being the only one which would allow us really to draw up a combined plan of operations.
>
> He was distinctly taken. He explained the position as follows: He was satisfied with Haig, but dissatisfied with Robertson. He was quite clear in his mind that we were not winning the war by our present plans, and that we never should on our present lines; but he did not know how, or what we should do, and he had no means of checking or altering Robertson's and Haig's plans though he knew they were too parochial. He said that he was not in the position, nor had he the knowledge, to bring out alternative plans and to insist upon their adoption, as it would always be said that he was overruling the soldiers. It was because of his profound disgust that he had thought of forming a committee of Johnnie and me and another, but he now quite agreed with me that that would not work and that my plan was infinitely better. He ordered me to go and see Milner and Bonar Law and lay my plan before them.
>
> I demurred, but he said that he wished it. He is evidently inclined to stop Haig's offensive in another ten days because of our losses, which, he says, we cannot stand. He was inclined to substitute Milner and Painlevé and Sonnino on my High War Committee, but I told him that, if he did, he must give those men the power to commit their

Two Months Unemployed 15

Governments, and to this he quite agreed. Altogether he rose well at my proposals.

He told Johnnie when I was out of the room that he would nominate me as the English soldier on this War Committee. He realizes that Russia is done and that America is a long way oif. I rubbed in the five months of mud and snow (½ November— ½ April)* during which we (and Italy) can do nothing, though the weather a little farther down the line in Asia Minor and Egypt is perfect.

Much encouraged by the favourable hearing which the Prime Minister had accorded him. Sir Henry seized early opportunities for placing his ideas before Milner and Bonar Law, and he also explained his project to Carson. They all three highly approved of his proposal, and he was well satisfied in consequence with the attitude which the War Cabinet seemed disposed to take up in connexion with a subject that had for a long time been dear to his heart. The setting up of the Supreme War Council at Versailles a few weeks later was indeed the direct result of these conversations which took place in England at the end of August. It should be mentioned that Wilson had a few days before this been telephoned for by Lord Derby to come to the War Office in connexion with quite a different matter, and Sir Henry recorded their discussion in his diary thus:

> He told me that at a meeting of the War Committee this morning they had decided unanimously that I should go to America and put the English case before them. I asked who I would be under, and he said he thought Northcliffe. I flatly refused to go. We then went over to see Bonar and he tried to persuade me to go; but I said that I could not see any good in it and that I would not serve under Northcliffe, which rather irritated Bonar because he said Northcliffe represented the British Government, to which I naturally replied by asking whether we had not got an Ambassador.

During these few weeks of unemployment he had spent several

---

* The B.E.F. was to find, to its cost, in the coming March, that March, at least, was not necessarily a "mud month."

days at Grove End, digging and gardening, as was his wont on such occasions. But he had also kept in touch with the progress of Haig's operations by studying the official reports as they came in. He had never shared the confidence entertained at G.H.Q. that the line would be pushed far enough forward before the winter to disengage Ostend and Zeebrugge. On the other hand, he fully realized the advantages that would accrue to the Allies, from the defensive point of view, supposing that all the high ground to the east and to the north-east of Ypres overlooking the great Flanders plain, extending to beyond Bruges and Ghent, were to be wrested from the enemy before the close of operations. Nor was anyone more alive than he to the vital importance of keeping the Germans occupied along this section of the Western Front for the present, so as to afford the French troops and the French people ample time to recover from the untoward depression that had descended upon them after the in ilitary disappointments of April and May under Nivelle.

Chapter XX – 1917: The Setting Up of the Supreme War Council

The Eastern Command — Lord French and Sir Henry at a War Cabinet meeting — The Caporetto disaster — Wilson proceeds to Italy with Lloyd George and others — Rapallo — Definite decision to set up the Supreme War Council — Wilson at the Italian Front — Clemenceau becomes French Prime Minister — Wilson returns to London — The Supreme War Council constituted.

Wilson took over charge of the Eastern Command from Sir J. Wolfe-Murray on September 1, and the arrangement suited him well. The pay was a consideration; owing to his head-quarters being in London he was able to reside at his house in Eaton Place, and, although he had every reason to expect that he would ere long be employed in some capacity more directly concerned with the actual prosecution of the war, the appointment in the meantime gave him occupation. The fact of being stationed in London, moreover, enabled him to keep in touch with his friends in the Cabinet, his friends at the War Office, and his friends in Parliament. He wrote in the diary on the 4th:

> Foch came to see me at 10 p.m. He came over because Cadoma, who is doing well (he took Mt. Gabrielle and 1,000 prisoners to-day), wants the help of some guns. Foch is in favour of giving him too heavy guns, but Robertson and Haig oppose him, with the result that

Haig has agreed to Antoine* sending 50 medium guns if Pétain can find 50 from the rest of his front — which Foch says is impossible, and Haig, who has 800 heavy guns at Ypres, won't send one. This is unfortunate, especially as Haig is not going to do anything really serious at Ypres this year.[†]

Foch says that Lloyd George was entirely on his side, but Bonar Law was against, and Curzon and Milner said little. Haig, Robertson and Kiggell are running the maxim of superior forces at the decisive point, etc., to death, and I told Foch we should never have any plan worth a d—— until we got my Superior War Council, and he agreed.

The next day he wrote:

I believe that Lloyd George, knowing that Haig will not do any good, has allowed him to keep all his guns, etc., so that he can, later on, say, "Well, I gave you everything. I even allowed you to spoil the Italian offensive. And now, owing to gross miscalculation and incapacity you have entirely failed to do anything serious except lose a lot of men." And in this indictment he will include Robertson, and then get rid of both of them.

On September 14 there appears:

The Lord dined last night with Montagu of Beaulieu. Montagu said that we were six months behind the Boches both in design and in output of aeroplanes; that we had only 1,100 aeroplanes on our front and were faced by 1,600 Boche aeroplanes; that the Boches would presently try and make life in London insupportable; that the Americans could not help us for a year, and so on.

I saw Amery before lunch and had a talk with him. I asked him what was being done about my plan for a Superior War Council. He replied— nothing. As I said — here we are at September 14 of our fourth winter, not only with no common plan for the whole front, but with no plan for our small section of front. I quoted the case of sending Cadorna 100 guns some 10 days ago, and now Montagu's

---

* General Antoine was in command of the French Army which was operating on the left of Gough's Army.

[†] So it turned out; but the Field-Marshal at this time still entertained hopes of consummating his far-reaching plan.

story of our 1,100 aeroplanes against 1,600 Boches, as proving once more the want of superior direction and of common plan. I quoted also a letter I had received yesterday from Sidney Clive from Compiègne, which said "the relations are very smooth here and will be for another three weeks. No letters pass between the C. in C.s. Each works out his own salvation." This is further proof of absolute failure in common effort.

On the following day Lady Wilson and he went to Chequets to stay with Sir A. Lee, and they found Sir E. Geddes, who was now First Lord of the Admiralty, there as a fellow guest. Geddes expressed himself as anxious to withdraw as many men as could be safely spared from France, so that they might be employed on shipbuilding, agriculture, and so forth, at home, but Sir Henry wrote in his diary:

> I told him that I also want to take troops away from France during the mud months, not to grow cabbages here, but to beat the Turks, and I asked him if he could ferry over 8 or 10 divisions; and he said that he certainly could. He told me that the Sinai railway had a capacity of 12 divisions. I would improve this, and also land troops on the Palestine coast, and see if I could knock out the Turk this winter. He described how he would tackle the U-boats. He will confine these to certain channels and certain seas, then nose them out with these wonderful new instruments, then go for them with destroyers and kites and deep-sea charges. He again said he could carry all the divisions I want to Egypt and Palestine this winter, but he must have good notice.

The Prime Minister had — amongst other projects — contemplated the possibility of dispatching an army from the Western Front to the Gulf of Alexandretta, to act against the Ottoman communications with Palestine and wim Mesopotamia. But Wilson's idea, as is evident from the above, was to land the troops — or, at all events, the bulk of them — at Alexandria, where ample facilities existed, a very different proposition from disembarking them in the Gulf of Alexandretta, where, for all practical purposes, there were no facilities at all.

Encouraging tidings came to hand from Flanders on September 21 and 22; for Plumer's Second Army had delivered an attack on the 21st which had resulted in the assailants gaining the whole of their objectives and also making large captures. This success was followed up by another satisfactory day's work on the 26th. But, even so, the progress of.the operations was proving slower than G.H.Q. had anticipated, owing very largely to the abnormal rains that had been falling at frequent intervals during the late summer. The steady decline in recruiting was giving the War Office serious grounds for anxiety, as the efforts of the Military Members of the Army Council to induce the War Cabinet to take the man-power question with the seriousness that the situation demanded, were proving of little effect. The closing days of September were also, it will be remembered, signalized by a succession of air raids by night over London, which caused both loss of fife and material damage, and which may have helped to strengthen the Prime Minister's dissatisfaction with the conduct of the war as a whole. Mr. Lloyd George, at all events, rang up Sir Henry at 10 p.m. on October 5, wanting to see him that night, and sent a car to bring him; and of the important interview that then took place, the following account appears in Wilson's diary:

> I found him at 20 Queen Anne's Gate (Sir G. Riddell's house). Johnnie French was there. We three [Lloyd George, Johnnie and I] had along talk. Lloyd George is mad to knock the Turks out during the winter on the plan that I explained to him on August 25, his difficulty being that Haig was hostile (which he thought natural) and Robertson was mulish, which he thought maddening. He wanted to know my advice. I repeated all I had said on August 23, and expressed the strong belief that, if a really good scheme was thoroughly well worked out, we could clear the Turks out of Palestine, and very likely knock them completely out, during the mud months, without in any way interfering with Haig's operations next spring and summer.
>
> I asked Lloyd George about a superior organkation, and he said that, of course, was the best plan, but the French and Italian Governments made it impossible to get such an organization started; therefore, he was reverting to his former idea of calling me in to examine Robertson's plans. Lloyd

1917: The Setting Up of the Supreme War Council

George told me to see Carson as soon as possible and try and persuade him to agree to action in Palestine during the mud months. Lloyd George said that Milner and Smuts were already persuaded to that view. Lloyd George wanted me to go down to Birchington to-morrow to see Carson, but I really thought this a little hot.

Lloyd George has no illusions about Haig's 'Victory" of yesterday.* At the same time I again insisted on Lloyd George giving Haig *all* the men and guns that he possessed, up to the time of the mud, to which he agreed. The fact is that Lloyd George is profoundly dissatisfied, but does not know what to do.

Wilson met Lloyd George and Lord French at dinner on the 10th, and he was then told that a meeting of the War Cabinet was to be held on the following day, at which French and he were to be present. The Prime Minister was much concerned at the very heavy losses that were being incurred during the Flanders offensive; and it was already only too apparent that the somewhat sanguine hopes that had been entertained by as to recovering possession of the Belgian littoral were going to be grievously disappointed. That the operations had been greatly retarded by exceptionally bad weather was a matter of common knowledge. But Sir Henry had, even at the time when the attack was opened and when there was no reason to suppose that the late summer and the autumn would be signalized by an unwonted rainfall, doubted the possibility of Haig's troops reaching Ostend before the winter.

Lloyd George and the War Cabinet did not, perhaps, sufficiently realize the vital importance of keeping the enemy occupied while the French troops were recovering from the events of May and June. How greatly enemy morale was suffering from the steady, if slow, pressure being exercised under Haig's directions has, moreover, only been made known to the Allies by Ludendorff since the conclusion of the war. But, be that as it may,

---

* The Second and Fifth Armies had made a substantial advance on October 4, securing some very valuable high ground and taking about 5,000 prisoners.

the Prime Minister's dissatisfaction in connexion with the Flanders offensive was to become a potent factor in bringing about the setting up of the Supreme War Council at Versailles. The Prime Minister had told Robertson, so he said, that "the patient after a three years' course of treatment not being yet cured, he thinks it advisable to call in another couple of specialists." This meeting of the War Cabinet therefore took place on October 11, and Sir Henry wrote of it in his diary:

> Lloyd George made clear, good statement of present situation. Invoked the precedent of August 5, 1914, for calling in Johnnie and me; no slur re Robertson and Haig. Referred to Russian collapse, which gets worse; to French cessation of fighting, and said my forecast had been fully justified. Haig says the French won't do any serious attack in 1918. Italy has ceased fighting, and is having grave internal difficulties. America is moving slowly, and tonnage is a terrible difficulty. Then Lloyd George referred to the condition of Germany, Austria, Bulgaria, and Turkey. He said that the present was a most critical period for all countries, and that this morning's meeting was a turning point in the war. He then gave four alternatives:
> 1. Concentrate all possible on West.
> 2. Fight on West with present forces, and use our forces now in Egypt, Mesopotamia, etc., to do as much as possible.
> 3. Military and diplomatic attack on Turkey, on Bulgaria, on Austria.
> 4. Wait for Russia and America.
> Johnnie and I are to be given all papers, etc., that we want.

Foch was over in London with Painlevé, and Wilson found that the French Chief of the General StaflF thought it too late by this date for undertaking a campaign in Syria, and held the view that the winter ought to be devoted to making guns, aircraft and other war material. Foch expressed himself as opposed to the idea that the British could do all the fighting, and could win, in 1918; and he told Wilson that the French were now constructing 2,000 aeroplanes a month, and that they proposed to have 4,000 on their front, whereas we only had 1,200. Sir Henry had that afternoon, as he wrote in his diary, "worked on papers in Johnnie's room at Horse Guards at Wellington's table," and during the following few days he was busy drawing up a memorandum for the War Cabinet.

1917: The Setting Up of the Supreme War Council

He was coming to think, like Foch, that it had now become too late in the season to plan and to carry out a decisive attack on the Turks during the coming winter. In the circumstances he came to the conclusion that the matters of most vital importance were to establish a superior inter-Allied war organization, and to increase the stock of war material of all kinds. He met Painlevé and "another Minister (with a snub-nose)," over from France, who expressed themselves as most anxious that he should go back to Paris; but he declared that, unless a Superior War Council were started, there was no place for him at the French capital. He wrote in the diary on October 16:

> I am getting on with my State paper. This morning Macready came over to see Johnnie French and me, and brought casualty lists. Some of the figures are startling. Since July 1, 1916, up to October 10 last, Haig has lost 900,000 in killed, wounded, and missing, not sick, and of these 80,000 are missing. As regards the future, it appears that our average monthly wastage in France is 50,000, and an optimistic estimate of intake is 30,000, though 25,000 will probably be nearer the mark. This shows a monthly deficit of 20,000-25,000. So that a year hence, with the past to guide us, we shall be 240,000-300,000 men deficient, all infantry; and we start to-day with a deficit of 48,000. This is a serious state of affairs.

Next day there is the entry:

> To-night Lloyd George, Johnnie and I dined again at Johnnie's house. It became very clear to me to-night that Lloyd George means to get Robertson out, and means to curb the powers of the C. in C. in the field. This is what I have been advising for 2½ years, and this is what the whole of my paper is directed at — not to getting Robertson out, but to forming a Superior Direction over all the CG.S.s and C. in C.s.
> Lloyd George said to-night that the French were favourably inclined, and this agrees with what Painlevé told me last week. Lloyd George refered to the Press campaign which is working up against him on the basis that he is interfering with the soldiers.

The memorandums which French and Wilson respectively were drawing up were practically completed by the 19th, and

Wilson wrote in his diary:

> It seems to me that there will be a holy row over all this, and, of course, the Frock Coats will quote Johnnie and me against Haig and Robertson. We must avoid this as much as possible. It is the system and machinery that I am aiming at, and not the men.

Sir Henry breakfasted with Lord Derby a few days later and the Secretary of State then mentioned that he had not yet shown the two memorandums to Robertson. "He said that Johnnie's was too personal and mine too unanswerable, and that if they were shown to Haig and Robertson there would be no end of a tow, which might lead to the resignation of Haig, Robertson and himself." Lloyd George also had thought that French's paper was too personal; so Wilson and Hankey went through it with the Field-Marshal, toned down some of its expressions, and a day or two later the two papers were handed to Robertson. But just at this juncture news arrived of the reverse to the Italians of Caporetto, and by the 28th of the month it had become obvious that a very grave position of affairs had arisen in Venetia, and that unless assistance was sent to Cadorna as speedily as possible the situation might become hopeless.

Wilson wrote in his diary on October 29:

> Robertson went off to Italy on Saturday night. Macdonogh tells me that he does not think we shall take Paschendaele village, and he says that there are not more than 8 or 9 Boche divisions down in Italy. I really am getting anxious about the end of this war, and I feel that if we don't get hold of the situation, it will take charge of us.
>
> Johnnie Baird and Edmund Talbot in after dinner. They had not much news, but Johnnie says that all programmes for the Air Services are held up because Smuts goes to Sheffield for the Freedom of that town, and now down to Tonypandy to try and placate those wretched South Wales miners. Tanks held up. Air Services held up. No superior direction. We may lose this war yet if we try.

Next day he wrote:

> I had a long talk with Winston. He is enthusiastically in favour of

1917: The Setting Up of the Supreme War Council

my paper, and has written a whole paper — which he sent me — on the paragraph in which I urge an enormous increase of material — guns, tanks, aeroplanes, railways, etc. Winston's paper is admirable, and full of ideas. Winston is quite clear that we must have a Superior Direction. He tells me that Lloyd George thinks this also, but is afraid to take the plunge because of the opposition of Haig, Robertson and Asquith.

I told Winston that I did not think Asquith would take up the challenge for one moment, for neither Haig nor Robertson would have a leg to stand on. I quoted the new case of the French sending 4 divisions to Italy and our only sending 2, as another example of how we lose a chance of getting a grip of the situation. Winston entirely agreed. I quoted also my example of the different strategies — ours and the Boches': 1. We take Bullecourt, they take Rumania; 2, we take Messines, they take Russia; 3, we don't take Paschendaele, they take Italy.

The Boches took Udine last night, the G.H.Q. of Cadorna. This is a serious blow. I rather doubt if the Italians now will stand behind the Tagliamento. We really must get on with our plans.

He was summoned to Downing Street to meet Lloyd George on the evening of the 31st, and he was then told that the War Cabinet had decided to set up a Superior War Council and had asked Painlevé, who was still in London, to assent. Lloyd George, moreover, showed him a draft laying down the functions of the British Military Member of the proposed Council. All plans were to be submitted to the Military Member by the C.I.G.S., and he would have the power to alter plans, and even to make fresh ones, without reference to the C.I.G.S. He could, furthermore, call for any information that he requited. Wilson was to be the Military Member, as indeed he knew already, and he was fairly well satisfied with the proposals. Lloyd George sent for him again two days later, November 2, to tell him that France and England had decided to establish a Superior War Council, that Pétain was in full agreement, and that Lloyd George, Smuts and he himself were to start for Italy nest day. "The whole future of the war rests on your shoulders," Lloyd George said to him; "you must get us out of the awful rut we are in. I don't like your politics, but I do like and admire you as a man and a soldier." Wilson wrote in his diary:

Kigg came in for an hour before dinner. He pleaded that in another eight days Douglas Haig would take enough of the Paschendaele Ridge to make himself secure for the winter, and that this operation ought not to he stopped. Also that Haig had another secret operation in view, which promised satisfactory results provided no more troops were sent to Italy. Kigg said that the Boches had skinned the whole front in a manner they had never done before, and that this was a great chance. I could not help sa5dng that, if this was so — i.e. the skinning — then all our attacks had had a very disappointing result, as they had not saved Russia, nor Italy, nor prevented the Boches weakening the front in face of us.

I got Tit Willow down here after dinner and told him I had been given this new appointment and that, of course, he would have to come with me.

Before leaving for Paris next day Wilson went to see Lord French, and he records in the diary:

Johnnie, with his back to me and facing the fire, said, "l want to apologize to you for not haying resigned when Asquith refused to allow you to be my Chief of the Staff." This was so sweet of him, and we shook hands without a word more.

The party for Paris consisted of Lloyd George, Smuts, Hankey, Maurice and Duncannon, and on the journey Wilson heard that a project was on foot of sending Haig to Italy to command the Italians, French and British in that theatre. He, however, expressed the view that the only thing we could reasonably hope for was that the French and British forces in that country should be combined as one army under a British general. It appeared that Pétain had put forward the proposal that the B.E.F. should extend its right and take over a considerable length of front at present held by the French, and that Pétain himself should thus be set free to extend his right and to include Italy and the Italian Army.

Wilson wrote in his diary before leaving Paris:

Breakfasted here in the Crillon, also General Pershing and his A.D.G. Smuts, Maurice and Hankey. Lloyd George was anxious to get Pershing to come down to Italy with us, and said that the President U.S. had agreed in principle to the Supreme Council. Lloyd George

1917: The Setting Up of the Supreme War Council

then explained to Pershing the reasons for the formation of this superior body. He quoted the Champagne offensive as having failed to save Rumania, and the present offensive as having failed to save Italy. He said that we were in a most critical condition and within a shade of final disaster, and that our one hope was the Superior Council. Lloyd George put his case very well indeed.

Later I met Haig walking with Lloyd George in the Champs Elysees — I was with Smuts. He is going on attacking for another 10 days along the Paschendaele Ridge in order to reach a certain point, which he says is essential for future defence. He is, of course, opposed to any more of his divisions going to Italy.

Lloyd George, Smuts, Maurice, and I lunched with Painlevé, Bouillon, Klotz, Barthou. A draft for the formation of the Supreme Council was put up by the Frenchmen; but we did not like it and took it away, and later Smuts, Maurice and I amended it and we take it down to Italy to-night.

The contingent from England, with Painlevé, Franklin Bouillon and other French representatives, left Paris that evening and they arrived at Rapallo on the following evening. Sir Henry mentions in his diary that Lloyd George remarked to him, as their train was passing Marengo,"You are our Kellermann and you must save us in our desperate situation. If you cannot, then no one can." They found Orlando, Sonnino, General Porro (the Italian Chief of Staff), Foch and Robertson at Rapallo, and a meeting of the French and British representatives was held at once. Foch explained the situation as he envisaged it, saying that the Second Italian Army (the one that had been involved in the Caporetto disaster) had practically ceased to count, that the First, Third and Fourth Armies, although still intact, were not in a satisfactory condition, that the High Command was virtually non-existent, that the staffs were inefficient, and that no orders were ever carried out. He thought that Cadorna ought to be removed, that the Duc d'Aosta ought to be put in his place, that the whole G.H.Q. Staff must be reorganized, and that if these changes were carried out, and with the assistance of the British and French who were on their way (or were arriving), the Italians might stand on the Piave. Robertson agreed, although he was rather more pessimistic.

Wilson wrote in the diary:

After dinner I had a long talk with Robertson. He is opposed to this Supreme Council. He does not see how it can work without responsibility, nor why it should be given responsibility. He thought that it might work if Maurice was member, but not otherwise.

I asked him if, looking back over two years, he was satisfied with the conduct of the war, and whether he would act in the same way again, and he replied in the affirmative to both questions. Since he has been C.I.G,S. we have lost Rumania, Russia and Italy, and have gained Bullecourt, Messines and Paschendaele.

I then (midnight) went to see Foch. Foch tells me that he keeps his present post as C.G.S, in Paris and comes to Versailles as well.* This is an amazing thing, as it is the essence of the plan that the Military Member of the Supreme Council should be absolutely detached and independent.

Next day (November 6) Wilson's record reads:

I saw Lloyd George, and then Smuts, separately. I told them both of the three points of last night, viz: 1. Robertson's opposition; 2. Foch's dual capacity; 3. The vital and pressing necessity of settling the question of command of combined British and French forces, and the relation (subordination?) of this officer to the Italian C. in C.

During the day we have had an interminable conference. The representatives were:

Lloyd George, Smuts, Robertson, Self.

Painlevé, Bouillon, the French Ambassador in Rome, Foch, Weygand.

Orlando, Sonnino, Italian War Minister, Porro.

The net upshot is that the position is very serious. Porro admitted to loss of 200,000 men, all prisoners and unwounded, and 1,800 guns "and more." He thought that, with the assistance of 15 British and French divisions, he could stand on the Piave. He was very nervous about the Asiago Plateau. In short the man does not know where he is, or what to do. Cordorna is being removed from the supreme command
and is put on the Supreme Council.

Finally, it was decided that the Supreme Council should be

---

* It had been proposed that the Supreme Council should have its seat at Versailles, but at the moment this was merely a suggestion, the Italians and the U.S. not yet having been consulted.

1917: The Setting Up of the Supreme War Council

definitely established, should have its first meeting to-morrow, and should then and there send its Military Members up to the front to see and report on the measures necessary. I got Robertson to wire for Plumer to come down at once and to take command — hope — of both French and English. This is the net outcome of all our deliberations, Foch also is to be taken away from his present post as C.G.S. in Paris.

The agreement, arrived at on November 7, at Rapallo, setting up a Supreme War Council, provided that this body should consist of two representatives from each of the Great Powers — the Prime Minister and another Minister of Cabinet rank. It was thus primarily a political and not a military body, its object being to secure such an adjustment of, and co-operation in, the national policies of the Allies as would render possible the framing and the execution of a single comprehensive strategical plan of operations on the part of their military and naval forces.

The working out of such a plan on broad lines in its technical military aspect was assigned to permanent Military Representatives, while it was also agreed that other counsellors capable of advising on various specialist aspects of the contest would be called in, as their services might come to be required. It was furthermore decided that the full Council should, if possible, meet at least once a month. The arrangements to be made as regards the staffs of the permanent Military Representatives, however, naturally only developed themselves gradually — as will be seen in the next chapter. At the time of the meeting which set up the Supreme War Council, it, moreover, was not known whether the United States would take part; but it was confidently hoped that this would prove to be the case, although it was recognized that the American representatives must be on a somewhat different footing from those of Great Britain, France and Italy, whose Prime Ministers would be in a position to attend sittings. In so far as the British Government was concerned, it was at once arranged that Milner was to be the additional Minister supporting Lloyd George, and that Wilson was to be the British Military Representative. The Supreme War Council held its first meeting on November 8, and it was then decided that its head-quarters were to be established at Versailles.

That night most of the Allied representatives travelled on from Rapallo to Peschiera, where a meeting was held next morning, with the King of Italy present. It was agreed that General Cadorna should be replaced by General Diaz, and the King expressed the opinion that the line of the Piave could be held; he also pronounced himself as satisfied with the state of discipline in his army. Lloyd George, Smuts and Robertson left for home after the discussion closed, while Wilson, with Duncannon, proceeded to Verona to see General Duchesne, who was in command of the French troops . From Verona Wilson went on to Vicenza, where he saw the Chief of Staff of the First Italian Army, and there he learnt that Cadoma had ordered the retirement of the First and Fourth Armies from their positions on the hills about the Upper Piave; these were strong tactically, and their occupation appeared to be vital, seeing that their loss would mean the turning of the line of the river. Sir Henry, much disturbed, hurried on to Padua, where Cadorna was; but the superseded Commander-in-Chief could not see him. Foch was at Padua, but was of opinion that nothing could be done in the absence of a Commander-in-Chief. "Bissolati is chasing Diaz and will bring him here when caught," Wilson wrote in his diary that night at Padua, "Why not telephone him? What a way of installing a new C. in C. — by the intermediary of a Socialist M.P.!"

Still, of whatever complexion Signor Bissolati's political views may have been, he did succeed in hunting his quarry down during the night watches, and at an early hour on the following morning triumphantly produced the new leader of the Italian hosts at their G.H.Q. It was a somewhat hectic experience for General Diaz, who was not, in fact, an especially well-known figure in Italian military circles at the time. The honour that had been so suddenly thrust upon him was quite unexpected. He had been conveyed to Padua by night without sleep, without personal staff, and without personal belongings, and now, almost before he had swallowed his early morning coffee with attendant roll, he found himself hustled off by his captor to be confronted with a trio of foreign officer who were in an extremely inquisitive mood. These (Foch, Wilson and Weygand) straightway started cross-examining him as to his plans, demanded information as to the present disposition of the forces of which he had just been ordered to take over the command, and questioned him as to all manner of matters with which his acquaintance at the moment was imperfect. Wilson's account of the meeting is to the effect that, after preliminaries, Diaz declared his intention to be to defend the line of the Piave at all costs. Troops, he said, were already drawn up on the right bank of the river, rear-guards were covering the retirement of troops still on the farther side, several bridges had been blown up, and the right bank was being appropriately fortified.

Sir Henry thereupon raised the question of continuing to hold the ground high up in the Piave valley, which Cadorna had ordered to be abandoned; in this Foch supported him, and Diaz pronaised to send counter-orders. Diaz was very anxious that the two British divisions that were on their way should concentrate at Vicenza, instead of at Mantua which was considerably farther back, as then arranged; but Sir Henry pointed out that this concentration could not take place in any case for ten days, and that much might happen in the meantime. He, however, thought that Verona, nearer the front than was Mantua, and on the left — the flank on which the French were to take their place — might well be substituted for Mantua, and he undertook to consult with Lord Cavan, who was commanding the British contingent at the moment, on this point.

It would seem that Foch, alienated by the obviously unsatisfactory state of affairs, had shown himself somewhat brusque in manner and didactic in the expression of his views during this prolonged discussion, and that Diaz had been inclined to resent this attitude. But Wilson had contrived to pour oil on the troubled waters, had restored good humour by his tact and geniality, had shown himself simpatico in the eyes of the Italian Commander-in-Chief, and had made a particularly favourable impression in that troubled quarter. When the distinguished quartet emerged from the apartment in which they had been holding their confabulation, to join a number of staff officers belonging to the three Allied Armies in an outer room, the tall British general, bent almost double, had his arm linked firmly through that of Diaz, a man of modest stature, and the pair were chatting confidentially and evidently already on the best of terms. The cordial relations thus set up at a critical juncture in Padua were to be continued by General Plumer and Lord Cavan during the months to come with no little advantage alike to British and to Italians.

The conference ended, Wilson started for the front and that day he saw the commanders of the Fourth Army, of the XIth Corps on the right of the Fourth Army, and of the Third Army. The commander of the routed Second Army was endeavouring to collect what was left of it, and Sir Henry failed to find him; but he met Lieutenant-Colonel P. D. Hamilton, who was in command of the British heavy guns which had been sent to this front from France, and which had only been saved with difficulty during the debacle. All were anxious, and were doubtful whether it would be possible to hold the line of the Piave. The Duc d'Aosta, commanding the Third Army, had received no orders for eight days, and Hamilton had a river behind him over which there was no bridge, he could not induce the Italians to throw a bridge, and he could get no orders.

On getting back to Padua in the evening and meeting Foch, Wilson found that no orders had apparently yet been issued by the new Commander-in-Chief, and he had moreover satisfied himself that no adequate steps were being taken to prepare rearward lines, supposing that the defence of the Piave line should break down. He wrote in his diary that night:

> I am coming to the opinion that we cannot hold the Piave, and that we had better fall back under cover of rear-guards. The loss of Venice means the loss of the Adriatic, and a serious threat, therefore, to Salonika and Egypt, but I am afraid this is coming.

Cavan had, however, arrived to see him, and it had been settled that the leading British division should detrain at Manma and march thence to Verona, while the next division should detrain at Verona. It had also been arranged that two more British divisions should be transferred from the Western Front to Italy, making four altogether. A fifth was placed under orders a few days later.[*]

Early next morning, the 10th ("as soon as it was daylight; there

---

[*] As illustrating the attention that Wilson paid to his diary and the historical value of the record, it may be mentioned that this day
(November 9) the entry runs to 1,300 words.

1917: The Setting Up of the Supreme War Council

was no electric light"), Wilson wrote to Diaz urging hm to prepare rearward lines, and this the Italian Commander-in-Chief promised to do. Foch and Wilson both felt considerable apprehension as to what might occur within the next few days, seeing that the Italian armies would necessarily in the meantime be in somewhat exposed positions without direct support from the French or British. The French had, at Cadorna's request, been concentrating to the west of Lake Garda; and to move them round from there to the threatened front, a distance of more than 100 miles, must inevitably take several days. Owing to the confusion prevailing on the Italian railways, Cavan's two divisions were taking longer to arrive from France at their detraining stations than had been anticipated, so that the whole situation remained disquieting and unsatisfactory. Just when Sir Henry was about to start, on the morning of November 11, for another visit to the front, he was summoned to join Diaz, Foch and Porro at a conference. He found that the Italian generals were urging Foch to push the French divisions forward to the extreme left of the Italian line, but that Foch was refusing to do so, as the roads were so encumbered with fugitives, troops, baggage and transport that these welcome reinforcements could only advance in driblets. Wilson records in his diary:

> There was much heated discussion, so, after an hour and ten minutes I asked if England might be allowed to say something. I asked point-blank "If either the Grappa or Montello* are taken, will the whole line fall?" Diaz replied, "Yes." He said that the army was not now in a state to hold on if either of these places fell; moreover, he did not know if he could stop the men if they once began to go.

Foch, however, adhered to his refusal to push his troops forward prematurely, and insisted that they must be properly concentrated near Vicenza and then moved forward as complete divisions to the fighting line. That afternoon Sir Henry had a conversation with an Italian general who was holding a section of the Piave front near the left of the front, and of what he then heard he noted in his diary:

---

* These practically represented the left of the Italian line.

> His Corps was very weak, not only because he did not get drafts, but because they took away some of all ranks to remake the Second Army. Also he had about 5-8 per cent, jail-birds, also a number of returned sick and wounded unfit to march. In short, with the exception of himself, his divisional and brigade generals, and some colonels and others, no one much wanted to fight. He had shot one officer and two N.C.O.s yesterday for giving up a post, and had spent many hours haranguing brigades. He read me a letter from his second son in the artillery now covering Vidol bridge. The bridge is indifferently blown up and the boy is trying to cover. He has no trenches or gun-pits, and has already lost a few men and a gun from enemy's fire.

Of next morning's discussion with Diaz;, Foch and Porro, Wilson wrote:

> Porro very tiresome about my trains and ships, and I refused absoutely to agree to any of his forecasts, because I have not yet received any programme. Then Foch and Weygand began to settle the dates of detraining my four divisions, and, to their entire satisfaction, they had the whole four detrained by the 19th. I refused to take part in building these "Castles in the Air," as I called them to Diaz, who was quite sensible. And, funnily enough, a couple of hours later Cavan sent me a wire to say his second division would not be completed till about 22nd or 23rd. I sent Foch a copy.

Sir Henry, however, agreed that the British contingent, when it arrived, should concentrate on the right of the French troops, and the requisite orders to ensure this were thereupon issued. He was glad to learn from Diaz that the construction of rearward lines was really being proceeded with at last. He had understood that Cadorna had been nominated as the Italian Military Representative on the Supreme War Council, but he was now informed that the late Commander-in-Chief was disinclined to accept the appointment. However, that evening after dirmer Wilson received a summons from the King of Italy, who was staying at a chateau a few miles from Padua, he drove thither at once, and this is recorded of what passed in the diary:

> I had an hour's interview with him in his bedroom. Camp furniture; 2 candles; all thoroughly uncomfortable. Speaks English

well. He liked Lloyd George very much. He said he had signed Cadorna's appointment to the Supreme Council, so he did not know how the old boy could get out of going. He had a high opinion of Diaz.

He said he had staked all on this war — his throne, the future of his wife and children, of his fortune, of Italy — and he begged me to accelerate our assistance all I could. Very touching. I replied that we were doing all that was humanly possible. He gave me both his hands when saying good-bye, and he said he hoped to see me before long again.

Alarming news arrived during the night to the effect that an Austrian battalion had succeeded in getting across the Piave in boats, that it had established itself in the middle of the Italian line, and that the defending troops stationed at this point were finding themselves quite unable to thrust the intruders back into the river. The consequence was that, when the usual meeting of the Allied chiefs took place on the morning of November 13, both Diaz and Porro were in a particularly despondent mood, and that Wilson realized that Italian G.H.Q. no longer felt any confidence as regards being able to hold the Piave line. Foch and Sir Henry therefore had a further private discussion after the meeting terminated, they could not disguise from themselves that the situation was the reverse of reassuring, and this appears in the diary:

> I told him of my talk with the King, and my general impression, which is that, if the enemy really attacks either in the mountains or on the Piave before we can get up to steady the Italians, they will give ground. Hence my anxiety to have good rearward lines established. I discussed with him the question of a fifth division, French or English, and I told him that if we were going to be on our present line I would wire for two more divisions now; but that if we got back to the Ivlindo I thought that if he had 6 and we had 4, i.e. if he had 54 battalions and we had 52, it would be enough, and that for this reason I was going to await developments. I told him that all the time I was thinking of next year's offensive, and was slow to commit divisions to defensive until I could see daylight. Also, there was still the question of relieving the French line in France. He agreed.
>
> I told him I was anxious to get off to Versailles as soon as I

could, so as to get on with next year's plans, and he said he was equally anxious. The streets of Padua are full of officers and men doing nothing. Shops open, women smartly dressed, etc. Plumer, Tim Harington[*] and Gathorne-Hardy[†] arrived at 5.30.

News was received at Padua on November 15 of the fall of the Ribot Government in France, and of M. Clemenceau becoming head of the new one and taking charge of the Ministry of War; and next day a telegram to Wilson intimated that the War Cabinet wished him to be at Versailles as soon as possible. He saw Orlando before leaving, and explained that the delay in the arrival of the British divisions was entirely due to the congestion on the roads and railways to the west. Foch, he found, thought that if the Piave line was to be held the number of British and French divisions ought to be increased to nine each, but was of opinion that a force of four each would suffice if it became a question of retiring and of merely holding the line of the Mincio and Po. Wilson, however, came to the conclusion that it would be best to wait before further decreasing the forces on the Western Front, the more so as the enemy's advance through Venetia appeared to be developing slowly.[‡] They agreed that the French and British forces ought to take up the left of the front, in the hills, leaving the Italians actually to hold the river line of the Piave, and they also agreed that it would be well to incorporate some Italian divisions in the French and the British Armies.

Wilson dined with the King before leaving, and he started for Paris on November 17, making a tour through the country about Lake Garda by car on the way to Milan, He arrived in Paris on the 19th, and there found Sackville-West and Amery waiting for him in connexion with setting up the British military advisory staff at

---

[*] Now General Sir C. H. Harington.

[†] Now Major-General Hon. G. F. Gathorne-Hardy.

[‡] This view turned out to be the sound one, for the Italians maintained their front successfully during the months to come, aided only by six French and five British divisions.

1917: The Setting Up of the Supreme War Council 37

the disposal of the Supreme War Council. "It is a maddening thing," he had written in his diary on the 17th in Milan, after his drive thither from Padua, "to see columns of French troops marching up to fight to save Italy when their own country is still invaded, and at the same time to see long columns of Italians marching away from the guns and passing the French troops going up," Sir Henry saw Clemenceau after reaching Paris. "The Tiger," he found, was not much interested in the Supreme War Council, very little had, in consequence, been done, and this appears in the diary:

> However, I pushed him about, and I got him to order Colonel Herscher to push about, and I will see about it myself to-morrow. Clemenceau told me he had ordered Foch to remain in Italy for the present — a stupid thing to do, as I told him; for the Superior Council has many important mings to deal with at once. Clemenceau talked about Unity of Command, but did not seem to know quite what he wanted. It is an impossible thing in my opinion.*

Next day arrangements were made in connexion with establishing offices in the Trianon at Versailles, and then V dson went to see Poincard, whom he found most friendly all in favour of the Supreme War Council; so Wilson seized the oppormnity to press for Foch's return to Paris. He saw Clemenceau in the evening, and at this meeting found "the Tiger" much more favourable to the Supreme War Council than he had been the day before. They again discussed the question of Unity of Command. Says the diary:

> I told him that I had heard that he was upset by the way Lloyd George had dismissed the possibility in his speech in the House of Commons. He said he was. I asked him what he meant by Unity of Command, and he said he meant that only two men should run the whole thing — a Frenchman (himself) and an Englishman (me). He wants the Supreme Council to have much more power than it now has, and I told him I would discuss this with Lloyd George direcdy I

---

* This shows that Sir Henry did not at this time believe Unity of Command to be a practicable proposition.

got back.

Sir Henry crossed the Channel to England in company with Amery and Duncannon that night.

He met with some obstruction from the War Office just at first. The Secretary of State, whom Wilson, on arrival, went to see at Derby House, declined to let him have either Sackville-West or Duncannon for his staff, objecting to the latter on the quaint grounds of his connexion with the National Party. "So I got cross," Sir Henry wrote in his diary, "and said, 'Very well then, Lloyd George can't have me.'" Next day (the 22nd) he lunched with Lloyd George and he records in the diary:

> I arranged with Lloyd George that I should send my reports to him and not to anyone else; also that I should get what officers I wanted; also, I told him about my work in Paris and about Clemenceau, and how nothing was arranged when we arrived and now all seemed going smoothly. Then I went to Derby and he withdrew his objection to Tit Willow, but he still stuck out about Duncannon.

He wrote in his diary on the 23rd:

> Breakfast with Derby. He still declines to allow Duncannon to come out. Derby said that Bonar Law agreed with him, so I went to see Bonar Law at the House of Commons, and he also tliinks that the Lord ought not to come out. He sent for Sir George Younger, who was more emphatic, and quite bitter against the National Party. I simply can't understand them. I got Duncannon down here after dinner and told him the situation, and Milner came in. Duncannon is to see Derby to-morrow, I told Bonar that I would refuse to move in the matter, for that, if I did, I would be turning myself into a politician, and that, as far as I was concerned, Duncannon should remain as my A.D.C. If Derby removed him, then that was Derby's concern.

The end of it was that Wilson, as might have been expected, got his way, and that the objections, raised on purely political grounds, to his retaining the services of his aide-de-camp were withdrawn. Difficulties were also raised as to Amcry

1917: The Setting Up of the Supreme War Council

accompanying him, but they were overcome by quiet persistence. A party comprising Lloyd George, Milner, Balfour, E. Geddes, Robertson, Wilson and several others started for Paris on November 27, and on the way over Wilson was able to acquaint Lloyd George as to the obstacles that were being put in his way. He also learnt from the Prime Minister particulars as to certain problems that were arising in Paris in connexion with the constitution of the Supreme War Council. Of these problems he that evening wrote in his diary:

> It appears, from what Lloyd George had already heard, that Clemenceau wants to change the whole Supreme Council, and put Foch on as C.G.S. and put Pétain on. This would mean Robertson and Flaig, and we should be where we have been all along. Then Clemenceau wants to make one C. in C. from the North Sea to the Adriatic, and this is to be a Frenchman, and in all others have English C. in C.s. It is curious how unpractical a clever man can be. Lloyd George is angry, and says that he will have a row with Clemenceau tomorrow, and if Clemenceau does not give in he [Lloyd George] will go straight back to London Lloyd George certainly must show his teeth. It is intolerable if arrangements come to at Rapido one week can be upset the next.
>
> Lloyd George realizes perfectly that his own future rests on the success of the Supreme Council, and he also is clear in his mind that unless we have it we shall lose the war. Clemenceau will give in tomorrow. He is in no position to quarrel with Lloyd George. House (the American)* will side with Lloyd George and has said so, and this is good.

Next day the entry appears:

> Lloyd George told me that he sent House at 9.30 a.m. tq Clemenceau, with a message to say that, if Clemenceau looked on the agreement come to at Rapallo as a personal agreement, and therefore not binding on the French Government, then Lloyd George had nothing further to do and he would return to London this afternoon.

---

* Colonel House had arrived in Europe with General Bliss, the Chief of the Staff and a large party of naval and military officers and civilian officials, a few weeks before this.

This brought Clemenceau to his senses and he, of course, said he would adhere to Rapallo. So Lloyd George and Clemenceau met at 10 a.m. and they had a talk.

Clemenceau said that Foch was going to remain on at Quatre-bis* and he [Clemenceau] had not yet selected a man for Versailles. This is make Quatre-bis superior to Versailles. We shall see what. If Clemenceau puts in Joffre he will show that he is playing to the public, specially America. If he puts in some subordinate of Foch's, he will be dancing to Quatre-bis. I daresay that. failing Foch, Gouraud would be best. But the whole thing is very disquieting.

In the meantime the British portion of the Supreme War Council was becoming settled at Versailles, offices had been secured, a residence had been arranged for, work had been started, and Amery and others had arrived to help Sackville-West. General Cadorna had made a beginning; but the French had done nothing, nor had the Americans. It transpired that Clemenceau had decided to make Weygand the French Military Representative on the Council, an appointment which Sir Henry regarded as highly objectionable. Owing to his very close relations of long standing with Foch, Weygand would, for all practical purposes, be simply a mouthpiece of the French C.G.S. The French "Technical Adviser" — this expression was a good deal used to indicate the "Military Representative" and was, in fact, a more correct one, seeing that the title "Representative," in the circumstances, rather suggested executive authority — would naturally be disposed to give the Allied Ministers forming the Council the same advice as Foch was giving the French Government. Lloyd George's and Sir Henry's conception of the Technical Adviser, at the outset, was that of a military expert who would be wholly independent of his War Office, whether French or British, and would be prepared to express views entirely different from those entertained, as the case might be, by Foch or by Robertson, the officers who were responsible to their respective Governments and to their respective countries. But Cadorna was the Italian C.G.S.; and in due course General Bliss, the United States Chief of Staff, was appointed the

---

* The French War Office.

1917: The Setting Up of the Supreme War Council 41

American Military Representative on the Council. Wilson's position was, in fact, going to be the exceptional one, and not Weygand's. Nor did Lloyd George show any disposition to raise objections with regard to what Clemenceau had decided.

Wilson wrote in his diary on November 30:

> I had a long talk with Geddes. He wants to give up his appointment as 1st Lord. He wants to form a Railway Commission in Paris and himself to be Chairman — or Commissary General, as he calls it — and then develop on the whole front from Nieuport to Venice the same railway facilities that he has carried out on the British front. There is a great deal in this. With the collapse of Russia, and to a certain extent of Italy, the Boches will once again gain the initiative and we may expect some heavy attacks. Until the Americans come in strength, our best defensive weapon is extreme mobility, and our railways must be developed to the utmost everywhere in France and in Italy.
>
> I then had a long talk with the American, General Bliss. The old boy knew nothing as to his future and had no plans whatever as to Versailles. I drew him up a graphic of what I was doing and rather enthused him, and he went off to House to get him to move at once.
>
> Clemenceau sent for me at 3 o'clock. While waiting in the ante-room I heard shouts of "Henri, Henri," and this was Foch who was with Clemenceau and heard I was waiting. Clemenceau was charming to me, told me to come to him whenever I wanted without appointment and without ceremony. He will give the Supreme Council every assistance, said he really could not spare Foch, said he had several subjects he wanted us to study, i.e. Belgian and Italian man-power, neutrality of Holland and Switzerland, Salonika, Rumania, etc. Altogether, I was satisfied with Clemenceau.
>
> I then went on to Foch, who was charming as ever and who I am sure will play up now that he has got Weygand to Versailles. We discussed all Clemenceau's points, and I added the necessity of great rail developments, to which Foch agreed.
>
> The news from Russia continues to be very bad. Italy is holding the Piave line, and we and the French are at Bassano and Montello.

The Supreme War Council had now been definitely constituted, and it held its first regular meeting at Versailles on December 1. That a wide difference of view existed even between Lloyd George and Sir Henry as to the proper organisation and procedure of this body is, however, indicated by the Prime Minister having wished to bring Balfour and Robertson over to this first meeting, thus tending to transform the gathering into one of those bloated conclaves that had been taking place at frequent intervals during the past three years, and which had never settled anything. Milner and Sir Henry, however, succeeded between them in dissuading Lloyd George from thus swelling the numbers present at the fest seance, and, as will be seen in the next chapter, the Council made a very promising start in consequence.

Chapter XXI – 1917-18: Two and a Half Months Military Representative on the Supreme War Council

Outline of the strategical situation on December 1 — Organization of Wilson's staff at Versailles — The question of the B.E.F. taking over more line — Differing views of Robertson and Wilson as to conduct of the War — Smuts and a High Commissionership — Meetings of the Supreme War Council on January 30, 31, and February 1 — Wilson, after strange indecision in high places, becomes C.I.G.S.

If the Supreme War Council was not actually a creation of Wilson's single-handed, if he could not perhaps claim it wholly as his child, its establishment none the less was to a far greater extent his handiwork than it was the handiwork of any other individual on the side of the Allies, whether civilian or military. Mr. Lloyd George is no doubt entitled to a share of credit for his successful pressing of the project, as conceived by its originator, upon the somewhat reluctant associated Governments. No sooner had Foch realized its merits than the future Generalissimo played an important part in disposing his civilian superiors to accept the arrangement. Colonel House and General Bliss helped by their advocacy very materially towards completing the structure, when urging the virtues of this new-fangled controlling body upon the President of the United States. But there can be no doubt whatever that Versailles would never have been set on foot had it not been for Sir Henry's foresight and administrative ingenuity, for his instinctive realization of the requirements of a complicated situation, for his gifts of dehneation and exposition when unfolding his ideas, and for the powers of persuasion which he exercised at the psychological moment for ensuring their adoption.

As far back as the autumn of 1915 he had, as we have seen, convinced himself that a small but authoritative body representing the British and French civil and military executives was imperatively needed, a body to be charged with examining the strategical aspects of this stupendous struggle, and with directing what course, broadly, was to be pursued in various sets of circumstances such as might arise. The big inter-Allied conferences were, already then, proving a failure — and they continued to prove a failure, and even a danger, up to the juncture when, under circumstances of no little anxiety and stress, the Supreme War Council was at last ushered in at the historic conclave of Rapallo. Wilson had at first merely contemplated a Franco-British "Committee of Six," composed of the two Foreign Ministers, the two War Ministers, and the two Chiefs of the General Staffs. Subsequent events, however, satisfied him that Italian representatives must also take part; and he came furthermore to realize that the respective Prime Ministers must be on the Committee so as to provide this with plenary executive authority, and that it therefore ought to consist of the three Prime Ministers and the three Chiefs of the General Staffs. Then, as it became apparent that the Prime Ministers could not always be present at meetings of the Committee, as he pictured it, he recognized that an additional Cabinet Minister from each country ought to be included, who would represent the Prime Minister when that official was absent. Finally, he came to the conclusion that the Military Representatives on the Committee or Council ought not to be, and in practice could not conveniently be, the Chiefs of the General Staffs, but that officers of high standing ought to be specially appointed to perform the duty, and that these must have appropriate staffs attached to them to aid them in their labours. That, in effect, was the arrangement that was agreed to at Rapallo.

The first meeting of the Supreme War Council was, as we have seen, held on December 1. But, before recording its proceedings, a brief summary of the situation as between the belligerents in the various theatres of war at this juncture will, perhaps, not be out of place. The really dominating event to signalize Ae past few months of conflict had been the gradual elimination of Russia as a factor in the struggle, following on the revolution of March. This had upset all the calculations of the Allied chiefs in the previous winter as to the course which the contest was likely to follow during the year 1917. The prolonged Flanders operations, closed without their achieving any successes of the first importance, and characterized, as they had been, by very heavy British losses, had, none the less, improved the situation appreciably in respect to the safety of the Channel ports. Haig's stubborn efforts had served, moreover, to keep the bulk of the German forces in this theatre so busily employed that Pétain had been enabled to restore the morale and discipline of the French armies, which had suffered owing to Nivelle's failure and to the political interference which that discomfiture had brought in its train. Although the Germans had hitherto brought across no vast forces from the Russian front to strengthen their fighting resources in the West, the French and British military authorities knew that such a transfer must be anticipated shortly, and that the enemy would therefore inevitably be very formidable during the first half of 1918, before the United States forces could seriously influence the strategical situation. Affairs in Italy, if still far from wholly reassuring, were becoming more hopeful from day to day, owing to the arrival of the French and British contingents at the front and to a gratifying recovery of confidence on the part of the Italian troops.

In the Eastern theatre, the position at the moment was that, the Bolshevists having gained the mastery in Russia, negotiations for a suspension of hostilities had been set on foot; and an armistice was actually adjusted on December 5. In Macedonia, stalemate was the order of the day; steps were, however, being taken to introduce considerable Greek forces on the side of the Allies into a theatre of war where French and British armies had too long been maintained, without their exercising an influence over the struggle as a whole at all commensurate with their numbers. After notable successes at Beersheba, Gaza and Jaffa, Allenby was about to advance on Jerusalem; while in Mesopotamia all went well, in spite of the Russian collapse that had taken place in Armenia.

Clemenceau was in the chair at the first meeting of the

Supreme War Council, Weygand being the other French representative. Lloyd George, Milner and Wilson were the British representatives, Orlando and Cadorna stood for Italy, and Colonel House and General T. Bliss were accredited by the United States. Besides these, there were present Foch, Robertson, Sackville-West, Hankey, and, for a time, M. Venizelos.*

Wilson wrote in his diary:

> The proceedings went off very well. Clemenceau was an admirable chairman, Lloyd George backed him well, Hankey drafted resolution after resolution, which Lloyd George read out and which Clemenceau put and which were instantly passed. A number of things were referred to the Council, viz.: Italy, Salonika, Rumania, rail transportation, Belgian army. These are quite enough to keep us busy for some time.

But while Wilson had already collected a portion of his staff, and his office was getting into working order, delay occurred before the French, Italian and American portions of the permanent staff of the Supreme War Council were definitely in being. Sir Henry, moreover, deprecated the attitude being taken up by the French with regard to the Council, and after a talk at the Elysee

---

* Sir Henry used to relate the story with gusto of an incident which apparently occurred at the opening of this meeting. But it may have happened later — on the occasion, for instance, of the first meeting of the "Executive Board" that was set up at a later date with regard to the General Reserve (to be mentioned on a subsequent page), or possibly when the Peace Conference was sitting.

It was suggested by the French, he said, that there was no need for each Ally to have his own shorthand writer present, as they would send round a translation of their notes for the various representatives who had been present to see. Henry at once leant across the table to Bliss and said, speaking between his hands, "We can't have that. We must insist on our own shorthand men." Then he turned to Foch and asked, "Did you hear what I said?" Foch pretended that he had not understood what had passed, although he knows English up to a certain point. "Well, I was telling him," explained Henry, "that we could not agree to that — that we don't trust you little Frenchmen for a moment." Foch roared with laughter. Henry's habit conversation to our gallant allies as "those funny little Frenchmen" when in company with French officers of rank who were well acquainted with English made one feel quite uncomfortable, until one saw that they rather liked it. C.E.C.

with Bliss, Cadorna, Foch and Weygand on December 3, he wrote in his diary:

> I have come to the following conclusions: That Clemenceau intends to direct the whole war by using Foch to work with Robertson, and then by sending Weygand here to impose his (Clemenceau's) will on Versailles by Foch through Weygand.

Bliss Started for America to bring over, or to send, a staff which was to be as far as possible a duplicate of Wilson's, and for some time after this Mr. Frazier, Counsellor at the American Embassy in Paris, represented the United States at meetings. Wilson wrote in his diary on the 6th:

> I went to Paris and had one and a half hours with Northcliffe, Sir W. Weir and Johnnie Baird about the part that the U.S.A. should play in aeroplane construction. Nothing clear and decided has been arranged, and it is evident to me that unless Versailles takes this matter up in a broad spirit we shall lose half our possibles. I impressed this on Northcliffe, and asked him to impress Lloyd George. He promised to do so and to get his brother Rothermere to come over here and see me.

Next day the entry appears:

> A letter from Derby to say he must insist on the Lord getting into plain clothes, and also that he had found out on inquiry that the French have only 2 officers, and therefore I cannot have more than I now have. I wired to say that the French have already 14, and are getting more, and that I was being much handicapped and quite unable to carry out the work ordered by the Prime Minister and the Supreme Council.

The following appears in the diary on December 9:

> Another bid by the Army Council to keep a hold of me, by an order to subpiit to them any advice that I was going to give to the Supreme Council. I wrote at once to Hankey, enclosing a copy of the order, and pointing out that I [Wilson] did not advise the Supreme Council, but was only one of four, and that all our advice was

collective and therefore could not be sent to the War Office of any one country.

In the afternoon I went to see Joffre, who was as nice as ever to me. I spent an hour with him. He is very anxious about the future, and if he knew the state of our man-power he would be more anxious still.

Then three-quarters of an hour with Nivelle, who also was as nice as ever, and he, too, was nervous about the future and especially of a German move through Switzerland with $0 divisions. He asked me what my estimate was of the number of divisions the Boches could bring over from Russia, and, when I said 50, he jumped out of his chair and said that was the exact figure he himself had given. There is no question, we are in for an anxious time in the next few months, and in fact all next year. Nivelle showed a correspondence with Haig, where Haig, being asked by Ribot on April 26 whether Nivelle's offensive should continue, emphatically declared in favour of continuance, that Ribot had then promised it should continue, and that he had then stopped it on the 29th.

One point significantly emerges from the above excerpts extracted from Wilson's diary. This is that the War Office was inclined to throw obstacles in his path just at first. Nor is this perhaps altogether to be wondered at. Rightly or wrongly, Mr. Lloyd George was dissatisfied with Robertson as his principal military adviser, and he was adopting circuitous methods of securing a different one. The C.I.G.S. had found himself wholly unable to support a succession of projects which the Prime Minister kept evolving out of a fertile brain. At one moment Mr. Lloyd George had clamoured for the dispatch of great Franco-British forces from the Western Front to aid the Italians in knocking their heads against the Julian Alps. At the next he wanted to filch divisions from Haig and to transfer them to the shores of Ayas Bay, near Alexandretta, under the impression that they could be back in plenty of time to secure the line in France against the formidable hosts which the enemy would be in a position to assemble in the mam theatre in the spring of 1918. He had at an earlier date hankered after effecting a multiplication of the Allied forces that were planted down in Macedonia, with the idea of their carrying out operations amongst the inhospitable highlands of the Balkan territory. To these and to other analogous strategical schemes devised by the Prime Minister, Robertson, who was convinced that the issue of the great contest would be decided on the Western Front, had offered a stubborn opposition. Which of the two was right may be a matter of opinion, but that strained relations had arisen between the head of the British Government and his principal official military adviser was a matter of fact, and indeed a matter of common knowledge.

Instead, however, of his having adopted the statesmanlike course of replacing Robertson by somebody in whom he had confidence, Mr. Lloyd George was resorting to the plan of making the British Military' Representative on the Supreme War Council a soldier entirely independent of the War Office, a soldier who would be in a position to express views to that exalted body which might be totally at variance with the views entertained by the military authorities in Whitehall. This may or may not have been a satisfactory plan, but Clemenceau's arrangement in connexion with expert representation on the Council was an entirely different one. Weygand was a subordinate of the French C.G.S., Foch; he represented Foch's views, and he was in no sense an outsider set up to tender counsel independently of, and in opposition to, the principal official military adviser of the French Government. As to the propriety of establishing a Supreme War Council there really can be no question, but the device which had been hit upon with regard to the British Military Representative does seem open to criticism.

This appears in the diary on December 12:

> Guillaumat, who goes out on Monday to replace Sattail at Salonika, came to see me. I told him I thought his first duty was to make love to the Serbs and to put a Serb on his staff, that Sarrail had treated the Serbs very badly, with result that if we retired from Monastir it was quite possible that the Serbs would leave us. Also, if we retired, it was certain that the Italians would fall back on Valona, and therefore it was necessary for him to ponder the problem that, if we had to fall back, we might lose both Italian divisions and both Serb divisions; and, of course, the Russians were useless. Therefore he would be faced with the situation that he must decide whether with 8 French divisions, 4 British divisions and 3 Greek divisions he could hold Salonika and also cover Greece; and if he could not do both,

then what would he do — would he hold on to Salonika, or would he cover Greece? In my opinion he must cover Greece.

Next day there is an account of a meeting which Sir Henry had with Clemenceau:

> The old man was difficult. He raged against the English, and then fastened on Haig and in a minor degree on Robertson. He told of the War Cabinet meeting this morning at which Pétain said that unless he was given 200,000-300,000 men from the interior for some weeks to dig backward trenches and put up wire, and unless we [English] took over the line to Berry-au-Bac — a front of 13 infantry divisions and 2 cavalry divisions of French troops — he, Pétain, would not be responsible for his front. This, said Clemenceau, had a very great effect on the War Cabinet. Clemenceau then undertook (a) to get the 200,000 men from the interior; (b) to make the English take over to Berry-au-Bac; or (c) to resign.
> Clemenceau repeated this three times to me, and he said that he was going to make out the case for this in his own hand-writing, and that this would take him about a week, as he was very busy with the "affair Sarrail," which, said he, he was confident he could win. We discussed Haig, Robertson and Lloyd George, and by degrees I got the old man a little quieter.
> He told me that Lloyd George had written to him a couple of days ago saying he understood Pétain had a plan of attacking without losing life, and would he tell Lloyd George the secret and send it over by an officer! Clemenceau said Lloyd George was a fool and the only way to save life was not to attack. But, when all allowance is made, it is perfectly clear that we must handle this business of relief and of the future with the greatest care and consideration. Before leaving old Clemenceau I told him to submit the whole case to Versailles and not to London, and I think he will.

On the day after this conversation Wilson proceeded to Montreuil to stay the night at G.H.Q. with Haig, and while there he in the first place discussed with Kiggell the question of the B.E.F. taking over line from the French. G.H.Q. raised very strong objections to taking over line to nearly so far as Berry-au-Bac (which was close to Rheims), although ready to extend as far as the Oise in a short time. Haig moreover informed Wilson that the Oise had actually been fixed upon as point of demarcation in agreement with Pétain. The situation as to numbers of the B.E.F., Wilson learnt, was very unsatisfactory. General Fowke, the AdjutantGeneral, calculating that there would be a deficit of 200,000 in establishment in March, and a deficit of 400,000 in October. "Before leaving," appears in Wilson's diary, "I had another talk with Kigg. I warned him again that Haig was going to have three attacks — by the Boches, by London, by Paris," and Wilson added, "we shall want D.H. badly when bad times come." In the meantime the British staff at Versailles was practically complete, and Sir Henry had organized it as follows:

There were three Sections: "A" ("Allies"), "E" ("Enemy") and "M" ("Material"); Section A was in charge of Colonel H. W. Studd and dealt with the Allies; Section E was under Hereward Wake and dealt with the enemy; Section M, under Brigadier-General (now Major-General Sir F.) Sykes, dealt with man-power and material generally. There was also a political branch under Amery. Section E collected information from all available sources as to the strength, disposition and so forth of enemy military forces in the various theatres of war, and regarded the strategical situation as a whole entirely from the enemy's point of view; Wake and his assistants in fact put themselves in the place of the enemy General Staffs, and thought out what would be the right course for the enemy to pursue in given circumstances. Sir Henry liked them to wear their caps when at work, and with the peak to the rear, so that when they looked up they would see themselves as Germans in the big mirror that was in their room. Section A had full information as to the strength, disposition and so forth of the Allies, and contemplated the various situatioris that arose, or that might arise, from the Allies' point of view. Section M, from the facts at its disposal as to man-power, air material, ammunition, guns, etc., was in a position to produce tables giving details of the resources of the Allies, and to give advice as to what might be considered as available.

Sir Henry had got together a personnel in whom he had complete confidence, no difficulties having arisen as regards his securing the services of the men he wanted, except just at the start. He made it his practice to discuss with them the various subjects that came up for consideration so as to get the full benefit of their experience and of their ability, and he always encouraged them to express their views freely, even when these did not happen to coincide with his own. One of those who served under him at Versailles at this time writes:

> He did love talking and haying others round him to talk to and to argue with — especially the latter. I remember his saying once, "Oh, we can't have So and So living in our mess — he never talks, and if people don't talk and argue there is no means of sharpening one's wits." That as he said, "they were so alert and bright in thought" was a reason for his admiring so many Frenchmen. Henry loved writing letters and receiving them; his first question in the morning always was as to the post, and then as to "what was the gossip." By gossip he meant political or military chat.

The British Military Representative on the Supreme War Council and his assistants formed in fact a very happy, as well as a very capable, family, and one which in consequence produced good work.

The procedure that was to be adopted by the Military Representatives as a body had also been decided upon by the middle of December. Their duty was to submit reasoned conclusions to the Council, collectively, with regard to any subject that the Council thought fit to refer to them. The conclusions were drawn up in the form of joint "Notes," the terms of which were argued out and agreed to at the meetings of the Representatives. The Notes were then signed by the Representatives and forwarded to the Council's secretariat as "Resolutions." The Council at its next meeting agreed to, or rejected (as the case might be) a resolution thus submitted to it. If the resolution was agreed to, executive action in accordance with its terms was supposed to be taken by the Government or Governments concerned. The British military personnel in reality took a very leading part in the transactions of the Council during this period, and also later. A Naval Liaison Committee was set up at an early stage, and this formed a link between the Military Representatives and the Inter-Allied Naval Council, which had its seat in London. An Inter-Allied Aviation Committee and an Inter-Allied Tank Committee were likewise established at a later date. With the process of thus expanding the functions of the military side of Versailles Wilson had much to do, his breadth of outlook, his gifts of organization, and his energy and driving power, all combining to make him take the lead in such developments.

Versailles: Allied military representatives and staffs

Almost the first question of importance that came up for consideration by the Supreme War Council was that of the B.E.F. taking over line from the French, a contentious subject which had been continuously cropping up at intervals ever since early in 1915. In the course of the discussions on this subject that had at different times taken place between the Governments concerned, and also between British G.H.Q. and French G.Q.G., the French were always in a position to point out that, relatively to their numbers, their troops were holding a far greater length of line than was the B.E.F. Against this contention the British could only insist upon the absolutely vital importance of the sectors situated between the Oise and the sea, seeing that penetration of these by the enemy inevitably jeopardized the Channel ports and therefore the communications of the B.E.F., and that a rupture in this quarter might bring about the separation of the British from the French host. Haig's offensives in Flanders and at Cambrai were now at an end, and Pétain was pressing the British Commander-in-Chief to take over a considerable stretch south-east G.H.Q. was not ready to extend its front at all at the moment, and was strongly opposed to extending it greatly even at a later date. Wilson's view was that the wishes of Pétain ought to be met to some extent; but he learnt on December 17 that, at a meeting between Haig and Pétain that day, no agreement had been arrived at. Sir Henry, therefore, went up to Paris and had an interview with Clemenceau, and he wrote in his diary:

> A memorable meeting. He began by saying, know where you been and what you have been doing. You have been to Haig's and you have told him that he going to have three attacks made on him — from Boches, from London, from Paris." This rather astonished me as I don't know how he heard it; but I was rather pleased that he should have, for, as I said to him, "Well, and is it not true?"
> I told the Tiger that Lloyd George had already ordered Robertson and Haig to make out their case and submit it to me, and I said I thought that the Tiger ought to do likewise, provided always that he was prepared to accept the Versailles decision as final. He asked who Versailles was and answered it himself by saying "Monsieur Wilson." He then thought a little and finally said, "Yes, I will agree to that proposal." I then suggested that he should wire that to Lloyd George. He took a bit of paper and a pen and said, "Will you dictate what you want me to say?" and I dictated as follows: "As Pétain and Haig cannot agree, I propose to submit the case to Versailles, and if you will also agree I am prepared to agree to the Versailles decision." He wrote this down in English and said he would send it off at once. He said he would have his case ready by Saturday. This is an epoch-making step, because it really calls Versailles into being as the supreme advisory (military) body, and as the supreme executive body also. I told the Tiger that I thought well of him and liked him, and he said he liked me too! The Tiger said that when I first spoke to him (on my return from Italy) he was hostile to Versailles, but that now he admitted that he was wrong. And so, with more chatter, this meeting ended with great goodwill between us.

Lloyd George wired next day to say that he agreed to Cleraenceau's proposal. But a decision as to this very contentious question was not finally come to by the Military Representatives on the Supreme War Council until January 10, when they laid down that the dividing line between the two hosts ought to be at a point a little east of the Laon-Soissons road — that is to say well beyond the Oise, but not so far as Berry-au-Bac. The extension was not, however, fortunately as it proved, carried out to the point proposed at Versailles, the B.E.F. only taking on as far as Barisis, about a dozen miles short of the Laon-Soissons road. For Haig and Robertson raised such strong objections that the British Government shrank from enforcing the recommendation of January 10. The progress made by the Military Representatives in other directions was more rapid, although the deliberations were not carried on without occasional friction — as is shown by an entry in Wilson's diary on December 22:

> Meeting this morning at which I put up three papers, one about Salonika and two about Italy. Weygand opposed all three! The Salonika one was on a question of principle. He said that as Foch had given Guillaumat his orders there was nothing more to be said. I replied that Foch had no business to have done so, and that an expression of opinion from us was absolutely necessary, and that Guillaumat should work on that, and in my note I made it clear that Guillaumat's plan must be submitted to us. Frazier, who was representing America, was warmly with me, and Cadorna coolly; but I carried the day.

Sir Henry proceeded to London at short notice on the 28th on receipt of a wire which ran as follows:

> Following for General Sir Henry Wilson, to be deciphered by himself personally. Very secret. In view of the determined peace movement on the part of the Central Powers, the Prime Minister is anxious to know your personal views as to prospect of our improving our position by continuance of war. The most vital factor to be military outlook. Subject of discussion cannot be dealt with otherwise than by word of mouth, and certainly not at this juncture except by ourselves. Could you come over at once for that purpose? I hope that the report on the Western Front is sufficiently advanced to allow of

your doing this. End of message. Milner.*

"This" says Sir Henry in his diary, "is an amazing wire and looks as though much would depend on my military opinion" Six different papers had already been drawn up by Wilson and his staff, and had been approved. They dealt with such subjects as the sending of further reinforcements from the Western Front to the Italian theatre, as the problem presented by the situation in Macedonia and Greece, and as recommending what steps ought to be taken in regard to stemming the tide of Bolshevism in the Ukraine, in Transcaucasia and elsewhere. Wilson was strongly of opinion that, until such time as the United States troops should have arrived in Europe in large numbers, the proper attitude for the Allies to maintain on the Western Front and in Italy was one of defence. That same attitude appeared also to be imposed upon the Entente — at least for the time being — Macedonia. But Sir Henry was very hopeful that Adlenby would be able to follow up the taking of Jerusalem (the Holy City had surrendered on the 9th) by prosecuting a war of movement which would carry his forces to Damascus and even to Aleppo. He had, moreover, initiated a war game on a comprehensive scale in his office at Versailles, a war game particularly designed to discover in what direction, and on what date, the Germans might be expected to deliver that great offensive against the Allies on the Western Front which was certain to be launched sooner or later during the course of the year 1918. Furnished with all the information that was available as to

---

* The report on the Western Front, which was referred to by Lord Milner in the telegram, was to be largely based on a memorandum prepared by Wilson's Section E and dated January 1. In this document ("Note No. 12") it was calculated that the Germans would have available for attack on the Western Front a force of 50 divisions on February 1, and that this number would be increased to 96 on July 1. After July 1 it was estimated that the German strength would remain stationary, whereas that of the Allies would be on the upward grade, thanks to the arrival of American divisions at the rate of two per month. On May 1 the enemy would have a superiority of 27 divisions over the increase to 37 in July, after which it would decrease. As regards probable date of a great hostile of a great hostile offensive, the memorandum suggested that the enemy's best plan from a purely military point of view would be to postpone attack until May 1, and perhaps even till July 1, but that it could be commenced on February 1.

enemy resources and enemy dispositions at the moment. Wake commanded the Kaiser's hosts, while Studd commanded the British, French and Belgian array; and much that was informative and useful had already been learnt from the exercise.

Wilson wrote in the diary on December 30, after arriving in London the previous evening:

> I went to see Milner at 10.30. The story is simply this. He wired for me because he and Lloyd George wanted to know my opinion. The question seems to be "Shall we be in a better position from the military point of view in 12 months, and if not why not discuss peace terms now?"
>
> In addition Milner told me that Lloyd George is so angry with Robertson that he proposes to kick him out and put me in. As I said to Milner again — I am opposed to this, though all in favour of Lloyd George giving me more power at Versailles, and reducing Robertson from the position of a master to that of a servant. Then I drove down to Walton Heath with Philip Kerr. Lunch with Lloyd George, Hankey and Philip.
>
> Before lunch Lloyd George gave me Robertson's answer to the Cabinet question which Mdlner asked me this morning — the effect of an inconclusive peace — ending with a demand for "more men" and "more ships," or it would be best to make peace. We talked for hours. I described my present war game at Versailles and our rough results, and Lloyd George was much interested. He made several valuable suggestions, especially about the Boches not attacking in the west, but going for Odessa and the north of the Black Sea, and holding us off meanwhile.
>
> I warned Philip before leaving that Lloyd George must not be allowed to kick Robertson out and put me in there, but much better for him to keep Robertson, and gradually give Versailles more power in the larger issues.
>
> Then to Carson and told him of my war game. He is angry with Lloyd George for his constant abuse of Robertson, in which he is quite right. A long day but, I think, good work, and I hope that I may save Robertson.

Next day Wilson wrote:

> Two long talks with Robertson; also read his paper on our chances of improving our position this year, the same paper as Lloyd

George showed me yesterday. I told him that I did not know what he meant about having adequate men and adequate ships, or else make peace. Then I discussed his Palestine paper, which amounts to doing nothing there, which I can't agree to.

Also long talk with Milner, who is in his house with a cold. He agrees with me that we ought to push about like the devil in the Caucasus, and if possible push on in Palestine. Allenby has had another success there yesterday. Also we must try and get command of the Black Sea.

Really we must change in 1918 our puerile, useless, costly strategy of 1916 and 1917. This past year has been a terrible disappointment, Russia and Italy failing so disastrously. Lloyd George has to-day handed over to Versailles the study of all these questions, and also of how we shall stand a year hence, of the Ukraine and Caucasus, of what chance we have of beating the Boches in the field in 1918 or 1919. All these questions have been sent to me to-day from the War Cabinet.

It should be explained that Wilson's underlying conception of the part which "Versailles" ought to play was that this should be in a position to examine, as a whole, all the various theatres of war, the man-power, the material and the communications at the disposal of the Allies, instead of these being considered separately for each theatre. Note No. 12 summed up these points, and it arrived at the conclusion that the Allies would not be strong enough to initiate attack on the Western Front in 1918, but that they could do so elsewhere, although they ought also to he fully prepared to take advantage of enemy mistakes, or of enemy exhaustion arising from the attacks which the Germans evidently contemplated in the West. Robertson, on the other hand, maintained that all available resources in personnel, other than those derived from India and those required for defensive purposes in distant theatres of war like Macedonia, Palestine, and Mesopotamia, ought to be employed on the Western Front — this in view of the vety formidable forces which the Germans would have at their disposal in that quarter in the coming spring and summer. Wilson believed that it might prove practicable to cause the Turks very serious trouble, and possibly even to detach them from Germany, without seriously prejudicing Allied prospects in the main theatre of war. Robertson, on the other hand, did not consider that the situation in the main theatre of war justified the devoting of resources to such ulterior objectives, however desirable they might be in themselves. (Leaving mounted troops and Indian divisions out of consideration, there were, on January 1, 17 British divisions in Macedonia, Egypt, Palestine and Mesopotamia, while there were 47 British divisions and 10 divisions from the Dominions on the Western Front.)

Wilson returned to Versailles from London on January 2, and saw Clemenceau next day in Paris. He found "the Tiger" somewhat out of humour; for Lloyd George was proposing a meeting of the Supreme War Council in London, and he was also proposing to discuss terms of peace. Clemenceau expressed himself as indisposed to set out what were the Allies' war aims, saying that these had been stated quite often enough. To this Wilson rejoined that those war aims were always changing, that there used to be talk about the independence of Poland, but that this subject had been dropped, and that little was ever mentioned now except Alsace-Lorraine. Clemenceau agreed, and he also intimated his concurrence in a proposal of Sir Henry's that aeroplane, railway and tank strategy should be brought under Versailles. Wilson afterwards saw Bonar Law, who was thinking about peace terms and believed that Germany might be disposed to restore Alsace-Lorraine to France and to make other concessions if given a free hand on the Russian side, and he wrote in his diary:

> I don't believe a word of this, but, as I said to Bonar, if she is feeling like that she must be nearly beat, and if she is nearly beat then let us beat her and have done with it. All this peace talk frightens me, for it creates a Boche atmosphere.

This appears in the diary on the following day:

> Leo Maxse to lunch. He said that on November 29 in Paris Lloyd George wanted to send envoys to meet the Austrians in Switzerland, that both Clemenceau and Sonnino objected, but that Lloyd George insisted, and that Smuts had been there once, and was going again. Curiously enough Esher told this to the Lord last night in Paris, and he passed it on to me.

I can't make out why Milner did not tell me about Smuts. It makes me uneasy, especially in view of Lloyd George's questions as to what we soldiers can do to better the situation in 1918, and, if we cannot better it, would it not be better to see what terms we can make now! All this makes me uneasy and suspicious.

Then, this afternoon brings me a letter from Macready in which he says that the last report on our man-power is dreadful reading, and amounts to this — that we must reduce our 56 divisions from 12 to 9 battalions, that in July we shall have to reduce from 56 to 44, and next winter from 44 to 30. This is simply damnable. I wrote Milner a long letter, in which I told him that if these figures were true then we must do one of two things: 1. Get more men. 2. Make peace now. Personally I rejected 2 as being cowardly and fatal in every way, at least until we were strained to breaking point. But I saw no difficulty in 1, which meant real conscription in England and Ireland, neither of which things have terrors for me compared with peace. But I confess that all this frightens me, and if Macready's figures prove true, and if Lloyd George won't take drastic action, then *I will*.

Next day Sir Henry had a talk with Clemenceau on the subject of Smuts's expedition to Switzerland. "He thinks Lloyd George is a fool, and an extra fool for choosing Smuts who 'didn't know where Austria was,' " Wilson wrote in his diary; but he at the same time came to the conclusion that "the Tiger" was not really anxious about this Swiss mission. The Military Representatives held a meeting at Versailles on the 7th (it was at this that their recommendation as to how far the B.E.F. should take over front from the French, already mentioned, was first considered), and after it was over Frazier had a talk with Wilson, of which Sir Henry wrote in his diary:

> It seems that Pershing has rather fallen out with Pétain, and then, in addition. Bliss who is coming here to Versailles is senior to Pershing. So poor Frazier is in a stove.

But the news that Bliss was coming back and taking up the appointment of American Military Representative on the Supreme War Council was very welcome to Sir Henry, who had found the United States Chief of Staff very practical and pleasant to deal with as a colleague during thek previous intercourse. A day or two later Robertson arrived in Paris, and accounts of the discussions that Wilson had with the C.I.G.S. appear in the diary on January 9 and 10:

> Long talk with Robertson. He gave me a paper written by Military Members of the Army Council in which they say that the man-power report only means 100,000 "A" men for the Army. This, of course, would settle the war. Robertson is very much ojpposed to Palestine. I gave him my proposal for keeping a certain number of divisions away from Haig and Pétain, and which those men could only draw on with permission of Versailles, or of Robertson and Foch.* He said that the politicians were taking increased charge of military affairs.
> Robertson came down and spent an hour talking to me. He told me of his meeting with Pershing last night and this morning, and of how he thought he had persuaded Pershing to agree to battalions of Americans being embodied in our army for training. The French want the same thing, and Pershing sees Pétain to-morrow before giving Robertson a final answer. Clemenceau told Robertson, just as he told me, that he did not care who they went to provided they came over as fast as possible.
> I told Robertson of our decision about the line, and then I talked again of the vital necessity of having a Central Reserve under Versailles or under him and Foch. Then I told him of the war game, and I took him up and showed him our maps, and Ollivant laid out his various attacks. He was a good deal knocked about by all this.

Of a visit to Clemenceau on the 11th he wrote:

> I found the old man tired and depressed. He said the Americans were going to come too late, and that he would be dead very soon. He told me he was losing his sleep, which is bad. He said I was to do as I liked about the railways. I told him my scheme for a Central Reserve under Versailles, which, he said, meant "under Wilson" — to which I agreed. And I spoke long and earnestly to him on this question, and of three Boche attacks, the third being launched when the first two had used up all Haig's and Pétain's reserves. This would be fatal, and my plan of Reserves under Versailles, or Foch and Robertson, is the

---

* This is the first mention in the diary of a General Reserve.

only possible solution.

Important changes were taking place at G.H.Q., Kiggell, whose health had been indifferent for some time, being replaced by Sir H. Lawrence, and a fresh Quartermaster-General and fresh Director of Intelligence being appointed. Wilson was also consulted just at this time by Lloyd George as to a project conceived by the Prime Minister of making Joffre generalissimo, with himself (Wilson) as Chief of Staff, and he mentions in his diary:

> I wrote Milner a long letter setting out that in my opinion we cannot have a generalissimo, but that, if this was tried, it would make it still more impossible if he was given a foreigner as Chief of Staff. I also told Milner of my proposal for a Central Reserve under Versailles.

Sir Henry was at this juncture giving special attention to Palestine and its possibilities, and on his receiving a message from Lloyd George not to send in a paper that he was supposed to be preparing on the subject until he had seen Smuts, who was on the way to Paris, he remarked in his diary, "I wonder what this trick is." He continued:

> I had a meeting of Studd, Hereward and Sykes on this matter, and I asked them to change their minds as to the best way to approach the problem, and first to find out whether we were safe in England, France, and Italy, and then, if the answer was in the affirmative, examine the Palestine and Mesopotamian problem and see what could be done. Not to approach the problem in the way that the War Office has done, by starting at the wrong end and ruling out Palestine and Mesopotamia to start with.

He wrote in the diary next day (January 16):

> Long talks with Smuts and Leo Amery. Smuts has been sent over by Lloyd George to ask my opinion on the following matter: Would it be a good plan to appoint Smuts as C. in C. and High Commissioner to Palestine — Mesopotamia — Armenia — Caucasus and Eastern Mediterranean. He is to be outside and not under the War Office; he is to remain a member of the War Cabinet, and as such to deal direct

with Government Departments, the Sirdar, the Viceroy of India, etc. At the same time he is to conduct operations and issue orders to the Admiral in the Mediterranean, to Allenby, to Marshall, and so on. Whew! Whew! Whew! After a tremendous wrangle I think I got it into their heads that such an appointment is quite out of the question. But on the other hand, there was much to be said for appointing one officer over both Palestine and Mesopotamia, and co-ordinating the whole movement against the Turks.

Much more talk again to-night about a drive against the Turk, and I told Smuts that my mind was travelling this way — that the Boche could not get a decision against us, that we could not get one against him in the West, and that therefore we ought to try and knock out the Turk.

At a conversation which Wilson had with Clemenceau on January 17 the latter told him that Haig, Pétain, and Pershing had met at Compiègne a few days earlier, and that an agreement had been arrived at to extend the British front to the Laon-Soissons road. Sir Henry, however, explained that only Versailles had agreed to this, and not Haig. He seized the opportumty to press his proposal as to creating a Central Reserve, taking the line that this Reserve ought to be under Versailles, and not, as he had been prepared to accept a few days earlier, under Foch and Robertson. Clemenceau appeared to be ready to agree to the proposed arrangement.

A day or two later Sir Henry was somewhat surprised to learn that, at a conference between the Commanders-in-Chief at Compiègne, Pétain had consented to the B.E.F. only taking over the line as far as Barisis. The whole situation was further complicated just at this time by the starting of a violent Press campaign in England directed against Robertson and, to a somewhat less extent, against Haig. Concerning this Press campaign Sir Henry wrote in his diary, "Now is this Lloyd George, and is he going to lead an attack of the 'You are butchers' type on a depth of 2 years from Loos to Cambrai?" After a talk with Foch on the 23rd he noted in the diary:

> He told me that he held to the Versailles ruling about the line. Foch is quite of my mind about the necessity of a Reserve and says

that Clemenceau will nominate him (Foch) as the French Military Representative to dispose of its use; and he wanted to know what Lloyd George would do. I told him I could not say, especially in view of this heavy campaign against Robertson. I did not myself see how either Robertson or Haig could last after such an attack.

We discussed Lloyd George, and Foch cannot understand why he can't or won't take any decisive action. I told Foch that Lloyd George is now in three holes: (a) The French line, where he must decide to back Haig and Robertson, or me; (b) The man-power and the "butcher's bill"; (c) Carson and the Irish Conference.* The President of the U.S.A, seems to be on the edge of barging in about Ireland, and there is a scandalous sort of threat in this morning's Paris *Daily Mail*.

Later we had a meeting of Military Representatives, and we passed a new resolution, which I had drafted, saying that the creation of a Central Reserve is imperative, but that, before laying out a scheme, the Military Representatives would like to know what the C. in C.s and the C.G.S.s think.

General Bliss had by this time returned from the United States, accompanied by a staff of officers who were to help him at Versailles, and he pronounced himself as in favour of America sending over 150 individual battalions, for them to be incorporated in the 150 brigades of the B.E.F. He declared himself ready to press this point upon his Government if Wilson thought such a course desirable. Sir Henry promised that he would be able to convince his American colleague next day; he set about doing so in characteristically original and trenchant fashion, and this appears in his diary:

> Bliss and 4 of his officers came this morning, and I gave them a lecture, wkh maps, on our war game. Then Bertie Studd and Hereward played the game for them, and they were immensely struck by the whole thing, and Bliss told me that he had never dreamt of such a thing and that it was intensely interesting, and that we had made out an overwhelming case for America helping us with every single man possible in every possible shape. So we did a real good

---

* The Irish Convention that had been sitting for a long time, trying to hit upon some solution of the Irish problem, had just broken down, and Carson had resigned from the war Cabinet in consequence.

Two and a Half Months Military Representative...

morning's work.

The understanding between the United States Government and those of the Allies in Europe was that America would send over two divisions a month. The 150 battalions above referred to were to be sent in addition to the divisions already decided upon. But although Bliss was anxious to see this plan of American battalions being attached to brigades of the B.E.F. carried out, General Pershing was, not altogether unnaturally, inclined to look askance at the project, Robertson, as it happened, arrived in Paris on January 27, in view of a meeting of the Supreme War Council that was to take place on the 30th, and Sir Henry had a long talk with him on the 28th at the Crillon with reference to this question of the American battalions, as well as other subjects. Owing to the man-power problem, the infantry in the divisions of the B.E.F. was very short of establishment, and the United States units would go far to compensate for this untoward shortage. The training of these units arriving in the theatre of war from the far side of the Atlantic would also assuredly benefit by their finding themselves alongside the war-worn battalions figuring in Haig's sectors of the Western Front. This is noted in the diary:

> I told him of what Bliss told me, and he quite agreed with me that we must force Pershing's hand by going straight to Wilson. I then discussed our Resolution 12, "the 1918 Campaign," with him. He asked why, when I knew that out effectives could not be kept up, I put in as a condition that the total aggregate of troops now in France must be maintained. I replied that it was quite simple, that, having studied the problem thoroughly, I had come to the conclusion that if our effectives were kept up we were safe, and if not then we were unsafe, and that I wanted to fix the responsibility on the Prime Ministers — which is where it must rest.
> We then discussed my paper about Reserve, and I told him that my original idea of having a small pool under Versailles, or under Foch and him, would not do, and that on working out the battle carefully I had come to the conclusion that all the Reserve must be under one authority. I told him that for the first time in the war I was wavering about a C. in C. But he said "We can't do that." So I left him to think over it.

Lloyd George and Milner, with others, arrived at Versailles to stay on the 28th, and the war game was played before them next morning, the whole party being much impressed and Lloyd George asking appropriate and intelligent questions. A meeting of Pershing, Bliss, Robertson, Haig and Wilson then took place on the subject of the 150 American battalions, and Sir Henry wrote in his diary:

> Nothing settled, but I had a talk with Pershing afterwards, and I am convinced that he would agree to recommend if only he is properly handled and if the case is properly put to him.

Nor was Wilson, according to the diary, by any means satisfied at the course taken by a discussion which he had with Haig and Robertson on the subjects of taking over line and of a General Reserve.* His account of the conferences held on the following day (30th), and of discussions that took place before and after the formal meeting, is therefore of particular interest:

> Clemenceau, Orlando, Smuts came here to my house at 10 a.m., and with Lloyd George and Milner they talked for 2½ hours. They discussed the loan of 11 Italian divisions to replace ours, and then the Central Reserve. They not only agreed that one was necessary, but Clemenceau insisted that it must be a big one of — he said — 40 divisions. He would not hear of my original proposal of 10 or 12 divisions. They then discussed the question of command, and were inclined to a board of officers, and Lloyd George was ready to accept Versailles; but Clemenceau said he could not agree to Weygand. Lloyd George, discussing the matter later with me, said that he found it very difficult to know what to do about Robertson and me, though he said he knew what he wanted.
> At 12 o'clock Haig, Lawrence, Davidson, Maurice and others came, and we played our war game for them. Pershing came to lunch, and Lloyd George got him to sign a paper agreeing to some 70 battalions coming to us for training.
> Then we had our 2nd Meeting of Supreme War Council at 3

---

* The term "General Reserve" gradually came to be substituted for "Central Reserve."

p.m., with Clemenceau in the chair. Clemenceau began at once on our Resolutions 12 and 14, viz.: the 1918 Campaign and the question of Reserve and he invited opinions from C. in C.s and Chiefs of Staffs. Foch, Robertson, Cadorna, and Bliss expressed themselves in favour of our note in so far as having an active defence and having a Reserve. Then Haig began and, having said he agreed, he went on to show that by the autumn his present 57 divisions would be reduced to 30! Such was the state of man-power. Pétain followed on this and showed that he would have to reduce by the autumn to the tune of 25 divisions if *he had no fighting*, and by 50 divisions if he had some fighting. This was all too much for Lloyd George, who said he was absolutely dumbfounded that 77 divisions were going to be wiped off in this manner, and that really he could not accept these figures, and that he must ask all the Chiefs of Staffs to furnish the figures on which these calculations were made by to-morrow morning. Now all this is extraordinary.

After dinner Lloyd George, Milner and I had a long talk. I advised Lloyd George to re-establish at once the power and prestige of Versailles by sitting as a Supreme Council and not as a Mass Meeting, then by sending for the Military Representatives, and then for any soldier they wish to ask questions of. I do so hope that he will do this, and I urged it as strongly as I could. As regards Haig and Robertson he does not know what to do. I told Milner afterwards that, if it would help them to solve the problem, I would resign with pleasure.

Orlando this morning paid me a charming compliment. He reminded me of a meeting I had with him at Padua in his bedroom, and he said he had always since called me "*le Rothschild des bons espoirs.*"*

Next day there was another meeting, also partaking rather of the nature of a mass meeting/" at which the talk was as discursive as was usual on such occasions, and Wilson that evening wrote in his diary:

And so another meeting 10 a.m. to-morrow, to discuss the campaign of 1918, which we were by way of doing all to-day. The three Prime Ministers sent a very strong wire to President Wilson to clear his railways and docks to allow of 2,000,000 tons of wheat

---

* "The Rothschild of good hopes."

to come over in February and March.

His record of the meeting next day (February i) reads as follows:

> At the conference this morning, with the same people present, we passed nearly all the fourteen Notes we have sent to the Supreme Council. The great fight was about our 1918 Note and the Reserve Note. Robertson fought both, but was over-ruled on the 1918 Note, and Lloyd George was angry with him.*
> After lunch we spent all the afternoon on the question of Central Reserve. Robertson fought this, and wanted the command to be given to Foch and himself. I wrote out notes for Lloyd George, showing the duties of the Commanders of this Reserve, and how impossible it would be for C.I.G.S. to be over here to perform them. Lloyd George entirely agreed, and showed that neither London, Rome nor Washington could spare their C.I.G.S., though Paris, of course, was different. Bliss suggested the Chiefs of Staffs of the C. in C.s, but I showed how impossible this was. There remained, therefore, only two solutions (as everyone agreed that a C. in C. was impossible) — one was Versailles, and the other was some Generals *ad hoc*, Lloyd George suggested an adjournment, and that each Prime Minister should bring a cut-and-dried scheme to-morrow morning.

Of the proceedings on the 2nd, Wilson wrote in his diary:

> Lloyd George, Milaer, Hankey and I breakfasted in my room, and Hankey turned my proposals, written yesterday, for creation, command and use of the General Reserve, into the form of a Resolution. This Resolution was later on adopted unanimously at the Conference, and so the long duel between me and Robertson has ended in his complete defeat. The Executive Board, now set up, consists of the Military Representatives here, less Weygand plus

---

* Clemenceau would appear to have sided with Robertson as regards the 1918 Note, being wholly opposed to the idea of weakening the forces on the Western Front for the purpose of overcoming the Turks; Foch seems to have expressed no opinion with regard to die question on this occasion. The Prime Minister's irritation against his C.I.G.S. was caused by Robertson having expressed views on the subject, contrary to his own. Sir William, both in his "From Private to Field-Marshal" and his "Soldiers and Statesmen," makes effective reference in this connexion to Mr. Lloyd George's evidence before the Dardanelles Committee.

Foch. Robertson fought to the last to be on it, but was badly beaten. I wonder will he resign? We then finished our conference by agreeing about taking over the line to Barisis, and making an *étude*[*] of taking over more,[†] and, all our Notes having been endorsed, the conference ended at 5 p.m.

The most far-reaching decisions were reached, and unanimously, and the most important of all our conferences is finished. Robertson was overruled about the 1918 campaign, and squarely beaten over the question of command of the General Reserve. In other words, our Cabinet and the Cabinets of all the Allies have backed everjrthing Versailles has devised. This really was a triumph.

The first meeting of the newly-formed "Executive Board" set up to control the General Reserve — Foch, Cadorna, Bliss and Wilson — took place on the following day, and it was proposed that this Reserve should consist for the present of 30 divisions — 14 French, 9 British and 7 Italian. It was also proposed that the French and 5 British divisions then in Italy should, for the time being, be included in the 30. But at a meeting of the Executive Board on the 5th a serious difference of opinion arose, for, according to Wilson's diary:

> Foch stood out for 10 British, 13 French, 7 Italian divisions, but

---

[*] "Study."

[†] In a letter to his brother-in-law, Price-Davies, then acting as Liaison Officer between himself and Cavan in Italy, Wilson on May 4 following told the story of what occurred in connexion with this question of the taking over of line: "D.H. very properly objected to taking over more line, but at a meeting of P.M.s last September (Robertson being present) it was agreed that, when the Paschendaele offensive was over, the exact amount was to be settled by the two C. in C.s. Well, in January, the two C. in C.s not being able to agree, the matter was referred to Versailles for arbitration! After three weeks of *most* careful and thorough examination, we (Versailles) said that the British should take over up to the Soissons-Laon road. Meanwhile, and while we were at work, the two C. in C.s agreed to the point of junction being at Barisis, i.e. about 2½ divisions less than we (Versailles) thought the British ought to extend to. At the meeting of the Supreme CouncE on February 2, the P.M.s agreed to Barisis, i.e. the decision of the C. in C.s, and overruled the decision of their own Military Representatives. So L. G. has a clean sheet."

could give no reason; and, when Bliss agreed with him and Cadorna with me, he jumped up and gave a casting vote and said 10, 13, 7, had been decided. Of course, I knocked out the casting vote, and then we broke up.

That same composition of the General Reserve was nevertheless agreed to at the next meeting of the Executive Board, subject to two British divisions being relieved by the Belgians up in Flanders. Then, on the evening of February 9, Wilson started for London in response to a telephone message from Milner asking him to go over at once, and he arrived at Eaton Place on the following afternoon. He wrote in his diary:

> I saw Milner at 6 o'clock, and he told me what had happened. Lloyd George had three plans, namely: 1. Send Robertson to York and replace him by Plumer; 2, send Robertson to York and replace him by Haig, replacing Haig by Plumer; 3, send Robertson to Versailles and bring me here as C.I.G.S. After tremendous discussion and vacillation he had now decided on 3, and had sent an emissary to Robertson, who is in the country for a few days, to offer either Versailles or a Command. This is pushing about with a vengeance. Milner said that he was sure Lloyd George now meant to carry this out, so that I really am afraid that I may find myself C.I.G.S. within the next few days.
>
> If, however, Robertson refuses Versailles, then Milner and I agreed that he should put in someone junior to me, and let me have a directing voice in Versailles if I was C.I.G.S, The whole thing is rather muddlesome.

Sir Henry's admission on the occasion of this meeting with Lord Milner that, in case he should be appointecl C.I.G.S., it would be well if the British Military Representative at Versailles should be an officer junior to himself so that he should possess a directing voice in that quarter, is one of peculiar interest. He was evidently coming to realhe that the British Military Representative ought to be in a measure subordinate to the C.I.G.S. just as Weygand was subordiuate to Foch. It was not, as will be seen, the plan that was actually in the first instance adopted when Wilson took Robertson's place at the War Office shortly afterwards; but it was adopted at a later date (after the "Executive Board" had virtually ceased to exist) and it thenceforward worked most satisfactorily. The meetings of the Supreme War Council a few days before had made manifest the objections to the Military Representative and the C.I.G.S. being officials of equal standing, of their being wholly independent of one another, and of their holding diametrically opposing views on questions of the very first moment.

There followed six days of chaos, of chaos that was apparently directly attributable to lack of purpose on the part of the Prime Minister. On the first day (February 11) Wilson saw Lord Derby, and the Secretary of State then showed him a note drafted by Mr. Lloyd George. This note laid down, clearly enough, what were to be the relations between Robertson and Wilson when Robertson became Military Representative at Versailles and Wilson became C.I.G.S. Under the new arrangement the Military Representative, although he was to be given a seat on the Army Council, was placed in a position to some extent subordinate to the C.I.G.S. One paragraph of the note indeed ordained that, when the Military Representative had decided upon the advice that he intended to give to the Supreme War Council on any matter, he was to submit it to the C.I.G.S. This, it will be remembered (*vide* the extract from Wilson's diary given on p. 47-48) Wilson had, when the Army Council had given directions to the same effect at the time when Versailles was first set up, taken strong exception to. In another paragraph of the note it was enacted that the position of the C.I.G.S. was to be reduced to that which holders of that appointment had occupied prior to the time of Robertson taking it up at the end of 1915 . He had then been given certain special powers, notably in connexion with giving orders to commanders in the field — Robertson had indeed made the granting of these prerogatives a condition of his accepting the post. The Secretary of State for War led Sir Henry to believe at this interview that it was now definitely settled that he (Sir Henry) was to be C.I.G.S. But next day there was quite a different story — as appears from the entry on the subject in Wilson's diary:

> Milner came in, 10 p.m., to say the whole place was in a mess, that Derby proposed to keep on Robertson, but thought that Robertson's special privilege of issuing orders should be curtailed

and the old Army Council revived, that Lloyd George (who is very seedy) had more or less agreed, that no decision had been reached, that in reality Robertson had won all along the line, and that the position of the Government was critical; that Curzon appeared to be backing Robertson, with Bonar Law washy, and only Barnes and he (Milner) standing up for bringing me here and sending Robertson to Versailles. Milner says this state of things cannot possibly last, and if Lloyd George does not catch hold he will be out.

The account in the diary of what happened next day reads:

I went up to Derby House and had a talk with Derby alone. I told him that in my opinion the Government had now better send Robertson to Versailles. I offered to come as C.I.G.S., or go on half-pay, or do anything that would help the Government. I can't do more. He said it was now intended to put me on the Army Council and take away Robertson's present superior position, reverting to the old manner of Army Council. I told him that Robertson would not agree, and as he had already won over refusing to go to Versailles so he would win again over this.

Went to see Milner at 2 p.m., and Milner is clear that a short statement must be issued, setting forth the real facts of the case; how Versailles had been made more important, how it had been offered to Robertson who had refused it, and how the old Army Council was going to be resuscitated and I was going to be made a Member. He said he would draft in that sense.

Then I went to see Robertson and we had a good talk; we differ fundamentally because he wants Versailles to be under him, and I say it cannot be. I told him that if I was Prime Minister I would order him out to Versailles, and that, as regards myself, I was perfectly content to go on half-pay. Our meeting was quite friendly. I then went over to Downing Street.

Milner read me out a draft, which was admirably clear and short, and Lloyd George had just agreed to it, if Derby would also. So I walked over to the War Office with J. T. Davies [Lloyd George's private secretary] with this draft. Creedy [private secretary to the S. of S.] took it in to Derby, and Robertson went in immediately after. In ten minutes Greedy came out with a note saying Robertson would not agree. I then went in to Derby and told him again that Versailles could not be deputy to anyone, and he went off to see Robertson in his room.

Two and a Half Months Military Representative... 73

I then went over to 10 Downing Street, and, after waiting till Lloyd George had finished with the Irish Conference, had a talk with him. I told him that Robertson wanted to get Versailles under him and that, in my judgment, this was impossible, and that Robertson should have his special powers — given to him by Asquith to cripple Lord Kitchener — curtailed, and that the Army Gouncil should resume its normal functions. Lloyd George gave me a draft of a proposed solution, in which I am made Deputy C.I.G.S., but given a certain amount of freedom. But I told him that I objected to the Deputy C.I.G.S., which I thought unsound and unworkable. He asked me to take this proposal to Milner and discuss it with him, which I did. He is writing to Lloyd George, as Derby and Robertson breakfast with Lloyd George to-morrow. So there we stand to-night and nothing has been settled.

The next day's (February 14) doings are recorded as follows in the diary:

I saw J. T. Davies, and he told me that Milner had last night written strongly to Lloyd George against the idea of my being a Deputy, and Lloyd George had said he was going to take charge of the whole thing mmself; and J. T. told me that Robertson had not breakfasted with Lloyd George this morning, only Derby. I saw Hankey and he told me that the Cabinet had finally decided to reduce the status of C.I.G.S. to its former place, to place the Military Representative at Versailles on the Army Council, and then they had offered Robertson the post. Arthur Balfour and Derby had been at 3 o'c. to Robertson with this offer.
I called round to see J. T. at Downing Street at 7 o'c., and J. T. told me Robertson had refused both, and that Plumer had been wired to and offered C.I.G.S. under, of course, the altered conditions. If Plumer agrees, then Robertson will be offered Plumer's command in Italy. Milner telephoned and corroborated all I had heard, and told me the vacillations and uncertainties all day had nearly killed him! But he hoped it would be all right now.

On the following evening (15th) Wilson went to see Milner by appointment, only to learn that he was with Bonar Law at 11 Downing Street, and on proceeding thither Sir Henry found the two Ministers in consultation with Hankey over a fresh development; Plumer, it appeared, had refused the appointment of C.I.G.S. and had, moreover, added that he did not agree with the proposals as regards the command of the General Reserve. This was telephoned down to Lloyd George at Walton Heath, who thereupon asked the three to repair thither at once, which, after a hurried dinner, they did. "At last I found Lloyd George in real fighting trim," Wilson noted in his diary. "He sees now, and fully admits, his weakness up to now, and how instead of leading he has balanced one interest against another." The diary goes on to relate how Lloyd George and Milner agreed that Milner should take Derby's place and should appoint Wilson C.I.G.S., and that they should then go over to G.H.Q. and consult Haig as to who had better succeed Sir Henry at Versailles.

At 5 o'clock next evening, the 16th, Wilson received a telephone message at his house from the Cabinet Secretariat Office to say that he had been appointed C.I.G.S., and adding that Haig was coming over to discuss the question of his successor at Versailles; also that Hankey, under the impression that Sir Henry had taken over the duties of C.I.G.S., was already sending some important wires from Smuts in Egypt for him to see. The notice to the Press announcing that Robertson had refused the position of C.I.G.S. under the new conditions and had also refused Versailles, and that he himself had been appointed C.I.G.S. was read to Wilson over the telephone from Downing Street a little later, and Milner shortly afterwards came in to announce that Derby was still War Minister. The diary mentions:

> Esher rang up to say that Haig was over and that Derby had met him. He asked me if I was C.I.G.S., and I told him I had just gone down to Victoria to buy a paper to find out, and that there was nothing in it.

Later in the evening Wilson, however, learnt that the official *communiqué* on the subject was posted up in the clubs.

The morrow was a Sunday, and Wilson in the first place went down to see Lloyd George at Walton Heath and afterwards went to visit Haig at his house at Kingston. "He said all these quarrels had nothing to do with him and that he was prepared to accept whatever was decided by the Cabinet, and he would then play up all he could," Sir Henry noted in his diary, and this also mentions that the Field-Marshal favoured Rawlinson for the appointment at Versailles.

This appears in the diary next day:

> The newspapers full of Robertson and me, and his resignation and my appointment. I had a talk with Gwynne on the telephone about his leader this morning, which was based on a fallacy. I then got on the telephone to Creedy to ask him who I was. Creedy[*] was amazed to hear that I had not had a "bit of paper" from Derby, and said he would ask Derby when he turned up at the office. I then saw Derby at 12.15 p.m. and he ordered me to take over C.I.G.S. tomorrow morning. He is not resigning. He told me Robertson had accepted the Eastern Command. I am still shown in the Army List as being there!

And so at length, ten days after Sir Henry had hurried to London and had there been made aware by Lord Milner that he and Sir W. Robertson were to change places, he was definitely appointed Chief of the Imperial General Staff, and his connexion with the Supreme War Council in the capacity of British Military Representative at Versailles came to an end. He had worked wonders while holding his previous appointment and developing its functions. In pursuance of a system which had in reality been devised by himself, all manner of questions affecting the future course of the war had been discussed by him in detail with French, Italian and American colleagues. What appeared to be the best course to pursue in each case had been committed to paper, and the document thus setting forth collective, expert opinion had been submitted to the Supreme War Council.

In preparing the original drafts of such documents, Wilson and his staff had taken the undisputed lead. "Nine-tenths of the detailed wotk of the inter-Allied Staff was initiated and carried out in the British section," according to an article on Henry Wilson's career which appeared in *Blackwood's Magazine* from the pen of Mr. L. S. Amery in August, 1922. He had, in fact, within the space of two

---

[*] Lord Derby's Private Secretary.

and a half months, made his recently created department at Versailles one of real authority in controlling the destinies of the Allies, in so fat as this was possible in the advisory as apart from the executive sense. He had furthermore played a conspicuous part in persuading the Supreme War Council to agree to the principle of setting up a General Reserve, and in prevailing upon that body to establish an Executive Board which would control the employment of the General Reserve. The acceptance of the principle of a General Reserve and the establishing of the Executive Board constituted a momentous step forward in the direction of securing that Unity of Command which the records of the past three and a half years of conflict had shown to be needed, but which had not even yet become an accomplished fact.

Chapter XXII – February and March, 1918: The Great German Offensive

Wilson C.I.G.S. — Difficulties as to General Reserve — The great Enemy Offensive launched near St. Quentin — The Doullens Conference — The Enemy checked short of Amiens.

The problem which principally engaged Sir Henry's attention at the outset, as it had engaged the attention of his predecessor, was that of man-power, and of the untoward diminution in the strength of the effectives in the various theatres of war, especially on the Western Front, that was taking place. He was far from satisfied with the attitude which was being adopted by the War Cabinet in reference to this vital matter; but the representations that he made proved of little avail until the crash came a month after his assumption of office. Far too many exemptions were, in his opinion, being permitted, and he held very strong views with regard to the imperative need of compelling Ireland to bear her fair share of the burden. Sir Henry, it may be added, felt even less sympathy with the so-called "conscientious objector" than did the vast majority of his fellow countrymen.*

---

* A story of his in this connexion, which he took particular delight in telling, ran as follows: "A soldier with three wound-stripes on his sleeve was listening to one of these shirkers, who was addressing a small company in the vicinity of the Marble Arch. The soldier presently demanded of the orator why he was not in

Wilson motored down on February 25 to where the Prime Minister was staying, in company with Milner, and the diary records:

> Lloyd George had received a wire from Clemenceau saying he had "certain" information that the Boches thought they would be in Calais on March 15 and Paris April 15. Rubbish. Rawly wires to say that Haig thinks my idea of General Reserve of 30 divisions much too big, and Haig thinks he can give 2 divisions, and Pétain thinks he can give 8. And Rawly agrees.

The C.I.G.S. also mentions that he discussed Ireland with Lloyd George during this visit, and that he seized the occasion to urge the Prime Minister to "govern" that country. He moreover makes reference to his having intimated that he was prepared to transfer a division from Mesopotamia to Palestine, but that there appeared already to be enough troops under Allenby in that theatre, and that what was really wanted for the purpose of an active campaign in the Holy Land was railways and rolling stock. Then, on the 25th, Sir Henry crossed the Channel, and he stayed that night at Montreuil, after having met Rawlinson at Boulogne on the way. He wrote in the diary:

> A talk with Haig about his ear-marking some divisions for the Versailles Reserve. He flatly refuses, says he won't be responsible for his line, and rather than do it he would resign. He is quite prepared to agree to any divisions we have in Italy being treated as General Reserve, but no others. All this is difflcult. Then, after dinner, a long talk with Lawrence. In the end he agreed to this alternative — which I must think over — viz., that no divisions should be ear-marked for Versailles Reserve, but that Versailles shorild have the power of moving such forces as they thought fit, when they thought fit. Of course, this is exactly the same thing, but dressed differently.

In connexion with Haig's attitude over this question of his

---

khaki. 'I am not one of the militarists,' rejoined the conscientious objector; 'I am a soldier of Heaven, and God is my colonel.' 'That so? ' ejaculated the soldier, 'then all I can say is, you're a —— long way from barracks.'"

February and March, 1918: The Great German... 79

furnishing divisions for the General Reserve, it has to be remembered that the Field-Marshal was just at this time taking over several miles of front from the French on either side of the Oise — i.e. as far as Barisis — and that he was finding the existing defence works along this new stretch of front very inadequate.* The majority of his divisions, moreover, were woefully short of establishment; nor did there at this time appear to be any prospect whatever of the yawning gaps in the ranks being filled up by the War Cabinet. The British Commander-in-Chief would appear to have held the view that, were he to deliver up a number of his divisions for the purpose of creating a General Reserve that would not be under his own orders, the loss of those divisions would so weaken the reserves actually under his own hand that he would be unable to prevent the effectual penetration of his line in case of a serious attack. Nor can it be argued that this view was an entirely mistaken one, seeing that his line was effectually penetrated even as it was.

Wilson's appreciation of the situation on the other hand was in effect that a General Reserve would be able, supposing the line to be penetrated, to prevent the disaster becoming worse, or becoming irretrievable. It is also conceivable that Haig may to some extent have been influenced by scepticism as to whether a body such as the Executive Board at Versailles could be trusted to carry out its functions in an effectual manner, in the event of a grave crisis occurring. Lord Milner has placed on record that, almost exactly one month after this talk of Haig's with Wilson, on the day after the Doullens Conference which appointed Foch virtually Generalissimo, the Field-Marshal remarked, "I can deal with a man, not with a committee." Haig also apparently had some reason

---

* This was largely due to the fact that a considerable portion of the front taken over was down in the valley of the Oise, which was very marshy — so much so that the French had not thought it worth while to take the fortification of such ground very seriously. But, as it happened, February and March of 1918 turned out to be particularly dry months, after the wet autumn which had so seriously hampered Haig's offensive in Flanders. The consequence was that terrain which the French had looked upon as virtually impassable, had changed its character — a fact of which the enemy took full advantage when the blow at Gough's Army was delivered on March 21.

to believe that Pétain was not prepared to find any divisions for the General Reserve — as appears from a conversation which Wilson had with Clemenceau next day; for the following entry occurs in the diary:

> At 6 o'clock I went up to Paris to see M. Clemenceau. He was as nice as ever to me, and we had a long talk before I brought in Rawly to be introduced. The Tiger swore that it was absolute news to him when I told him that Foch had wired to Robertson advising the withdrawal of two of our divisions from Italy. He also did not know that Loucheur had told Haig that Pétain would not give any divisions to the General Reserve. But the situation seems to be this: The Tiger was up staying with Haig yesterday, and went round some of our lines (Vimy) etc., and saw some of our troops, and was very favourably impressed with all he saw. Haig told him flatly he would not hand over any of his divisions to the General Reserve, and Clemenceau thinks Haig would resign rather than do so. Clemenceau thinks this would be a disaster at this juncture. Then, in addition, the Tiger finds Pétain much in the same mood and does not want to quarrel with him, and he told me that he had not discussed this with Foch at all. On the whole therefore the Tiger favours the General Reserve being composed only of those troops which we can withdraw from Italy, and then perhaps let it grow later. I confess I don't agree, and said so bluntly, but I am not in a position to overcome the Tiger, Pétain and Haig.

Next day (February 27) he wrote:

> I told Rawly this morning that he must summon a meeting of Military Representatives, and also of the Executive Board, and he must take stock of where we are and what we are doing, otherwise Foch will begin ordering troops about on his own. It seems from a wire I received this morning from the War Office that Foch has ordered some 2,500 scallywags to Egypt without consulting us.
> At 11 o'clock Rawly and I went to see Foch. He took up a perfectly legitimate stand as regards Haig and the General Reserve. He said that the Governments had ordered the Executive Board to form and command a General Reserve. On that the Committee had drawn up proposals and sent them out to the C, in C.s. Pétain and Diaz had answered, the one with 8 and the other with 6 divisions. Haig had not answered, but had told Clemenceau he would not give

anything.* Foch claimed a written answer from Haig, giving his reasons, etc., and also saying whether he could not get 2 Belgian divisions to relieve 2 of his up to the Langemark railway. All this was perfecdy fair, and, of course. Rawly agreed to get it from Haig.

I asked about Guiilaumat's plan, and Foch said it was now actually on its way from Salonika. I asked about those scallywags going to Egypt, and he assured me our Foreign Office knew all about it!

Wilson got back to London on the last day of February, and Smuts arrived home from Palestine immediately afterwards. At a meeting of the War Cabinet held on March 4, after Smuts's return, it was decided to transfer a division from Mesopotamia to Palestine, and also to transfer several native Indian cavalry regiments from France to that theatre. Although of opinion that Haig was mistaken in refusing to furnish divisions for the General Reserve, Lloyd George agreed with Wilson that the Field-Marshal could not be compelled to do so at the existing juncture. One of the five British divisions in Italy was being transferred to the Western Front, and there was a question of another following; but, although Wilson was anxious that the move of the second division should take place at once, he was overruled on the subject by the War Cabinet. Plumer was, at Haig's request, wired for just at this time to return to the B.E.F. and to take up command of the Second Army, Cavan assuming charge of the British contingent in Venetia in his stead. Sir Henry learnt on March 5 that Haig had written officially, declining to find any divisions for the General Reserve, also that Rawlinson supported him in this attitude; and in communicating this fact to the War Cabinet on the following day he expressed the belief that Clemenceau was siding with Haig and Pétain against Foch in the matter. He wrote in his diary on the 8th:

> After lunch Lloyd George had an enormous Tank Committee, at which Winston said he would build 4,000 tanks by April, 1919. This

---

* It has been alleged that the proposals had not been sent officially to G.H.Q. till just about this very date, although they had been sent to Diaz and Pétain at the time when they were decided upon by the Executive Board. But this does not appear to be correct.

will require at least 100,000 men. Geddes doubted if Winston would get the steel. I doubted if I could get the men. But we decided to go on with the tanks, which I think on the whole was wise. There seem to be three answers to tanks: (a) Low-flying aeroplanes; (b) guns; (c) mines.

The last the most dangerous.

Then I saw Johnnie French, just back from a tour in Ireland. He says the country is in a shocking pie, but from a military point of view safe, because aeroplanes, armoured cars, maxims, etc., terrify the natives.

Next day there is the entry:

Letters from Rawly and Tit Willow. Rawly is combining with Douglas Haig and Pétain and the Tiger against the formation of the General Reserve.

On March 11 he wrote:

War Cabinet. The Boches have now 186 divisions over here, of which 92 face us. They ought not to attack until they have another 20 at least. Much talk at Cabinet about the Japanese joining us and going to Siberia. I have written a paper saying they must come in.

This appears on the 12th:

Proofs grow that the Boches will attack on the Arras front.

It had been arranged that a meeting of the Supreme War Council was to be held in London on the 14th, and Haig and Rawlinson arrived two days earlier so as to be present, followed on the 13th by Clemenceau, Orlando, Foch, Bliss and others. Wilson's diary contains much that is of particular interest during the few days when so many prominent figures, at the head of affairs in connexion with prosecuting the war, were in England. On the 13th, for instance, he wrote:

An Army Council meeting at which Guy Granet* explained the American shipping and rail situation in France. The Americans promised to send over engines and trucks to work their L. of C. They have done neither. We have lent them 10,000 trucks and a lot of engines. Now we have to find 10,000 trucks for coal for Italy, and we are quite incapable of doing so. I think that 600,000 tons of Dutch shipping now in American ports should be pinched to ease the situation.

Then a long talk with Douglas Haig, who came to see me. He says he can't and he won't give any divisions to the General Reserve. He explained that he had not enough for G.H.Q. Reserve, so the thing was impossible, and he said that, if I wanted a General Reserve, I must make some more divisions and I must get more man-power, I could not get him to see the problem in any other light. I impressed on him the fact that by refusing to contribute to the General Reserve he was killing that body, and he would have to live on Pétain's charity, and he would find that very cold charity. But I was quite unable to persuade him. I arranged for him to see Lloyd George tomorrow at 10 a.m., so that all this may be settled quietly and not at one of our mass meetings. Personally he was very nice to me.

I saw Nash,† who repeated all that Granet had said about the American railway problem, and told me we were in the devil of a tight place, as the French wanted 200,000 tons of strategic coal at once, and Italy wants 10,000 trucks.

I told Hankey to explain the situation about the General Reserve to Lloyd George, and to tell him that if Haig said he would resign if ordered to contribute to it, then in my opinion we ought to give up the idea of the General Reserve for the present. At this juncture I am clear that, if we have to choose between a General Reserve and Haig, we must choose Haig, wrong as I believe him to be. Then I saw Bliss, just over from Versailles, and I told him that I thought we must give up the General Reserve for the present. He rather wanted to make me believe that we had got it, but I was able to persuade him that I was right; also that we must reduce our programme of bringing over American troops to France and substitute engines and wagons. He

---

* Sir Guy Granet and Sir Sam Fay were Members of the Army Council at this time in connexion with railway work of all kinds.

† Major-General P. Nash was Inspector-General of Transportation on the Western Front at this time.

agreed to this also.

Then I saw Foch and Weygand and told them what I thought of the General Reserve and of the American question. Foch, of course, wants me to order Douglas Haig to contribute to the General Reserve, but, as I told him, this question is greatly complicated by the fact that Clemenceau and Pétain agree with Haig. He had no answer.

Then I saw Milner and told him that Douglas Haig was to see Lloyd George at 10 a.m. to-morrow, and if Lloyd George could not persuade Douglas Haig to contribute divisions to the General Reserve, then in my opinion the General Reserve and the Executive Board ought for the present to remain in abeyance. He agreed. Leo Amery there also, and in the end he agreed also.

Next day (March 14) Wilson wrote:

I saw Rawly and Bliss about necessity of giving up the programme of two American divisions a month, and getting over rolling stock in their place.

Then meeting of Supreme War Council at 11.50 at 10 Downing Street. Two hours' talk about General Reserve and no decision, then adjournment for lunch. I lunched with Lloyd George and Hankey, and at lunch we drafted a Resolution, afterwards adopted, to the effect that, to begin with, no divisions in France should be put in the General Reserve, but that our 5 and the French 6, with a quota of Italians — all in Italy — should form the nucleus. Of course, in a sense this is nonsense, as it does not give us any General Reserve; but it does keep the main idea alive, and it does save the position of the Executive Board. So that on the whole I think it is our best course. Foch protested against this arrangement, but Clemenceau accepted in the name of France. On the whole I was satisfied with to-day's work in the Supreme Council.

On the following day (the 15th) there is the entry:

I went to the Ritz at 10 a.m. and had a long and private talk with Foch. I knew he was up for fighting the decision reached yesterday, and he showed me a long statement he had drawn up, in which he claimed that the Supreme Council had gone back on its own ruling and had stultified itself, and that there was now no General Reserve and no possibility of making one, and that everyone was upset and no one was the better. I confess his case is sound, but I advised his not saying too much, but to be content with having his protest recorded; and this he did at the meeting later on.

Then Supreme War Council, where we decided to requisition 800,000 tons of Dutch shipping, and where the Tiger and I had a passage of arms about the state of the French railways, and where we finished our agenda and Foch made his protest.

Meeting of Granet, Nash, McMorrogh (American) about the state of the French ports and railways for carrying American traffic, and all three are absolutely agreed that it will be impossible to keep any more American troops up in front without more locomotives, trucks, sidings, etc., etc.

Sir Henry wrote next day:

Bliss came to see me, and I explained the French port and railway situation to him, and I think he has got it well into his head. Then Foch in. He discussed present situation with me. He is still very sore about the collapse of the General Reserve and the Executive Board, and he complains about the lack of information about the British Army. I think he wants to send a swarm of his own liaison officers to find out all about us. Of course this is impossible, he must get all information about us through Rawly. I discussed this year's campaign with Foch. He does not quite agree with me. I think the Boches ought to threaten us on our front and the French, and fall on the Italians about May and June. He does not think the Boches will try Italy because it would be too advantageous for the Austrians. He thinks the Boche will threaten as I do, and then turn all his attention and energy to the East.

I went to see Haig off at Charing Cross at 2 p.m. and congratulated him on his heir, born yesterday.

This appears in the diary on March 17:

I had a talk with the Tiger and told him that the real difficulty was that Foch and I were right, whilst he [Tiger], Haig and Pétain were wrong, and yet Foch and I had to give way, Foch with a bad grace and I with a good one. The Tiger agreed absolutely.

Clemenceau was almost the last of the foreign representatives to quit London; most of the others, as well as Rawlinson, having left a day or two earlier.* One of the last acts of the Supreme War Council had been to send a cable message to President Wilson, urging him to agree to Japan undertaking operations in Siberia, a matter to which both the British War Cabinet and the British military authorities attached very great importance. The only representative of the United States at the sittings of the Council in London had been General Bliss, whereas Lloyd George, Milner, Clemenceau, Pichon, Orlando and Boyelli — two Ministers from each country — had represented the other three principal Allies.

The references to the question of railways and rolling stock in connexion with the American forces that were gathering in France, which appear in the extracts from Wilson's diary previously quoted, make manifest what difficulties the Allies were labouring under at this time — just when the great German offensive was about to be launched against the Western Front. Both the British and the French armies were shrinking fast in numbers, and, in default of drastic steps as regards available man-power being taken on the part of their respective Governments, those armies were certain to shrink still more rapidly in the event of serious fighting taking place. And yet, at a juncture when troops from the United States, if only they were transported across the Atlantic on a sufficient scale and at a sufficient rate, might be expected to counterbalance this untoward diminution of Franco-British fighting strength, it was becoming necessary to stay the movement of the American reinforcements because rolling stock appeared to be even more urgently needed than soldiers.

Another point deserves to be noted in connexion with the extracts. This is that, just as Wilson when Military Representative on the Supreme War Council had differed profoundly from

---

* Sir Almeric Fitzroy, in his "Memoirs," mentions meeting Rawlinson and Sir Henry on one of these days at the Travellers' Club, and hearing that Rawlinson was succeeding Wilson as Military Representative at Versailles, "I expressed my pleasure to Rawlinson," he writes, "adding that it was a position requiring more suppleness than was perhaps usual in men of the British race, whereupon Wilson grasped my arm and asked me what I meant by the term; when I replied that, of course, it was used in its most complimentary sense, as indeed it was; but the interruption, for all its perfect good humour, was not without significance."

Robertson, then C.I.G.S., on the subject of the General Reserve, so now Rawlinson, Military Representative on the Supreme War Council, was differing from Wilson, C.I.G.S., on this same subject. Whichever side was in the right on an admittedly somewhat contentious question, the fact remains that the responsible military adviser of the War Cabinet was in either case overruled by the independent Military Representative at Versailles. Such a clash of opinion and authority could not have occurred in the case of the French military advisers of their Government, seeing that Weygand was for all practical purposes the mouthpiece of Foch, so that their attitude in respect to the General Reserve was consistent throughout.

Wilson made a sigrxificant entry in his diary on March 20:

> Signs of more aerodromes, etc., on our Front, and certainly the signs are cumulatiYe of a big attack, but I still think that the Boches, while pressing us, should wait and fall on Italy later.

It was known in London and at G.H.Q. that the number of German divisions in the Western theatre had, during the winter, been increased by no less than 46; and by the middle of March it had become estabhshed that great hostile forces were massed facing the British Third and Fifth Armies under Generals Byng and Gough. These consisted together of 29 divisions, with three cavalry divisions; 10 of the 29 divisions were in reserve. The French reserves were at this time grouped behind Rheims, behind Verdun and also on the extreme right of the line, near Belfort, prepared to meet the eventuality of a German attack through Switzerland; for in spite of the grouping of the enemy forces. General Pétain and his staff were msposed to assume that the blow would fall on the French and not on the British. An agreement had been arrived at between Haig and Pétain that in the event of the German blow being Erected against the B.E.F. the French would either intervene in the actual battle with a force of from six to eight divisions, or else they would take over an equivalent length of front, and by doing so would release British divisions for transfer to the point of danger. But the French reserves were by no means appropriately disposed for carrying the agreement into effect, and when the anticipated crisis came some of the troops that were hurried by Pétain to Haig's assistance were drawn from far away on the borders of Alsace.

Wilson recorded the following on the 21st:

> The Boches started their big attack this morning. Two hours intense artillery, and then infantry attack on an 85 kilometre front from the Scarpe to the Oise. This is a big affair. We seem to have fallen back on all this line from our outpost line to our battle position, and the Boches appear to have got a lodgment in about five places in our battle position. We ought to kill them all off. Long discursive and useless discussions at War Cabinet about Russia, Japan and U.S.A. It appears that President Wilson has become still more opposed to Japanese intervention. But Bonar Law and Smuts agree with him and trust Trotsky.

The above references to what had occurred about St. Quentin suggest that the extreme gravity of the situation on the Western Front had not yet been realized in London, owing, no doubt, mainly to the inevitable delay that took place in news coming through from the fighting front. That the enemy was greatly helped on the morning of the 21st by the prevailing fog is well known, and it was to some extent thanks to this that the first day of the great German offensive proved so disastrous to Gough's Army. Although well aware of the gathering of vast hostile forces opposite to his Third and Fifth Armies, Haig seems to have felt some confidence that these would be able to withstand whatever pressure was put on them, at least for some time, and also to have expected that succour would, at the worst, be very speedily forthcoming from Pétain. In both anticipations he was to be disappointed. Had the General Reserve, as conceived by Foch and Wilson, been in existence, the discomfiture of the B.E.F. at the outset would in all probability have proved even more serious than it was, owing to the line attacked in that case necessarily being thinner. But it is, on the other hand, a reasonable assumption that the arrival of troops from this central body would have brought the enemy's thrust to a standstill sooner — and at a greater distance from Amiens — than actually proved to be the case. Be that as it may, the entries in the C.I.G.S.'s diary on March 22 and 23 indicate how the realities gradually came to be grasped at the War Office and by the War Cabinet, as fuller reports came to hand. On the 22nd he wrote:

> The Boches are pushing on in an awkward way at Croiselles, and Roisel and south of the Oise. I don't understand why we are giving ground so quickly, nor how the Boches got through our battle zone apparently so easily. Our casualties yesterday are estimated at 30,000 by G.H.Q., and I am afraid will have been heavy again to-day, and we have no reserves beyond 50,000 men on which to draw. Douglas Haig is asking the French to take over up to St. Simon, and they must take over much more. They must take over at least half of this immense battle front if the Boches continue to attack on it. I am afraid we must have lost a good many guns to-day, as we have given up so much ground.

On the 23rd:

> An anxious day. The Fifth Army seems to be beaten, and has fallen back behind the Somme. The Third Army is conforming, but is fighting well. Telephoning at 7 p.m. to me from G.H.Q., Lawrence said the French had agreed to take over up to Péronne, but that this would take three days, which would be critical days. There is, roughly, the situation to-night.
> I was about five hours with Lloyd George. I lunched at Bonar's with him, and Lloyd George and I sat in the garden at Downing Street till 4 o'clock, when we had a War Cabinet till 6 o'clock. For hours I insisted on the importance of taking a long, broad view of the future, of conscription of everyone up to 50, and, of course, on Ireland. I think I did good, and Winston helped like a man. Smuts was good, but more cautious. Milner disappointing. Bonar Law ditto. A.J.B. rathet uninterested. Curzon not there. We took following steps. I telegraphed early to Reading asking him to press on Wilson the vital importance of sending over infantry. I telegraphed to Allenby to pull out a white division and hold it ready.* I telegraphed to Cavan to send up one division and the 4 brigades of field artillery with the Army. At the War Cabinet we decided to send out the 50,000 boys (trained) of

---

* A second division and several individual battalions were ordered to the Western Front during April.

18½ years and up to 19, and some other lots which will make up 82,000, which, with the 88,000 returning from leave, will mean 170,000 in the next 17 days if we can ship at that rate.

Marvellous fine day, but with fog on Channel and haze in France, but no mud. *Le bon dieu est boche.**

A general officer, who was at this alarming juncture serving on the staff of the B.E.F., writes of Wilson:

> I remember one thing about him that I always thought very typical of the man he was. It was on the day after the beginning of the big Hun attack in March, 1918, and all of us who happened to be on leave in England at the moment had been recalled. He was C.I.G.S. at the time; he came down to the returning ''staff'' train at Victoria, and he made a point of speaking to all of us whom he knew. I suppose that he realized even better than we did what was going on in France, and what we had to look forward to.

The following three days were amongst the most critical passed during the war, and the various accounts of what occurred in connexion with the higher direction of the Allied forces, that have appeared, are not all in complete agreement. The record of events as contained in Sir Henry's diary is therefore of a very special value. The Prime Minister had at night on March 23, after the War Cabinet meeting, asked Lord Milner to go over to France so as to consult with the French Government and the French and British military authorities as to what was to be done in view of the defeat of the British Fifth Army and of the retirement of the Third Army. Milner, therefore, left London on the 24th, passed through Montreuil on the evening of that day, where he saw Davidson the Deputy C.G.S. (Haig and Lawrence being at advanced headquarters at Beaurepaire), and he reached Versailles in the small hours of the following morning. The military situation on this 24th day was in the highest degree disquieting, owing to the tardy arrival of the French reinforcements that were moving up on the right of the B.E.F. to aid in staying the German advance. That

---

* "The good Lord is a Kraut."

February and March, 1918: The Great German... 91

night, about 11 p.m., Haig met Pétain at Duty to discuss what was to be done. Pétain then informed the British Commander-in-Chief that, if the enemy should continue to press the attack in the direction of Amiens, the French divisions that had come up on the British right had received orders to fall back south-westwards so as to cover Paris. This meant that if the Germans should act as they seemed at the time likely to act, and as they in fact did act, a wedge would be driven between the British and French armies. Convinced that such an eventuality must be averted at all costs, the Field-Marshal, unaware that Milner was in France and actually at the time motoring to Versailles, telegraphed to London asking Milner and Wilson to come over at once. He had at an earlier hour, as will be seen, telephoned to Wilson asking him to come; but owing to his moving about he had received no reply. Sir Henry's account of the day's doings on the 24th, as given in his diary runs as follows:

> Mr. Page (American Ambassador) and Mr. Baker (War Minister)[*] in. I explained the present dangerous situation and the urgency of immediate dispatch of battalions from America. Not complete divisions, as Pershing wants.
>
> I saw Milner off at Charing Cross at 12.50 for Versailles. Milner was nearly as strong as I was for the necessity of *levée en masse*[†] in England and Ireland, which could be carried out with real conscription. At 1.30 I heard the Boches had taken Sailly-Sailliselle. This shows the tremendous danger of this colossal attack. At 5 o'c. a telephone message to say Combles and Péronne had fallen, and our troops were retreating to the Ancre. I telephoned at once to Lloyd George at Walton to come up. At 5.30 Foch telephoned asking me what I thought of the situation, and we are of one mind that someone must catch hold, or we shall be beaten. I said I would come over and see him.
>
> At 7 o'c., meeting at Downing Street of Lloyd George, Bonar Law, Smuts and me. We discussed, and I said I was going over. There is no mistaking the gravity of the situation, nor the entirely inadequate measures taken by Haig and Pétain in their mutual plans for

---

[*] Newton D. Baker, the U.SA. Secretary of War.

[†] "Mass collection."

assistance. While we were discussing, a telephone from Haig to say Third Army was falling back to the Ancre. and asking me to go over. So I go by special, 6.50 a.m. to-morrow, and then destroyer.

I dined with Winston and Mrs. Winston, and Lloyd George also there, and Hankey after dinner. Winston backed me up well when I pressed Lloyd George hard to really conscript this country and Ireland. I finished by saying to Lloyd George, "You will come out of this bang top or bang bottom," and Winston cordially agreed. I want Lloyd George to summon Parliament, conscript up to 50 years of age, and include Ireland. I am not sure that he sees the gravity of the situation yet.

A moving day. We are very near a crash. Lloyd George has on the whole been buoyant. Bonar Law most depressing. Smuts talked much academic nonsense. Winston a real gun in a crisis, and reminded me of August, 1914.

Haig's telegram arrived at Eaton. Place during that night, but Sir Henry makes no mention of it in his diary, no doubt because he had already made all arrangements to start early in the morning. Those present at the discussion in Downing Street on the evening of the 24th were not aware, it must be remembered, of the full gravity of the situation. They knew nothing of Pétain's intentions, which even Haig only heard of two or three hours later at Dury.

Milner discussed the situation with Rawlinson at Versailles on the morning of the 25th, and he then saw Clemenceau in Paris. The French Government had apparently entertained some idea of a unified command being set up under Pdtain; Imt to this arrangement Mlilner, having perhaps discovered that general's inclination to sacrifice the junction between the British and French armies for the sake of covering Paris, felt bound to demur. It was, however, arranged that a meeting should take place at Compiègne, Pétain's head-quarters, and It was hoped that it might prove possible for Haig and Wilson to be present at this, Milner having learnt that Wilson was to meet Haig in the forenoon. Messages, however, went astray, and neither Haig nor Wilson appeared at Compiègne; but a meeting was held there of Poincaré, Loucheur, Foch, Pétain and Milner, and at this Foch insisted on the vital importance of massing reserves so as to stay the enemy's advance on Amiens, and thus to ensure that the French and British armies

February and March, 1918: The Great German... 93

should not be separated. Milner returned to Versailles after this meeting at Compiègne. Wilson's account of the day's proceedings on the 25th explains how it was that he did not arrive at Compiègne. He wrote:

> Got to Montreuil 11.30 a.m. Interview at once with Haig and Lawrence. After much talk I told Haig that in my opinion we must get greater unity of action, and I suggested that Foch should co-ordinate the action of both C. in C.s. In the end Douglas Haig agreed. I could not help reminding him it was he (Douglas Haig) with Clemenceau's assistance, who killed my plan of a General Reserve, nor could I resist reminding him of what I had both told him and written to him on the 6th March — that without a General Reserve he (Douglas Haig) would be living on the charity of Pétain. An impossible situation, for here is the attack I foresaw and predicted in January in full blast, and really no arrangements to meet it.
>
> I had arranged for Clemenceau and Foch to come and meet me at Abbeville at 4 o"c., so Douglas Haig and I motored there, only to meet Weygand, who told us that Clemenceau and Foch and Milner were going to Compiègne at 4 o'c. to meet Pétain. I at once decided to go to Versailles, to see Milner on his return from Compiègne. I arrived at Versailles at 8.15 and Milner got back at 9 o'c. Milner told me they had had this meeting, but nothing had been decided as I was not there. I rang up Foch and got to his house at 10.30. After talk with him and Weygand, I arranged that at our meeting at Dury to-morrow I would suggest that he (Foch) should be commissioned by both Governments to co-ordinate the military action of the two C. in C.s. I got back to Versailles at midnight.*

In the course of the talk which Wilson had had with Milner at Versailles, before going on to Paris to see Foch, the plan appears to have been mooted of giving Clemenceau the authority to co-ordinate, with Foch acting as his technical adviser; but Foch would seem to have pointed out to Sir Henry the weak points of such an arrangement. Next morning (26th) Milner and Wilson motored north from Versailles, making for Doullens (which had been

---

* Opposed as Sir Henry had been to the idea of a generalissimo up till the end of 1917, he had to some extent changed his view while at Versailles, as was shown by his conversation with Robertson in Paris on January 28 (vide p. 65).

substituted for Dury as the meeting place), and during the drive, the car being frequently delayed by military traffic, they fully agreed as to making Foch the co-ordinating authority. Milner was in a difficult position, seeing that he was furnished with no authority from the War Cabinet to commit that body to a step which necessarily went a long way towards setting up Foch as generalissimo.* Wilson, however, was insistent and, convinced by his companion's arguments that the proposed measure was urgent and imperative, Milner accepted the responsibility of assenting on behalf of the British Government.

Wilson described the day's doings in the diary as follows:

> Left with Milner at 8 a.m. and went to Dnry. Gongh just established his head-quarters there, but as our meeting had been changed to Doullens we pushed on through Amiens, which was fairly quiet and not being shelled. A certain amount of natives on the move. Doullens at mid-day.
>
> Poincaré, Clemenceau, Loucheur, Foch, Pétain, Milner, Haig, self (and Plumer, Byng, Horne in attendance). Milner, Haig, and I had preliminary talk, and Haig agreed to my proposal for Foch to co-ordinate. Then meeting of Poincaré, Clemenceau, Foch, Pétain, Milner, Haig and self. After discussion, in which I fell out with Pétain for contemplating a retreat, Milner put up proposal for Foch to co-ordinate, and, all agreeing, Clemenceau and Milner signed the document.
>
> Then I discussed removal of Gough, and told Haig he could have Rawly, and Rawly's old Fourth Army staff from Versailles, to replace Gough. Haig agreed to this. Both Lawrence and Haig are delighted with this new arrangement about Foch. So is Foch, and so really is Clemenceau, who patted me on the head and said I was *un bon garçon*,† Milner and I (and the Lord) lunched at the "Quatre Fils" at Aymon — reports that Boche tanks and cavalry were through Pas and that we had better clear out! All rubbish.
>
> Back to Montreuil for tea. I saw Douglas Haig, just going out for a ride, and he told me he was greatly pleased with the new

---

* Four months before this, November 17, the Prime Minister had in the House of declared himself "utterly opposed" to the appointment of a generalissimo.

† "A good boy."

arrangements. I told him and Lawrence at Doullens that much would now depend on the officers he chose for liaison with Foch and that, of course, he could have anybody he liked. Douglas Haig is 10 years younger to-night than he was yesterday afternoon. Milner and I over by destroyer at 7 o'c. Boulogne. Got back to Victoria at ½ to 11.

Milner, Winston and I to 10 Downing Street, and we told Lloyd George and Bonar Law and Hankey result of our labours and, as I summed It up for Lloyd George, "the chances are now slightly in favour of us."

One noteworthy point in connexion with the historic Doullens Conference receives no mention here. When Clemenceau in the first instance drew up the resolution on the subject of the superior command, it was expressed to the effect that Foch was to be appointed "to co-ordinate the operations of the Allies about Amiens." But this wording was changed on the representation of Haig, with the result that Foch's powers were expanded, that he was entrusted with co-ordinating authority over all operations on the Western Front, and that he was in reality to all intents and purposes appointed Generalissimo in the main theatre of war. General Pershing was too far away to have attended the conference, but the American Chief wrote in cordial terms to Foch two days later, agreeing that the provisions of the Doullens arrangement should apply fully to the United States forces in France.*

The victorious Germans continued their forward movement during this day, but their progress north of the Somme was slow in face of the steady resistance offered by the Third Army. To the south of the Somme they were less stubbornly opposed by the remnant of the British Fifth Army and by the French troops coming to its assistance; they gained a considerable amount of ground, and they were already beginning to approach inconveniently near to Amiens and to the main line of railway between that city and Paris.

Wilson wrote in the diary on the 27th:

---

* General Pershing at the same time declared that "America would feel greatly honoured if its troops were engaged in the present battle."

Breakfasted with Lloyd George and Winston. I warned him that if we now blocked the Boches in this attack they would turn on Italy in May and June, and then come back to us in the autumn. Winston agreed. Then to see the King, tell him of my trip and suggest to him to go out for a few days, and the King goes to-morrow. Then War Cabinet. Described my visit, and wound up by saying the chances were in our favour now. Milner described his work. Then War Cabinet again at 5.30 on Irish Conscription. A lamentable exhibition of ignorance and weakness.

Next day there is the entry:

Winston telephoned he wanted to see me, as he was off to France. I caught him in the train at Charing Cross. He was being sent out to Foch by Lloyd George. I told him I could not agree and I must have this changed, and he must go to Clemenceau and not to any soldier. Lloyd George did change this during the morning, and before I spoke to him at lunch at Derby House.

War Cabinet on Irish Conscription. I urged importance of haste, so did Milner, A, Geddes and Johnnie French. All others hanging back for report of Convention.* Convention is, of course, dead, but these men won't or can't see it. I insisted that every day lost was a disaster, and that we were bound to go on from one crisis to another, and that men were essential. Eventually decided that conscription should be out after the Convention had reported on April 6. I told Duke† that when the Convention heard that the moment they had signed the Government would put on conscription, it would be found that they would all get measles and the whole Convention would fall down. He disagreed.

Lunched at Derby's, with Lloyd George also. I told him that Winston could not go to Foch's head-quarters, but he told me he had already changed this to Clemenceau, and J. T. Davies later showed me the wire in which Lloyd George said Botiar Law and I were opposed to his [Winston's] going to Foch, so he was going to Paris to Clemenceau.

---

* The Convention which had been sitting in Dublin for a long time past, composed of Union and Nationalist representatives, but in which no Sinn Fein representatives would take part.

† The Chief Secretary for Ireland.

Next day (29th) Wilson wrote in the diary:

I tried again at the War Cabinet to get some Marines out of Geddes and Wemyss [now First Sea Lord], but no success, and I tried again with Wemyss at 5.30, with possibly a little success. I warned the War Cabinet this morning of the danger of secret plans leaking out, and Lloyd George taking this as a hint to himself was annoyed. Bonar Law and Milner both warned me of this afterwards.

Lloyd George agreed to ask America to send us 100,000 infantry a month for three months, and during the day Philip Kerr, Maurice and I drafted a long wire to Reading, and in this we put that here we were going to comb out and ruin all industries not absolutely vital, and conscript Ireland, so, if Lloyd George has sent this to-night, the fate of Ireland is sealed. I put in a short paper to the War Cabinet to say that I was not afraid to take 100,000-150,000 recalcitrant, conscripted Irishmen into an army of 2½ million, fighting in five theatres of war.

Hereward sent me a map, dated March 20, showing the dispositions of the French and British Reserves on that day, and there is shown the cause of the present disaster. News to-night not so good. French counter-attack east of Montdidier is not getting on, and we have lost Mezières, north of Montdidier.

On the 30th there is the entry:

The news is not so good, as the Boches have pushed the French out of Montdidier and have got nearly to Moreuil; Winston from Paris reports well on the Tiger and on the pace at which the French are coming up. President Wilson seems to have sent his congratulations to Foch on being made C. in C. I pressed hard for the publication of our Doullens agreement, and in the end it was agreed to do this in to-morrow's Press. I warned Johnnie French that in my opinion he might have trouble in Ireland when, over there, they realized that they were going to have conscription. Johnnie said he was absolutely ready for any contingency.

Milner came to see me at 6.30 p.m. at No. 36. We went for a walk in the Park. He told me he had been sitting all the afternoon on this Committee, with Cave as chairman, to draft a Bill for further combing out and for conscription for Ireland, As regards the latter, the Committee proposed to apply conscription to Ireland, but to give a month's law during which men might enlist voluntarily. I don't like this, as it will give the Sinn Feins a month in which to get ready. And Lloyd George and the others, especially Bonar Law and Barnes and Smuts who are against conscription for Ireland, still seem to have a simple faith in the Convention! Wonderful.

At this morning's Cabinet, Lloyd George read out portions of two wires received from Winston. To-night in our walk Milner referred to this, and said that he was going to tell Lloyd George that either he (Milner) must have Lloyd George's full confidence or else he would leave the Government. I agreed with Milner. This sending Winston over — first with the idea of going to Foch, which I killed, and then to Clemenceau — is a direct snub to Milner, who, after all, represented the Government at Doullens, and has all along been the Cabinet Member at Versailles.

The situation to the south of the Somme continued to give grounds for anxiety during the 28th and 29th owing to the persistent pressure of the German legions — this in spite of determined counter-attacks on the part of the French, who had by this time come up in strong force. But to the north of the river the position of affairs had been greatly improved from the Allies' point of view. This was due to a severe repulse suffered by the enemy in course of a violent attack delivered on both sides of the River Scarpe. The Allied front was here held by portions of the First and Third Armies, and the collapse of this effort was so serious a blow to Ludendorff, that his offensive north of the Somme was brought to a standstill. But how important and farreaching had been the results of the German effort is shown by the enemy on the 29th claiming to have captured in the week's fighting no less than 70,000 prisoners and 1,100 guns. An entry in Wilson's diary on the 31st likewise shows how grave had been the losses incurred by the B.E.F. during the past few days:

> We stand this way. From March 21 to March 29 we have lost 114,000 infantry. We have sent out, or will have sent out by April 4, 101,000. They had some 20,000 out there (in depots?), but we have sent all boys of 18½ who are trained, so we have nothing more except driblets for three or four months. In home defence we have still 39,000 boys under 18½, and 20,000 B.1s. I told Macrcady to put this 20,000 under orders. He and I went to see Johnnie French, and he agreed, I promising to put the whole case before the Cabinet to-

February and March, 1918: The Great German... 99

morrow. We shall have nobody for the defence of England except untrained boys of under 18½. The next three months will be anxious, even if the Americans send us 100,000 a month. Macready showed me a letter from Fowke which said that he must begin breaking up divisions, and would start with the 16th and 66th.

During dinner Lloyd George rang me up from Walton to say that President Wilson had wired to say that he would send 120,000 infantry a month for four months, but asked that conscription be not put on Ireland, as his task would be rendered very difficult. Lloyd George said that the President was evidently in a fright, and that he wanted Lloyd George to make the first announcement over here. The whole thing sounds a little fishy. I will see to-morrow. At 11 o'clock Milner came in to see me. I told him of Lloyd George's telephone message, and he quite agreed that the whole matter wanted examination and careful and accurate scrutiny. I told him of my conception of the next Boche move if we stop this attack on approximately the present ground, and that is that he will put Amiens Junction and roads under his guns, and then mount an attack either against our Line north of the Somme or against the French south of the Somme, and trust to his guns on Amiens preventing the one wing from reinforcing the other. I told him I believed we could frustrate this by having a central reserve astride of the Somme, west of Amiens, with extra bridges, etc., which would enable these troops to reinforce where and when required.

Wilson's grasp of the military situation, and those gifts of lucid exposition when dealing with the uninstructed which he possessed in so eminent a degree, proved of immense value to the War Cabinet during these anxious and critical days. His courage and confidence exercised a soothing effect upon Ministers, who were sensible of their great responsibilities and were constantly being called upon to give decisions of vital moment in respect to questions that they could not be expected to understand otherwise than imperfectly. Mr. G. N. Barnes, who was one of the Prime Minister's colleagues on this innermost Council, pays a handsome tribute to the services of the C.I.G.S. at this juncture in a passage in his book, "From Workshop to War Cabinet" which runs:

> It would have been impossible for Sir Henry Wilson to be other than first favourite in any company in which he found himself. Genial,

effusive, and even at times boisterous in manner, he was the typical Irishman and the same to all men, whether gentle or simple. But when discussing military projects or forecasts, he spoke like a book. In front of a large map he woiild talk for about ten minutes or a quarter of an hour with machine-like precision, and would finish without a single superfluous word by way of fringe or peroration. It was a good thing that he was at Downing Street in the spring of 1918, for he knew almost exactly what would happen — and what did happen — and, having foreseen it, had come to the conclusion as to what would follow.

Although the condition of affairs on the Western Ftont remained an extremely precarious one at the end of March, the situation was no longer quite so ominous as had been the case on the eve of the Doullens Conference a week earlier. The effectual rupture of the Allied line no longer appeared to be absolutely imminent. The risk of French divisions that were gathering at the danger point retiring south-westwards so as to cover Paris, and of their thereby allowing the Germans to sweep through the gap that such a movement would create between Haig's and Pétain's forces, was — thanks to Foch now exercising the supreme military control in this theatre of war — virtually at an end. Still, the state of things to the south of the Somme remained disquieting, seeing that, although the advance of the enemy towards Amiens had been checked, it had not been brought completely to a standstill. Ludendorff's legions were in great strength, and they were enjoying all the advantages that are automatically conferred on an army in the field by the possession of the initiative. Furthermore, although the British War Cabinet was now, belatedly, making a supreme effort to provide man-power for the front, and although the dispatch of American troops to the scene of danger was about to be very appreciably accelerated, several weeks must inevitably elapse ere the balance in numbers as between the respective belligerents on the Western Front could possibly be restored.

A definite form of Unity of Command had, however, been set up by the Allies, and for this important development Wilson had been more responsible than had any other individual, civilian or military, representing the interests of the British Empire. His services in bringing it about had been by no means confined to the prominent share that he had borne in discussions with Lord Milner when they were driving from Versailles to Doullens, as also in discussions at Doullens itself, on March 26. The way for the Doullens decision had been paved by the creation of the Executive Board, intended to control the General Reserve; this, again, had been prepared for by the acceptance on the part of the Supreme War Council of the principle of a General Reservethe principle of a General Reserve, again, was one direct result of the Supreme War Council having been established. In causing each successive step to be taken by the Allied Governments — Supreme War Council, General Reserve, Executive Board — Sir Henry had played a conspicuous, if not indeed a pre-eminent, part.

Chapter XXIII – 1918: From April to the End of June

Conference at Beauvais, April 3 — German offensive on the Lys — Question as to Haig's line of retirement if it becomes necessary — Divergent views of Foch and Wilson — Conference at Abbeville, April 27 — German offensive towards the Marne — Grave situation — Lively meeting of the Supreme War Council — Haig's American divisions.

A most satisfactory message was received by the War Cabinet from Lord Reading at Washington on April 1, endorsing that received on the day before (mentioned in the previous chapter), and having for purport that President Wilson was prepared to accede to the request on the part of the Allies that American infantry should be hurried across the Atlantic, and conveying a definite promise that 120,006 should be dispatched each month for the coming four months. The message, however, to Sir Henry's disgust, concluded with a warning that the imposing of conscription upon Ireland might cause difficulty in the United States. "Of course Lloyd George fastened on this as a sort of excuse for leaving Ireland out of his Bill," appears in the diary. A belated Man-Power Bill, raising the military age to fifty, and providing for the extension of the Military Service Act to Ireland, a Bill which ought to have been introduced months earlier, was being drafted; it was introduced to the House of Commons on the

1918: From April to the End of June 103

9th, and it was passed three days later.* But its effect could naturally not make itself felt during the critical weeks of April and May that immediately followed the passing of the measure.

Arrangements had been made for a conference (at which Generals Bliss and Pershing were to be present) to be held at Beauvais on the 3rd. Churchill had moreover wired from Paris to the Prime Minister to come over. So Wilson crossed the Channel in company with Lloyd George that morning, and they met Churchill by arrangement at Boulogne. "I am anxious to get Winston back," the C.I.G.S. (who had looked askance at that statesman's mission to France from the outset), had noted in his diary on the previous day; and when recording the proceedings which had taken place at Beauvais, he wrote that same night:

> Winston came nearly to Montreuil with us. Lloyd George, Winston and I in one car. Winston said Clemenceau wanted Foch's position strengthened. I agreed, but not up to C. in C., especially as the Tiger wished this principally to allow Foch to coerce Pétain, and not Haig who is working smoothly. We picked up Haig at Montreuil, Winston having got out before we got there, Lloyd George and Haig in one car, Lawrence and I in next. Lord, Hankey and J. T. following. Lloyd George told Haig that Gough must go. Also told him of his new arrangement with Americans of getting 120,000 infantry a month. Then we changed at Abbeville, and I went with Douglas Haig, and Lloyd George with Lawrence. Lunched Beauvais 1.30 p.m.
>
> The Tiger came and sat with us, and after lunch the Tiger, Lloyd George and I had a talk. Tiger produced a note as follows: "*Les gouvernements britanniques et français confieront au général Foch la direction stratégique des operations militaires sur le front occidental. Les C. in C.s des armies britanniques et françaises exercent dans sa plenitude la direction tactique de leurs armées.*"† I thought it was a pity to substitute this for the Doullens agreement,

---

* Under its terms compulsory service could be imposed in Ireland by an Order in Council.

† "The British and French governments will entrust General Foch with the strategic direction of military operations on the Western Front. The C. in C.s of the British and French armies will exercise in its entirety the tactical direction of their armies."

which I considered was the stronger of the two, as this latter raised the question of the difference between strategy and tactics, which the C. in C.s might exploit; but the Tiger and Lloyd George were in favour of the change.

At 3 p.m. we had a meeting in the town hall. Tiger, Foch, Pétain, Bliss, Pershing, Lloyd George, Douglas Haig and self. Tiger said position of C. in Cs wanted more definition. Foch said Doullens only "co-ordinated" action, but that if there were no action there would be no co-ordination; hence "direction" should be added in order to bring about "preparation," to be followed by action. I replied that Doullens already gave Foch that power — "*co-ordiner l'action des armées alliées sur le front ouest*"* — and I was afraid the new definition would raise the question of what was strategy and what was tactics. Lloyd George said British public wanted Foch to have real power; did Doullens give this power? Bliss said that Foch must be given — if he had not already got them — powers for the future as well as for the present.

I drafted a part of Tiger's new declaration into the middle of the Doullens agreement, and added at the end a paragraph of right of appeal of each C. in C. to his Government if he received from Foch any instructions which he thought would endanger the army. The American Government, with Pershing's and Bliss's approval, was added to the other two, and everyone agreed, Haig and Pétain agreeing. All this was agreed to and adopted. Douglas Haig then urged an early French offensive, Lloyd George and I pressed this on Foch, and Clemenceau and Foch agreed. We then discussed some points with Pershing and Bliss about the 120,000 American infantry to come over a month, but, as Pershing apparendy knew nothing of this, I arranged that Bliss should come over to London and see Bridges, Hutch and Graham Thompson before they sail.†

The party from England got back to London that same night, but within a couple of days Clemenceau was already wiring to suggest that Foch should be put over the Italian theatre of war as

---

* "To coordinate the action of the allied armies on the western front."

† Major-General Sir T. Bridges, Colonel R. Hutchison and Mr. Graham Thompson of the Ministry of Shipping, were about to cross the Atlantic to confer with the United States authorities on various matters, Bridges taking charge of all the British Military Representatives in the United States.

well as the Western Front. This project Wilson strongly opposed in the War Cabinet, pointing out that Foch had not yet got the Western Front properly in hand, and that he had not succeeded in ingratiating himself with the Italians. So no more was heard of the matter. Sir Henry also deprecated proposals that were being made within the War Cabinet to remove Haig from his position as Commander-in-Chief of the B.E.F. He was only too well aware that the primary cause of the disaster to the Fifth Army on March 21 and the following days was insufficiency of numbers, due to the War Cabinet's failure to make full use of the principle of compulsory service, and he realized the greatness of the Field-Marshal's services in having insisted that Pétain must regard maintenance of connexion with the British forces as of even greater importance than the covering of Paris. It did not, on the other hand, appear to him that either Haig or Foch were sufficiently convinced of the importance of improving the communications across the Somme below Amiens so as to ensure their being able to move reserves in either direction at will. The enemy had by this time, it should be explained, been definitely brought to a standstill on both sides of the Somme; but the German line was nevertheless perilously near to Amiens, and therefore to the great line of railway skirting the city. So Wilson wrote in his diary on April 6:

> I wired to Foch and Haig saying that I thought a senior British officer (Du Cane, for instance) should be at Foch's head-quarters, and that my fear was that the Boches would put their guns on Amiens and then attack the British, that the real answer to this was either that the French took over much more of our line, or that Foch should have a General Reserve down river and astride the Somme below Amiens.

Next day there is the entry:

> Long talk with Maurice and Hereward in the office only confirms me in the belief that, once Amiens is denied to us, the Boches will mount a great attack against Haig between Albert and La Bassée.
>
> I read Minutes to-day of yesterday's Cabinet on conscription for Ireland and, except for Bonar Law and Barnes, who wobbled rather badly, it seemed to be all right, except that they mean to bring in some

farcical Convention Home Rule as well, though of course they will never pass it.

On the following day (the 8th) he wrote:

At 4 a.m. I got a wire from Haig to say he agreed to my appreciation of the situation and had put it yesterday to Foch, who refused to take over line and only meant to put a small reserve behind Amiens, which Haig thought quite inadequate. Haig wants me over at once, so I wired at 4 a.m. to say I would be over to-day or to-morrow. Told War Cabinet this, and was given full powers to do what I thought best.

Derby read a letter from Haig to him to the War Cabinet, saying he only wished to remain C. in C. so long as he had the confidence of the Cabinet. Later on Lloyd George asked me if I did not think we ought to take Haig at his word; but I said that, failing some really outstanding personality, and we have none, I thought we ought to wait for Haig's report. Goughie has returned and reported himself to Derby, and has taken his recall very well.

Wilson wrote on the 9th:

Left Folkestone at 6 a.m. Had much talk with Hereward on way over. It seems that the Boches can attack us with 35-40 divisions this week, and Foch must take steps to help.

Got to Douglas Haig's house at 9.15 and had a little breakfast, and then a long talk with Haig and Lawrence, and then Haig alone. He is afraid of French troops taking over our line in front of Amiens, and suggests their taking over a 6-division front at Ypres, but this does not appeal to me; it is too far away, it would take too long, and if we lose Amiens it would be a bother to feed, draft and ammunition them. No, either take over on our right, or put substantial reserves about St. Pol and Doullens, or both. Douglas Haig says the French have not enough troops for a big attack between Noyon and Montdidier, such as Foch was contemplating last Wednesday when I was at Beauvais. He tells me that the two Portuguese divisions are to be pulled out to-night. As we were discussing this a wire came in to say that the Boches were attacking the Portuguese now.

Foch came at 12.30, and we talked for a couple of hours. Foch would not hear of relieving us either up at Ypres or opposite Amiens. He simply would not hear of it. On the other hand he will put a

1918: From April to the End of June 107

reserve astride of the Somme, heads of columns to be within 24 hours of Arras front. He wants to move 4 infantry and 3 cavalry divisions up at once. That area is very congested; but in the end Haig agreed to this proposal, though I advised him to register a note showing the disadvantages. On the whole I still remain of opinion that a big French Reserve behind Amiens is the best answer to an attack by 40 divisions about Arras. Foch agrees to having Johnnie Du Cane attached to his staff.* Foch wants a title for himself.

Wilson went on in the evening to Versailles, where Sackville-West was now installed as British Military Representative, Rawlinson having gone to command the Fourth Army; and nest morning he drove into Paris to see Clemenceau, "who began by saying that never, never, never would he make peace. I believe him." They discussed the question of a title for Foch; Sir Henry objected to Clemenceau's suggestion of "Commander-in-Chief of the Allied Forces," pointing out that Foch's authority was confined to France, and he proposed "Commander-in-Chief of Allied Forces in France" instead, to which Clemenceau assented. Sir Henry also urged "the Tiger" to back up Versailles; and they then debated what the B.E.F. ought to do in case Haig was compelled to make a big retirement.

> The Tiger said we should swing on out right and come back to the Somme,† but I was very soon able to dispose of that, saying that it was death to uncover the ports, and so our right must fall back; and if the French would hold the left bank of the Somme we would never lose touch with them.

---

* Colonel E. Dillon was at this time acting as Liaison Officer between Foch and the British Commander-in-Chief, having acted in the same capacity in 1916 at the time of the Battle of the Somme. Foch was quite satisfied with the existing arrangement, and when Du Cane arrived at the Generalissimo's head-quarters he was not just at first welcomed with open arms, while his A.D.C. was received with even less effusive cordiality. But within a very short space of time Foch and Du Cane were on excellent terms and the plan worked extremely well during the months to come.

† Evidently meaning that the B.E.F. should wheel its left back, pivoting on the Somme.

Wilson after this had a discussion with Bliss at Versailles, and he was much pleased to find that the United States Military Representative entirely agreed with him as regards the employment of American battalions with the British troops. The news that came in during the day indicated only too clearly that the enemy attacks in the sector immediately to the south of Ypres, of which General Plumer in command of the Second Army was in charge, were being delivered in formidable force and with great resolution, and that the Portuguese had been compelled to give way. After his conversation with Bliss Sir Henry motored north, and that night he discussed the situation very fully with Haig and Foch at G.H.Q.; Foch entirely agreed with him as to the imperative necessity of covering the ports. He returned to London next day, during which the news arriving from the battlefield south of Ypres became most disquieting, and he wrote in his diary:

> A War Committee at 6 p.m. where I frightened them properly about this attack of the Boches, and I am frightened myself as I am afraid it will end in the loss of Dunkirk.
> At 9.30 p.m. Lloyd George telephoned that he wanted me, and I went to Winston's, where he was. I told him I was anxious, and that it looked as though we might lose Hazebrouck, and if so everything north of Hill 63 would have to come right back, and our line would be Dunkirk — Aire, and later on this would probably mean the loss of Dunkirk.
> From Winston's, Lloyd George and I went to the Admiralty, and then I went on to the War Office and sent a wire to Foch reminding him of my warning to him the day before yesterday to get the floods of Dunkirk and Aire — St. Omer ready. I wish there had not been this awful delay of moving the French Reserves across the Somme behind Amiens. I wired to Foch last Sunday (7th) begging for this move, and it is only to-day (11th) that the heads of the French columns are moving towards the Somme; 3nd they won't have reached Doullens before the 13th.

Next day there is the entry:

> The news this morning is bad. Merville and Hill 63 are gone, and Bailleul threatened. The danger is Hazebrouck, for if we lose that we must retire our whole left, and we shall lose Dunkirk later. I warned

1918: *From April to the End of June* 109

the Cabinet. The other danger is that we cannot any longer make good our losses, and so we are a fast dwindling army. This is desperately serious.

But the enemy's progress in this region was fortunately checked on the 13th, and the situation in consequence became for the time being somewhat less alarming. A wire asking Lloyd George to cross over to France for a consultation nevertheless reached London from Clemenceau, and Sir Henry was not a little disturbed thereat. He feared that "the Tiger" contemplated interference in the military operations, and he dreaded what might happen were the Prime Minister also to take a hand. Sir W. Furse, who was Master-General of the Ordnance at this time and a colleague of Wilson's on the Army Council, contributes the following sprightly account of the attitude taken up by the C.I.G.S. in this emergency, and of the means by which Lloyd George was prevailed upon to stop where he was:

> In the morning I went on business as M.G.O. to H. W.'s room, and, just as we began, his private secretary came in to say that L. G. had telephoned to say that H. W. must come over at once to see him, and that the two must go back to G.H.Q. that evening. H. W. said to me, "I must go to him, Fuzz, but I'll be back in half an hour. I'm d——d if he, or I, goes back to France."
>
> When I went to see him about half an hour later, he was smiling. I said, "Well, did you dissuade him?"
>
> H. W.: "We are not going, but it was the devil to get it home to him. After much talk I said" [very slowly, with many pauses and in his deepest tones] "There are times — and seasons — when a Prime Minister's presence is worth — his weight — in diamonds. — There are other times — and seasons — especially when a decisive battle is in the fighting — when a Prime Minister's presence — is nothing but — an infernal nuisance."
>
> W. F.: "Did that settle it?"
>
> H. W.: "Yes! Arthur Balfour was the only other present, and when I said that he exploded with laughter, put his hand on my shoulder with a clap, and said, 'Quite right. Quite right.'"

On learning that Lloyd George did not intend to go over, Clemenceau telephoned asking Wilson to come instead "with fall military powers." "I told Capel to tell him," Wilson wrote in his diary, "that I was under the Prime Minister of England and not under the Prime Minister of France." Lord Milner, however, crossed the Channel that night to confer with Haig; and two days later he sent a message asking Wilson to follow as, although the German advance in Flanders had been partially checked, they were stUl attacking in force, the French reinforcements were very slow in arriving, and the situation along this important sector of the front remained extremely critical. Sir Henry therefore proceeded to France on the morning of April 16, and that day a meeting was held at Abbeville, of Milner, Haig, Lawrence and himself with Foch and Weygand. Of this conference he wrote in the diary:

> This morning we lost Wytschaete. The loss of this and of Bailleul shows the seriousness of the situation. Foch announced that he had summoned a meeting at 7 p.m. at Blondecques of Plumer and Robillaud (the French General), that he considered Plumer had sufficient troops now that he had been reinforced by a French infantry divisions and 3 French cavalry divisions, that out tactical handling was not good and that he was going up to see and inquire *sur place*.*
> Lawrence, who had just come down from Plumer, said that Plumer was doing all that was possible, but that he had not sufficient troops, that the British troops were exhausted, and that without teal assistance he would have to give ground again. Foch brushed this aside. Haig raised the question of inundations, and showed by map and the engineers' calculations that most of the serious inrmdations were salt water and would take 25-30 days, and he urged, as he had already done and I have also, that these should be started at once. Foch said he had on the 12th given orders for a "barrage" inundation of fresh water to be commenced. This seems to be quite insufficient. I put to Foch in the plainest terms that I thought he must inundate to full at once, and send up much more reinforcements. Nothing was settled, and he went off to Blondecques leaving Weygand behind to go back to his head-quarters and to prepare another division should one be necessary. I had a talk with Weygand about Du Cane, telling him that I thought Du Cane should be a staff officer on Foch's staff for the British Army, and that all orders should be sent through him, and that he ought not to be only a liaison officer.

---

* "On the spot."

After dinner another long talk with Haig. I told him that in iny opinion the time had come when we should look into the future and decide whether we ought not to cut our losses and fall back with our left on the St. Omer inundations. We should lose Dunkirk, but it looked rather as though we would lose that in any case. What was certain was that our army would soon be reduced to impotence, if the French did not direedy intervene and take some of our punishment off us. Haig agreed with all I said.

Next day (the 17th) Wilson wrote:

I was over at Blondecques at 8.30. Plumer had a long talk with me before Foch came m. Plumer is quite clear that, if the Boches attack heavily, he cannot hold the line of the hills much longer. He says he cant trust his troops; they are untrained and, although as brave as possible, simply don't know their business.

Then Foch carne in and we talked, and Foch gave Plumer his instructions, which consisted of holding his present ground and tidying up. As I pointed out to him, all this is quite simple provided one has the necessary troops, and quite impossible if one has not. Then Plumer and I had a long talk alone. I told Foch that there were two courses open to him— to accept battle, or to retire with left on inundations. He was entirely in favour of accepting battle on our present ground, his reason being that we shall save Dunkirk and that we are fighting on the strongest battle line we possess in the north. I told him that, if he did accept battle, then he must act accordingly and bring up troops; and after he left — to go up to see the Belgians — I wrote him a note on the situation as I see it, and the steps which seem to me necessary. I sent copies of my note to Haig and Plumer.

Wilson returned to England that evening, and on the following day he asked the First Sea Lord to prepare a memorandum indicating what were the Admiralty views as to the effect which the loss of Calais and Boulogne, assuming it to occur, would have upon the communications of the B.E.F., and whether in such circumstances full connexion could be kept up with France. Upon the opinion that the Navy expressed on the subject would, so it seemed to the C.I.G.S., depend the attitude to be taken up by the Allied forces that were now so seriously threatened in Handers. If the loss of Calais and Boulogne wordd involve the loss of the

Channel as a line of military communications, then it might even, for the purpose of preventing the fall of the two ports, become necessary for the B.E.F. to accept separation from the main French armies. If, on the other hand, the Admiralty should intimate that the loss of Calais and Boulogne would not involve the loss of the Channel as a line of military communications, then the proper course in the event of the German Flanders offensive achieving further substantial successes might be retirement south-westwards, so as to ensure the maintenance of unbroken touch with the French. Wilson regarded this maintenance of touch with the French as vital, and he was therefore pleased to gather from the Admiralty memorandum that the Navy hoped, even if the two ports were to pass into the enemy's hands, still to ensure communication across the Channel; the situation to the south of Ypres and towards Hazebrouck had, however, in the meantime become less critical. Lord Derby, it should be mentioned, had accepted the Embassy at Paris a few days before this. Lord Milner had just been appointed Secretary of State for War in his stead, and Wilson wrote in the diary on April 22:

> Milner held his first Army Council meeting as S. of S, At War Cabinet Lloyd George much upset by some figures of comparative strengths of Armies published in Maurice's weekly notes for circulation to the Cabinet. It was decided that Smuts should go to Kola to see Trotsky.
>
> After lunch General Niessel came to see me, just back from Russia and Rumania, where he was head of the French Mission. He was very interesting. He says Trotsky is a pure revolutionary who cares nothing for any country, including Russia, but a great deal for himself. Absolutely unreliable and without any principles of any sort, and therefore a man to be measured. I sent him to Smuts.

On the 24th there appears the entry:

> At 6.30 I was sent for to Downing Street, and Milner was there. I explained that there were two problems of first magnitude facing us.

One was Foch's proposal for a *roulement** of our divisions down to Alsace, and to this I had grave and weighty objections unless it was kept within strict limits. The other was the question as to whether we should, in case of further serious retirement, give up Calais and Boulogne, or give up the French and cover the Channel ports. I told them that, now that the ist Sea Lord had written me a paper to say that the loss of the Channel ports did not mean the loss of the Channel, I had absolutely no hesitation in saying that we ought to fall back with the French and give up Calais and Boulogne.

I told Lloyd George that some days ago I had set a scheme to both the War Office and Versailles asking certain questions, and when they were answered I would write a paper on the subject, and he and Clemenceau would then have to decide, as it was a question of high policy, based on military and naval strategy. I pointed out that Haig's opinion was that we could not retreat south, but that in my judgment this was not so, provided the decision was taken in time. Of course, if the Boches are allowed to push down the Somme it would soon be impossible to get across the river, and consequently we would be forced to fall back northwest and lose touch with the French, and then, later, we should be forced to lay down our arms. These are momentous decisions, and, although I trust they may never have to be carried out, yet they certainly oueht to be determined.

Lloyd George was full of abuse of Ireland, and said he wished my d——d country was put at the bottom of the sea; but I said this was simply that he would not, or could not, govern the country. Altogether, Lloyd George's Government is in rather a rocky condition.

Wilson noted in the diary on the following day:

I had a talk with Milner before the Cabinet meeting, and I told him that if a Home Rule Bill was brought in putting the North under Dublin we would have civil war, and in that case we had not enough troops in Ireland to compete with such a situation, and this was quite apart from the deplorable effect all this would have on the army. Milner said there was "no question" of putting the North under the South, and I hope this is so.

---

* "Rolling."

A violent attack delivered by the Germans on the 25th on the junction of the British and French Armies in the Amiens sector south of the Somme, in which the assailants gained capturing Villers-Bretonneux, gave force to Wilson's views as to the imperative necessity of deciding in good time whether the B.E.F. was, at the worst, to be prepared to retire south-westwards, maintaining touch with the French, or whether it should retire westwards with the idea of covering Calais and Boulogne. As it turned out, however, the enemy's further advance towards Amiens was effectually barred by the Allied troops that were available on the spot; and thereafter this sector of the front, which had been threatened so gravely at one time, gradually ceased to be a point of pressing danger. Very severe fighting, however, took place to the south-west of Ypres on the 25th and 26th, fighting in which the Germans at first gained a decided advantage and in the course of which they captured Kemmel Hill from the French. But the enemy's progress was ultimately arrested here also; and by the end of the month the struggle in Flanders, which had upon the whole gone so badly for me Allies, had died away without its involving the loss either of Ypres or of Hazebrouck.

Wilson had in the meantime paid another visit to France in company with Milner on the 26th, for the express pxirpose of holding a conference with Clemenceau and Foch. And it may here be recorded that these very frequent passages across the wayward Channel were keenly enjoyed by the C.I.G.S. for their own sake. Few take pleasure in such maritime trips. To only too many travellers indeed are they wont to prove a discomfiture and a trial. But Sir Henry almost always made his way on to the bridge, whether he was aboard a packet or aboard a destroyer, no matter what the weather was like, and he always showed himself conversant with nautical methods and keenly interested in the handling of the vessel. Still, although an excellent sailor himself, he sympathized with the discornfort which others, and particularly me rank and file, were apt to suffer during the brief periods spent between port and port. In anticipation of their coming discussion with the French representatives, Milner and he spent a night at Montreuil, considering the present military situation in all its bearings with Haig and Lawrence, and looking into the future. It

1918: From April to the End of June 115

transpired that Foch had not yet started the salt-water inundations, this in spite of the urgent representations on the subject which the C.I.G.S. had made ten days before. "Haig agrees," Wilson wrote in his diary, "that in the last resort we should fall back south. I asked him specifically twice, and both times he agreed." The conference took place at Abbeville next day, the 27th, and Wilson wrote a full and interesting record of the proceedings in his diary:

> We had a meeting at 10 a.m. of Clemenceau, Foch, Weygand, Milner, Haig, Lawrence, Du Cane and self. Tiger complained of our recent agreement with Pershing, come to in London a few days ago,* also of my proposal to withdraw 12 battalions from Salonika. After considerable wrangling, and some warmth, it was agreed that we should refer both these matters to a meeting of the Supreme War Council.
>
> I referred to the astonishing proposal of the Tiger to send over two colonels to-morrow to examine our man-power. The Tiger, being caught red-handed, at once bit Spears† for telling me! Milner then referred to the relief of our troops in front of Villers-Bretonneux, and Foch agreed to do it as soon as possible. Foch said that, later on, he meant to retake the Bretonneux plateau, as it was a menace to Amiens but that this could not be done as long as there was fighting going on at Kemmel. The loss of Kemmel is a sore subject.
>
> I then raised the subject of *roulement* and punishment. I pointed out that our 60 divisions had had 300,000 loss, and their 100 divisions had had 60,000-70,000 losses. I pointed out that if this went on, and we started a *roulement*, the British Army would disappear and we should lose the war; and then I proposed that the French should take some of the punishment. Foch said he would not relieve during a battle, and there was no use relieving where there was no fighting. Haig proposed that the French should relieve us up to the Belgians, and in the end Foch agreed to consider. Foch said all inundations were under de Mitry and the fresh water was going well.

---

* This was in connexion with the 120,000 infantry per month, promised by President Wilson. Pershing had been in London on the 22nd and 23rd, but, although mentioning meetings taking place, the diary does not say what exactly was decided.

† Spears was acting as "liaison" between Wilson and the French Ministry of War.

We broke up, Milner and Tiger going for a walk. I then tried to find out whether Foch favoured covering the ports or retiring behind the Somme. I tried hard, but he absolutely refused even to consider the problem. He said that he would not go back a yard, that he would stop me Boches, etc., etc. Of course, this must not rest here, and I mean to have It out. The attitudes of Foch and Tiger were difficult, and it is clear to me that we must assert ourselves much more.

Milner went back to G.H.Q., and the Lord and I came here (Versailles). Tit Willow gave me the answers to my two problems of withdrawal to cover the ports or south. Then Spears came out at 10 p.m. He says there is a dangerous campaign on foot to depreciate the British Army and exalt the French. A dangerous article had appeared in the *Matin* and another in Clemenceau's paper *Homme Libre*. We talked it over, and I am sure we must assert ourselves more. I will discuss with Milner. We must take over high policy everywhere, command of the Mediterranean, etc.

The truth was that just at this time, the end of April, the French had been more impressed with the fact that the enemy had gained substantial successes over the B.E.F., first of all about St, Quentin and at a later date on the Lys, than with the fact that their troops had been slow in coming to its assistance when it was in serious difficulties. Nor was it probably fully realized that the reason why their troops had been so slow was that their reserves had been most faultily disposed in view of the strategical situation existing at the time when the Germans started their great offensive on March 21. That the immediate cause of Foch having been created Generalissimo on the Western Front was Pétain's readiness to sacrifice the connexion of his armies with those of Haig for the sake of covering Paris was moreover not generally known. Our Allies, too, were dissatisfied with the efforts being made in this country in connexion with the utilization of man-power — not without some justification perhaps in view of the failure to impose conscription on Ireland — and, as usual, they ignored the services of British sea-power to the cause. They were disposed to be critical, and to show it. But when about three weeks later Pétain's forces gave way before the enemy thrust which carried the invaders to the Marne, the attitude of the French underwent a characteristically sudden transformation.

1918: From April to the End of June

Milner and Wilson returned to England on the 28th, but they recrossed the Channel on May 1, this time accompanied by Lloyd George and Admiral Wemyss. For it had been agreed that there must be a meeting of the Supreme War Council, and Abbeville had been agreed upon as the place of assemblage. At this Clemenceau, Foch, Pétain, Bliss, Pershing, Frazier, Orlando, Haig, Lawrence, Sackville-West and one or two others were present, besides Milner and the C.I.G.S. Wilson's account of the meeting runs:

> Clemenceau led off about the agreement come to on April 24 by Milner and Pershing for May, and vanted it extended to June. Much argument. At 5 o'clock, still arguing, we formed a small committee in another room of dinner and self, Pershing and Foch; presently Clemenceau and Lloyd George joined, and in the end Pershing agreed to extend May agreement if Lloyd George would guarantee tonnage for 130,000 men in British bottoms.
> Then we discussed Salonika, and my proposal to reduce our force by 12 battalions. Guillaumat strongly protested. In the end it was arranged to send out a British and French general to report. Then Orlando said that he proposed to apply the Beauvais agreement (about Foch as C. in C.) to the Italian Army. I pointed out that this would make Foch C in C. of Italy. Orlando did not realize and fumbled about, and, after mv warning this morning, Lloyd George joined in and asked for postponement till to-morrow. He will square Orlando to-night. Then we abolished the Executive Board.

Of the meeting next day Wilson wrote:

> I at once raised the questions of the Channel Ports and the Somme. Foch said if retirement was necessary he would conduct ah along the line. I said that this was no answer to my question, and I asked my question again. Haig said that it was vital to ho] d on to the French. In his opinion to get separated from the French meant absolute disaster, as both army and ports would be lost. Foch said that such a retirement as we were considering would never occur, but, if it did, he would fall back to the south and base himself on France. Wemyss and the French admiral both seemed to think that if we lost the ports we lost everything. Foch asked for more labour. Pétain underlined my question and Foch's final answer, and that it had now been decided that for the British to hold on to the French came first, and the ports second. *This was unanimously agreed to.*

Some other matters were finally settled at the meeting and Sir Henry, with the others, returned to England on May 3.

The situation in Ireland had in the meantime been growing worse, the question of sending over a fresh Viceroy had come up for consideration just at this time, and Lord French accepted the appointment. Wilson met French at dinner with Lloyd George, Churchill and Mr. Fisher (who was drafting the Honae Rule Bill) being the other guests, and he mentions in his diary that:

> Lloyd George impressed on Johnnie the wisdom of putting the onus for first shooting on the rebels. The Prime Minister moreover declared that he was going to table the Order in Council for conscription in Ireland at the same time as he tabled the Home Rule Bill.

This appears in the diary on the 7th:

> A letter from Fred Maurice in the Morning Posf, giving Bonar and Lloyd George the lie direct about replies and speeches they made in the House of Commons about Douglas Haig taking over the line, and about Army, etc. This will lead to trouble.
>
> When I got to the office I found that Lloyd George and Bonar Law had both sent for me. I first of all got the A.G. to write at once to Maurice, asking for his reasons in writing. Then went over to Downing Street. There we had a long argument and wrangle, and in the end the cabinet agreed to keep Maurice's military offence quite separate from his imputation of want of truthfulness to Bonar Law and Lloyd George, we (Army Council) dealing with the military offence. The Cabinet agreed to set up a "Court of Honour" to consist of two judges of the High Court, to examine into the questions of fact in Maurice's allegation.

The sequel to this incident was that Maurice was called upon to resign his commission, and that Mr. Asquith moved a vote of censure in the House of Commons, which was defeated. Maurice, it should be mentioned, had recently given up the position of Director of Military Operations and Major-General P. de B. Radcliffe had taken his place. The appointment of D.C.I.G.S. had also recently changed hands. General Whigham being given a division in France, and General Harington succeeding Whigham.

1918: From April to the End of June 119

A number of very interesting points are touched upon in Wilson's diary on the 11th, 12th and 13th — for instance, on the 11th:

> At the War Cabinet a long discussion about Russia — whether we should occupy Archangel and Murmansk and Vladivostok, whether we should blow up the Russian Baltic Fleet, and so on. I have a simple rule, which is to help my friends and down my enemies.
> During the meeting Colonel Tanaka (Japanese Military Attaché) came to see me, to say that he thought the time was ripe for Japanese intervention, and what did I think. Later in the afternoon I wrote a note for him, which I read to Milner, Smuts and Wemyss, saying that from a military point of view, the Japanese Army could not intervene too soon nor go too far, and that I was always impressing this on my Government, and hoped that the Japanese G.S. would do the same to their Government.
> After the Army Council* broke up I tried to get a decision from Lloyd George and Milner as to Johnnie French's successor. Johnnie went to Ireland last night. I could not get Milner and Lloyd George to make up their minds. On the whole I advised Haig being brought home. But Lloyd George and Milner would not decide.
> At the War Cabinet meeting Wemyss read out a proposal he was making for the command of the Mediterranean to be taken over by us. This is right.
> Tit Willow and Arthur Capel in at 9 p.m. A long talk about the way in which the French are trying to take over from us militarily and economically.
> *May 12.* The French mean to take us over body and soul. They are proposing to pool oats, and to have a Frenchman to say how many horses each country is to have, and how much ration, etc, A paper this morning from Du Cane says that Foch and Weygand are saying that our battalion estimate is too big and ought to be lowered, etc. Numberless signs of increasing interference.
> *May 13.* I did not speak to Milner or Lloyd George to-day either about Johnnie French's successor or about the French absorbing us, but it is the first day for a week I have not done so. Macready sent me a paper on man-power recapitulating all the warnings given, and giving a forecast of reduction of 25 divisions in August at our present estimate of 930 [per battalion], or 29 divisions at an estimate of 800. This will make the Cabinet sit up.

---

* War Cabinet?

H.M. the King and Sir Henry Wilson

1918: From April to the End of June 121

The question of who was to succeed Lord French as Commander-in-Chief of the Home Forces was not finally settled until just before the end of the month; Robertson was then selected, and he accepted the appointment.* It will be seen in a later paragraph mat Wilson, who would have been pleased to see Plumer in charge of the B.E.F., quite frankly informed Haig of his recommendation made on the 11th (as mentioned in the diary quoted above) that the Field-Marshal should be transferred from G.H.Q. to the Horse Guards. Many, bearing in mind the great achievements of the British Armies under Haig's direction during the last three months of the war, achievements for which in some quarters insufficient credit has been given to the British Commander-in-Chief, may think that Wilson was mistaken in making such a recommendation. But it has to be borne in mind that the remarkable succession of British victories had yet to come, and that at the moment the record stood at two very severe reverses suffered by the forces serving under the Field-Marshal within the past two months, while the equally severe reverse to the French under Pétain only befell them, as it happened, a few days after it was settled that the Field-Marshal should remain where he was. Whatever opinions may be formed on the subject, it will not be disputed that Sir Henry displayed candour and good faith in making Haig acquainted with the attitude that he had taken up in the matter.

The C.I.G.S. paid another visit to France on May 20, and he in the first place had a meeting with Foch and Weygand at Abbeville, where they discussed a number of pressing questions. Foch gave Sir Henry to understand that the Dunkirk inundations had actually risen so high that it had been found necessary to run off some of the water, and the Generalissimo also expressed complete

---

* There had been a question of sending Sir W. Robertson out to India as C. in C. and bringing Sir C. Monro home to take Lord French's place. For Sir Henry's diary records on the 1 6th: "Lloyd Grorge and Milner decided to bring Monro back from India to Horse Guards and send Robertson out there as Commander-in-Chief. Milner to go and see the King." But on the following day there is the entry: "Curzon and Austen object to Monro being moved from India, so this plan of Lloyd George's has collapsed."

confidence as to his ability to block the Germans, whatever might happen. This appears in the diary:

> A long talk with Haig to-night. I told him of the extra men I hoped to send over, and we settled that they should for the most part go into the cadre divisions. I discussed sending over Moir, the engineer* to inspect, and he was willing. I told him that I wanted to put transportation back under Q.M.G. This he did not like much, but later Lawrence quite agreed. Haig says the Americans are not trained at all and talk all manner of languages. I told him that I was denuding Home Defence, so he must be prepared to send me 30,000 any day I called. He agreed that it was most reasonable.
>
> He was as nice as could be. I told him that I had suggested to Lloyd George that he should bring him [D.H.] home to succeed Johnnie, because of the altered status of Commander-in-Chief here. He did not say anything, but said the way I was being criticized was hateful.

Returning to England next day, Wilson proceeded north to visit Sir David Beatty and the Grand Fleet in the Firth of Forth.

> He showed me where the Boche High Sea Fleet had got the other day, and how he only missed them by 50 miles. He explained his plans for drawing out the High Sea Fleet by weak convoys, etc., and I was pleased by all I heard. We went round the Fleet. A wonderful sight, lying in the Firth of Forth. Beatty told me that the other day, when he went to try and catch the High Sea Fleet, he started in thick fog at full speed with 191 ships of all sorts and sizes. Wonderful!

After Sir Henry's return to London on the 27th there appears in the diary:

> The Boches attacked our IXth Corps (Hamilton-Gordon) down at Berry-au-Bac, and the French along the Chemin des Dames, on a front of 50 kilometres, and have thrown the whole line over the Aisne. This is really rather an amazing business, as all that country is so naturally strong. I don't like this sort of thing at all. The King sent for

---

* Sir E. Moir.

1918: From April to the End of June   123

me at 7 o'clock and was much upset.*

Wilson wrote next day:

> This retirement of our IXth Corps and the French over the Aisne and Vesle is very disquieting. The Boches are increasing their attack on the Aisne up to 35 divisions† and quite possibly may turn it into their main attack. I hope so. This would be good. Their wireless tonight claims 15,000 prisoners, but I am afraid there is more — and guns— to come. Milner just back from G.H.Q. and Versailles. He cannot account for this retirement on the Aisne, and from all he heard he thought badly of it. He saw aemenceau yesterday, but this was before the big retirement. The Tiger was full of fight.

The German offensive continued to gain ground during the next few days, especially so immediately to the west of where the IXth Corps was slowly falling back under heavy pressure. The enemy had reached the Marne by the 30th, was forming a deep pocket between that river and the Aisne directed towards Paris, and for two days the situation on the Western Front appeared to be more critical than it had been at any juncture since just before the Battle of the Marne. But by June 2 Foch had moved up sufficient divisions from his reserves to bring this formidable hostile advance

---

* Our IXth Corps, composed of divisions that had suffered very severely during the fighting in April up in Flanders, had been lent to Pétain on the understanding that they were going to be placed in a quiet sector of the French front. It had indeed at first been intended that the Corps should act as a Central Reserve in the hands of the French Army Commander, Franchet d'Esperey. Owing to the losses that they had suffered, the divisions were very short of experienced officers, and the ranks were full of immature and half-trained lads. But it was pointed out by the French staff, when the divisions on their arrival from Flanders were placed in front line to the west of Rheims, that no attack was expected and that the troops could therefore continue their training. The French intelligence was sadly at fault, for, even so late as the 25th, French head-quarters declared that there were no indications of an early ofensive on the part of the enemy in this quarter.

† The five divisions of the IXth Corps was opposed by eleven German divisions.

at last to a halt.*

Wilson had written in his diary on the 30th:

> News to-day is bad, the Boches have taken Soissons and Rheims, and to-night I hear Château-Thierry. This is serious. And as far as I can see, not a single division from Rupprecht's Army has been used, and so we are still liable to attack on the Arras — Amiens Line. This is rather anxious.

Rheims, however, fortunately had not been taken, and the historic city in the event never was taken. But the extreme gravity of the situation, as it presented itself at the end of May, is made manifest by what Wilson wrote of it on the evening of the 31st after arriving at Versailles, and also by what he wrote on the two succeeding days. He had made the journey via Dieppe with Lloyd George, Milner, Balfour, Geddes, Wemyss and others, as there was to be a conference, and he entered in his diary:

> During the voyage I had much talk with Lloyd George, Milner, Geddes and Wemyss. I said that Foch was trying to hold too long a line with the troops at his disposal, and that either he must shorten or he would crack; that the only place to shorten was in the north, and that we must now do what I begged Foch to do on April 17, i.e. come right back to the floods, and put our left on St. Omer. Try and hold Dunkirk, but as a separate operation. By good salt- and fresh-water floods I calculated we could save nine divisions. There was the question of the Belgians, and there was the much greater one of the loss of Dunkirk, which, Wemyss said, would be very serious and probably lose us the Dover barrage, etc. Geddes told me of the amazing Martello towers he is going to plant in the Channel. Sixteen of them, with 6-inch guns and searchlights. These Martello towers will completely block the Channel; but, of course, the loss of Dunkirk might, and the loss of Calais would,, make this scheme impossible. Dunkirk or no Dunkirk, we must shorten our line.
>
> Johnnie Du Cane, up from Foch's head-quarters, was here

---

* The Germans had found the Marne a very serious obstacle to penetration southwards, and they had then endeavoured to push their right flank westwards. But they found their opponents too strong — this phase being signalized by the fine work of American troops, arrived from the north.

(Versailles) when I arrived. The news is bad, there is no question of that. The French have lost Château-Thierry and Villers-Cotterets. This last must mean that they are not fighting. If this is so we are done, and Lloyd George and Milner at once went on that assumption and talked — nonsense. Du Cane told me that when Douglas Haig was discussing matters this morning at Sarcus, Foch got a message from Pétain to say that he must see him at once, so Foch bundled straight off, and Weygand coming back into the rooms, before starting, said that things were "*très graves*"[*] and "*les troupes estaient très fatigues.*"[†] We know what that means. To-morrow will be a critical day. If Rupprecht now attacks south from Montdidier to Noyon and takes Compiègne the French are beaten. It is not easy to follow what will happen after that.

June 1. Writing now, before breakfast, I find it difficult to realize that there is a possibility, perhaps a probability, of the French Army being beaten. What would this mean? The destruction of our army in France? In Italy? In Salonika? What of Palestine and Mesopotamia, India, Siberia and the sea? What of Archangel and America?

During the day there was little information, but on the whole we seem to be giving ground, but much slower. Haig came to the Villa at 11 o'clock and we had a long talk about the Americans. Lloyd George has managed well and, from a promise of having 12 battalions in front in 6 weeks, we have got 4 divisions, i.e. 48 battalions by the end of this month, i.e. 4 weeks.

Then we began with a small meeting at the Trianon Palace of Clemenceau, Foch, Weygand, Lloyd George, Milner, Haig, Lawrence, self. We discussed American programme of 200,000 for June and July. The Tiger made a heavy attack upon us, and Foch went still further and gave figures. This gave Lloyd George his chance, and he made Foch withdraw his paper as being entirely misleading. Foch insisted on necessity of Haig to keep up his total of divisions, and said bluntly that, if he did not, we should lose the war. In all this I agree and backed Foch. Lloyd George offered to allow the Tiger to send a man over, to go through Auckland Geddes' arrangements and see if he could find any men. I think this is wise, as if there is a crash, it will be well to have shown transparent *bona fides*. The President, U.S.A., has now ordered Bliss not to back Japanese intervention.

---

[*] "Very serious."

[†] "The troops were very tired."

We then went to our Mass Meeting where, after a prolonged and heated discussion, it was decided that Jellicoe should go as Admiralissimo in the Mediterranean.

Then, 7 o'clock, another small meeting of Milner, Foch, Pershing and self to settle June and July American contingents. June was settled at 170,000-200,000 infantry. But it then appeared that there was no more trained infantry to come over, and that there would only be the May recruits to bring in July. Pershing wanted to use July shipping to bring 200,000 artillery, engineers, L. of C. troops, etc., and I think he is right. Foch wants the May recruits. Lloyd George, who had joined, backed Foch. The Tiger and Foch had pressed me very hard to withdraw nine battalions from Italy. I refused because of the effect in Italy. Five minutes later I got a wire from Cavan saying that he was sure at last of coming attacks both down the Brenta and on the Piave. This confirms me in my decision.

June 2. Long meetings all the afternoon, and nothing settled except the numbers to come over in June and July, i.e. 170,000 June, 150,000 (infantry) July, of whom 100,000 will be May recruits. During one of these meetings Tiger made more attacks about manpower, and Foch said he could not continue the war unless we kept up our present number of 53 divisions. After many inaccurate statements (such as that he only had 150 divisions whilst the Boches had 210 — the real figures being; American, 4; Belgian, 12; British, 53; French, 103; Italian, 2; making 174). Foch asked how many divisions the British could keep. I replied 47, of which 27 British, 10 Colonial, 10 American. Milner at once said he could not accept my figures, but I would not change.

The decision reached yesterday to appoint Jellicoe as Commander-in-Chief Mediterranean was cancelled to-day, because the Italian admiral said he might be ordered to sea. There was terrible waste of time all day, what with Foch and his inaccurate figures, with Pershing, and with the Italian admiral. And all the time the Boches are gaining ground below Chateau-Thierry, and towards Villers-Cotterêts, and west of Soissons, and south of Noyon. A council is a pathetic and a maddening thing.

But this day, June 2, may, as already mentioned, be said to have marked the end of the third — and last — great, successful German offensive of 1918. Wilson had, in the meantime before returning to England, paid a visit to General Franchet d Esperey at his head-quarters at Provins, and had seen Hamilton-Gordon and other British commanders who had been concerned in the recent fighting to the west of Rheims. He noted in his diary:

> Gordon told me he had only the 19th Division on its legs. The 8th and 50th were quite knocked out, and the 21st and 25th much used up. All the same, his impression was that, if his troops were removed and replaced by French, the whole line would go back. Franchet praised Gordon and the IXth Corps warmly.

Before going on this expedition he had told Lloyd George and Milner at Versailles that in his opinion Foch was making a serious mistake in not taking some of the French divisions away from Flanders for service at more critical sectors of the line. He maintained that the Generalissimo was putting it quite out of his own power to carry out the engagement entered into at Abbeville on May 2, when it had been decided that, in case of extreme necessity, the B.E.F. would fall back behind the Somme and so keep touch with the French. "By weakening his centre, by not carrying out salt-water floods, and by not shortening his line, Foch is making certain that this decision cannot be carried out." Lloyd George had in consequence promised to make representations on the subject to Clemenceau. From what he had heard at Provins, Wilson, however, came to. the conclusion that the German offensive that was in progress at the moment had been stopped; and this proved to be the case. He returned to England with the rest of the party on June 4; but Milner and he were back in France again two days later, in consequence of a decided difference of opinion having arisen between Foch and Haig, in which the C.I.G.S. and me War Cabinet were on the side of the Field-Marshal.

Foch had already denuded Haig's front of four French divisions and of five newly-formed American divisions, and he had now sent an order to the Field-Marshal to move down three British divisions from die north to the sector astride of the Somme. Wilson regarded such a weakening of the front between the Somme and the sea as most dangerous, unless the line was to be shortened at its northern end, and unless greater use was made of salt-water inundations in the Dunkirk region than was at present the case. He indeed entirely disapproved of Foch's strategy in this matter, and he told the War Cabinet so at its meeting on the 5th. "It is simply d—— nonsense saying he won't '*lâcher un pied*'* and then run from the Chemin des Dames to Chiteau-Thierry" he remarked caustically in his diary, and the War Cabinet consequently decided that Milner and he must go over to Versailles and make representations to Foch and Clemenceau. "This will be a delicate business," he remarked in the diary, A further discussion took place in Downing Street before Milner and he left, and of this he wrote:

> I told Lloyd George that if Foch would not agree to our proposals viz. either to take four of his French divisions from the north and to leave us our Americans, or else to shorten the line in the north, and in any case to allow Haig to fight his line in any way he may choose then Lloyd George would get a letter from me to say the British Army would be lost.

The truth indeed was that, excellent as "Unified Command" was admitted to be in principle, and valuable as it had proved to be when Amiens had been in danger at the end of March it was giving rise to serious difficulties in practice. Milner and Wilson spent that night at Montreuil, and Wilson wrote in his diary:

> Much talk after dinner walking round the garden with Haig, and then in his room with Milner and Lawrence. Haig says in his opinion we would be mad to go south and join the French, but in addition he thinks it is already late. Lawrence and he both expect a big attack on Montdidier — Noyon within two or three days,† also about Kemmel, also about Arras. If this is so it is certainly getting late.

The next day he records:

> We had a meeting at the Crillon Hotel at 2.45 p.m., Milner, Haig, Lawrence, Du Cane, seif. Haig read a draft note to Foch saying he

---

* "Drop one foot."

† This anticipation proved correct.

was willing to help in every way, but so long as Rupprecht's reserves (49 divisions) remained intact, he could not agree to any more troops being taken from his command. His front had already been weakened by the withdrawal of 8 French divisions and 5 American divisions, and now he was asked to place 3 British divisions astride the Somme. He thought that he ought to be consulted before such withdrawals were decided upon and carried out. We agreed to his text, with certain alterations.

We then went to the Ministry of War, where we had a meeting in Clemenceau's room. Clemenceau, Foch, Weygand, Milner, Haig, Lawrence, Du Cane and self. Milner opened discussion by saying that me Government had been made rather anxious by the constant withdrawals of troops from Haig's command, while Rupprecht's divisions remained intact, and now Haig had been asked to move down 3 divisions to astride the Somme. The Field-Marshal, while not thinking that a disastrous point had been reached, did nevertheless consider that if further reductions were made he would have formally to appeal to his Government, unless Rupprecht's strength was sensibly reduced.

Foch read a letter of his to Haig, dated June 4, to which he had had no answer, saving that he wanted Haig to prepare plans for sending down all his reserves, and even thinning his line, should the Boches join battle on an 80 kilometre front from the Somme to the Marne; such action would show that the enemy was employing the whole of his forces. Haig then read his note prepared at the Crillon. Foch said that up to date there was no [ground for?] protestation, as he was only asking Haig to make plans for moving his divisions away. Haig agreed, and said he was hard at work on these plans already. Foch then said he was sure that Haig would only protest in future if he [Foch] committed "*des imprudences*,"* and that in that case he [Foch] would agree with the Field-Marshal.

Foch repeated that, if the Boches attacked on a big front from the Somme to the Marne, he would call on Haig for all his reserves, as this would mean that the whole Boche strength was being used. Haig agreed to this, but asked why Foch thought such an attack was likely, as all information pointed to heavy attacks south of La Bassée and between Hazebrouck and Kemmel, and as preparations were now so forward that these could be delivered in 48 hours. Milner pointed out that Foch had only said "if" such an attack as he suggested took place,

---

* "Carelessnesses" or "recklessnesses."

he would call on us, etc. The Tiger said we were all agreed that preparations for all eventualities should be made.

Milner said the journey had been long, but had been well worth carrying out. He said our Government were anxious owing to the constant reductions. However, the misunderstanding had now been cleared away. He asked if it were Foch's intention to withdraw any more American divisions, and Foch said it was not. Haig complained that Foch had withdrawn both the American and the French divisions without informing him. I never saw old Foch so nonplussed. He simply had not a word to say. Clemenceau said such a proceeding was impossible, and must never happen again.

I then asked Foch if our Abbeville agreement of May 2 *re* ultimate directions of retirement held good, and if Foch's dispositions were made with that in view. Foch replied that the continuous touch was of primary importance, but he also said that he would not uncover the ports. After a pause he asked Haig if he agreed to touch being maintained, and Haig said certainly.

"This meeting has done a vast deal of good and has been well worth the trouble," was Wilson's conclusion as to what had passed. It had led to a clearer understanding as to what relatively were the positions of Foch and of Haig under the existing conditions, and it had afforded an example of the power possessed by the British Government to intervene if they saw reason to believe that either the safety of the British Army in France or the prospects of the Allied forces were being jeopardized by injudicious dispositions for which Haig was not responsible. Such intervention was unquestionably to be deprecated if it could be avoided. But it was expedient that the existence of a vetoing power should have been so clearly indicated at this early date after the principle of unified command under the direction of Foch had been set up.

The five American divisions which had been withdrawn from Haig's command had been under training. Their progress had been rapid, and all ranks had shown the utmost eagerness to profit to the full by contact with the more experienced British troops. Before the end of June another five American divisions had been constituted and were already considered sufficiently advanced to garrison some of the defences in the second line. Three of them remained under Haig until August, when they were moved east to be incorporated in Pershing's army; the remaining two, the 27th and 30th, were then incorporated in the British Fourth Army under Rawlinson. General Pershing and his staff had, as was only to be expected, been anxious to collect the United States troops as an Army or a Group of Armies as soon as possible — contrary to the recommendations of the French and British staffs. These latter realized that the best value would be got out of the troops from the far side of the Atlantic were they, for at least several months after their arrival in France, to be distributed as divisions among the various French and British Armies, so as to be under leaders and staffs who were now, after three years' experience in the field, fully versed in the management of great masses of men.

Wilson got back to London on June p, and next day he noted in his diary that the enemy had opened an attack on the line Noyon— -Montdidier, as Haig and Lawrence had predicted. In the meantime the Prime Ministers of the oversea Dominions had assembled in London for an Imperial Conference, the first meeting of this took place on the 11th, and Wilson gave a short account of the present position in France. Of the second meeting, which took place on the 13th, he wrote in his diary:

> Borden made some open remarks on our strategy and tactics, on our Corps commanders, staff, etc. Massey (New Zealand). who followed, agreed. I must try and answer as best I can on Tuesday.

Of that day (the 18th) he wrote:

> At 11.30 I gave my lecture on the military situation, past and future, to the Imperial Cabinet. It lasted 70 minutes. I traced the armies from July, 1914, to to-day. I explained the strategy of the Boches and of the Allies, and I looked into the future and the fact that no decision on the west can now give a decision in the east, so we must get a decision in both theatres. I was much congratulated.

The question of forming an army in northern Russia had attracted attention at various times during the past few months, and Poole, who had come home to consult with the Government and the rmlitary authorities, had proceeded to Murmansk in May to start operations in this direction. The Supreme War Council had, moreover, during its conferences at the beginning of June, agreed to the command of any joint Allied force in that quarter being placed in the hands of a British general, and a number of additional officers had been sent out to Poole to assist him in his task. But the advance of Russian Bolshevist forces to the Caspian and in Siberia, was at this time causing the Cabinet and the C.I.G.S. some anxiety. He wrote in his diary on the 19th:

> At our morning "conversation" of Lloyd George, Milner and me, Lloyd George started a plan for Knox to go to Siberia in plain clothes. Milner and I pressed for Japanese intervention in Siberia, but Lloyd George hangs back for some unaccountable reason. Later on, at War Cabinet, I again said that I would have to ask for the withdrawal of Poole and all his command if the Japanese did not come in, as we shall lose all our men there at Pachenza, Murmansk and Archangel.

The Imperial War Cabinet met next day, and it was agreed to dispatch a cable message to Washington in the name of this very influential assemblage, urging upon the President the need of Japanese intervention in Siberia. A special meeting of the Prime Ministers from oversea with Lloyd George, Milner and the C.I.G.S. took place on the day following, at which, amongst other points, the question was discussed of bringing some more troops back from Palestine to the Western Front. Two such divisions had already been transferred, brides a number of battalions. Wilson, according to his diary, advocated withdrawing another division from Allenby, and this was agreed to.*

> Then Hughes wanted to know about the conduct of the war, the promotion of New Army officers, the future, etc., and we had an interesting talk. Hughes said he was out for fighting on, even if we were driven out of France. Lloyd George gave his *resumé* of position and of fighting in Flanders, etc., of civil versus military opinion, and on the whole was very fair. A useful discussion.

---

* The move of this division, the 54th, was not carried out — apparently owing to the improvement in the situation on the Western Front within a few days.

1918: From April to the End of June

Such was Wilson's summary of the proceedings, and on June 21 he started for Italy, as Cavan had asked him to come out. The Austrians had, some days before, delivered an attack which had partly fallen upon the British contingent and had been momentarily successful; but all the ground lost had been speedily recovered, and the situation was quite satisfactory when Sir Henry arrived. He met Cavan at Vicenza and proceeded with him to the Asiago plateau, afterwards visiting Diaz and dining with the King; then, he spent the 25th, 26th and 27th visiting the different British divisions and the superior Italian commanders. He was most favourably impressed by the difference that he observed between the condition of affairs obtaining now and the confusion and despondency that had prevailed when he had last been in this theatre of war seven months before. Diaz expressed himself as somewhat anxious concerning the possibility of a number of German divisions arriving, and Wilson noted in his diary:

> I said that if the Boches sent 10 divisions I would certainly try and send him three or four; but he must remember that Foch, and not I, was Commander-in-Chief in France.

But a meeting of the Supreme War Council was to be held on July 2, so Wilson journeyed back from Italy, arriving at Versailles on June 29, and he wrote in the diary:

> Much talk with Tit Willow and Studd and Capel, and before dinner with Derby and Du Cane. What is clear is that Clemenceau is trying to grab more and more power, and is trying to brush on one side anybody who gets in the way.

Thanks to the reinforcements in men sent out, and to a lull in the German activities along its front, which had enabled the existing line to be greatly strengthened and certain reorganizations to be carried out, the B.E.F. was now far stronger than it had been in March, and Wilson, writing in his diary on the last day of the month, expressed the opinion that me enemy ought therefore to attack the French rather than launch a further offensive against Haig's command.

Several passages, quoted from Sir Henry's diary in the course of this chapter, have recorded instances of his finding himself in disagreement with the great French soldier who was now saddled with the tremendous responsibility of holding the supreme command on the Western Front, and point to his watching the bent of M. Clemenceau's for taking charge of Allied conduct as a whole, with marked concern. To express opinions as to which of the two friends of long standing, Foch and Wilson, was right as a rule, or on any particular occasion, would be out of place. To comment on "the Tiger's" somewhat acquisitive propensities is unnecessary. But one point stands out clearly. The C.I.G.S. had, during the three and a half years of war antecedent to his coming to be the principal military adviser of His Majesty's Government, undoubtedly been looked upon as somewhat unduly pro-French in high places within the B.E.F. To this impression may indeed have been due the fact that, saving for a few months spent at the start as Sub-Chief of the General Staff, and for the year 1916 which saw Sir Henry at the head of the IVth Army Corps, he held no genuinely responsible position at any time under command either of Sir J. French or Sir D. Haig on the Western Front. But now, during the very critical months which followed the setting up of Unity of Command in the main theatre of war, the attitude that he adopted on more than one occasion proves that, granting him ever to have shown himself most sympathetic in reference to French sentiment and always striving to ensure that French susceptibilities should not be offended, he was quite prepared to insist that the British side of any question which might come to be at issue should receive the consideration to which it was fairly entitled.

Chapter XXIV – 1918: July to September. The Turn of the Tide

The Generalissimo's confidence — Differences of opinion on the Supreme War Council— Lloyd George, and Foch's action in withdrawing divisions from Haig— Foch's counterstroke — Meeting of Imperial War Council— Rawlinson's victory of August 8 — Confidence of Haig and lie B.E.F. — The Police strike, Macready becomes Commissioner of Police — Haig breaks the Hindenburg Line— The Bulgars surrender.

In view of the meeting of the Supreme War Council that was to take place on the morrow, Wilson was glad to be able to pay a visit to Foch at his head-quarters on July 1. Foch, in the course of conversation, expressed the opinion that the Germans were puzzled as to what to do next, and he also thought that Austria-Hungary might soon be in a state of revolution. He remarked to Wilson, rather to the latter's surprise, that all great anxiety would be over within ten days' time, and Wilson noted in his diary:

> I don't think it will be over till September 1, nor that we shan't still be anxious right up to the mud in November, after which we ought to be quite safe.

His account of the meetings of the Supreme War Council on the following three days makes plain that these were signalized by some sharp differences of opinion. Thus he wrote in his diary of the meeting on July 2:

> We discussed a telegram to President Wilson urging Siberia

intervention, and this was agreed to.* Then Tardieu gave a long discourse about the Americans, the 100 divisions and the tonnage required, etc. I had warned Lloyd George that the French, especially Clemenceau, were steadily taking us over, and so, at this tonnage question, Lloyd George boiled over. He said be had never been consulted, that the French had no tonnage, it was all British and American, that he would not accept Tardieu's figures, and that the British and Americans would work it out. It was a complete "deflate" for the French.

Later we had a small meeting to discuss Versailles. Lloyd George said he wanted to strengthen Versailles. The Tiger saw no use for the place. Foch asked if he might put problems to Versailles, and suggested that it should be placed under turn. I was in arms at once, and asked if Foch could put problems about theatres other than France. I said that the French had never made use of Versailles. The Tiger made an attack on me, which made me smile. We broke up, with nothing decided; but Lloyd George said he would bring proposals to-morrow. Leo Amery and I got these out to-night, and they amount to Foch having France and "co-ordinating" Italy, and all other theatres, being over the salt water, fall to me. This will give some fun to-morrow.

This appears in the diary next day:

A long discussion this morning after breakfast as to what we are to say to the French about Versailles and Salonika. I remain of opinion that I had expressed at the time of the Doullens and Beauvais agreements, that when we handed over our army to Foch, we should announce that we took over all the salt water and theatres over the salt water except France and Italy. Neither Lloyd George nor Milner agree with me. I pointed out that I should probably want 4 or 5 divisions from France for Palestine in the autumn, after the French front was safe, and that we ought now to make this clear to the French. But, although Lloyd George and Milner quite agreed, and were all in favour of my going on with preparations, they were against saying

---

* A considerable Czecho-Slovak contingent had succeeded in reaching Siberia early in the year and was upholding the Allies' cause against Bolshevism; but it was getting into difficulties and it sadly needed Japanese support. Masses of munitions, procured by British credits in America for the Russian Army previous to the peace of Brest-Litovsk, were collected at Vladivostok and were in danger.

anything about them to the French. This is quite wrong. Lloyd George agreed to take up the question of Salonika, and Foch's and Clemenceau's orders for an offensive there.

The afternoon sitting was rather a warm affair. Foch and Tiger tried to get the Belgian Army under them. The Belgian Chief of Staff flatly refused. The Tiger said some plain things. Then Lloyd George attacked Tiger about Salonika. I had prepared a case, showing that Foch and Tiger were both issuing orders for big offensives in the Balkans, in flat contradiction of Notes 1 and 4. Lloyd George wandered off into abuse over Franchet d'Esperey's appointment and got rather bogged, but recovered over my brief and came out top at 8 p.m.

On July 4 there is the entry:

We made up our programme for the afternoon of submitting the case of offensive at Salonika to the Military Representatives, of cancelling Clemenceau's orders to Franchet to attack, and of the French submitting the names of C in C.s in France and Salonika, before appointing. All these points were carried without a murmur.

At 2.30 Milner and I met Foch, Weygand and Johnnie Du Cane. Foch wanted to know when our B. Divisions would be out, and urged adding another division to our 59, making 60. Neither Milner nor I would promise. Then Tiger and Lloyd George joined us, and Lloyd George said he wanted to make quite clear that we could not promise always to keep up 59 divisions, because either our man-power would not allow it, or we might require to send some divisions to the Near East. This greatly incensed Foch, who said we must always keep 59 divisions, otherwise we should lose the ports, and England would be done, whereas France could still go on. Of course, this was all rank nonsense, but I was astonished at Foch's attitude. He never referred to the prospective and enormous increase in American strength. I did.

All the same, I am glad that I got Lloyd George to raise this matter, as I think it is only fair to the French, and later I told Du Cane that he was to explain more fully to Foch that there never would be any idea of taking away our divisions so long as France was in danger, but that in the autumn, when we were safe here and mud was on us, it was my present intention to exploit outside theatres.

The larger meeting passed off peacefully, and we finished amicably. This (7th) meeting of the Supreme War Council was the angriest we have had, but I was very anxious that we should give the

French clearly to understand that they were not going to take us over, body and bones, and take charge of every theatre. We have done this plainly — if a little, and unnecessarily, roughly.

At 7 o'clock this evening, when I was working in my bedroom here with Tit Willow and Hereward, Clemenceau, Foch and Weygand arrived to say that, if the Resolutions we had passed this afternoon concerning the duties of the Military Representatives at Versailles held good, Foch said he would resign. We worked till 9.15 at an alteration of wording, not of substance, and then Foch was satisfied.

"The Circus" (the expression at this time employed by the C.I.G.S. in his diary for designating the party from England that used to assemble when a gathering of the Supreme War Council was about to take place) returned to London next day, and three days later an interesting discussion took place at the War Cabinet on the subject of a proposal to publish the British casualties in America for purposes of propaganda. This appears in Wilson's diary with regard to what passed:

> Cabinet against it, saying that people of this country would be horrified. I was in favour, saying that the more we tell the truth to the people the more they will respond. But neither Lloyd George, nor Curzon, nor Barnes, nor A.J.B. were of my opinion. Milner alone agreed.

Then, on July 14, Sir Henry, who had stayed at Wargrave the previous night, wrote in his diary:

> Wires and letters from the War Office tell me that Foch has ordered 4 of our divisions south, as he thinks he is going to be attacked in Champagne, and 4 more have to stand by. Douglas Haig only went back to France this morning. Then, at 5 o'clock a telephone from Lloyd George, who is near Brighton, to say he wants to see me, so I came up. P. de B. [General Radcliffe] met me at No. 36 . We started at 7.30 p.m. and got to Hassocks at 9 p.m. Long discussion till midnight, when P. de B. and I drove home.
>
> Lloyd George began by saying he would not allow 4 of our divisions to go south unless Haig could give a guarantee that Rupprecht would not attack him. Smuts talked about his fear of the Boches attacking the French and us, and, of course, they may. Milner

1918: July to September. The Turn of the Tide

was quite sensible, and in the end we got Lloyd George to agree to send Haig a wire to say that if he thought his force was being put in danger, or if he thought Foch was being pushed to this by Clemenceau for political reasons, he [Haig] was to appeal under the Beauvais agreement. Lloyd George will send over somebody to G.H.Q. to insist upon 5 more American divisions training behind our lines; I think that this will be reasonable in ordinary times, but, of course, absurd at the minute.*

Most soldiers would agree that the Prime Minister's action in this matter was to be deprecated, although the representations made by Milner and Wilson had served to minimize its magnitude. Haig had appealed to his Government a month before, at a juncture when he thought his line was being endangered in somewhat similar circumstances; and the whole matter had then been thrashed out at the French Ministry of War on June 7 (vide p. 129). The Field-Marshal understood his position perfectly, and he was quite aware that he could appeal to his Government if he thought it necessary. He did not think it necessary. He accepted the responsibility of reducing the numbers on his front so as to meet the wishes of the Generalissimo, realizing that this was imperative in the common interest. For Foch had foreseen that the Germans were about to launch another great offensive, this time on either side of Rheims; and that offensive was actually launched on the 15th. But, although Foch had his plans all ready, he required to have some additional troops at his disposal. The counter-stroke was delivered by General Mangin between Soissons and Chateau-Thierry on July 18 with far-reaching results, and what it accomplished represents the turning point of the conflict on the Western Front. But Smuts had in the meantime visited G.H.Q., only to find that the British Commander-in-Chief had no intention of appealing to his Government on this occasion, and that the demands of the Generalissimo had been met with promptitude and

---

* It is not quite clear what this last passage as to American divisions means, but the Prime Minister apparently wished that there should always be a reserve of 5 such divisions in case of eventualities, G.H.Q. obviously possessed no power to order additional American divisions to come under its control.

loyalty— this in spite of indications of an onslaught possibly being delivered by Prince Rupprecht at almost any moment on the B.E.F.

The following appeared in the diary on the 16th:

> Lloyd George was very fractious and difficult this morning, with complaints against Haig and commanders and organization of the Army, said nothing was being done, and was quite rude to Milner. At the Cabinet A.J.B. brought up Reading's objection to Knox going to Siberia, saying President Wilson was opposed to it. I was very angry, and Lloyd George and Bob Cecil backed me; so Knox goes to-night by New York and Vancouver.

The German offensive on either side of Rheims was in the making little progress. So Wilson came to the conclusion that, as only 27 divisions appeared to be taking part in it, the enemy did not contemplate a great effort in this region, but would make the principal stroke against Haig. He was confirmed in this idea when news came to hand on the 18th of Mangin's very successful counter-attack, and of the amount of ground that this was rapidly gaining, for he wrote in the diary on the 19th:

> I am more and more convinced that the Boche attack on either side of Rheims was never meant as a great offensive, but only to draw Foch's reserves to that area, and then their real offensive will be on our front. And now it seems they are succeeding in this plan, even though Foch's counter-attack continues to be successful.
> Douglas Haig sent me a copy of his letter of yesterday to Foch asking for the return of his 4 divisions, and at 8 p.m. a letter from Du Cane by aeroplane to tell me Foch would not return those divisions at present, but that Douglas Haig was fairly satisfied, as Foch had told him on the 15th of this proposed counter-offensive. The French have taken 16,000 prisoners and 300 guns.

This is noted in the diary on July 20:

> Our 4 divisions on loan to Foch appear to be going into the fight, 2 near Chiteau-Thierry and 2 under Mangin in the counter-attack. The French are gaining ground everywhere in their counter-attack and also south of the Marne. All this is good. I still think that Rupprecht will weigh in with his big attack.

Next day he wrote:

I left Charing Cross 2 o'c. with the Lord, and got to Douglas Haig's at a quarter to eight. Long talk after dinner. He began by telling me that he had never had such a free hand, never been so little worried and therefore never been so happy as under me. Tim [Harington] also was working admirably. Then I discussed our falling recruiting, men for tanks, exchange of staff and commanders from other theatres, my fixed point of 900 estimate for a battalion. In all these things he said he would help me in every possible way, and was most nice. The Boches have fallen back from the nose of Chateau-Thierry, our a divisions west of Rheims have had heavy fighting, our other two under Mangin will probably go in to-morrow.

This entry occurs on the 22nd:

Met Rawly at Abbeville, 8 a.m., he does not believe that Rupprecht will attack anywhere, nor that he will do much good if he does. He wants Douglas Haig to give him 5 or 6 divisions and tanks, and let him push out from Villers-Bretonneux; and this is certainly worth thinking about. He defies the Boches to take Amiens.

Drove Johnnie Du Cane on to Bom Bom, where I arrived 3 o'c. Foch delighted to see me and as nice as ever. Long talk. He is very pleased. Said this counter-attack was originally prepared as one of his attacks, and not as it now appeared, but that when the Boches attacked on the 15th, Pétain at once gave up all idea of counter-attack and ordered troops round from Mangin; Foch counter-ordered, and on the 15th fixed the 18th as day for Mangin's attack. Foch said he had much opposition both from soldiers and from Paris, but he stuck to it. He now hopes to push Boches back over the River Vesle, and possibly to the Aisne. He is already contemplating an attack out from our lines, and I told him of Rawly's propose, which we discussed and which pleased him. He has again flooded the Dunkirk area; he is greatly pleased with our defensive lines; he is going to refit his tired divisions under the Somme so as to have them centrally placed. He pushed me about for more men and more divisions, and I countered by asking him why he did not fill up his divisions by boys of 18½ as we were doing, and this was a greater "punch" than I thought. Altogether, although looking tired, he was well and happy and contented. He says the Tiger does not now interfere. Curious, he does not think Rupprecht will attack.

Back again to Paris to see Clemenceau. He was looking well and said our politicians were fools, but I was a good boy! He was well pleased with the turn of events, but not boasting.

Versailles, 8.15. Tit Willow thinks the Boches will attack between Noyon and Montdidier, which seems reasonable, I confess I don't think Rupprecht can stand fast, but Douglas Haig, Lawrence, Rawly and Foch all think he won't attack because we [British] are too strong. In that case we must attack.

Wilson returned to London on July 25, and next day he dined with Lord French, Lloyd George also being of the party. French declared himself to be determined to have conscription in Ireland in October, and that he did not believe in there being any real difficulty; nor did Lloyd George raise any objections. The Prime Minister was, however, much put out next day on hearing that Foch was forming two American Armies, one on the Marne and one below St. Mihiel in Lorraine, as he assumed that this was a first step towards withdrawing the five United States divisions that were serving under Haig from the Field-Marshal's command. "Lloyd George said he would withdraw our tonnage from bringing over Americans," Sir Henry noted in his diary, "and that he would not be bullied by Clemenceau and Foch, etc."

A reference must be made at this point to a somewhat awkward misunderstanding with regard to the question of arms in Ulster which arose at the end of July, and of which Wilson gives certain details in his diary — a misunderstanding to which, as soon as he took a hand in the matter, he speedily put an end. Lord French had come to the conclusion that it would be well to carry out a modified form of disarmament in the province, in view of possible eventualities. But Mr. Shortt, the Chief Secretary, precipitated proceedings by informing Colonel Sharman-Crawford, one of the leading figures in Ulster, that all the arms, even those that were kept stored in armouries, would have to be delivered up — a far more drastic measure than Lord French had ever contemplated. Wilson acted as intermediary between the Viceroy and Sharman-Crawford, and thanks to his good offices the arrangement was come to that all outlying arms, those in possession of individuals, were to be collected into armouries by the Ulster leaders, that the armouries were to be registered, and that their sites and their

1918: July to September. The Turn of the Tide

contents were then to be made known to the military.

A gathering of Prime Ministers took place at 10 Downing Street on July 31, and at this a memorandum of Sir Henry's, setting forth his views as to the course which the campaign of 1919 would be likely to take, came up for discussion. Of the proceedings of this meeting he gives the following account in his diary:

> Milner is clear that we shall never thrash the Boches, and he suggests holding them on the West with 35 British, 65 French, and 65 American divisions, and sending 10 British divisions to other theatres. Hughes thought that we must smash the Germans in France. Borden favoured aeroplanes and economic war after the war. Smuts said my paper was very able, and agreed in the main that the Boches would have one more try in France, and then one in Italy. He disagreed with my proposal to disengage the Ypres hills, Bruay mines and Amiens; on the other hand, he favoured our having an attack in the Trentino. Time, space and season of the year have nothing to do with these strategists! Smuts agreed with Milner that we could not beat the Boches in the West next year and that therefore all our spare troops should go against Austria.
>
> Hughes dissented and said that we must lick the Boches in the West. Smuts thought we could never beat the Boches. (What price his speeches?) Lloyd George began to sum up, when Borden had to go and we adjourned to to-morrow.

The account of next day's meeting of the Prime Ministers runs:

> At the meeting of Prime Ministers, the same present as yesterday, Lloyd George was very captious about my paper, saying that no calculation had been made about losses for the coming 12 months, and so on. But I was able to knock him about rather severely by showing that the paper itself, and the "graphic," gave the whole of the information.
>
> Practically all the Prime Ministers, i.e. Lloyd George, Borden, Hughes (but not so much), Smuts, Massey, and Milner, are of opinion that we cannot beat the Boches on the Western Front, and so they go wandering about looking for laurels. Hughes sees clearer than the others, and sees that we must beat the Boche army if we want a real peace. However, we all ended peacefully. News from France is good and French are advancing north of Fère-en-Tardenois.

The views given vent to by these distinguished gentlemen make strange reading to-day. This consensus of pessimistic civilian opinion was set down in writing by the C.I.G.S, just one week before the great Allied offensive was set in motion on the Western Front, which ended three months later in the abject craving of the beaten enemy for a cessation of hostilities. Nor is it unlikely that a fuller, and possibly an even more damaging, record of the convictions to which the lot of them, with the honourable exception of Mr. Hughes, subscribed on this unfortunate occasion, is to be found amongst the treasured archives in charge of Sir M. Hankey. But, be that as it may, Wilson's serves as a sufficient exposure for all practical purposes. It must, however, in fairness to the politicians be admitted that even the military leaders of the Allies, such as Foch, Haig and Sir Henry himself, hardly realized to the full how critical had grown the position of the hosts under the control of Ludendorff, nor how bright had suddenly become the prospects of the Entente.

News had arrived of the landing of General Poole at Archangel without opposition; but, on the other hand, matters were proceeding none too well in Transcaucasia, for Turkish forces were seriously threatening Baku, which had recently been occupied by a British brigade. Nor was the situation satisfactory in Siberia where, owing to the obstructive attitude of President Wilson, action on the part of the Japanese was being very seriously delayed, and in the end failed to materialize. But all was going well on the Western Front, and on August 5 Wilson wrote in his diary:

> I am puzzled by the Boche, and am beginning to think he must be more tired than we have been giving him credit for. The French are over the Vesle with light troops, and I really believe that the Boches are going back over the Aisne. It is an amazing business. They are falling back over the Ardre at Montdidier and over the Ancre at Albert — Hamel. What the deuce is it all about?

Then, on the 8th and 9th came to hand news of Rawlinson's attack, delivered on the 8th to the east of Amiens, and of its very gratifying progress — "the black day of the German Army in the history of this war," as Ludendorff calls it in his "My War

1918: July to September. The Turn of the Tide 145

Memories." But the far-reaching importance of this triumph was not at first fully realized even at the front.

Wilson crossed the Channel on the 10th; he spent two days in Haig's train, moving about, and he had a meeting with Foch at Sarcus on the 11th, where the discussion that took place would seem to have been of a controversial character. For Sir Henry wrote in his diary:

> He has not yet mounted his Marshal's clothes,* but will tomorrow when he sees the King. He very soon began about the 59-61 divisions. I told him that we could not keep up that number, and might drop to 40-43. He said he would resign, that England was prolonging the war by two years, that she had the men and would not use them, and so on. He presently said that we did not send wounded back to the front. I jumped in at once. I said he totally ignored our efforts in other theatres, our Navy, mercantile marine, coal, industries, etc., and that his observation about out wounded was untrue.
>
> I pretended to be much more annoyed than I really was, and it did him good. I told him that if he wanted more divisions all he had to do was to put his boys down to 18½ in, as we were doing, and then to turn the American divisions from 12 battalions of 1,000 men to 9 battalions of 900. He said he did not command the American Army, and I said, "nor do you the British." It was nice and breezy while it lasted, but it did good, and we were as good friends as ever after it.
>
> Du Cane came to the train for lunch and told me Foch's plans for this year and next. Foch wants this year to disengage the lateral railways at Amiens and Hazebrouck, Compiègne, and St. Mihiel.† Next year he wants to seize the Boche lateral railway of Lille — Herson — Mezières — Metz; when that is done he thinks he can deal with the Boches, as it were, in two theatres — north and south.
>
> After lunch I went out to the monument at Villers-Bretonneux. Amiens is much more damaged than I thought, and Villers-Bretonneux is a mass of ruins. I met Douglas Haig and Lawrence there. Then I fell on a conference of Rawly's just outside V.B., at which Clemenceau and Klotz were present. I had a long talk with the

---

* General Foch had just been raised to the rank of *Maréchal de France*.

† This modest programme serves to show that the Generalissimo had at this date little expectation of the triumphs about to take place.

Tiger, and told him of my talk with Foch in the morning, and warned him that Foch must really keep off our internal affairs or else there would be trouble. Then I took Rawly back to the monument, where he had not been. It is a desolate place — a modern battlefield. Then I had tea with Monash* and his five divisional generals. Monash told me it was the first time the six of them had ever been together in a room.

Back here for dinner. Haig at dinner said we ought to hit the Boche now as hard as we could, then try and get peace this autumn. Foch came over to ask Douglas Haig to go on pushing so as to get the Boches over the Somme. D.H. agreed.

Wilson returned to England on August 12 well satisfied with what he had seen of the situation on the Western Front. With regard to Haig's promises to Foch on the evening of the 11th to the effect that he would go on pushing so as to drive the enemy over the Somme, it should be mentioned that the Field-Marshal two days later satisfied himself that the German divisions which had been driven back from about Villers-Bretonneus, were now strongly posted between Roye and Chaulnes. He foresaw that Rawlinson's forces might suffer discomfiture were they to continue attacking with the idea of driving the Germans over the Somme river, which to the east of Chaulnes runs south and north. The British Commander-in-Chief consequently decided on a more scientific plan, which consisted in utilizing Byng's Third Army on Rawlinson's left to attack farther to the north, and in utilizing Home's First Army at a later date still farther to the north. A sharp difference of opinion appears to have occurred; but the Field-Marshal was firm and Foch eventually acquiesced in Haig's plan. Wilson, however, makes no mention of the incident in his diary. He wrote on the 13th:

> At War Cabinet this morning. A.J.B. gave us 1½ hours of delightful description of the condition of Europe at the Peace Conference, vnth absolutely no indication of what we should do except that we should not agree to the Brest-Litovsk Treaty. Ye Gods! The fact that we have no foreign policy will ruin us, as it has ruined

---

* General Monash now commanded the Australasian Army Corps.

1918: July to September. The Turn of the Tide

us all along. Then desultory talk, and then Borden came out with the amaaing opinion that after the war we [British] should have no annexations, and that all our gains, i.e. Palestine, S.W. and S.E. Africa, Mesopotamia, Persia, Pacific Islands, be handed over to the United States. Reading said he thought U.S. would take Palestine but not the rest, but that the President [Wilson] would strongly object to our having any gains. Meanwhile Wilson seems to have annexed San Domingo! Hughes was straining at the leash, but discussion was postponed till to-morrow.

Then the entry appears next day:

War Cabinet 3.30 o'c. Massey entirely opposed to Borden's proposal to hand over German colonies we have seized to the United States. Hughes said, "If you want to shift us, come and do it," he also claimed the right to help to shape our foreign policy, adding that we had none.

Smuts enumerated all points made by A.J.B. yesterday, all of which would require decisive victory in the field. Smuts does not believe in a decisive victory against the Boches in the west, and does believe in Boche victories in the east, therefore the moment the tide turned in our favour — and it almost has, now — he would make peace, even if by so doing we carted our Allies! He would try a fall with Austria, and would give Constantinople to Bulgaria so as to make trouble between them. He suggested an International Board for all tropical Africa, with an American as Chairman. Fantastic! And he never mentioned the sea!

On Wilson's next visit to the front he found the Field Marshal to be very confident, although somewhat disappointed at Pershing having taken away three of the five American divisions that had been with the B.E.F. for several weeks past. Byng and Rawlinson were making steady progress, and Wilson saw them both, as well as many others of the generals. "All are confident that we shall get the Boches back to the Hindenburg Line," he wrote in the diary, "and it certainly looks like it." Our airmen were bringing in most encouraging reports as to the confusion that was noticeable behind the German front. When the C.I.G.S. got back to London he was therefore able to make a highly satisfactory report as to the existing situation and as to the prospects of further successes to the War

Cabinet, although the general impression in the B.E.F. at the time seems to have been that the enemy would only, during the campaign of 1918, be driven back as far as the Hindenburg Line.

The plan which Wilson had adopted at Versailles of organizing most of his staff as two opposing sides, one representing the Allies and the other the enemy, had proved so appropriate and satisfactory that he had latterly been anxious to organize his staff at the War Office on similar lines. In place of having one branch as an Operations Directorate and another branch as an Intelligence Directorate, he wanted to rearrange them, and an opportunity for carrying out the desired transformation presented itself just at this time. For, as a consequence of the strike of the Metropolitan Police at the end of August, General Macready was, on September 1, appointed Commissioner of Police, and a few days later General Macdonogh, from being Director of Military Intelligence under Wilson, succeeded Macready as Adjutant-General. Sir Henry thereupon brought in Major-General W. Thwaites in Macdonogh's place, and he divided the duties up between Thwaites and General Radcliffe on the Versailles lines. He had been highly indignant at the conduct of the Police in striking under the circumstances existing, and he wrote in his diary on the 31st:

> Small Cabinet of Lloyd George, Bonar Law, Milner, Macready, Cave and self to discuss the Police strike; Macready was of opinion that the increase of pay must be admitted, that Tiele should be allowed back, but that the Union should not be agreed to.* If the men did not agree to this, he thought they ought to be conscripted and made to carry out their police duties as soldiers. I said I thought that if the men did not agree to these terms they should be put in the trenches. Bonar Law and Lloyd George agreed with me. At mid-day Lloyd George received a deputation and spoke very straight to them, and to-night the men have agreed. Crowds of police everywhere in plain clothes, and the whole thing a very disgraceful affair. They undoubtedly had a grievance, but it was a scandalous way of behaving.

---

* Tiele was a constable who had been dismissed and whose reinstatement was demanded. The matter was settled on the lines suggested by Macready.

1918: July to September. The Turn of the Tide   149

There had, however, been some delay in filling up Macready's place as Adjutant-General, as is indicated by an informative passage in Wilson's diary dated September 3, which runs:

> Milner tackled Lloyd George about Macdonogh succeeding Macready Lloyd George rather opposed to it, and said he had some scheme for amalgamating the A.G. and Q.M.G. and putting it all under a civilian! Ye Gods! So the matter rests to-night. But I certainly can't agree, nor will Jack Cowans. And Macready, who said good-bye to-night, was equally emphatic.

The Army Council, including its civilian members, were naturally up in arms at so mischievous a project; and, as Lord Milner took up a strong line, the Prime Minister dropped it, Macdonogh thereupon became Adjutant-General, and Sir Henry, as already mentioned, instituted the new system of operations and intelligence in the General Staff Department of the War Office, and it worked very satisfactorily. Haig's forces were in the meantime acting with tremendous effect. The First, Third and Fourth Armies, pressing forward simultaneously, were carrying all before them. 57,000 prisoners and 650 guns had been taken by them during August, a fresh 25,000 prisoners were captured during the first four days of September, and by the 7th of that month the enemy was in full retreat for the Hindenburg Line. The Second Army was also moving steadily forward, and it had already recaptured much of the ground near Ypres that had been lost in April.

The situation in the Balkans also now appeared to offer favourable prospects, should the Allies decide upon undertaking a general offensive in that theatre. General Guillaumat had explained plans for operations in Macedonia that he had in view at a meeting of the War Cabinet on the 4th; these plans had Wilson's full support, and they were in due course put in execution by General Franchet d'Esperey, who was now in chief command in and around Salonika. Sir Henry, who had been gazetted full General on the 4th (dating back, however, to June 3), proceeded to France on the 9th, and a meeting took place at Cassel between him, Foch, Haig and Plumer on that day. At this the Generalissimo announced that he had arranged with the King of the Belgians (who now commanded all the Allied Forces on the left of the British First Army) for a general forward movement to take place between Ypres and the sea. This also appears in the diary:

> Douglas Haig and Lawrence again thanked me for the extraordinary way in which I saved them trouble. Douglas Haig said he had absolute peace, nobody worried him, nobody interfered with him, and he wrote to nobody except to me. They were off home by my destroyer, as Douglas Haig wanted to impress on the Home Authorities the importance of hitting as hard as we could up to the mud time, and Douglas Haig wanted to know, before he said all this, whether I approved.* I do. He said there was now ample evidence of the deterioration of the Boche, and I believe this.

Sir Henry had a meeting with Foch at the latter's headquarters on September 11, but their talk was chiefly on manpower, and this is noted in the diary:

> He told me nothing of his further plans and said they were always changing. I told him that I only wanted to know so that I could assure my War Cabinet I was satisfied, otherwise there was a distinct danger of Lloyd George wanting to interfere.

Wilson also saw Clemenceau, whom he found inquisitive as to what was going to happen in Ireland, but whom he reassured on the subject of conscription coming in that country. Clemenceau expressed himself as opposed to a meeting of the Supreme War Council, seeing that there was nothing to discuss except manpower over which there might be a quarrel. Du Cane arrived from Foch that evening with information as to the Generalissimo's contemplated plans, and they proved to be quite simple.

> Everyone is to attack (Belgians, British, French and Americans) as soon as they can, as strong as they can, for as long as they can. He will also attack the Hindenburg Line. He will begin again April 1.

---

* The Field-Marshal on this day told Milner that the conflict had changed its character and was on the eve of decision.

1918: July to September. The Turn of the Tide

Although the tidings from all sectors of the Western Front continued to be most encouraging, the C.I.G.S., back in England, was much disappointed at hearing on the 16th of Baku having been lost to the Turks. The small British force that had been sent there had, however, been safely withdrawn from its isolated situation. "This is a bother," he remarked in his diary "as it breaks the chain from Baghdad to Archangel."

Sir Henry had been doing his best for a long time past to persuade Diaz to give Cavan command of an Army, and he was much pleased to hear, from Cavan himself who was home on leave, that this had now been arranged. Then, on the 20th, most satisfactory reports arrived to the effect that Allenby had commenced a great forward movement on the previous day, and that this was proceeding very successfully. This early information from the Palestine theatre was followed during the next two or three days by continuous reports of rapid advance and of huge captures in a region in which Wilson had, for months past, felt convinced that great things might be accomplished in furtherance of the Allied cause. The gaps which had been caused in Allenby's forces by the hasty withdrawal of troops for service on the Western Front after the German offensive in that quarter of the preceding March, had to a great extent been made good since that time by the accession of additional, newly-raised units, sent from India; while the splendid body of mounted troops that had even then been available, had been appreciably augmented by the dispatch of Indian cavalry from France.

Wilson wrote in his diary on September 23:

> Long talk with Milner this afternoon on his return from 10 days in France. He thinks Haig ridiculously optimistic and is afraid that he may embark on another Paschendaele. He warned Haig that if he knocked his present army about there was no other to replace it. Milner saw many generals in France and they were all most optimistic. The manpower is the trouble, and Douglas Haig and Foch and Du Cane can't understand it.
>
> I spoke on the telephone to Lloyd George, who is at Hassocks near Brighton. I told him I wanted to send Allenby a telegram of congratulation from the Cabinet, and also a wire saying that, if he would like to try a cavalry raid to Aleppo, the War Cabinet agreed.

To both of these propositions Lloyd George agreed, and, Milner having already agreed, I sent the two telegrams. The news from Allenby to-night is 25,000 prisoners. The news from Salonika is also excellent; the Bulgars seem to have started a general retreat. Allenby's success has already resulted in a Turkish division from the Caucasus being ordered back to Palestine via Black Sea and Constantinople.

This appears next day:

At War Cabinet I told of Allenby's capture of Haifa and Acre and Es Sault. Then long discussion about the Railway Strike.* The G.W.R. and parts of the L.N.W.R. defy all authority, and it is really a challenge to the Government of the country. We agreed to accept the challenge and call out the soldiers this evening. Bonar was quite good and firm, and so was Barnes. Later in the day the strike spread, and to-night I hope the soldiers are out taking charge, I lunched with the King and Queen and Princess Mary.

On the 25th there is the entry:

At Cabinet I told of Allenby's 40,000 prisoners and 265 guns and booty, and in Macedonia of Allies being over the Rivet Vardar on a 45 kilometre front. French in Prilep.
Douglas Haig writes for Yeomanry, cyclists, motor machine-guns, lorries — anything to make him more mobile in the coming great attack. This is the first I have heard of this big attack, except that Bonar Law said yesterday that Hughes had given him all details of the British — French — American attack. The railway strike seems to be dying out to-night.

Wilson motored to Hassocks on September 26 to see Lloyd George, who had been ill and whom he found quite determined that Clemenceau and Foch should be told definitely about the situation in the United Kingdom as regards manpower, and also satisfied that conscription must be applied to Ireland. On the following day a wire arrived from General Milne to say that the Bulgars had sent

---

* This strike was not supported by the Unions.

1918: July to September. The Turn of the Tide 153

in a flag of truce, and had asked for an armistice. The C.I.G.S., Bonar Law and Balfour agreed that an armistice must not be granted, but that properly accredited representatives might be allowed to come and discuss matters, and this appears in the diary:

> I asked what our Foreign Office was going to do if Turkey followed suit, and A.J.B. did not know. I put in a strong plea for making love to Turkey, not to Bulgaria.

In the meantime news from the Western Front continued to be excellent, as the First and Third British Armies had broken through part of the Hindenburg Line on the 27th, and, besides the progress that Haig's forces were continually making, French and American armies in the Argonne were also advancing. So that when Wilson crossed the Channel (on the 28th) and again spent two days in Haig's train, he found every reason for feeling well satisfied with the military situation in all quarters, and he wrote in his diary on the first day:

> No further news of Bulgaria to-day, nor of Allenby, except that his prisoners are now 50,000. Over here in France things are going well. The Belgians have taken Langemarck and Houthoulst Forest and Polecappele and 4,000 prisoners. We have got on towards Cambrai, and Rawly attacks to-morrow. The French and Americans in Champagne and Argonne are going slowly.
> Long talk with Douglas Haig to-night. He hopes to be in Valenciennes in a few days, and in Brussels before the winter; he thinks the Belges will go on to Roullers to-morrow and later on to Ghent. The two American divisions under Rawly are attacking, with Australians behind them, to-morrow.

Next day there is the entry:

> The news this morning is good. The two American divisions under Rawly have taken all their objectives, and the Australians are passing through now, at 11 a.m., to push on. Plumer got Wytschaete yesterday. Mangin reports that the Boches are falling back from the western end of the Chemin des Dames, and that Laon is being cleared. It looks to me as though Ludendorff either could not, or would not, make up his mind for a real shortening of his line, and that now he is

too late and that his retirement will be a very costly thing. Everyone here very hostile to Lloyd George for not having given Haig a "puff."

News all day good. Douglas Haig showed me all his plans, which seem sensible and good. After lunch I went over to Rawly's headquarters near Péronne, where he has a wonderful camouflage camp. He does not know where the two American divisions which attacked this morning have got to. Otherwise all is going well, and on my return I passed through the cavalry going up to the Omignon Valley so as to be ready for to-morrow.

On September 30 Wilson wrote:

Another talk with Douglas Haig about the present situation. He believes that the Boches are going to copy the Bulgars and ask for peace. I hope to God they are not, as one never knows what the politicians will do. Foch turned up at 9.30. He is looking very well and of course, mightily pleased with everything. He insisted again upon our keeping up 61 divisions, building less ships, less aeroplanes, less tanks, etc. The same story. He is delighted with Allenby's success, which he thinks "*très chic.*"* He wants me to reinforce Milne, so as to occupy Bulgaria and get on up into Rumania. I caught the 2 o'c. boat.

It seems to me that the French are taking complete command of the Bulgarian situation without consultation with us, and this is all wrong. I spoke to Bonar Law on the telephone, and told him that in my opinion we were tumbling into peace in just the same way as we tumbled into war. No concerted action, no far-seeing plans — just haphazard.

The French news to-night continues good. I think the Belges and French are in Roullers. Horne, Bungo and Rawly got on well; some 10,000-1 5,000 prisoners. Berthelot has opened an attack west of Rheims. The two American divisions with Rawly have disappeared, and the Australians who are following them cannot use their guns as they do not know where the Americans are!† Allenby has got another

---

* "Very elegant."

† It should be explained that of the two American divisions (27th and 30th) the 30th had advanced rapidly, apparently carrying all before it, but had omitted to secure me ground after capture. This was due to inexperience, British New Army divisions had committed exactly the same error along half of the front attacked on

1918: July to September. The Turn of the Tide   155

10,000 prisoners of the Turks east of the Jordan.

The "cease fire" went in Macedonia at 12 midday to-day. This is the beginning of the end.

Major Bacon, Mr. A.J. Balfour, Sir Douglas Haig, Sir H. Wilson at Versailles

Thus the month of September, 1918, drew to its close under circumstances that were full of encouragement for the Allies on the Western Front, even if the progress of the French and the Americans in the Argonne region, on the right of the great combined movement which Foch was developing, stretching from the Meuse to the sea, was being somewhat inconveniently delayed by the difficulties of the country. The Allied victories of July, August and September had constrained the enemy to abandon all the furthest advanced areas of that huge salient within French territory, which German hosts had been holding in their grip since the early days of the war. But a blunt salient still existed, and the

---

the first day of the Battle of the Somme. But, whereas the result at the Battle of the Somme had been that the victors had been driven out again and back to their own lines, the Australians, following behind the Americans, had consolidated what these had won. There had been confusion, but no question of failure. The 27th Division was stoutly opposed and gained little ground except at first.

Marshal was taking full advantage of this by pushing forces forward on the two flanks, eastwards from Flanders and northwards from Lorraine, while Haig in the centre dealt with the problem presented by the formidable Hindenburg Line where it was at its strongest. In that formidable line a huge gap had been created by the armies under Horne, Byng and Rawlinson, and Ludendorff's position had thereby been rendered precarious, if not indeed actually desperate.

In the remoter theatres of conflict the triumphs of the Allies had if possible been even more pronounced and far-reaching. For the last day of September was rendered memorable by two events occurring in regions far removed from the Western Front and from each other. Bulgaria surrendered, accepting the Allies' terms in full. Damascus was taken by British troops and Arabs, and the fall of that ancient city signified the final collapse of the Ottoman legions which had been striving in vain to stay the rapid advance of Allenby's forces through Syria.

Chapter XXV – 1918: Last Six Weeks of the Great War

Difficulties between the Allies — The Turks surrender — President Wilson ignores his Allies — Problem of the terms to be insisted upon — The question of conscription for Ireland — Austria-Hungary requests an armistice — November 11.

The collapse of Bulgaria, eminently satisfactory as was this development from the point of view of the Allies, gave rise none the less to some embarrassment, for it produced inconvenient differences of opinion between the Allied Governments, as also between their military advisers. Nor did President Wilson's inopportune interventions, and the attitude which he took up in reference to questions of moment that came up for consideration, tend to ease the situation. Sir Henry's diary during the month of October, 1918, provides much that is of especial interest, owing to the light that it throws on these subjects, and also because of the evidence which its pages provide of the diarist's clarity of view in respect to problems that were hedged round with military and political complications. We find on the 1st:

> At the Cabinet this morning I explained military situation in Bulgaria if army was disarmed and demobilized. How the country would be at the mercy of the Austrians; how we could not save it, nor march on Constantinople (as Prime Minister wants), for some time. My Cousin seems to have barged in and said he wanted to settle the

Bulgarian affair, and the Tiger rapped him over the knuckles. All the news from France is good.

At 3 o'c. A.J.B., Milner, Hankey and self had a meeting in my room. We redrafted the wire which Lloyd George wants to send to the Tiger, and I agreed to take it down to Lloyd George. We ought to have a meeting in Paris or Versailles. At 5 o'c., a meeting about conscription for Ireland of Johnnie French, Shortt, Auckland Geddes, Macdonogh and self. All arrangements to be made to carry it out.

Motored down to Hassocks to Lloyd George, Johnnie French and Rosie Wemyss there also, and Hankey, Philip Kerr and Riddell. Long talk about Bulgaria and Turkey, and I persuaded Lloyd George to have a meeting. So I go over to Paris to-morrow, and Lloyd George comes when I wire. We must walk warily or we shall be getting into a mess down in the Balkans. Lloyd George quite agrees about conscription the moment the House meets.

Next day there is the entry:

There was a curious wire in from Rome to say the Austrians, through the Roman Church, had offered terms to Italy. They would give up Trentino, make Trieste international, and use their good offices about Alsace-Lorraine. Orlando had replied that they must send in a flag of truce.

The Lord and I left Victoria by special, 11.35 a.m. Tit Willow glad to see me. There has been no further news during the day, but Tit Willow had a copy of the instructions now being issued to Franchet d'Esperey (Guillaumat is not now going out). These instructions are, no doubt, in addition to those I have seen, which Guillaumat got, but are still incomplete.

On the 3rd Wilson wrote:

Du Cane sent me a letter, 4 a.m. this morning, to say he had discussed Balkan situation with Foch yesterday. Foch is entirely opposed to any action against Turkey. He wants to get up on the Danube and talks of joining up with Rumania. How he is going to join Rumania without getting command of the Black Sea I don't quite

1918: Last Six Weeks of the Great War   159

know.*

I saw Clemenceau and Guillaumat this morning. Tiger very nice to me. He wants to hit Turkey as soon as possible, but he does not a bit realize that the Bulgarian and Serbian questions are not nearly finished yet, and that we are working for trouble if we add to our commitments at present. Foch, Guillaumat, Berthelot and Franchet are for the Danube, Lloyd George and Tiger are for Constantinople, I am for examining the question a little more before giving an opinion. Tiger quite clear he won't stand any interference from my Cousin; he wants to see Lloyd George to-morrow when he arrives, so I wired Lloyd George my news. Tiger told me he had reliable information that the Boches would not help the Turks. I doubt this. It is possible they may not send troops to Turkey, but I should think they are certain to occupy Nish and Sofia, and so threaten any movement of ours to the East.

We have taken Lens and Armentières and Aubers Ridge and La Bassée, and our cavalry and tanks have taken Fresnoy north of St. Quentin. All this is good. Spent the whole afternoon studying present situation in the Balkans. Tit Willow and his staff advocate a landing of two divisions in Saros Bay, clearing the Gallipoli, landing also at Kum Kale and clearing southern shore, and then passing up Fleet. I am not persuaded.

On the following day, the 4th, Wilson had a long talk with Foch at his head-quarters, and he found the Marshal now very hopeful of bringing about a German disaster before the winter, by keeping up constant pressure along the whole front between the sea and the Meuse. "He gave our troops the highest praise," appears in the diary. Sir Henry afterwards had a meeting in Paris with the Rumanian Colonel Rosetti, who, like himself, looked upon the French plans of co-operating with Rumania as impracticable until command of the Black Sea had been secured. Mr. Lloyd George arrived in the evening, he proceeded with Sir Henry to Versailles, and Wilson wrote on the 5th:

At 10 a.m. General Alby arrived from Clemenceau,

---

* Bulgaria's abandonment of the contest had rendered operations by land against Turkey in Europe a practicable proposition.

bringing with him notes on Balkans by Guillaumat and by Berthelot, and instructions by Clemenceau to Franchet and Berthelot. The most fantastic proposals. They all ignore the Dardanelles. They all promise to "isolate" Turkey by occupying Bulgaria and Varna and putting submarines in the Black Sea. They are all incapable of estimating the value of salt water. They propose to join up with Rumania across the Danube.

I told Lloyd George what we ought to aim at, viz: Occupation of as much of Serbia as we could; occupation of the least of Bulgaria we could; occupation of Maritza line and up to Demotika bridge, and then an attack on Constantinople and Gallipoli with Greek and British troops. We (Lloyd George, Hankey, Admiral Hope and I) went in to the Tiger. Orlando was there, and the three Prime Ministers had a private talk. After half an hour I was sent for and found them discussing Balkan strategy on a small hand-atlas map of Europe, the whole page of Europe being about 8 inches by 6 inches! And this after four years of war. I suggested another meeting at Versailles, which was agreed to, Lloyd George told me that he had suggested to Tiger that Allenby should arrange to knock out the Turk in Europe as well as Asia, but Tiger would have none of it.

Back to Villa Romain at 3 o'c. Delmé-Radcliffe to see me. He has no news as to where Diaz's coming attack is going to be, but imagines it will be on the Asiago, as Cavan was recalled from leave. Then Derby came out here to see me; he does not think that the French had any secret information that the Bulgars would chuck it if they were attacked. I think the French had.

Then a meeting here of Lloyd George, Tiger, Orlando, Foch, Admiral Le Bon, Hope, self. Lloyd George advocated a transfer of troops — and Allenby — from Palestine to European Turkey, via Dedeagach, Saros, etc,, and that we should knock out the Turks as soon as possible. Foch agreed that, to knock out the Turk, you must go to Constantinople and via Dardanelles. He thought, however, that we should first cut the railway in Bulgaria near Adrianople, and then occupy strategic points in Bulgaria, and put troops along the Danube, which he thought would be a matter of 15-20 days! Lloyd George, however, claimed that Foch was in agreement as to the necessity for knocking the Turk out, and, this being so, he bowed Foch out, and then he and Tiger and Orlando continued their talk.

I impressed on Lloyd George the necessity of getting Tiger to agree to Allenby having command against the Turks in Europe, as he would have to use Salonika as his principal base, and also on the importance of getting Tiger and Orlando to agree to allow Greek troops to be used in this operation of Allenby's. Nothing much was really settled at this Prime Ministers' meeting; but Lloyd George said he had pushed so far that I could send Allenby a wire. I sent him one to say it had been decided to transfer troops from Palestine to Salonika and ports in the East, and he would have an independent command of Palestine and of all troops to be employed against Turkey in Europe, while Franchet d'Esperey would remain in command of all operations in Serbia and Bulgaria. Of course, this is vague to a degree, but, as I said in my wire, it will allow the Bull[*] to think, and to begin ear-marking and collecting troops, ships, etc.

Wilson farther records in his diary:

> Clemenceau brought us news that yesterday Germany, Austria and Turkey had notified President Wilson that they were ready to treat on his 14 points, and asking for an armistice pending discussion. Pretty piece of impertinence. As I have always said, let the Boches get behind the Rhine and then we can discuss.

On the following day a telephone message from the Admiralty came to hand to say mat a Turkish envoy had reached Mitylene on his way to Athens to discuss terms; Sir Henry continued to press upon the Prime Minister the urgent need of some decision being arrived at as to the command of the forces that would act against

---

[*] The name that Allenby was very generally known by in the British Army.

the Turks in Europe, and also as to the Greek military forces being employed against the Turks. The three Prime Ministers on this day devoted their attention to discussing what answer was to be given if Germany and Austria were to ask for an armistice, and Lloyd George afterwards told Sir Henry that what they contemplated was insisting upon the evacuation of Belgium, France, Alsace, the Trentino, Italy, Serbia, Bulgaria and Rumania, The Prime Minister wished Wilson to examine these proposed terms from the military point of view, but Wilson remarked in his diary:

> I think the whole thing is wrong, and that we ought to say "The Boches will get behind the Rhine, and the Austrians out of Italy and Trentino, and then we will talk." Bonar flew over, and Bob Cedi came by boat and car, and after dinner we had an interesting discussion. Lloyd George took the line that we pandered and bowed much too much to President Wilson. Bob and Bonar Law were all in favour of conciliating him. I agree with Lloyd George, and am certain that a few good home truths would do the President good.

On October 7 there is the entry:

> At 10 a.m. Foch and Weygand arrived. Lloyd George led off on manpower. Foch went through all his old arguments about population aeroplanes, tanks, Hindus, navy, etc. Nothing, of course, settled. Lloyd George asked for Foch's photograph, so all went well.
>
> Spears sent me Franchet's proposals for his coming campaign. Milne to go to Sofia and Danube, and a French general to attack Turkey. Very hot stuff. Meeting of Prime Ministers at Quai d'Orsay at 3 o'clock. I was in attendance. Lloyd George flatly refused to accept Franchet's plan, and after much wrangling it was agreed that Milne, with nearly all our troops and some French, Italians, Greeks and Serbs, should command the operations against Turkey. This cancels my orders to Allenby, so I wired at length to him and to Milne.
>
> Then the 'Frocks" discussed terms of a possible armistice with Germany and Austria, and I was told to consider the steps necessary. No answer from President Wilson to Boche offer to discuss his 14 points.

Next day, the 8th, there is the entry:

1918: Last Six Weeks of the Great War 163

Long discussion with Tit Willow on problem set me yesterday by Prime Ministers about armistice. My opinion now is that we must make immediate disarmament a condition. Then keep Boche troops under Boche command and discipline (leave 5 p.c. armed), and march and train over the Rhine, leaving all arms, munitions, depots, factories, etc., intact. During the morning we got out a M.R. paper on the lines of disarmament, fall back behind Rhine, our occupation of Metz, Strasburg, Neu Breisach, Lille. Had a talk with Lloyd George and Bonar Law about my armistice terms. They both think them too severe. It is curious how nervous these politicians are. I don't see what guarantee we shall get worth having unless we disarm the brutes.

There was a "Frock" meeting at 3 o'c., which I did not attend, at which our armistice proposals were discussed, and Hankey tells me that the proposal for disarmament was thought too severe; a copy, however, was wired to Washington. Foch did not propose disarmament, but he proposed a bridge-head over the Rhine with 30 kilometre radius.

On the following day Wilson wrote:

At 10 a.m. Frazier telephoned to say Wilson's answer had been received, and was to the effect that he was not clear what Prince Max meant— whether he meant that he was prepared to accept the 14 points unconditionally, or only as a basis of discussion, but that in any case he would not consider an armistice until the Boches had cleared out of all occupied territories. Lloyd George was angry about this, because he nad not been consulted and because no mention was made of Alsace-Lorraine. Half an hour later, heard that Wilson's reply is in all the London papers. He really is the limit.

Meeting at 3 p.m., Quai d'Orsay. Agreed not to add a Belgian to Supreme War Council, but one might attend when Belgian questions were being discussed. Then we discussed President Wilson's answer to Prince Max. Clemenceau and Pichon were for taking no notice. They said they had no official cognizance, so could take none. Lloyd George pressed that an answer, not for publication, be sent, pointing out that if the Boches accepted the 14 points we should be in a difficult position, as we could not agree to Point 2, "Freedom of the Seas," and that therefore we should tell Wilson plainly that evacuation of occupied territory was a necessary preliminary to any exchange of views about an armistice, which would then be a matter for the Military to settle. Further, Bonar Law pressed my point that

> President Wilson should come over here, or send someone with full powers. In the end Lloyd George got his way about both these points.
> At 6 o'c., the same crowd being reassembled, we all agreed to the two draft telegrams, one about the armistice and the other about Wilson, or someone with full powers, coming over. Foch gave Haig and our Armies great praise, so I got a telegram of congratulation to Douglas Haig from Lloyd George. We are off to-morrow by special and I am very sorry my week here is over. It has been a week of wonderful change, and it really looks as if we were coming near the beginning of the end in all theatres except Russia.

The Allies had made advances at almost all points on the Western Front during the week, and the Third and Fourth British Armies had pushed forward well beyond the Hindenburg Line on the 8th, capturing over 10,000 prisoners and 150 guns. Haig's forces had taken 110,000 prisoners and some 1,200 guns since August 21; and they followed this up by occupying Cambrai on the 9th and Le Cateau on the 10th. The French in Champagne, and the Americans under Pershing farther to the east, also made good progress on the 9th and 10th. Sir Henry spoke to Lloyd George on their way back to London on the subject of conscription in Ireland, and he found the Prime Minister quite firm about putting the Order in Council on the subject on the table in the House on its reassembling. But on arrival in London he learnt to his dismay that the Cabinet were now opposed to its imposition.

> Milner told me that, while we were away last week, at a Cabinet at which Curzon, Barnes, Austen, Smuts and he were present, all were opposed to conscription for Ireland except himself. Milner thinks that if Lloyd George presses the conscription he will break the Cabinet. And a good job too.

This appears in the diary on October 13:

> I saw in the paper this morning that the Boches have accepted my Cousin's proposals, viz., evacuation of all occupied territories and 14 points. Milner telephoned to say I had to go down to Hassocks to Lloyd George for lunch. I found there Lloyd George, A. J.B ., Bonar Law, Milner, Winston, Reading, Wemyss, Hankey, Philip Kerr. We discussed: 1. What we were now to say to President Wilson; 2. What

1918: Last Six Weeks of the Great War 165

we were to say to the Press.

As regards Wilson, we agreed that we would wire to say that he must make it clear to the Boches that his 14 points (with which we do not agree) were not a basis for an armistice, which is what the Boches pretend they are. As regards the Press, we agreed that they should be told that Wilson is acting on his own, that the war is *not* over, that the 14 Points are *not* an armistice, and that an armistice is *not* a peace. It was a very interesting afternoon. Everyone angry and contemptuous of Wilson,

We discussed conscription for Ireland, and Lloyd George was angry with Curzon, Long, Smuts, etc., who, at the meeting Milner told me of the day before yesterday, were afraid to apply conscription. Lloyd George reminded me of those meetings some months ago, when Curzon and Co. were brave as lions, and when he (Lloyd George) hesitated.

At the meeting I insisted strongly on my plan of disarming the Boches where they stand, and then marching and training them back behind the Rhine unarmed, in opposition to Foch's plan of telling them to go back behind the Rhine and claiming three bridge-heads at Rastadt, Strasburg and Neu Breisach over the Rhine. The meeting became all in favour of my plan.

On the 14th the entry occurs:

Bill Sykes[*] came to see me, and we discussed his giving up all Air schemes for 1920 and anticipating all that, and by so doing he thinks he could now put the equivalent of another 50 squadrons in the field. I told him to do it at once. I also told him to bomb Berlin now. He has one machine that can do it.

Griscom[†] came to see me and to ask what I thought of the future. I told him the main thing for my Cousin was not to mix up three separate things, viz. Armistice, Peace terms, League of Nations.

Next day there appears:

---

[*] He become Chief of the Air Staff on the resignation of General Trenchard.

[†] L.C. Griscom, lawyer and ex-Ambassador of U.S.A. in Italy, was a lieutenant-colonel on General Pershing's staff, acting as liaison officer.

At War Cabinet we considered Wilson's last answer to the Boche. It really is a complete usurpation of power of negotiation. He practically ignores us and the French. He won't treat with the Hohenzollerns — thus making sure of Bolshevism. He won't treat as long as the Boches sink ships and have other frightfulness. And he is sending a separate letter to Austria. And all this without consultation with his Allies. We discussed all this, and I was strongly of opinion that we should go over to Paris at once and register a note to Wilson putting him in his proper place; but I was not able to persuade Lloyd George, and after lunch he went off to Walton Heath. Either he is seedy or is meditating a speech. I am certain we (British, French, Italians) ought to get together and put the truth baldly before Wilson. He is now taking charge in a way that terrifies me, as he is only a super-Gladstone — and a dangerous visionary at that.

On October 16 he wrote:

At the War Cabinet (Lloyd George was away at Walton Heath) I gave warning against too great optimism, and I pictured our army as tired but willing and able to fight, the French Army as very tired and neither willing nor able to fight, and the Americans as unfit to fight.[*] True, the Boches are in a bad way, but we are not in a position to take full advantage of their weakness.

Before lunch Ian Macpherson came to see me, and to tell me that all idea of conscription for Ireland was over. This is simply the devil, I called a meeting of Military Members after lunch. I pointed out that we had been promised 50,000 recruits by October 1 (later October 15), or in default we were to have conscription, i.e. 250.000. Now we had neither. We got 9,000 men (useless) instead of 50.000, and we were not to have conscription. All our promises to the French to keep up our divisions were broken. We had no means of replacing casualties in Italy, Salonika, Palestine, Mesopotamia, etc., and we were raising a bitter feeling in the army.

---

[*] This was, of course, an exaggerated picture, although effective. The French were making satisfactory progress at almost all points in face of relatively feeble opposition, and their casualties during the last 4½ months of the war mounted up to 530,000. The Americans were fighting with characteristic determination; but owing to lack of experience in the handling of great bodies of men, indifferent staff work in rear of advancing divisions was retarding the advance of what in fact constituted the extreme right wing of Foch's huge converging host.

1918: Last Six Weeks of the Great War 167

Serious as the man-power question had become, the news from the Western Front continued excellent — that from the north of the line especially so just at this juncture. For the King of the Belgians' forces were now pressing forward rapidly in Flanders, Lille had been occupied by General Birdwood's recently formed Fifth Army, and a naval force had landed at Ostend. Allenby's troops were, moreover, steadily pushing north through Syria, heading for Aleppo, and General Marsha's forces north of Baghdad were about to make their final advance on Mosul. General Diaz was preparing to launch a great offensive in Italy; and the Austro-Hungarian Empire was already crumbling to pieces even before this commenced, for a Czech Republic had been established at Prague and Yugo-Slav independence had been proclaimed at Agram. Sir Henry nevertheless remained anxious, and he could not understand the Prime Minister's present attitude. His comment on the 18th was:

> He runs away at the last moment from conscription in Ireland and now he does not catch hold of a situation which to me is frightening, as it is drifting in an aimless way down-current and it will ground on a mud-bank and not be brought into harbour.

Haig arrived that evening from G.H.Q., and the CJ.G.S. anticipated — quite correctly — that the Field-Marshal's armistice terms would prove to be more lenient than his own. He wrote in the diary on the 19th:

> Douglas Haig came to see me in War Office 10.15 a.m. I explained the position here at home to him — the surrender to Ireland of imposition of conscription, the fear of the Trade Unions, of strikes, of General Election, etc. But I maintained that we ought to insist on the disarmament of the Boches and the occupation by the Allies of all Boche territories up to the Rhine.
> Then we went over to 10 Downing Street. Present — Lloyd George, Bonar Law, Milner — and later A.J.B. and Wemyss. Douglas Haig said he would be satisfied if the Boches went back to the 1870 frontier, and if we occupied at once all Alsace and Lorraine and particularly Metz and Strasburg. He is of opinion that, although the Boches have been roughly handled, chiefly by us, they are not yet

reduced to accepting either my terms or Foch's. I expressed myself that the 1870 frontier was not good enough. True, France would recover Alsace and Lorraine; but the Allies would have no real asset with which to enforce all the terms which they thought absolutely essential to peace, i.e. Poland, Yugo-Slav, indemnities for Belgium, Rumania, Italy, etc. I kept on repeating, with some success, that once "Cease fire" sounded, we could never go to war again (in this war), and that therefore, unless we held real guarantees, i.e. occupation of Boche territory, we would never be able to enforce terms which would give us a durable peace.

Lloyd George and Milner rather agreed with Haig. Bonar Law and A.J.B. rather agreed with me. Wemyss (and David Beatty) wanted the surrender of practically all surface and submarine craft, and the continuance of the blockade. I said that in my opinion it would be impossible to continue the blockade indefinitely once an armistice was agreed upon, and once we began to discuss terms of peace. In the end it was agreed that we should think over all these points and meet again on the 21st.

A number of telegrams in this evening. They show on the whole that Germany and also Austria are in a tight corner, and my own opinion is that if we keep up all possible military pressure, and if we conscript Ireland, thus showing our determination to "go all out," the Boches will agree to my terms of disarmament.

News reached the War Office next day of Geneal Townshend's arrival at Mitylene from Constantinople with peace proposals, and Wilson wired to him to proceed to Mudros and await further orders. The morning's newspapers of the 10th published President Wilson's reply to Austria-Hungary, intimating that the Government of the Dual Monarchy must consult the Yugo-Slav nation — which the President had just recognised. "'This makes a fair pie of things," the C.I.G.S. commented in his diary, "and he does this without consulting Lloyd George or Clemenceau." The Belgians had taken Zeebrugge and Bruges on the 19th, and the British on the 20th forced the passages of the Selle River and pushed on towards Valenciennes. The French in Champagne also gained an important success north-east of Laon on this same day, and they broke through the Hunding Line on a broad front. Wilson then gives an arresting account in his diary of the discussion that took place on the 21st, on the subject of what terms should be imposed when

1918: Last Six Weeks of the Great War 169

granting an armistice on the Western Front:

> Beatty argued that terms of armistice should almost be terms of peace, and practically all the Boche fleet and submarines should be handed over; and — apart from submarines — he based this on the result that he would obtain from a fleet action. I thought this was very sound reasoning. Lloyd George and Milner thought the terms too stiff. I did not. Much discussion.
> Then Curzon, Austen, Smuts and Barnes joined us. A wire just in from Townshend from Lemnos giving the Turkish terms of peace, which were fantastic. So we wired to Calthorpe, the admiral in the Ægean, that he was not to discuss peace, but that if the Turkish Government sent a properly accredited person we would at once discuss armistice.
> Then we all lunched at 10 Downing Street and sat on till 6.10 p.m., from 11 a.m. After lunch the Boche wireless answer to my Cousin came in. When we examined the answer, it was quite adroit. The Boche agrees to my Cousin's proposal to evacuate occupied territory and suggests that a military commission be set up to arrange details. No mention of Alsace-Lorraine, nor any mention of the salt water. My Cousin is trapped. My own opinion is that, unless Lloyd George and Tiger catch a hold, my Cousin will cart us all. Reading, who had joined us, heard some true things about the President, A.J.B. drafted an excellent wire to Wilson, pointing out that the Boche is taking advantage of one sentence in Wilson's first telegram of terms, and is now taking it for granted that only "occupied territories" should be evacuated, but that, of course, this was ridiculous. And A.J.B. then went on to say that we were of opinion that Wilson should not wire again without consulting the Allies. This was approved and sent off.
> I was asked to write a paper on what the secession of Turkey would mean. I did this after dinner, and I showed that if Turkey gave in, and we had free access to the Black Sea, we could presently develop an attack from the Danube and Rumania of 50-60 divisions, and that the Austrians could not prevent us getting to Budapest, not the Italians to Laibach; that this would knock out Austria, and that then we could move into Germany from south and west and defeat the Boche armies on Boche territory.
> A very interesting day.

That, as a sequel to so protracted a session at 10 Downing Street, as was this one of October 21, which lasted from n a.m.

until past 6 p.m.. Sir Henry should have sat down after dinner and drawn up a memorandum for the War Cabinet setting forth what would be the effect of the Ottoman Empire, ceasing to be a belligerent, furnishes us with a striking illustration of the amount of work that the C.I.G.S. was capable of getting through within the twenty-four hours. It has to be remembered that he probably, in addition to this, entered some, at least, of the long account of the day's proceedings (not nearly the whole of which has been quoted above) in his diary before he closed his labours for the night. On the following day he discussed with Admiral Wemyss the question of how to occupy the Dardanelles and Bosporus forts in case the Turks gave in, and he then sent a wire to Milne asking for his opinion with regard to this problem, as he [Milne] and Admiral Calthorpe would have to carry out the operations between them. Sir Henry also drew up a memorandum showing the absolute necessity of conscription in Ireland, seeing that, unless compulsory service was enforced on the farther side of St. George's Channel, the army would by June 30, 1919, be 200,000 men short of establishment in infantry alone. He wrote that night in the diary:

> At 7 p.m. Lloyd Geotge sent for me, and then for Milner. This was to show me Franchet's dispositions in the Balkans, to arrange for Milner to go over to Paris to-morrow to see Clemenceau and soothe him, as the old Tiger had protested through Cambon against our making an armistice with the Turks simply on the basis of their handing over the Bosporus and giving us direct access to the Black Sea. Also to try to persuade the Tiger that our Admiral should command there. Also to try to persuade the Tiger that Foch should force Pershing to spread out the American army over the French and over ours, as no one was getting full value for it now.
>
> Reading and A.J.B. were also present, and we discussed a wire from Lansing in answer to A.J.B.'s telegram of yesterday. It appears from Lansing that Wilson is again going to answer the Boches without consulting us or the French,
>
> To-night I dined with Johnnie French (over from Ireland), Lloyd George and Winston. We discussed Irish conscription. Johnnie vehemently in favour of it. Lloyd George and Winston both of opinion that in the present state of uncertainty it would be suicidal to try it, but that if all hopes of armistice disappeared then we should apply it at once. I strongly advocated application at once both as a

war measure and as a peace measure. As war measure to give us 150,000-200,000 more men, as peace measure because I cannot conceive Ireland uncompelled and garrisoned by English conscripts. There is no answer to this, and Lloyd George agreed that there was none except practical expediency. I hope that my Cousin will send an uncompromising answer to the Boches, and that we can then bring in conscription for Ireland.

The Italian offensive on the Piave was successfully launched on the following day (the 24th) by the Tenth and Twelfth Armies, the Tenth being under command of Cavan. Valenciennes had been occupied by the First British Arrmy on the 22nd, and the Americans had experienced some hard fighting on both banks of the Meuse north of Verdun on that same day. The First and Third British Armies, moreover, delivered an attack between Valenciennes and Le Cateau on the 23rd — which was completely successful, 9,000 prisoners being captured on that and the preceding day.

Lord Milner proceeded to Paris on the 24th as arranged, to discuss the question of naval command in the Ægean with Clemenceau, and to propose that American divisions should again be distributed between the various British and French armies along the Western Front, so that fuller advantage should be taken of their remarkable fighting capabilities than could be expected when they operated as an American Army,* Sir Henry was, moreover, informed by Du Cane over the telephone that afternoon that a difference of opinion had arisen between Foch and Haig with regard to Plumer's Second Army. This had for some weeks past been included in the forces operating north of Lys under command

---

* The struggle on the Western Front had become to a great extent a war of movement, and the problem, alike for Sir D, Haig, for General Pétain and for General Pershing, was coming to be one almost as much of organization in rear of the fighting fronts as of defeating the enemy in actual battle. The region for which the American troops were heading was largely hilly and broken, with comparatively few roads, and only a very experienced staff could have been expected to triumph over the administrative difficulties which the supply of food and munitions for great bodies of men traversing such country was bound to present.

of the King of the Belgians, but it had now crossed that river, and it was abreast and alongside of Birdwood's Fifth Army. The Field-Marshal had very naturally asked that in the circumstances it should come under his orders again, but to this the Generalssimo had refused his assent. Shortly after the receipt of Du Cane's telephone message, another arrived, direct from Haig, requesting that the C.I.G.S. would intervene in the matter. So, after a consultation with the Prime Minister, Sir Henry made arrangements to cross the Channel on the 26th. He took the precaution to ensure that a preliminary meeting should take place between Milner, Haig and himself, and he wrote in his diary:

> What a bother. It sounds to me as if Haig was right. Foch wants us to do all the work. The French are not fighting at all, and the Americans don't know how, so all falls to us. We took 8,000 prisoners and 200 guns yesterday, and no one else did anything. Both in the Ægean and in France the French are being very tiresome.

As regards the question at issue in the Ægean, news arrived from Paris on October 25 to the effect that Clemenceau was prepared to fall in with the British proposals. On that same evening Sir Henry attended a meeting of the War Cabinet at which were discussed certain suggestions on the part of the French Prime Minister as to what armistice terms ought to be considered at a meeting of Foch, Haig, Pdtain and Pershing fixed to take place on the following day, and Wilson wrote in his diary:

> Clemenceau suggests as a basis for discussion of armistice (*a*) that our armies should be safe during armistice; (*b*) that if armistice breaks off we should not be in a worse position than we are now. We all disagreed with this ridiculous proposition, and wired to Derby to say so and to say that the generals should discuss on the terms we laid down three weeks ago in Paris, now endorsed by President Wilson, and also outlined in A.J.B.'s wires on October 13th and 21st. I also telephoned to Milner to make sure that Haig knew the wishes of the Cabinet before he went to the meeting.
>
> Then A.J.B. read a wire he was sending to the capitals, to say that we did not agree at all to Wilson's 14 points and speeches, and we had other points to add. Again, we none of us know who is the next party to move.

Lloyd George then raised the point — do we want peace or not? Austen wants a good peace, i.e. rather easy terms. Bonar Law the same. Curzon rather stiffer. Lloyd George undecided. Smuts has written a paper (which I have not seen) agreeing apparently to any terms. Lloyd George then raised the question of quarrel between Douglas Haig and Foch about the Second Army coming back from the King of the Belgians. The Cabinet were unanimously of opinion that Douglas Haig was right, and authorized me to give Haig the necessary authority and to tell Foch.

Wilson proceeded to Versailles next day. Milner told him that Clemenceau had agreed to the arrangement that Admiral Calthorpe should have control in the Ægean, and had also given way as to assenting to an armistice with the Turks on the basis of the Straits being placed under control of the Allies. It also transpired that Clemenceau's views as to the terms on which an armistice might be granted to the Germans (which the War Cabinet had disapproved of on the previous day) had been misunderstood owing to faulty wording in a telegram, and that "the Tiger" was by no means in favour of such terms being of a benevolent character. Generals Pétain and Pershing had not, it transpired, been present at the discussion of generals on the previous day with regard to armistice terms, Foch and Haig alone meeting. They had afterwards debated the matter of the Second Army, and, as the Generalissimo had declined to give way, Haig had written an official complaint to the War Office.

Lord Derby came on the following morning to propose that he should see Clemenceau, and should suggest that Foch ought to let the Second Army come back to Haig. This was agreed to; and Haig and Lawrence shortly afterwards arrived. They explained how very necessary it was that the matter should be adjusted, and they showed Sir Henry a copy of the official letter that had been sent to the War Office on the subject. The following appears in the diary:

> Then Derby came out again to lunch and told Milner and me that he had seen the Tiger, who entirely agreed with him that the Second Army should be given back to Haig, and that he would go out to Senlis and see Foch, but that, in the event of there being difficulty, he gladly accepted a proposal made

by Derby that he [Derby] should go and see Foch and try to persuade him.

On thinking this over after lunch I decided that it would be dangerous for Derby to see Foch, and, after discussing with Milner, who agreed, I went in to the Embassy and saw Derby and told him I thought he ought to keep out of it, Derby went off at 6 o'c. to see Clemenceau after his return from Foch, and he reported that the Tiger had been quite unable to persuade Foch, and even that he [Tiger] had greatly weakened in his opinion that the Second Army should come back to Haig. Clemenceau said that Foch had said that he would be glad to see Derby at 9 a.m. at Senlis. This was just what I was afraid of, so I persuaded Derby to let me telephone to Foch to say he could not go to-morrow, and that I would go instead. If I can't persuade Foch to give up his position I shall have to order him. But this, of course, is the last thing I want to do.

It seems from the newspapers to-night that Ludendorff has been *degomme*.* Does this make for peace or war? Tiger thinks for war. I am inclined to think for peace.

Wilson wrote next day, the 28th:

> I went to Crillon at 10 a.m., saw Haig and had a talk, and he gave me a letter, which he read to me, to Foch restating his reasons for wanting the Second Army back. I then went out with this to Senlis, and saw Foch and Weygand, who have moved there from Bom Bom. I had rather a stormy meeting with Foch, but I think I was able to put my case strongly, but quietly. We parted excellent friends.
>
> Then back to the Embassy for lunch. Douglas Haig also there, and as he had to go and see Foch at 4 p.m., I told him I was sure the old boy would meet him halfway now, and I suggested asking for the Second Army to be given back when it reached the Scheldt. This he did, and both he and Du Cane telephoned to-night to say that everything had gone splendidly at the meeting, and flowers, and tea, and delights! So that corner is turned. Meantime this afternoon Austria-Hungary has replied to my Cousin that they accept his conditions about Czecho and Yugo-Slav States and are prepared to

---

* Ludendorff had resigned on October 26.

1918: Last Six Weeks of the Great War

treat, without their allies, for an armistice. It is clear that the enemies are breaking up,

Lloyd George, Hankey, etc., arrived. Lloyd George showed me a wire from Calthorpe, which shows that the Turks are going to allow us to occupy Dardanelles and Bosporus if we do it only with the French and ourselves. We have wired to Calthorpe to agree.

On the 28th:

This morning's papers give the Boche reply to my Cousin's last note. So, the pea is under the Boche thimble. The reply says that serious Government changes are going on, that the Army is now under the Government, and that the German Government awaits the proposals for an armistice preliminary to a just peace "as the President has described it in his public declarations." A wonderfully interesting day, with the note from Germany and the other from Austria. We must walk warily now and we shall get all we want, Lloyd George favours Geneva as place for Peace Conference. I prefer St, Moritz.

Terms proposed by Foch for an armistice with the Germans amounted to this: Within fourteen days of signature the enemy must evacuate the occupied territories and Alsace-Lorraine; within eight more days German troops must evacuate the Rhenish provinces; within three more days they must evacuate a strip 40 kilometres wide on the right bank of the Rhine; 5,000 guns, 30,000 machine guns and 8,000 trench mortars must be handed over to the Allies. Lloyd George was disposed to think these terms too harsh, but he was, on the other hand, coming to favour stiff naval terms. "In any case I think the Frocks now agree that Douglas Haig's terms are too mild," Sir Henry wrote in his diary, and in a talk which Milner and he had with General Bliss they found the American general to be more extreme than anybody, and to favour total disarmament of the Germans.

What Sir Douglas Haig no doubt had in his mind was that a cessation of hostilities before the winter must be ensured. At a time when he had accepted the responsibility of launching his armies against the Hindenburg Line he had been hampered by his Government sending him a cipher telegram indicating that they would become anxious if severe casualties were incurred in carrying out this formidable operation. He had ignored this communication. But he was fully aware of the difficulties that were arising over man-power in the United Kingdom, the casualties incurred during his triumphs of September and October had necessarily been heavy, and in the circumstances he was justified in holding it to be imperative that the negotiations for an armistice now being set in train should put a term to further fighting. President Wilson, Colonel House and General Bliss, with ample resources in money and man-power at their back, did not view the continuation of the struggle into 1919 with the same apprehension, and they naturally favoured the imposition of extreme terms. Foch and Wilson, realizing what must be the effect upon the predominant partner in the enemy coalition of Bulgaria, Turkey and Austria-Hungary all craving for peace, and interpreting Teutonic mentality quite correctly, felt satisfied that the Germans would be prepared to agree to severe and humiliating conditions — and they proved to be right. This appears in the diary on October 29:

> Several wires from Cavan. He and his Tenth Army are well over the Piave, and it looks a little as though the Austrians were going to have a Caporetto. It looks to-night as though Austria was tottering to a crash and I expect any day to hear of our occupation of the Dardanelles and Bosporus. Remains only the Boche, and he is *done*.

Wilson wrote next day:

> Another squeal from Vienna this morning begging for an armistice. The Italian offensive goes well — 16,000 prisoners up to last night! Further screams from Emperor Karl to Diaz to stop fighting in order to save the crops in the Venetian plains. They are in a parlous condition, are the Austrians.
>
> Lloyd George, Milner, and I discussed pulling out the Austrians at once, and Lloyd George asked me what terms we should offer. I wrote on a bit of paper: 1, Demobilization down to ? divisions; 2, retire to the line of the London Pact; 3, free use to Allies of all roads, railways, and waterways; 4, occupation of strategic points, as Allies may decide on Lloyd George put the paper in his pocket and bundled

off to meet Tiger and House. Was telephoned for at 2 o'c. to the Embassy. Lloyd George told me my 4 points had been passed unanimously. Hankey being there I added another (5) — repatriation of prisoners and civilians and Lloyd George went off to a meeting of Frocks at 3 p.m.

I motored out to Trianon to discuss these points with Tit Willow and had only just got there when I was telephoned for to go back at once to the Quai d'Orsay. There we had a meeting of self (Chair), Pershing and Bliss, Belin, Robilant, and Tit Willow, with the Lord as interpreter and Philip Kerr as secretary. We enlarged and defined my 5 points, and laid them down as complete terms for an armistice.

On the 31st there is the entry:

> The Turks last night signed our armistice terms, swallowing them whole, to date from noon to-day. Now we shall get the Austrians out. Lloyd George, Tiger, House, Orlando had a "hush" meeting this morning, and made some alterations (nothing material) in our Austrian armistice proposals of last night, and adopted them.
>
> Venizelos came to lunch. He made a curious remark. He said that those monarchs who claim to base themselves on the Almighty had fallen (Tsar, Austria, Germany, Bulgaria, Greece), whilst those who based themselves on the will of the people were strengthened — England, Belgium, Serbia, Italy.
>
> Meeting of Supreme Council. Foch gave résumé of present military situation. Our last night's Austrian armistice proposals passed with minor alterations. Then naval ditto passed. We meet again to-morrow to discuss terms of armistice with the Boches.

At the meeting of the Supreme War Council held on November 1 the severe terms which Foch proposed to insist upon in granting an armistice to the Germans were provisionally approved. The news from the Italian theatre of war was now in the highest degree encouraging, as 50,000 prisoners and 300 guns had been captured, and Wilson wrote in his diary:

> All the evening I pondered about the new military situation arising in Russia, in the Balkans, in Austria, and so forth. I think we ought to look after Turkey and let Europe stew in its own juice.

At a meeting of Foch, Haig, Pershing, Bliss, General Robilant and Wilson next day a paper was drawn up which urged that a force of from 30 to 40 divisions should now be deployed between the Inn and the Danube for action against Bavaria, so as to bring effective pressure upon Germany from the south. Austria-Hungary accepted the Allies' armistice terms on the 3rd, Germany was, therefore, left the sole belligerent still opposing the Allies, and Wilson wrote in the diary on the 4th:

> Meeting at 11 a.m. at Colonel House's house. Present — House, Tiger, Foch, Lloyd George, self. Tit Willow, Orlando, Robilant and secretaries. Discussed and passed our very stiff military terms of armistice for the Boches. These include 5,000 guns, etc., and retirement of Boches to a line 40 kilometres on far side of Rhine. Then we discussed future action in Rumania, Bohemia, bombing Berlin, etc., and these matters were handed over to Foch and me. Then discussed our proposals to deploy a force of 30-40 divisions on Bavarian frontier. All agreed to.
>
> Discussed naval terms, which were thought too severe and were referred back to Naval Council, to see if they could agree to interning all Boche ships in neutral waters instead of making them prisoners.
>
> Then out to meeting here [Versailles] of Supreme War Council. We endorsed our military terms of armistice for the Bochies. We endorsed amended naval terms of internment, which I thought a very stupid thing, and after we broke up Foch and I had a long talk about the future of Franchet d'Esperey's army.
>
> As far as I can see now, it will take all, or most of, the Serbian 6 divisions to look after Serbia and her marches. It will take 2 or 3 divisions to look after Bulgaria, 2 or 5 to look after Turkey, 3 or 4 to help Rumania, 1 to Batoum and Trebizond (?), and this will leave Franchet with only 7-10 to play with. Foch agreed with me in my warm opposition to occupying strategical points in Austria-Hungary, unless they were directly connected with lines of communications or with operations against the Boches. And therefore I think that, if we can find the shipping, we ought to ship as much as we can to Trieste or Fiume. A long talk to-night with Milner on these lines,
>
> Lloyd George went off home at 2 p.m. this afternoon. Rawly, Bungo and Horne attacked on the Valenciennes — Mormal front and took 10,000 prisoners and 200 guns, and Debeney alongside took 3,000 more. A good day's work, which will make the Boches shake their heads a bit.

1918: Last Six Weeks of the Great War

This appears in the diary next day:

> Very peaceful now Lloyd George has gone home. Much talk with Milner this morning about our future action in Europe, in Russia, in Siberia. We are entirely agreed to keep out of Austria-Hungary, Poland, Rumania, Ukraine and north of Black Sea except in so far as is necessary to beat the Boches. But on the other hand, from the left bank of the Don to India is our interest and preserve.
>
> The military and naval terms of armistice we settled yesterday are being telegraphed to-day to President Wilson. I suppose he will agree, because House has. Then he will inform the Boche that if he sends flag to Foch and Beatty he can get terms. Boche might do this about Saturday or Sunday. Then I suppose he will take 2 or 3 days to consider, and will then start haggling. So that early next week we may hear what the Boche thinks of out terms. We had a great success to-day in front of Rawly, Bungo and Horne, driving 26 Boche divisions before us.

Sir Henry returned to London on November 6, and events thereafter moved very rapidly The German white flag was expected to come in to Foch on the 7th, and on that day the C.I.G.S. wrote in his diary:

> Rosie Wemyss is with Foch and will be present when the Boches come in. I envy him this, as I feel that I have been longer in this war than any other soldier or sailor.

The story of the historic meeting of the German delegates with Foch at Rethondes near Compiègne on the 8th, of his refusal to consent to a provisional armistice, of his insistence upon his terms being agreed upon by 11 a.m. on the 11th, and of the actual signature of the famous document at 5 a.m. on that day, is a familiar one. The War Cabinet was kept constantly informed of the progress and movements of the German delegates, and Wilson, who had dined at the Mansion House on the night of the 9th, where Lloyd George made a fine speech, wrote of a meeting at Downing Street which took place on the following day:

> Cabinet 6.30 to 8 p.m. Lloyd George read two wires from Tiger describing Foch's interviews with the Boches, and Tiger is afraid that

Germany will break up and Bolshevism become rampant. Lloyd George asked me if I wanted this, or would rather have an armistice, and I unhesitatingly said "armistice." All the Cabinet agreed. Our real danger now is not the Boches but Bolshevism. Wires came in during the Cabinet to say Kaiser and Crown Prince had escaped to Holland, and German towns were in the hands of Revolutionaries.

Next day, the 11th, there is the entry:

> At 6.30 a.m. I got a wire from Wemyss, who is with Foch, to say that Armistice was signed at 5 a.m. Hostilities to cease at 11 a.m.
> Cabinet 9.30 a.m, Lloyd George, Bonar Law, Barnes, Smuts, Geddes, Milner, self. Robertson was sent for, and it was decided to play bands, ring bells, &c., at 11 a.m. Then Geddes read wires to show the Boches' fleet was under the Red Flag and challenged us for keeping up blockade. Another wire from Rome to say Austrian fleet under Czechos was also chaos. Calthorpe reports he is in the Marmora.
> Then we (Army Council) went to Buckingham Palace. We were received by the King and Queen alone. The King made us the most charming little speech, and the Queen cried. A *delightful* little informal human ceremony. Much work all afternoon at demobilization, which is such a thorny subject.
> Dined with Lloyd George at 10 Downing Street. Only Winston and F.E. Smith. We discussed many things, but principally the coming General Election. Lloyd George wants to shoot the Kaiser. F.E. agrees. Winston does not; and my opinion is that there should be a public *exposé* of all his works and actions, and then leave him to posterity! Incidentally he has shown he is a coward by going to Holland. Wonderful crowds in the streets, showing wonderful loyalty.

Wilson walked home from Downing Street to Eaton Place that night, passing the enthusiastic swarms of cheering citizens that were still gathered even at that late hour in front of the Palace. As he made his way along Buckingham Palace Road he came upon an elderly well-dressed woman, a pathetic figure in deep mourning, alone and sobbing her heart out. Distressed at such a spectacle amid the tumultuous rejoicings on all sides, he went up to her, stopped and murmured, "You are in trouble — is there anything that I can do for you?" She looked up bravely. "Thank you. No," she replied. "I am crying, but I am happy, for now I know that all my three sons who have been killed in the war have not died in vain."

Chapter XXVI – The Close of the Year 1918

Disinclination of H.M. Government to consider the new military situation — Sir Henry present at the Belgian King and Queen's entry into Brussels — Foch and Clemenceau in London — Problem of demobilization — President Wilson in London.

During the few weeks immediately succeeding the announcement of the Armistice concluded on November 11, entries in Wilson's diary demonstrate in no uncertain fashion how strong was the disinclination on the part of H.M. Government to grapple with the military situation, as it stood on the sudden termination of active hostilities in the main theatre of war. Party politics, which happily had been virtually in abeyance since August, 1914, began straightway to engage the attention of most Ministers of the Crown. Preparations for a coming General Election excited far livelier interest amongst the heads of State departments in Whitehall than did vital questions such as the strength to be fixed for the fighting forces that were to be maintained to preserve peace and as the measures that must be devised to provide reasonable national security. But even on the day of the Armistice, while excitement over the tidings from the Forest of Compiègne was at its height, and while gladness at the great deliverance was manifesting itself on every hand, the C.I.G.S., as we have seen in the last chapter, was already hard at work in his office, preparing plans for such incipience of

The Close of the Year 1918

demobilization as the conditions now created would permit of, and examining problems likely to arise in the immediate future.

After attending the inspiring Thanksgiving Service in St. Paul's, at which the King and Queen were present, he spent the rest of the 12th at the War Office, and he was seriously concerned to learn on arrival that Sir Auckland Geddes had incontinently stopped all recruiting. He wrote in the diary:

> I kicked up a row, which may do good. It is impossible to carry on if this sort of rubbish is allowed. I spoke strongly to Milner tonight.

Nor did he find matters any more satisfactory when he presented himself at 10 Downing Street on the following day. He wrote:

> The most useless War Cabinet I have ever attended. I brought up the question of a post-bellum army, but entirely failed to get up any interest in anyone. We shall have chaos. Nor could I get anyone to be interested in my proposal not to allow our troops from Italy and Salonika to be dragged into European complications, I am tired out.

And he goes on to mention dining at Lord French's house that evening:

> At Johnnie French's there were some 25 Americans dining. All through dinner they were flattering me and praising President Wilson and American idealism — especially and all the time as regards Freedom of the Seas, which they interpreted as being equal navies for America and England. They were very clear that America would build against us if we tried to have a dominating position on the salt water. Where are we all going?

Next day there is the entry:

> At War Cabinet this morning I made another attempt to get a decision on our 150,000 Volunteer Army and on our post-bellum Army, but was ridden off again. It is marvellous.

This appears on the 15th:

No War Cabinet, much work in office. No particular news from Germany. Rumanians and Bulgars now fighting on the Danube. Italians and Yugo-Slavs almost fighting in Fiume and Cattaro. Our election announced for December 14.

He crossed the Channel in a destroyer on the 21st with Duncannon to be present at the entry of the King and Queen of the Belgians into Brussels. Landing at Dunkirk, they proceeded to Ostend and thence on to Zeebrugge and Bruges; early on the following morning they reached the rendezvous on the Ghent road on the outskirts of Brussels, and of what followed Wilson wrote in his diary:

> The King and Queen and children drove up in cars at 10.30, and got on horses in a small garden. He sent for me, and both the Queen and he were charming to me. He said he knew the part I had played and thanked me. He was also nice about Lloyd George, and charming about our troops.
> Then the procession started, and I followed the King's procession, driving my Rolls. He wanted me to ride, but I did not wish to take part. Enormous crowds, cheering and enthusiasm and flowers, I have never seen such a sight. The King and Queen's reception was quite wonderful. The Lord and I lunched with him at the palace. About 40 officers, no Ministers. Our Prince Albert, and Athlone and his wife, Roger Keyes, Vivian, the Lord, Jack Churchill, Birdwood and self were the English. After lunch the King again came to me and had a long talk. He recalled our many meetings, and again the part I had played, and was most flattering. He said he had never thought the Boches would collapse like this, and had thought it would take another year. The palace was full of flowers, chrysanthemums, orchids, etc., and the King told me that the Boches had not taken his plate, glass, linen, etc., which had been well hid. The servants were in scarlet and breeches, and in fact the whole thing looked as though he had never left the palace. Yet the Boches were here last Saturday.

On the following day they drove round to Louvain and Malines and back to Brussels, spending some little time on the field of Waterloo, ascending the Mound, and Sir Henry noted in his diary:

> It was extraordinary to stand on the top and to see the 29th

Division file by on their way to Ohain for the night; I met Freyberg on the top; he commands a brigade in the division.

He, moreover, recorded with pride that his car with its red ensign was given a great reception everywhere. They returned to England via Montreuil, and Wilson at once went to the War Office, where a discussion took place as to the organization and recruitment of the Army of Occupation on the Rhine.

He wrote in his diary:

> I am quite clear that Lloyd George will get into a regular mess if he does not explain the situation to the country before the General Election.

This appears on the 28th:

> At the Cabinet this morning we discussed whether we ought to try the Kaiser. F.E. Smith gave the opinion of the Law Officers, and said they were unanimously in favour of trial. He made two points which were very convincing: 1. How could any subordinates be tried if the Kaiser was not? 2. The surest way to prevent a repetition of frightfulness was personal responsibility and punishment. The Cabinet unanimously agreed to try the Kaiser. Lloyd George asked me, and I agreed too.

It had been arranged that Marshal Foch and M. Clemenceau were to visit London on December 1, so Lords Curzon and Stamfordham, with Wilson, acted as a small committee to elaborate the procedure to be followed. The procession from Charing Cross to Claridge's Hotel went off well, the Italian representatives. Orlando and Sonnino, arriving by the same train and sharing in the welcome. The streets were lined with troops, and the visitors, and especially Foch, were accorded a stirring reception by the crowds. On arrival at the hotel the Duke of Connaught and Wilson spent some time in conversation with the Marshal in his private room, and Wilson records:

> Foch said very nice things to the Duke of Connaught about our army and about Haig. Then Duke of Connaught went off, and I

remained on with Foch and Weygand for an hour and a half, and we had a long talk.

Foch showed me his paper with his proposals. He proposes to throw all the Rhenish Provinces into the Western Group, to consist of France, England, Belgium, Luxembourg, and an autonomous Palatinate, but under the eyes of France and England. He does not see by what other means he can guard his left flank. This is going rather farther than my plan of forbidding any Boche troops on left bank of Rhine.

At 5.15 we had a meeting at 10 Downing Street of Lloyd George, Bonar Law, Foch, Weygand, Hankey and self. At this meeting Foch developed his proposals that, in order to face the 65-76 million Boches over the Rhine, he wanted to combine all the French, Belgian, Luxembourg and Rhenish Provinces in one Confederation, amounting to 54,000,000, which, with the help of the British, might hope to cope with the Boches. Both Lloyd George and Bonar Law were opposed to this, as making of the Rhenish Provinces another Alsace and Lorraine. I think that Foch is going too far, but at the same time it is clear to me that neutrals like the Luxembourgs and the Belgians unduly expose the flank of the poor French, and that therefore some precaution must be taken, such as that no Boche troops should be quartered over the Rhine, and possibly no Boche conscription in the Rhenish Provinces.

Next day (December 27) there is the entry:

Allied Cabinet. Lloyd George, A.J.B., Bonar Law, self, Clemenceau, Foch, Weygand, Orlando, Sonnino. Agreed that the Allies should discuss terms, and then present them to the Boches; after that we are to have a Peace Congress. Agreed to exact indemnities. Agreed to try the Kaiser. Agreed to Paris as place of Conference.

Meeting in afternoon, same as morning, with Reading and Wemyss. Foch got permission to extend Armistice after 16th, and to exact more if terms not being complied with. Naval terms are being carried out. Much warm talk about the Adriatic and Yugo-Slavs. Foch and Clemenceau getting the most tremendous receptions everywhere.

This appears on the following day:

Imperial Cabinet at 10.30, followed at 11.15 by an Allied

Cabinet. We discussed Army of Occupation in Germany, and Foch put a minimum of 30 divisions, of which we should supply about 10, with some divisions in rear for relief. Then, Labour claimed to hold a Conference in Paris at the same time as the Peace Conference. It was decided Labour must sit in a neutral State. Duke of Connaught, Princess Patsey, Foch Weygand, Aileen [Lady Roberts], and Susan Dawnay lunched. Crowds cheering outside the door.

Then, 4 p.m., our small Allied Cabinet like yesterday. We discussed and decided about: Feeding Germany, Milne's command, Turkey and Batoum; the state of Constantinople.

Foch, Clemenceau, Orlando and Sonnino returned to the Continent on the 4th, their visit having gone off most satisfactorily, and Sir Henry now found himself a good deal occupied with the question of honours and rewards to be granted for services during the war. He had ascertained that Foch was of opinion that this country ought, even after Peace was signed, to keep 10 divisions in the occupied territory, as well as another 10 divisions in Belgium or France. The railway men were in the meantime threatening to strike; this disagreeable matter came before the War Cabinet on December 6, and Wilson wrote in his diary:

> War Cabinet on railway strike for an 8-hour day, and, of course. Cabinet agreed to all the men's demands. This giving in to all demands means ruin for the country. The War Cabinet discussed demobilization, and Milner and Macdonogh were sent for. Lloyd George in one of his difficult moods because we were not getting the miners home quicker, and rather rude to Milner and Macdonogh.
>
> At 5.50 Miner sent for me and told me he would not work any longer with Lloyd George, and he was going to resign. That he had a growing feeling for some time that he would not work with Lloyd George, and this morning decided him to go now. He told me, a thing I did not know, that when he accepted Secretaryship of State, Lloyd George promised that he should be the Cabinet Minister to attend at the Supreme Council's meetings, and that Lloyd George had systematically broken his promise in this matter. I could not, and did not, urge Milner not to resign; for I felt, and said, after Lloyd George's exhibition this morning at the Cabinet, in front of a crowd of railway and Board of Trade officials who remained in the room, that a great public servant like Milner had just cause for resigning. Of course, Lloyd George's irritability is all due to this cursed General

Election.

On the 9th there is the entry:

> Office all day and Eastern Committee this afternoon, when Bob Cecil and A.J.B. advocated our not going to the Caucasus. Wonderful.*
> Milner told me to-night that Lloyd George had asked him to stay on, but he would only do so as a temporary measure. Lloyd George said he was not complaining against Milner but against the army!

On the following day:

> At Cabinet we discussed how soldiers could vote, and Lloyd George insisted on men getting leave, etc. All bribes, and disgusting, as it is against the law. Then we discussed Russia, and Lloyd George wanted to come away from Murmansk because he thought our occupation there was unpopular. Again, all votes. Luckily, as I pointed out, we can't do that, as we should leave the Americans, French and Italians at Archangel in. the lurch.

Sir Henry's persistence at last earned its reward, for he succeeded on December 12 in extracting a decision from the Cabinet approving his proposal that from 14 to 20 British divisions must be maintained for some time to come, in addition to the voluntarily recruited Regular Army. He may not have foreseen — it could hardly be expected that he would foresee — the delays that were to ensue before peace terms were signed, owing to the action of President Wilson and to the ineptitude of the Allied Prime Ministers arrayed in Council. But he clearly realized that Europe remained in an extremely disturbed state, that Russia presented a very serious problem, and that in the circumstances, and till the situation should become more settled, the nation's military forces must remain at an approximation to a war footing. (Sir R. Borden and Mr. Hughes had intimated that Canada and Australia were not

---

* General Denikin was at this time initiating the anti-Bolshevist movement in Transcaucasia that for a time was to achieve very important results in the following year. Wilson wished to afford it support.

prepared to provide troops for the Army of Occupation on the Rhine.)

"The bribing of Lloyd George at this election is simply disgusting," the C.I.G.S. wrote next day. "I won't vote to-morrow." General Milne came to see him on the 15th, and entirely agreed with him as to the expediency of clearing out of the Balkans, a course which he had advocated ever since the Turks had made their first overtures for peace. On the following day he had Mr. Churchill as a visitor, who came to announce that he was to succeed Milner as War Minister, and Wilson's only comment in his diary on the subject is, "Whew!" Then, on the 19th, Sir D. Haig and his Army commanders arrived in London, and they drove in procession through the streets to Buckingham Palace; Wilson met them at Charing Cross, and he was afterwards present at the luncheon given by the King. He dined with Churchill that evening, and he then learnt from the prospective Secretary of State that the Prime Minister proposed to combine the War Office and the Air Ministry — a plan which did not wholly commend itself to Sir Henry. "What of the Navy and what of Commercial Air?" he asked himself in the diary.

On the 20th there appears the entry:

> Imperial War Cabinet discussion about captured German colonies, etc. Much discussion about what we could — or ought to — give up. I was opposed to giving up anything, on the double ground of the safety of the Empire and of the good government of the peoples concerned. Curzon and Hughes excellent, Austen not bad, Milner wobbly, Lloyd George very poor.

Wilson wrote in Paris on December 20:

> The Lord and I got here by train at 9.45 p.m. Crankshaw met us at the Gate du Nord and said Derby wanted us to go to the Embassy, where he was having a reception for President Wilson. So we went straight there. I was introduced to the President and had to minutes' talk. He did not impress me in the least. He told me his grandfather and grandmother both came from Ulster, but met for the first time in America. He said he had a keen sense of humour. He has not yet been for his trip round the devastated country, and he is so angry with the

Italians that he has given up his Italian trip. No. He did not impress me in the least. But my conversation was too short, and our subjects too general, to allow me to form an opinion yet.

But Sir Henry had not, it must be confessed, been by any means predisposed in the President's favour even before this meeting of theirs in the stately mansion off the Rue St. Honoré. The C.I.G.S. had fully realized early in the year the vital importance of prevailing upon a not unwilling Japan to undertake military operations for the purpose of stemming the untoward tide of Bolshevist advance into Siberia. The great stumbling-block to such action on the part of the island empire had been the opposition of the White House in Washington. Nor had the attitude taken up by the President with regard to Ireland been of a nature to appease Sir Henry. Finally, there had been that odd bent, frequently displayed by Woodrow Wilson during the closing weeks of the war, for negotiating with the enemy without reference to his Allies, a bent which had provoked the C.I.G.S. at least as much as it had provoked the British, the French and the Italian Governments. This appears in the diary on the 22nd:

> Out to Senlis at 11 a.m. to see Foch, who was as nice as ever. He is not happy about the way everybody is demobilizing. He now wants us to keep up to preliminary peace being signed, 30-40 divisions, the French 60-65, the Americans 22-25, the Belgians 6. After the peace he only wants us to keep 12-15 divisions. He says the Boches are keeping 60-65 divisions. He insists on the line of the Rhine being the only line to hold till the danger is passed.
>
> Then back to the Embassy. Wilson wants America and England to share equally the Command of the Sea. He wants a League of Nations, and the representative of each nation to carry equal weight, i.e. a Czecho carries equal weight with us over, say, a sea question! All matters of dispute to be referred to the League, which would be composed of Ambassadors sitting in Switzerland. Any country going to war to be punished even if right in going to war! All German colonies to be administered by small States, with the League in the background. If he has any sense he will get back to America as soon as he can. Wilson has not yet been to the devastated country.

Returning to London nest day. Sir Henry on the 24th wrote in

The Close of the Year 1918

his diary:

> Imperial War Cabinet this morning, at which they all talked about Peace and the League of Nations, and the whole thing such rubbish that I went away. Why not face the facts, that there are still wars going on in several countries and that until these are crushed out it is no use talking about peace?
>
> Curiously enough, I had a long visit from a Canadian (Colonel Boyle) who has been out in Russia and Rumania for 2½ years on railways, and who has just brought the King of Rumania's son for school here. Boyle firmly believes that if we don't attack and crush Bolshevism in Russia it will spread all over Europe and lead to a most frightful state of affairs. He really was very terrifying.

President Wilson arrived in London for his visit on the 26th, and on the following day the C.I.G.S. dined at Buckingham Palace to meet the President, with whom the Prime Minister and Mr. Balfour had enjoyed long discussions during the day. "No one present, not even Hankey," Wilson remarked in the diary, "so I am sure they have made an awful pie of it."

Prince Feisul came to see him that same day, accompanied by Colonel Lawrence as interpreter, and the C.I.G.S. promised his visitor some guns, tanks and camels. A luncheon was given to President and Mrs. Wilson at the Guildhall on the 27th, at which Sir Henry was present. The result of the General Election was announced that day. Mr. Lloyd George secured a great majority at the polls. That night Wilson dined at Downing Street to meet the President and the War Cabinet; this appears in the diary:

> Much talk about this amazing election, and all agreed that it was a bad business, having no opposition. Winston tells me that it is settled he takes over both War Office and Air Ministry. Milner told me this afternoon that nothing would get him to go on.

Then, on the 30th, an important meeting of the Imperial War Cabinet took place, and of this Wilson gives an interesting account in the diary:

> It appears that President Wilson wants to form a League of

Nations first, and then refer everything to it. He has no clear idea of what he meant by such a League. His position in America becomes increasingly difficult, and he will probably have to go back soon and is desperately anxious to take something back. He has no clear idea of whit he means by Freedom of the Seas. He thinks that Germany must be disarmed, but he does not know down to what. He wants to get his men out of Archangel, and out of all Russia, and he wants to let Russia stew in her own juice — and his promises.

He is very angry with the Japs, and would even break the agreement we made with them about the acquisition of all their island captures north of the Equator and in the Pacific. He thinks we should ask the Bolshevists, through Litvinoff, what they want. He is in favour of Turkey being put out of Constantinople and a small State installed as Mandatory. He is opposed to America being a Mandatory anywhere.

He will not agree to our Dominions keeping the German Colonies they have captured, and thinks they should be handed over to a small State as Mandatory of the League of Nations. He is opposed to any of us having indemnities. He is very angry with the Italians. These were the salient points which Lloyd George told us.

Hughes tore Wilson's proposals to tatters, and Curzon and Long agreed with Hughes. Borden said we could have no peace until the Russian problem was solved, A memorable meeting.

I dined at the "Senior" with Milner, who gave a dinner to Douglas Haig, Bungo, Birdie, Horne and the Army Council; Rawly and Plumer away. Milner and Douglas Haig both made nice speeches, the latter giving me great praise.

On the last day of the year Sir Henry wrote in his diary:

Imperial War Cabinet. I brought up the case of Russia, and asked for some policy; and Admiral Fremantle asked the same for the Baltic. It was agreed that this should be the first topic in France on the 14th, when we meet. I was told to leave our two battalions in Omsk meantime, and also not to demobilize our troops in Murmansk and Archangel, and at the same time not to send out any more conscript troops there until some Allied policy for the whole of Russia had been settled on in Paris. Also, the Admiralty were told to withdraw our Baltic Squadron, which will, of course, result in all the poor Esthonians, etc., having their throats cut. This all comes of no policy in our Russian theatre, which at this time of day after all our

The Close of the Year 1918

discussions for months and months is an absolute *disgrace*.

He concluded his record for 1918 with a brief reference to what he justly described as "a wonderful year" — to his becoming C.I.G.S. in February, to the critical days between March and July, to the great Allied advance, to the collapse of Bulgaria, Turkey and Austria-Hungary, to the Armistice, and he concluded:

> What is the outlook for 1919? Lloyd George ought to last out a year, Clemenceau won't. President Wilson will be discredited. We shall have serious troubles in Ireland and many wars in many parts, and Bolshevism frightens me. The Bolshevists are approaching Reval, Riga and Vilna, and will soon get into Poland. I don't like it.

Chapter XXVII – 1919: January to March. The Peace Conference in Paris

Aftermath of wanton Election promises — Opening of the Peace Conference — Its slow progress — Trouble amongst the smaller States — Force to be allowed the Germans — Difficulties at Constantinople — Experiences at the Conference — A gathering at Fontainebleau.

Sir Henry had been not a little disturbed at the unwarranted note of optimism sounded by the Prime Minister in public during the weeks intervening between the Armistice and the General Election. Wayward, illusionary promises, promises which could not possibly be fulfilled, had been freely given utterance to. People who did not think for themselves had been led to imagine that national prosperity would return, in full flood and as a matter of course, immediately upon the cessation of actual hostilities. The lessons of history on the subject had been studiously ignored. An impression had been created amongst the general public that demobilization of those huge fighting forces which the country had built up in its dire peril would be carried out practically at once, and that a return to a peace footing was feasible, without even waiting for the signature of a formal treaty of accommodation by the belligerents. This impression had as a natural consequence come to be entertained amongst the troops on service in the various theatres of recent war, and the C.I.G.S. was only too soon to find that his apprehensions had been fully justified.

For a serious situation arose during the very first week of the

1919: January to March. The Peace Conference in... 195

new year, 1919, in connexion with large numbers of men on leave from the Western Front at the time, whose period of leave had expired. Some 2,500, so situated and under obligation to return to France, refused to embark at Folkestone on January 3, and the number of recalcitrants had swelled to 10,000 next day. They demanded another week's leave. The Army Council therefore dispatched a wire to G.H.Q. intimating that no men on leave would henceforward be demobilized, so that the position would be made known to the troops.

Sir Henry wrote in his diary:

> The whole of demobilization has been completely boxed up by Lloyd George, who, in his anxiety to get votes at the recent Election, kept adding every sort of authority to help (?) in demobilizing the army, a thing which we soldiers could have done alone and without a hitch.

This appears on the 6th:

> I saw Milner at midday. Told him that Lloyd George was responsible for the mess we were getting into, and that he must make a clear pronouncement that the 'war was not over and that the soldiers must obey orders, otherwise we would have no army in a short time. Milner quite agreed.
>
> I held a Military Members' meeting at 12.30, when I proposed, and they all agreed, that we [soldiers] should put in a short statement of our position and advice; and they all agreed that Lloyd George must make it clear to the country that the war is not over, that we are demobilizing quite fast enough, and that, above all, the men and the public must have confidence and trust in their officers and in the War Office. If he does not do this the whole army will be turned into a rabble.
>
> A long talk with Milner at 7 o'clock and I told him all this, and he quite agreed and hoped that I would put it before Lloyd George to-morrow. He returns to-night to Walton, so I suppose we shall have a Cabinet to-morrow. The whole of this trouble is due to Lloyd George and his cursed campaign at election for vote-catching. Now he is faced up against something ugly and real, as I repeatedly told him he would be. At meeting of Military Members this afternoon we agreed that the A.G. should draw up a paper showing how constantly civil

interference had wrecked our carefully worked out scheme for demobilization, and explaining clearly that unless we soldiers were allowed to run our own show we would have a disaster.

Next day there occurs the passage:

At 6.15 I went to 10 Downing Street. Prime Minister, Eric Geddes and Bottomley (!) there. Bottomley talked much vain nonsense. When he had gone I told Lloyd George plainly what I thought — viz., he must come out in the open at once and back the War Office and the officers. He must crush out the poisonous part of the Press. He must say the War is not over. He must prepare the public mind for armies of occupation in India, Gibraltar, Malta, France, etc. I spoke very plainly and I frightened him. He agreed to all my proposals, and then sent for Milner, who will draft an "interview" for submission to Lloyd George tomorrow.

This appears on January 8:

A War Cabinet this morning at 11 a.m., but nothing of importance, so I did not stay. At 1 o'clock I was sent for again, and found a soldiers' demonstration outside Downing Street, and had to work my way through the soldiers to the door. The men were quite respectful and quiet, but not much saluting.

Lloyd George, Barnes, Bonar Law, Curzon, Milner, Weir, Robertson and self. Lloyd George was going to see a deputation of the men, but I stopped that, and eventually Fielding got the men on Horse Guards Parade and Robertson saw a deputation. The urgency of Lloyd George getting out a pronouncement increases every hour, and at 6 p.m. we had another meeting to settle this, Milner's draft was an excellent one but had been cut about and not made half so good. Robertson objected to one paragraph as being too strong, so this was weakened and one of Milner's paragraphs put back, and then we passed it. It is only fairly good, but I hope will give us soldiers a chance of catching hold again.

On the following day, the 9th, it was finally announced that Lord Milner was leaving the War Office, and that Mr. Churchill was coming in his place and was also to have under him the Air Ministry — an arrangement that, as we have seen, Wilson did not believe would work well. He indeed asked the new Secretary of

State at their first official meeting, where the Admiralty came in, and, according to Sir Henry's diary, Churchill was unable to say. A big party — the Prime Minister, Bonar Law, the Dominions Prime Ministers, were, together with Wilson, to proceed to Paris on the 11th; and at the Cabinet on the day before the C.I.G.S. brought up the question of there being absolutely no policy as to Russia. So it was agreed that this must be the first subject to be discussed in Paris. The C.I.G.S. was very critical as to the manner in which foreign policy as a whole was being handled at this time, and he had written in his diary on the 2nd:

> I had a long talk with Bob Cecil, Bob, having resigned his post owing to "Welsh Disestablishment," is now, quite naturally. Foreign Secretary; for Balfour is at Cannes and there is no one else! So Cecil sits in Balfour's room and "carries on." We both agreed that the situation is as ridiculous as intolerable, Cecil is not even a Minister, and has no power, and ought not to be in the Foreign Office at all, and says so.

On arrival in Paris on January 11, some of the more prominent members amongst the British representatives, including Wilson, were housed at the Villa Majestic, and he soon ascertained that nothing was as yet settled about the Peace Conference, that no meetings were arranged for, and that no agenda had been drawn up. He impressed strongly upon Bonar Law the urgent need of a discussion as to Russia taking place at once. "If we can solve Russia," he remarked in the diary, "we have almost solved the League of Nations." He lunched with Lloyd George on the following day (Balfour, Bonar Law and others being of the party), and they discussed Russia. He wrote in the diary:

> Lloyd George is opposed to knocking out Bolshevism, he does not even like my proposal to arm Russian prisoners now in Germany, even if they express a wish to go and fight against the Bolshevists. This tacit agreement to Bolshevism is a most dangerous thing.

He was summoned to attend the first meeting of the Allied representatives; but, after discussion had been proceeding for an hour, Lloyd George "discovered that he had wanted a meeting of

Prime Ministers and Foreign Office to discuss the broad lines of the coming Conference, and the room was cleared of all but those named." Sir Henry dined with the Prime Minister in the evening, and, according to the diary:

> Lloyd George was in tremendous spirits. He told us of the meeting after Foch and I had left. They discussed the representation of our Dominions, and Wilson was opposed to their being present. Lloyd George reminded him that both Australia and Canada, with tiny populations, had lost more than America with her 100,000,000. This was a facer. Later on it was agreed that they should be represented. The strain between French and Americans seems to be considerable.

One of the problems which was causing Sir Henry searchings of heart was that of how to extricate Milne's forces from the very scattered situations in which a large part of them found themselves. There now were British detachments at Batoum and other points in western Transcaucasia, and also in Armenia, whose position might well become insecure if Bolshevism continued to gain the upper hand. The position of affairs all round the Black Sea was in fact anomalous, and its manifest inconveniences and dangers were one of the causes of the persistent, if unsuccessful, efforts of the C.I.G.S. to induce H.M. Government to adopt some policy with regard to Russia that was intelligible and was capable of being carried out. He was, however, beginning to hope that some other one of the Allies might possibly be prevailed upon to take over charge of the regions to the east of the Black Sea, and it occurred to him that, if President Wilson refused to do so, the Italians would form excellent substitutes. Sir Henry was most appreciative of the admirable work that was being done by our troops in this out of the way part of the world, but he realized that we did not possess the military forces requisite for undertaking police work in territories in which the Empire was not vitally interested.*

---

* In an article written by him after he had ceased to be C.I.G.S. he a special reference to what had been accomplished by our troops in this quarter, as had been set forth in a dispatch of Sir G. Milne's. "I have always quoted Sir George's dispatch as being a fairy tale," he wrote, "of what a handful — and they were only a handful — of regimental officers and British soldiers were able to do in those

1919: January to March. The Peace Conference in... 199

Another "mass meeting" took place at the Quai d'Orsay on the 13th, at which the question of Armistice terms was discussed, "President Wilson being rather tiresome and Lloyd George for the most part asleep," and that evening Sir Henry started for England. He crossed the Channel next day in company with Haig, Lawrence and Fowke, they described the state of the army as deplorable, and Wilson noted in his diary:

> The real fact being that, owing to the General Election and indiscriminate promises, we have turned the period of the Armistice from a period preparatory to demobilization into the demobilization itself. Result — chaos.

An elaborate scheme based on the compulsory system had by this time been drawn up in the War Office, so as to secure the necessary forces for the Rhine and for other theatres. The new broom, Churchill, proved himself most energetic and helpful in the matter, and Wilson mentions in his diary having a long conversation about it with the Secretary of State on January 17:

> I told him that when we got our scheme through the War Cabinet on Tuesday [the 21st] both he and I ought at once to go over to Paris and get Lloyd George to agree to it, and then get it out without a moment's delay. We are sitting on the top of a mine which may go up at any minute. Ireland to-night has telegraphed for some more tanks and machine guns and are evidently anxious about the state of the country.

This appears in the diary on the 20th:

> Lloyd George has written Winston a cross letter for getting out a scheme for Armies of Occupation without his seeing it. Winston has

---

somewhat restless countries, and in somewhat turbulent days. For example, you will find a young subaltern, a couple of sergeants and five-and-twenty soldiers keeping law and order in a part of the world as big as Yorkshire, administering justice, collecting revenue and generally speaking, 'running a small country to the enormous benefit — economically financially and materially — of the natives of that country."

replied that it was no use showing him a half-baked scheme, and he wanted to complete it before going over with it, or sending me over with it, to Paris.

Some fortnight ago I wired to Knox, suggesting that John Ward, who commands a battalion at Omsk, should wire in clear to Barnes his views on Bolshevism. An excellent wire from Ward arrived this morning, but Lloyd George, or someone in Paris, has marked it "secret." It must get out somehow. Winston all against Bolshevism and therefore, in this, against Lloyd George. I can't understand Lloyd George being such a fool.

Next day there is an entry:

After lunch I went to see Bonar Law, just back from Paris. He told me that Lloyd George was angry with Winston, but I explained that he had no reason to be. Douglas Haig in to discuss our new scheme, and he is in absolute agreement with me about the necessity of carrying it out. I saw Winston at 7 p.m. He had just received a message from Lloyd George, strongly objecting to our scheme. He must be made to agree. Lloyd George won't let Winston place our scheme before the Cabinet to-morrow, but has no objection to all the members meeting in '"conversations." This will give him the chance of denying later on that we put the scheme before the Cabinet. I wired to Lloyd George this morning, or rather the Lord telephoned to P. de B. Radcliffe, to take my message of "grave concern" to Lloyd George.

On the 22nd Wilson wrote:

Lloyd George writes, wires and telephones from Paris that our figures are fantastic. He knows nothing about it, and I have not seen a trace of statesmanship in any of Lloyd George's work. At 3 o'clock we had Cabinet "conversations," Bonar Law' having intimated that no decisions were to be taken. Winston stated the case for our scheme. I emphasized the urgency of the situation, pointing out that unless we carried out our proposals we would lose not only our Army of the Rhine, but our garrisons at home, in Ireland, Gibraltar, Malta, India, etc., and that even now we dare not give an unpopular order to the troops, and discipline was a thing of the past. Douglas Haig said that by February 15 he would have no army in France. Much talk round the plate. But Winston and I stuck to it, and in the end we got an unwilling assent to our proposals. Austen very frightened of the expense. Bonar Law very determined not to give an opinion. Curzon not present, so Foreign Office not represented. No secretary, so no record of the proceedings.

On the following day Churchill, Haig, Wilson and others crossed the Channel, and the Prime Minister agreed to the plan, subject to some modifications of no great importance. Sir Henry was at the moment suffering from a bad sore throat and was confined to his room, and he was incensed on hearing of the project that was on foot for dispatching Sir R. Borden on a mission to Prince's Island near Constantinople to meet Bolshevist emissaries. It was settled that Churchill and the C.I.G.S. should return to London on the 27th to meet the Cabinet next day, and that there should be a meeting with representatives of the Press that same evening; Wilson described the contemplated procedure in his diary.

> Then all the Press to bring out '"puffs" on Wednesday, and we follow with an Army Order on Thursday; and then the great adventure of "compulsing" a million men in time of peace, to serve abroad, will have begun. There is not a moment to lose, as all our power over the army is slipping away. We shall get about a million men, who will be compelled to serve for 12 months. Of course, if these men really refuse to serve, we are done; but I have no fear of this if the case is properly put to the men, and if Winston and I can get the support of the Press.

This appears in his diary next day (January 26):

> I could not go to the meeting to discuss strengths of the Allied forces on the Rhine, but Douglas Haig went and then came to see me to tell me that he had told Foch we were prepared to put 10 infantry divisions, 2 cavalry divisions and 3 Colonial divisions as our quota. Foch was quite satisfied.
> At 5 o'clock Foch and Weygand came and had tea and talked for an hour. Foch is quite satisfied with our 10 infantry and 2 cavalry divisions, provided we keep them up. We discussed the possibility of limiting the enemy's number of trained men, and we were both agreed that it was quite impossible. Just as in Ulster and the south and west

of Ireland clubs and associations can carry out drills, etc., and arm, etc., right under the nose of our police, so infinitely more could be done in Germany. As Foch put it: we can no more limit the number of men trained to arms in Germany than the Germans could limit the output of coal in England. Then we discussed the possibility of checking and limiting guns, rifles, lorries, etc., and again we came to the conclusion that it would be quite impossible. Foch is determined to stick to the line of the Rhine, and I agree that this is much the wisest, and in fact the only, plan until we have secured the fruits of victory.

Wilson wrote next night:

Dr. Beauchamp would not let me out till I came to the train 10.15 p.m. A lot of visitors. A long talk with Douglas Haig after breakfast. He is clearly of opinion that our proposals for a clean cut and extra pay will produce a force that can be disciplined. He is anxious about his railway situation, and I must continue to press Foreign Office for permission to use the Scheldt and the Rhine for all purposes, i.e. armed men, munitions, etc.

After he left, Winston sent me over a long letter from Bonar Law, in which he shows he is terrified of our scheme coming out now because it is against "election speeches."

A.J.B. came to see me this evening. He was not at the meeting which decided on the disgraceful Prinkipo proposal, and he does not approve of it. It looks this evening as if no one would go except the big Powers, and, if no Russians go, then Borden and the others can't go, and the whole thing will be a damaging blow to the Peace Conference. And I shall be glad, for I am convinced that this Peace Conference, -with Wilson leading, will land us in endless wars, and so the sooner it is smashed up the better and the sooner we shall work our way back to a balance of Great Powers.

Winston writes to-night before he goes to dine with the Prime Minister, and he addresses a note to the Prime Minister in which he says that he is very unhappy about Russia. I attached a short note saying that I had been writing about Russia for months without result, that I was in favour of clearing out of Omsk now, if France would agree, and getting ready to clear out of Murmansk and Archangel next summer, but on the other hand I would want to strengthen our position on the line Batoum — Baku — Krasnovodsk — Merv. Winston, Lord and I caught the 10.30 train.

After a meeting of the War Cabinet next day, Churchill and Wilson saw representatives of the Press at the War Office, The Secretary of State explained the new scheme and its objects, and Wilson added a few words about the great responsibility that was, for the time being, being transferred from the officers to the Press, seeing that the men and officers were strangers to each other, that the whole army was, at the moment, in a state of flux, and that the men were disposed to take their opinions largely from what they read in the newspapers, Robertson, who was present, added a few words in the same sense. This meeting led to most happy results, for the Press behaved loyally and, by its commendatory attitude, greatly assisted the military authorities in their introduction of the new system. This, as it turned out, proved a complete success,

Wilson found himself recalled to Paris at the end of the month, and he gives an interesting account in his diary on February 1, of a conversation that he had with the Prime Minister on arrival in the French capital:

> Prime Minister wants to clear out of Constantinople, Batoum, Baku, Transcaspia and out of Syria. He means to force the pace, and to force President Wilson to take his share in garrisoning, or to name the Mandatory. I have no objection, and indeed I am all in favour of obliging my Cousin to decide on something. Wilson wants to leave the nomination of Mandatories to the League of Nations. Lloyd George argues that the League of Nations does not exist, and may not exist for months or years, and he refuses to occupy territories at vast expense and inconvenience meanwhile. Lloyd George wants me to help him to force the pace. I pointed out that all this is Foreign Office work, but he and I know well enough that with A.J.B. here and Curzon in London we have no Foreign Office. So I will see how I can help.
>
> Worked in office up to 6.30, then went to see Botha and Smuts. Botha goes to Warsaw next week, and he wants a soldier to go with a sub-commission to keep peace between the Czechos and the Poles. The Poles seem to be at war with the Bolsheviks, the Ukraine, the Czechos and the Boches. I suppose the League of Nations will settle all this.
>
> Had a long talk with A.J.B. I find him in favour of clearing out of Caucasus and of Constantinople and of Syria, but not of Mosul. I asked how he proposed to tear up the Sykes-Picot agreement, and he

did not know. [This was the agreement that had been come to between Sir Mark Sykes and M. Picot in 1916, partitioning Turkey in Asia.] I urged him to bargain with all we have got and not just to throw things away, and above all to bargain the grant of the Saar Valley against the Sykes-Picot.

Next day (the 2nd) there is the entry:

A.J.B. sent for me to tell me the Czechos under the guidance of some Major Crossfield, a lieutenant-colonel in the French Army, a major in the Italian Army, and a lieutenant in the American Army, had attacked the Poles about Teschen. I dori't know who Crossfield is, but a man called Kenny, who had just arrived from Warsaw, said he was in the Flying Corps.

Wire in to-night shows Glasgow in riot, and troops are beginning to occupy the streets, and that other strikes in Liverpool and London are getting worse, and that a railway strike is imminent.

On February 3 there appears:

Dined with Foch and Madame Foch. He is very anxious about the general situation and the total inability of the Peace Conference to come to any decision on any subject. He says his men won't stand it much longer, and will demobilize themselves just as the Belgians are doing. Foch has a supreme contempt for such ideas as League of Nations, Mandatories, etc. I cordially agree with him. I am so glad that we [English] have got out our scheme for Armies of Occupation, and all the reports I got to-day about the way the men are taking it are good. In three months we shall be the only nation with an army.

Of a discussion with Foch on the 5th, he wrote:

I talked longly on the dangers of a French occupation of Syria, and I told him I was convinced that, if the French insisted upon occupying Damascus, Homs and Aleppo, they would be at war with Feisul and the Arabs, and that this would be disastrous. I suggested the French becoming Mandatories for Constantinople and Thrace instead of Syria. Altogether I think I did some good. He is very anxious about the way the Peace Congress is getting about its business, and thinks that unless they give up talking about the League of Nations and come to some practical decisions there will be a real crash in Europe.

I saw Milner after dinner, he has just arrived from London. He told me that we are in chaos in England as regards these strikes, which under Lloyd George's regime are being dealt with by every sort of man and every sort of department, each acting on a different principle from the other.

Sir Henry found it necessary to return to England on the 7th, as a number of important questions required attending to at the War Office; and he learnt on arrival that a certain amount of trouble was still arising from time to time in connexion with soldiers on leave, who were due to return to the Continent. The Army Council therefore decided to bring home the Guards Division, a move which was also rendered expedient by the fact that serious unrest amongst the railway men and the miners was causing the Government a good dem of anxiety. Sir Henry attended a War Cabinet meeting on the 12th (the Prime Minister having arrived in London), and at this the question of food distribution in the event of simultaneous strikes on the part of railway men, transport workers and other industrial bodies was considered. He seized the opportunity to raise the question of what military policy was to be pursued in Russia. The War Cabinet showed no disposition to approve of warlike operations being undertaken against the Bolshevists; and in the circumstances the C.I.G.S., who had lost confidence in General Denikin and also in General Kolchak (who was opposing Bolshevism in Siberia), declared that the only course to pursue was to withdraw our troops. No definite decision to that effect was, however, arrived at. He therefore proceeded to Paris in company with Churchill on the 14th, in hopes of bringing the matter up for consideration there, and he wrote in his diary:

> Winston and I went to Quai d'Orsay at 5 p.m., where a plenary meeting of the League of Nations was sitting (Mrs. Wilson was present!), and where one delegate after another talked nauseating nonsense about peace, etc. After this was over at 7 o'clock we had a small meeting in Pichon's room of head Frocks, about putting pressure on Holland to allow our troops up the Rhine, and then Winston asked about the Russian situation. Did Prinkipo still hold the

field or did it not? If not, then what? This drew from Wilson the statement that (*a*) he would withdraw all Allied troops from Russia, and (*b*) he would meet Bolsheviks alone at Prinkipo.

Of a meeting next day. President Wilson having started for America over-night, he wrote:

> Tiger in the chair. We tackled Prinkipo. Lansing, House, A.J.B. and Winston in favour of wiring again and fixing date. Tiger opposed altogether Prinkipo. Sonnino then pointed out that the first invitation to Prinkipo *did* gave a date, viz., February 15, and this completely changed our outlooks.

On February 17 the entry appears:

> Peevish wire in early from Lloyd George saying the country was in a dangerous state, that war against the Bolsheviks was quite impossible, etc., etc. Winston quite calm. Later in the day Winston and I found that Lloyd George had wired to Philip Kerr to send copies of these telegrams to Colonel House.
> We had Supreme Council in Pichon's room at 3 o'c. We discussed Russia, and whether we should submit the problem to Military Representatives at Versailles. House objected to this, and A.J.B. backed House. Clemenceau exploded. House said neither Americans not material would be allowed to go to Russia. Tiger said, that being so, the others would discuss Russia without America. He said it was a pitiful thing to see the victors of the Boches afraid to refer the Russian problem to Versailles. Winston and I and Sonnino were entirely in sympathy with Clemenceau. I said nothing; but Winston spoke a little, and well. And so in the end it was agreed that each country should ask its Military Representative, who should report separately, no joint note being allowed. I think this is the greatest depth of impotence I have ever seen the Frocks fall to. I advised Winston to go home as he was doing no good here and would get tarred, so he went to-night.

Sir Henry now found himself to some extent in disagreement with the French as to what sort of military force Germany was to he permitted to maintain. He favoured that country being allowed a voluntary long service army of limited proportions. The French

1919: January to March. The Peace Conference in... 207

advocated a conscript army of one year's service, only 100,000 men to be enrolled each year; they maintained that long-service men would all be fitted to become officers on emergency, and that under the voluntary plan the Germans would come to possess a vast cadre of officers and would in consequence be enabled to expand their army rapidly in case of war. Sir Henry contended, against this, that cadres were of no use if there were no trained men to fill them. Wilson remained in Paris until the 20th, devoting his time largely to consideration of the Russian problem, and satisfying himself that nothing further than giving some support to the border States against the Bolshevists was feasible in the circumstances now existing. He was much distressed on hearing on the 19th of the attempted assassination of M. Clemenceau and greatly relieved to learn before returning to England that his old friend was not very seriously injured.

Immediately on getting back to the War Office he prepared a memorandum which dealt with all the various theatres in Russia, "advising delimitation in the west" (according to his diary), "evacuation of Archangel, instructional staffs only with Denikin and Kolchak, and handing over Transcaucasia to Italy." The Cabinet agreed to the principles laid down in this document; and Wilson went over again to Paris on February 27, in connexion with the question of the military force that was to be allowed the Germans, and also to come to an understanding as to the position at Constantinople, where the French were showing a disposition to take complete charge. So he went to see Clemenceau on the last day of the month, and of their interview he wrote in his diary:

> I found the old man very little changed, but looking a shade thinner and rather tired. Very nice to me. I unfolded my complaints about Constantinople, and told him that they all came from Franchet d'Esperey facing south instead of north. The old man was struck with my arguments and way of putting my case, and I gave him — or rather he pinched — my copy of the Notes of our case which Curzon had drawn up and sent to Derby. I read these last week, and got a copy of them from the Embassy this morning; but I was not quite sure as to the wording, so — as I told Tiger — there may be some truths put in a blunt fashion. For they were not drawn up for presentation to the French. As I was going away I said to Clemenceau, "Tiger, you

really are a wonderful old boy." To which he replied, "Why old?" I feel sure he will do as I asked him about Franchet.

Then I went and had 1½ hours with Foch. He enlarged on the vital necessity of the French holding the whole of the Rhine down to Holland, then taking in all the Rhenish Provinces! Then we discussed my Russian proposals, with which he entirely agreed, except that he has no belief in either Denikin or Kolchak — and I am afraid I agree. Milner and I dined alone and had a long talk. He says Lloyd George must come over, as nothing is being settled.

Wilson had further discussion with Foch next day, and he found the Marshal absolutely convinced that the line of the Rhine must be held for good, and that its acquisition would prove the cheapest form of insurance. "From a purely military point of view this undoubtedly is so," Sir Henry remarked in his diary, "but from any other this is impossible," He returned to London on March 2, after giving a sitting to Sir W. Orpen in Paris for his portrait ("Result clever, but appalling").[*] He was becoming very anxious about t h e interior condition of Germany, owing to the want of food that was reported, and about the spread of Bolshevism that was taking place in consequence, and, of an interview which he had with the King on the 3rd he wrote in his diary:

> I told him that I was getting very frightened of Germany going smash altogether, and that these fools who went on talking about Leagues of Peace, etc., instead of acting and feeding the Boches, would be responsible for the most awful chaos the world has ever seen.

The Cabinet, like himself, considered the permanent holding of the Rhine by the French to be quite out of the question; but they thought well of his suggestion that the Rhenish Provinces might be

---

[*] This was the first of several sittings. Of these, Sir W. Orpen wrote in his "An Onlooker in France": "When I painted Sir Henry, he gave me his views on the brains and the merits of many of the delegates, but when I had finished painting him I came under his kindly lash. He called me 'a nasty little wasp,' and he kept a 'black book' for any of his lady friends who said the sketch was like him. With all his fun, Sir Henry was a deep thinker, and towered over the majority of the 'Frocks' by his personality, big outlook and clear vision."

demilitarized, and they were unanimous as to quitting Archangel, Murmansk and the Caucasus. He was only at home for two days on this occasion, as he re-crossed the Channel with Lloyd George and A. Chamberlain on the 5th; and on the journey to Paris he seized the opportunity to impress upon them the outstanding importance of feeding the Germans. Discussions thereafter took place in Paris, and at a meeting of the Peace Conference held on the 6th, Lloyd George gave those present clearly to understand that he was opposed to Foch's idea of allowing the Germans a conscript army, as opposed to a voluntarily enlisted one after Sir Henry's plan.

On March 6 Wilson remarked in the diary:

> I feel very strongly that these terms ought to be presented to the Boches at once, and that they will agree; that we should then collect all the arms and ammunition we can, because I feel more and more every day that the Boches are going to crack, and the sooner we get their guns and ammunition the better. The Frocks are to blame for our present parlous condition, because for three months they have been discussing nonsense like the League of Nations and never once have tackled any of the really serious problems, with result that instead of taking charge of the situation the situation is taking charge of them.

Of a meeting of the Peace Conference on the 7th he wrote:

> We had rather a heated meeting about passing food to the Czechos from Trieste, the Italians saying that the Yugos had insulted them! And then about my proposals for making the Boches hare a voluntary army, as opposed to Foch's proposals for a conscript army. In the end the meeting seemed to pass a Resolution that the future army of Germany should be based on the voluntary principle, and the matter was referred to the military experts.

So the organization and strength of the proposed voluntarily enlisted German army were gone into thoroughly by the military experts, and the strength of the force was fixed at 140,000, although the French objected to the plan as a whole and wished the establishment to be reduced to 100,000. Wilson explained the position to Lloyd George, with the result that the Prime Minister accepted the arrangement and the 140,000. But the diary mentions that the Prime Minister, House and Clemenceau met immediately afterwards, and that they then agreed to the figure 100,000 — and that was what was decided upon at a plenary meeting of the Peace Conference in spite of Foch contending for the conscript system. "So," as Wilson remarked in his diary, "I got my principle, but not my numbers, and Foch got his numbers but not his principle. An amazing state of affairs." He was not in the meantime forgetful of the vitally important question of provisioning Germany, and he was largely responsible for bringing about the very practical arrangement, eventually come to, under which supplies were sent to that country in exchange for ships of the Teutonic mercantile marine. During the course of his stay of three weeks in France at this time. Sir Henry enjoyed opportunities of observing the futilities that were usual at the Peace Conference. Some meetings he was present at. Of what used to occur at others he heard from some of those whose fate it had been to take part in the proceedings. A few entries on the subject, culled from his diaries, deserve to be quoted in view of the light which they cast upon the methods and the workmanship of the "Big Four."

> *March 12.* — Nothing done to-day except to turn down ridiculous claims by the Czechos.
> *March 13.* — Long discussion as to how to get the Emperor of Austria safely out of Switzerland, who does not want him, unless the Paris Conference promises not to ask for his extradition, and no one was ready to promise. Then we discussed our air terms to the Boches, which to me are fantastically severe and illogical.
> *March 14.* — President Wilson[*] and the other Prime Ministers had a long meeting this afternoon and did absolutely no business. Wilson talking of League of Nations and other nonsense. Curiously enough, Wilson wants to change our military terms to the Boches and to impose conscription. If he brings this up to-morrow when we are to agree to the voluntary principle, it will be curious.
> *March 15.* — After lunch I had a talk with Lloyd George about our military conditions for the Boches, and then I walked down with him to the Quai d'Orsay. A big meeting, and then it was found that Wilson was not coming, as he had not sufficiently studied the

---

[*] He had returned to Paris from the United States on the 12th.

question! This is the most barefaced waste of time that I have seen perpetrated up to now, as well as being impudence on the part of Wilson, since both House and Lansing had already agreed in principle and detail to our military terms.

March 17. — Meeting at Quai d'Orsay at 3 p.m. Wilson came down with intention to challenge our voluntary-principle army for the Boches, on the ground that he had not been present when the decision was reached, although both House and Lansing were. Lloyd George at a private talk with Wilson made it clear that he would not tolerate this and said that if he persisted he — Lloyd George — who was not present when the League of Nations was agreed to, would challenge that decision. Wilson collapsed. We discussed and passed our military terms and naval terms and nearly all our air terms. In my opinion they are *all* much too drastic, but the French insisted on them, and the Frocks agreed.

Then Foch raised the question of Poland and her immediate danger, especially her loss of Lemberg which the Ukrainians are threatening. Lloyd George and I went into another room, and I told him that Foch was going to raise the whole Border States question. On the other hand Lemberg did not belong to Poland, and therefore it was very difficult to fight the Ukraine, who had at least an equal right to the town. At the same time, something must be done to stop the Bolsheviks, and I thought we ought to tell Poland to clear out of Lemberg, and at the same time tell them we would give them Danzig. Then Lloyd George and I went back to the Council room and he gave an amazing strategical lecture, winding up by saying he would never be a party to forming large armies and invading Russia. Foch asked if he might by an Allied Staff *étudier** the question of moving Haller's forces† from France to Poland, and in the second place of moving up Rumanians to save Lemberg. The first was agreed to, not the second. Foch very angry. The whole discussion was ignorant and amateurish to a degree, but it was anyhow a first discussion on the fringe of the Russian question. And this after over four months of Armistice! Nothing has been more scandalous and futile than this ignoring of Russia by the Frocks in Paris.

March 18. — Went to Foch to meet Stephanik, the Czecho from

---

* "Study."

† General Haller was in command of a considerable body of Polish troops at present in France.

Siberia. He makes out that the Czechos cannot now get back to Europe and that we [the Allies] have sacrificed them. He is right. He says the Czechos will turn Bolsheviks, and then the Kolchak government will disappear and all Siberia will be gone. I agree again. This Paris Conference is heading straight for disaster. It has never really examined the Russian question, and it alone is to blame for the scandalous want of policy and consequent disorder and chaos reigning in every part of Russia.

March 19. — I went to the Quai d'Orsay, but Foch and I were told we were not wanted, so we went back to our offices. An hour later we were sent for again. I found the Frocks discussing Ukraine and Poland, and wiring to tell them to stop fighting at Lemberg. Then they began to discuss the Polish west frontier — a report by a sub-committee. But, when General Le Rond began to read the report, President Wilson objected, saying that frontiers had nothing to do with soldiers. So Foch and Bliss and I went off. This was a *tour de force* on the part of my Cousin. Frontiers have nothing to do with soldiers! "Whew!"

By this time the C.I.G.S. was becoming very anxious to get back to London to attend to his duties at the War Office; but Lloyd George refused to let him go because a meeting of the Conference had been arranged to discuss a refusal on the part of the Germans to allow Haller's Polish troops to reach Poland by way of Danzig. This meeting took place on the 21st, and Wilson wrote of it in his diary:

> We discussed Danzig and the Boche refusal to allow Polish troops through, and for three hours we wrangled and came to no decision of any sort. It was a miserable exhibition of unashamed incompetence.

He had, a few nights before, given Hankey a strategical lecture; the Prime Minister had heard of this, and the result was that an arrangement was come to for a discussion on analogous lines to take place at Fontainebleau. Thither Lloyd George, Wilson, Hankey and Mr. Montagu repaired on March 22. They remained for three days in these enjoyable sylvan surroundings, and of his first lecture to this exclusive party. Sir Henry wrote in his diary:

1919: January to March. The Peace Conference in... 213

I began by saying that to build on the League of Nations was to build on shifting sands. I pointed out that, on the one hand, we were railing numberless young nations into being and patting them on the back, and at the same time we were creating a League of Nations which internationalized the world, and which in truth was a machinery set up to interfere with everyone's business, and this by 3rd or 4th rate men and by 10th rate Powers. Then I became a Boche. I explained my present situation, and my wish to come to an agreement with England and France, but saw no hope, for I read into the crushing terms they were imposing on me a determination on their part to kill me outright. As I could not stand alone I would turn to Russia, and in the course of time would help that distracted country to recover law and order, and then make an alliance with her. I would under no circumstances join so crazy and so rotten a thing as the League of Nations, nor would I sign the peace terms which I understand are soon to be presented to me.

On the second day he presented the picture from the point of view of a French woman, "showing how sore she was both morally and physically, and how loath to look into the mirror of the future from a dread of what she might see." Lloyd George, having listened attentively to these two expositions proceeded to give utterance to his views as to what should be the peace terms, which, he declared, must not be such as to crush Germany. France was to be given Syria; the United States was to occupy Constantinople and Armenia; Italy was to take charge of the Caucasus; the British Empire was to keep the German African colonies, Palestine, Mesopotamia and the conquered Pacific Islands; the newly-created States were to be handed over to the League of Nations to knock into shape. As a result of these discussions, a memorandum was drawn up and a copy of it was sent to Clemenceau. On getting back to Paris, Wilson was visited by General Dm, and they came to an understanding with regard to the Italian preparations to take over the positions at present held by Milne's forces in and about Transcaucasia. The Allied representatives were somewhat concerned on learning that Bolshevism had suddenly broken loose in Hungary; so Foch worked out a plan for dealing with this new situation by military force, and a meeting took place at the French Office on March 27 to discuss the whole question. Of this meeting

Wilson wrote in his diary:

> Foch exposed his plan, and urged its immediate adoption. Lloyd George and Tiger took me separately to one side to ask me if I approved of the plan. I said, "Yes, if military action is decided on." The Tiger first asked Diaz his opinion. The Tiger caDed on me next. I said that it was not for me to say whether military action was now an answer to Bolshevism. If the statesmen decided that it was, then Foch's plan would do all right for a beginning, but it was not possible to forecast what would follow. If, however, the Frocks elected for military action, there was not a moment to be lost. The fact that Bolshevism had got hold of Buda had already lengthened our front by 500 kilometres, and if, a week hence, Vienna succumbed, then the line would be yet another 1,000 kilometres longer. Lastly I pointed out that if military action was not the answer to Bolshevism, then, if Vienna and Berlin went Bolshevist, military action would be quite unable to enforce terms of peace.
>
> After dinner I went round to Lloyd George. No one there except the Hankeys and Eyre Crowe. We discussed for an hour, and Lloyd George said that he was much struck by my remarks this afternoon, and that after we soldiers left, the four Frocks unanimously decided that military action was not the answer to Bolshevism. But the Frocks were unable to say what was the answer. I said, and Crowe warmly agreed, that it followed that the Boches would, under cover, real or simulated, of Bolshevism, refuse to sign. And then what? No answer. I put on Lloyd George's silk hat, which delighted him, but gave no ideas.

There appears next day:

> I think the Frocks have gone mad. They sit and talk all day; but, as no secretary attends no records are kept, and Hankey is crazy.

On the 29th there is the entry:

> At midday the Boche answer to our wires about Danzig arrived. To me it is quite simply impudent. It offers Stettin, Konigsberg, Memel or Libau, Refuses Danzig, and entirely ignores Foch's offer to meet a plenipotentiary at Spa. At 3 o'c. we met in the Tiger's rooms at the War Office. To my amazement the Frocks saw no refusal in the Boche wire, but almost an acceptance, and after much talk they

settled for Foch to wire to say he would explain everything at Spa on April 3, if the Boches would send a plenipotentiary. I hope the Boches will do no such thing and thus force the Frocks to act. The Boches are making fools of Paris.

At the end Wilson said, "And I would affectionately ask General Foch to act more as a diplomat than as a soldier." The old boy's face was a study, and he put his hand up to his mouth and said in an audible whisper to me (I was sitting beside him): *"Ce n'est pas commode, Henri!"**

But the German authorities did accept the proposal for a discussion with the Marshal at Spa on the date indicated. In consequence of their doing so, a meeting of the Peace Conference was held on the last day of March for the purpose of deciding what line Foch was to adopt, and the Marshal then read two separate papers, each of which insisted upon the vital necessity to the French of their holding the left bank of the Rhine. As usual, however, nothing was settled with regard to this fundamental question, which clearly must be decided one way or the other before Allied plenipotentiaries could approach those of Germany with definitely expressed conditions of peace.

---

* "That's not easy, Henry!"

Chapter XXVIII – 1919: April to June. The Peace Conference in Paris

The Hungarians defy Paris — The difficulty over Fiume — The Russian problem — The Peace Terms handed to the German Plenipotentiaries under extraordinary circumstances — Three of the "Big Four" give Smyrna to Greece behind the back of the Fourth — Syria — The signing of the Treaty of Versailles.

Quite apart from the irritation that he felt at the dilatory proceeding of the Peace Conference, and from his fear that the terms offered to the Germans would be unduly severe, Wilson had at this time other grounds for anxiety. The news from Murmansk and Archangel was by no means satisfactory, as some of the Allied troops in that theatre were reported to be discontented and even mutinous. There appeared to be a growing disposition on the part of the "Big Four" (Clemenceau, Lloyd George, President Wilson and Orlando) to ignore Foch. The news from both Egypt and India was by no means reassuring. He also feared mat, if the French occupied Syria, war would break out between them and the Arabs. Trouble furthermore was brewing between the Hungarians and the Rumanians, and on April 1, Smuts took his departure from Paris for Budapest, with the object of endeavouring to keep the peace. "A curious business," Wilson remarked of tins in his diary. "A Welshman sends a Dutchman to tell a Hungarian not to fight a Rumanian." Clemenceau, in answer to the Fontainebleau paper, admitted that there was much to be said for making the terms easier for the Germans, and he then went on to suggest that the British

1919: April to June. The Peace Conference in Paris 217

should return them some of their colonies and some of their ships. The following appears in the diary on April 2:

> Went round to Lloyd George after breakfast to get him to speak with Wilson about allowing the crews of the two American cruisers, that are going to Murmansk to-day, to land if the situation demands. It was agreed that, as the Americans were going to Constantinople and the Italians to the Caucasus, these moves should take place at once. Lloyd George told me te had not yet told Wilson about the Italians, but would do so this morning. Lloyd George is beginning to lose heart as to an early settlement. He says Wilson is boiling up against the French and had a violent explosion, not in front of the French, saying he would never sign a French peace and would go home rather than do so.
>
> I went to see Foch at 3 o'c. He was in despair about the Frocks, and he prophesied that within a week from now the Paris Conference would crash. To-night I cannot see daylight, and, for the first time, I thought Lloyd George saw about where he stood. Hankey told me to-day that the four Frocks had now held 17 Meetings *of which no records had been kept and at which no decisions had been reached.*

On the 4th, Wilson wrote:

> Millet (of the *Temps*) in to see me 9.30 a.m. He is in despair, and says the Frocks are done and that they will never make peace. I was guarded in what I said, but I suggested that the Frocks should take a complete holiday week, and go away and come back with fresh minds. Millet said I was the only person who could pull the whole thing together, and would I undertake it? I told him such a proposal was not practical.
>
> Admiral Hope brought me a wire, 3 p.m., from our Admiral in Black Sea, to say that the French were clearing out of Odessa. The Bolsheviks will now cut the throats of the Greeks there. Hope says the loss of Odessa will not affect our command of the Black Sea. It will, however, have a dangerous effect upon the Rumanians, and we shall presently have the Bolsheviks in command of the Danube.

Wilson saw Foch on the 6th — the Marshal had returned from Spa the previous night. "He says Germans agreed to all his terms. They cried out about Bolshevism, but got no sympathy from Foch." A meeting of the Supreme War Council was held next day, at which the Marshal reported the result of his visit, and that Haller's Polish troops were to be transported across Germany to Poland by rail. A wire had just come in from Smuts to announce that the Hungarians declined to withdraw their troops from a strip of territory on the Rumanian frontier, which the Paris Conference had declared must, for the time being, be regarded as neutral, and Sir Henry wrote:

> So Smuts is coming back disgruntled, and once again (4th time — Prinkipo, Danzig, Lemberg, Hungarian-Rumanian No Man's land) Paris has been snubbed. Absolutely fatal all this is for the final peace.

Of an interview with Marshal Joffre on the 8th he wrote in his diary:

> The old man was so pleased to see me. He was wearing his red trousers, which pleased me. We chatted about the state of affairs. He is profoundly dissatisfied with all the Peace arrangements. He told me that last night at dinner he met White (the American) who said openly that, as the Americans could not get the Allies to work a reasonable peace, the Americans themselves would make a separate peace with the Boches. Joffre said that would be the act of a traitor.
> At 5 o'c, a meeting of Foch, Diaz, Bliss and self to discuss proposals we soldiers should make if (*a*) the German, Austrian, Bulgar or Turkish Governments — or all of them — refuse to sign our terms of peace; (*b*) no governments exist in the four countries; (*c*) Germany signs, but not Bavaria. We agreed that in (*a*) we should march on the capitals and put the governments out; that in (*b*) we should occupy rich territory like Westphalia; that in (*c*) we should surround and knock out Bavaria.
> I went to Lloyd George's flat after dinner to see what Bonar — who flew over to-day — had to say. Bonar was ultra pessimist. Ireland was going into revolution, labour was once more hostile, Eric Geddes impossible, Winston very difficult, the House of Commons hostile to Lloyd George, and so on. I told Lloyd George that in my opinion America would soon make an alliance with La Bochie. I don't think he agreed, but I think I made him think.

This appears next day:

1919: April to June. The Peace Conference in Paris

Venizelos came to see me to ask me to get the Bulgarians disarmed, and offered to march 10 Greek divisions to Sofia if the Bulgarians did not instantly agree. After that, he said, I could count on 6 divisions as available for fighting in Asia Minor.

Denikin wants more assistance and is steadily giving ground; Denikin also angry with us for being in the Caucasus. What will he say when he finds the Italians going to replace us! Finance and the Kaiser's head talked of to-day; no great decisions. Smuts back from Budapest after his snub there — a futile and harmful mission, proving once more the impotence of Paris.

Next day (April 10) Wilson wrote:

C. B. Thomson to see me; he came back yesterday with Smuts. There is no doubt that Smuts's visit was a dismal failure. Smuts has put in a long paper proposing a Mandatory for the States formed out of the Austrian Empire, and military intervention. Dined at Lloyd George's. I discussed my proposal, alternative to Smuts's, i.e. that we should send out a man like our Speaker of the House of Commons to summon and preside at a meeting of all the new nations, viz. Austrians, Hungarians, Czechos, Yugos, Rumanians, Poles, but without any force other than ids own personality and impartiality. To my amazement Lloyd George did not agree, preferring to enforce the decisions of Paris by force of arms — which is, of course, impossible in all these minor theatres. He told me he did not see why we should not be in a position to summon the Boches and Austrians to Paris on Wednesday week, 23rd of this month. Whew!

On the 11th there appears:

Admiral Hope and I drew up a paper against President Wilson's proposal to raise the blockade on Germany. My Cousin is the limit!

Went to see Foch. We discussed the Frocks. Foch says that last night's speeches and resolution in the Senate are only the openings of trouble for the Tiger, and that France will never agree to come back from the Rhine. It looks to me as though the Tiger and Foch might have a fight over this, and that would be a thousand pities. Foch told me that it was the four Frocks who gave the order for Odessa to be evacuated, that he [Foch] had refused to send it, and that it had been sent by Clemenceau, the real author being Wilson because he won't fight the Bolsheviks.

Admiral Cowan, who was commanding in the Baltic, had wired that chaos now prevailed at Riga, where the Bolshevists were carrying on outrages of all kinds; and he reported that the Germans could not march on the place and restore order because we had cut off their supplies. He also wrote privately to Wilson — they had been on Lord Roberts's staff together in South Africa — asking if something could not be done, and he made certain suggestions of a practical kind concerning the matter. To this letter Wilson replied:

> You want me to send a general to help in the Baltic Border States. Yes, on one condition. That is that the Big Four lay down a broad policy. Otherwise — No. Since November 22 of last year I have been trying to get a policy — trying, trying, trying, and not a shadow of success.
>
> That being so, my whole energies are now bent to getting our troops out of Europe and Russia, and concentrating all our strength in our coming storm centres, viz. England, Ireland, Egypt and India. There you are, my dear. Since the statesmen (?) can't and won't lay down a policy, I am going to look after and safeguard our own immediate interests, so that when all the hot air now blowing about Leagues of Nations, Small States, Mandatories, turns to the icy cold wind of hard fact, the British Empire will be well clothed and well defended against all the bangs and curses of the future.

Lloyd George proceeded to London on April 14, and Wilson, following next day, then spent nearly a fortnight at home; he found plenty of work to attend to in Whitehall after his prolonged absence. Allenby had wired for reinforcements in view of the state of Egypt, and the War Office were in difficulties as to how to meet the call as the regular army was very short of establishment. A message, moreover, arrived from India on the 19th announcing serious trouble with Afghanistan, and asking the military authorities at home to hold four divisions and four cavalry brigades in readiness to be sent out as reinforcements. "I really have not enough troops to cope with our possible difficulties" Sir Henry wrote in his diary on the 23rd.

A serious difference of opinion in connexion with Fiume had occurred between the Italian plenipotentiary, Orlando, and

1919: April to June. The Peace Conference in Paris 221

President Wilson while Wilson was away from Paris. The Italians claimed that the city ought to be allotted to them, although that had not been contemplated under the London Pact of 1915, and Orlando and Sonnino had quitted Paris in consequence of the dispute, of which Wilson wrote in his diary:

> The Italians have to guard the American Embassy in Rome. All this is due to the miserable Frocks, who tried to build on a rotten base of small nationalities and of League of Nations. President Wilson was guilty of a flagrant act in rushing into print and appealing to the Italian people over the head of the Italian Government.

Lloyd George was back in Paris, and on receiving a summons. Sir Henry returned to the French capital on the 27th to learn that the German representatives were to arrive on the 30th and that they were to be given fifteen days to think over the terms. From Lloyd George and Hankey he learnt details of what had been going on while he was in England, and this appears in the diary:

> Lloyd George told me he had a row with my Cousin yesterday and beat him. It was over some question of reparations, and Wilson said some sanctimonious things about "right and justice." So Lloyd George flew into a temper and said that, if right and justice were meted out to the Boches, they would be crushed out of existence.

Wilson wrote next day:

> Two hours with Foch, who is more maddened than ever with the Frocks. He tells me that the Tiger never sees him nor tells him anything. I showed him the paper Hankey gave me last night, setting out that the Frocks contemplate armies of occupation for 15 years, but giving up Cologne bridge-head in 5 years to retire to a line detailed in the paper, then after 10 years to retire to Coblentz to another detailed line, and after 1 5 years to retire from Mayence to the Saar line.
> This was the first that Foch had heard of all this, and he and I got out the proposed new frontiers. It took us half an hour to find all the places, and to lay them out on the map. And all this has been done by the Frocks without Foch, or me, or any soldier, being consulted. An amazing thing. Foch is very anxious that Clemenceau and Lloyd

George should not meet the Boches until Orlando returns, and if Wilson wants to meet his Boche friends, let him, I think that Foch is right, and that we shall be made to make a Europe hostile to us, on the 1,000 to 1 chance of gaining a friendly America. There was a Plenary Meeting to-day, at which the League of Nations Convention was passed. What futile nonsense.

On April 29 there is the entry:

I spent the whole morning examining the amazing proposals for falling back from the Rhine adopted by the Frocks, and in preparing an answer for them. Also in considering a message I am sending to Kolchak, advising him as to the strategy of his summer campaign. Then Bob Cecil came to see me about the Danube and the best way to utilize it for distribution of food from the Banat.

Weygand came to see me to discuss various points, and to ask me for a copy of the Rhine paper, which, of course, I gave him. Orlando has made his speech in the House about Fiume, and got an enormous majority and enthusiasm in favour of retention by Italy. He has published a note of Wilson's and one of Tiger's and Lloyd George's. How all these beauties are going to make up their quarrels I can't imagine.

Next day there appears:

Bill Thwaites was with Weygand this morning to discuss the terms about Army of Occupation after Arrmistice ceases and peace begins, i.e. powers of billeting, movement over railways, etc. Bill found that Foch had never seen the Frocks' clauses about demilitarizing the Rhenish Provinces. I wrote a note on the Frocks' amazing paper about falling back from the Rhine in 5 and 10 years, and sent it to Lloyd George,

I lunched with A.J.B. We discussed the *affaire* Orlando, and he sees no way out of the *impasse*. While we were at lunch, Lloyd George sent for A.J.B. to discuss whether we ought not to call up the Austrians and Hungarians to Paris. But I said to A.J.B., "How on earth do you imagine you can make peace with Austria or Hungary whilst Italy is absent?"

After dinner Hankey told me that the Frocks had changed our military and air terms, which they had agreed upon and passed a month ago. They are marvels.

1919: April to June. The Peace Conference in Paris

Sir Henry's fondness for motoring stood him in good stead during these prolonged periods spent in France in connexion with the Peace Conference, and his car was not often left idle. He was constantly running out from Paris to Versailles, and making short trips immediately round the French capital; but he was also able to enjoy a complete holiday on most Sundays, and he used then to go on long drives, always at the wheel himself. He was as a rule accompanied on such occasions by Colonel W. Pitt Taylor, who was now his Personal Assistant in place of Lord Duncannon. He used to plan these excursions in advance during the week, and he always keenly looked forward to them — they appeared indeed to give him a much needed rest from the mental strain of working days. On one Sunday they proceeded from Paris as far as Metz, and made their way back by a roundabout route — a distance of over 420 miles; but Sir Henry enjoyed every minute of the drive and did not seem in the least tired when they got back to the Arc de Triomphe after a day's run which would have exhausted many professional chauffeurs.

General Kolchak's forces were gaining important victories during the months of March and April over the hastily collected troops which the Bolshevist leaders were able at that time to oppose to him. They had swept forward westwards from Siberia into European Russia, and were approaching the Volga in the direction of Kazan. The Allied troops under General Ironside, operating in a south-easterly direction from Archangel, had also gained some successes during April. So there was a reasonable prospect that they might be able to join hands with Kolchak's forces, and might by doing so form a screen to cut the Bolshevist levies off the more effectually from Siberia. Wilson thought well of this project, the more so as Denikin was beginning to make his presence felt in southern Russia, and as preparations were being made by an anti-Bolshevist force under General Yudenitch for an advance from Esthonia direct on Petrograd. The Bolshevists had, however, invaded Bessarabia, taking advantage to some extent of the fact that the bulk of the Rumanian forces were at this time advancing into Hungary and were consequently unable to watch the Dniester.

Wilson wrote in his diary on May 1:

Bill Thwaites went to see Bliss about our occupation clauses. The old boy had never heard of them and complained bitterly of the President never seeing him nor consulting him. Bliss had never heard of the wonderful Tardieu paper of 5-10-15 years. I find that the Frocks yesterday changed Clauses 45 and 46 of our military terms without any reference to Foch or me. I am finding out what the changes mean.

At 4.30 I went to see Foch. He is kept in complete ignorance of all that is going on. Clemenceau tells him nothing. I tell him everything I can think of, and show him all my papers. He was delighted with my Note to Prime Minister on Tardieu's 5-10-15 years paper. He thinks that the Boches, seeing our irresolution and divisions, will play a bold game and we shall lose the peace. I agree.

Bonar and I dined alone with Lloyd George. We had a long talk about Russia. After great struggles, Lloyd George agreed to my proposal to let Ironside join Gaida at Kotlas. I persuaded Lloyd George to bring up the question of Tardieu's 5-10-15 years paper and tear it up, and he promised to bring it up to-morrow. We discussed the situation at length. I put my case as strongly as possible, but neither Lloyd George nor Bonar agree. I said that Lloyd George must now decide whether he was going to be a European or an American, and that in my opinion he must be European. I declared that my Cousin was Boche, that we could never have peace in Europe without the goodwill of the Italians, that we could not have Orlando and Wilson in the same room at the same time, and that therefore Wilson had better clear out. It is quite clear to me that Lloyd George is out of his depth and in these matters is weakly following my Cousin, who himself has no idea where he is going.

Next day there is the entry:

Richard Haking* arrived, and we had a long talk. He does not think the Boches will sign. And when he and I and Bonar talked it over, this became more apparent, because Richard was quite clear that the Boches would not sign to giving up the Silesian coalfields to the Poles, nor would they sign to handing over their culprits to be tried by hostile and interested courts. Paris is going to crash, but I always thought it would because the fools built on the shifting sands of Small States and Leagues of Nations, without power of enforcing

---

* Haking vas at Spa, in touch with the German Commissioners there.

conditions.

I went over to see Foch. He told me he had not seen nor heard from Tiger for a fortnight. I brought him copies of all my papers and proposed changes in, and additions to, the military conditions, with all of which he agreed. I heard later that on my representations the Frocks replaced Article 45, which yesterday they cut out. Wonderful! Foch says he won't attend at Versailles next week when we meet the Boches unless he is told beforehand — and has approved — the military clauses.

There was no development during the day about Italy, but news came in that the Yugos were attacking the Austrians, and had taken Klagenfurt. So much for League of Nations. Then Tchaikovski, the President of the Archangel government, came to see me. He sees no reason why Kolchak should not reach Viatka, Vologda and even Petrograd this summer. All this is good.

On May 5 there appears:

The Tiger wanted to see me 9.30 a.m. When I got there he pretended he did not know what it was about, but I told him that it was Tardieu's paper of 5-10-15 years! He then remembered! After talking it over, he said that he would submit my note to his military advisers, but that he thought my proposal of retiring first from the south was impossible because the last troops to go would be those in Cologne, and these would have to retire through Holland! I told him that I had never thought that I would have to teach elementary French geography to a Prime Minister of France. Later on he admitted that he wished to God the soldiers were still running the show as we did it so much better than the Frocks.

At midday Foch rang me up to say he was coming up at once to see me, as he had most urgent business. Five minutes later he turned up, and this was to tell me that last night he had seen a complete book of the Treaty of Peace, that it was an immense volume, that it spoke of the "German Empire," commenced with the League of Peace, did not allot the German colonies to anyone, kept referring to the League of Peace on which (Foch declared) the Boches would sit, was a mass of cross references, paragraphs changed. Articles substituted, etc., etc., with net result that no one could possibly know what he was signing unless he could study the book as a whole. That nobody had studied it, that Tiger and Lloyd George had no notion what was in the book, and that consequently it was impossible to present the thing to the Boches until we had had a chance of examining the whole thing closely,

I entirely agreed, and said I would try and get a copy. A good talk with Bonar. He quite agreed that we must examine the Treaty as a whole, and we got a scrambled copy (the only one he had) from Hankey. Bonar Law says Lloyd George does not realize how serious the position is made by the withdrawal of Italy, and I know this is so.

Long afternoon in office. Every day instance after instance crops up of the shifting base on which we are building. Now the Esthonians — a small State — threaten to make a separate peace with the Bolsheviks, now the Finns are marching on Petrograd, now the Yugos are attacking the Austrians and have taken Klagenfurt, now the Rumanians are throwing the Hungarians over the Theiss, now the Bulgars are becoming truculent and have imprisoned some Greeks — and so on *ad infinitum*. And Paris remains paralytic and impotent, owing entirely to her own action of building on small States, and on Leagues of Nations without power to enforce decisions.

Sir Henry ushered in his record of the occurrences of Monday, May 5, with the remark: "An amazing day." And so indeed it would appear to have been. The German Plenipotentiaries, it must be remembered, had already in accordance with formal arrangements made their appearance in Versailles. They had been there since April 30, and they were patiently awaiting the handing over to them of a copy of the proposed Terms of Peace. This was to take place on the 7th, and Sir Henry's diary of the proceedings of the 5th runs as follows:

I began with a walk at 10 a.m. with Lloyd George and Borden. We discussed the Balkans, and Lloyd George is convinced that the Italians are going to carry out a coup in Bulgaria, where they have the 36th Division, 30,000 strong, and in Anatolia, where they seem to have landed in several places. They also are having some naval demonstration, as the Tiger told us later that they had seven battleships off Smyrna. I don't believe half these things, but Lloyd George greatly excited. I took the opportunity of urging that I be allowed to withdraw from the Caucasus, and I did good business. We finished our walk by sitting on a bench in Nite Place, studying strategy on a small map.

Then Lloyd George brought me to Wilson's house, where there was a meeting. Imperiali arrived just after to say that Orlando and

Sonnino would be back on Wednesday morning. I could not make out, and Imperiali did not say, on what terms they are coming back, but I should think on the Treaty of London, which my Cousin will not agree to. We shall see. Then our meeting — Wilson, Lloyd George and Clemenceau. I showed the military situation in the Balkans and in Asia Minor, and Lloyd George pressed for a *fait accompli* in settlement to be reached before the Italians come back on Wednesday. Lloyd George still wants the Italians to go to the Caucasus, although he told Wilson their presence there would create "Hell" — which pained my Cousin. Then he wants the Americans to take over Constantinople and Armenia, give Smyrna to the Greeks, Syria to the French and Palestine to us. With much nonsense, the above is in brief Lloyd George's proposal.

My Cousin was much pushed about over all this. I suppose he knows quite well he cannot supply the troops. However, he asked me how many he would require. I suggested one big American division for Constantinople and the Straits, and anything up to five for Armenia. This terrified him, and he asked me to see Bliss and Benson,* and himself telephoned to them to come to my office. Tiger amused and listening. My Cousin said he knew nothing about our coming away from the Caucasus and the Italians replacing us, and Lloyd George said he did. I said the Italian military and naval Mission must now be at Constantinople on its way to Batoum-Baku to make arrangements for taking over. My Cousin more useless and hopeless than ever.

I then went to the Astoria, and Bliss and Benson arrived. I explained the situation to them and gave them maps and figures. They both were agreed that Congress would not look at the idea of America going to Constantinople and Armenia, and said my Cousin would be crushed out over such a proposal,

I went to see Foch, as he rang me up. He showed me a letter he had written (one to each of Lloyd: George, Wilson and Tiger) asking for a copy of the Treaty it is proposed to give the Boches on Wednesday, as he had not seen it and, as Commander-in-Chief, he might have to act on its provisions. Foch is wise in writing.

Then, at 5 o'c. a meeting of British Empire Delegates, Lloyd George, Bonar Law, Barnes, Borden, Hughes, Massey, Botha, Smuts, Hope, self. Lloyd George read out some extracts from a "Summary of the Treaty," but he said it was the only copy, although he hoped his

---

* Admiral Benson was the U.SA. Naval Representative in Paris.

colleagues would have this Summary in the morning. As regards the Treaty itself, no one has ever seen it in its completed form, for it does not exist. Both Bonar Law and Smuts, who have been struggling to get completed copies, told me they had been unable; and both told me the whole thing was in a hopeless mess. In short, we are at this pass; we are going to hand out terms to the Boches at 3 p.m. on Wednesday, and to-night — at midnight — no one has ever seen them in their completed form. There is no British Empire Delegates meeting to-morrow, and the Treaty won't be printed till to-morrow night — if then, and even then incomplete. So that we are going to hand out terms to the Boches without reading them ourselves first. I don't think in all history this can be matched. Incidentally, at the B.E.D. meeting Lloyd George said that he thought the constitution of the League of Nations was a most "ridiculous and preposterous document." And the Treaty opens with the League! And there were serious differences of opinion at the meeting on several questions of *principle*! And this at this hour.

I spoke to Bonar Law, Smuts, Borden, Massey and others, and they were all equally at sea and hopeless. I saw Bob Cecil and Hankey after, and they also agreed that the whole thing was terrible. I dined at the Embassy, a big party. A.J.B. there, and I spoke to him about the Terms, and he, of course, like the others, has not seen them. He was openly joking, in front of ladies, etc, about the farce of the whole thing — and yet he has to sign!

At midnight Philip Kerr came to my room to say Lloyd George wanted me to advise as to how many troops it will be necessary to keep on the Rhine after peace is signed. I asked whether they were purely frontier guards, or were to have power of persuasion to keep the Boches up to the peace terms. Philip did not know.

Of next day's proceedings Wilson wrote in the diary:

I went across to see Lloyd George and had a long talk. He tells me the Tiger is watching for an opportunity to remove Foch and put in Pétain. Lloyd George asked me to see Foch and tell him that he, Lloyd George, had told both Tiger and Wilson that, in answer to Foch's letter of yesterday, the Marshal must be given a copy of the Terms, and to-day, and that Foch must be treated with the greatest consideration. Lloyd George said the difficulty of sending Foch a copy of the Treaty lies in the fact that it is not ready, and that he himself has never seen it, and that neither Bonar Law nor Smuts had

1919: April to June. The Peace Conference in Paris 229

been able to collect up a complete edition. And Lloyd George sees nothing odd in this, although we are to present the Terms to the Boches at 3 p.m. to-morrow!

After lunch I went to see Foch. He showed me Clemenceau's answer to his letter of yesterday. The Tiger said he would send him a copy of the Treaty as soon as one was ready. Foch very anxious and disturbed about our leaving the Rhine.

I went on to the last Plenary Conference before handing the Peace Terms to the Boches. Everybody there. Before we went to the Conference Room Lloyd George got hold of me and Venizelos, and told us the three Frocks had just decided to put the Greeks into Smyrna at once. Not a moment to be lost, as the three think Italy is up to tricks. I asked Lloyd George if he realized that this was starting another war, but he brushed that aside. We then went in to the Coherence. The Tiger began by saying that the first subject was "responsibilities for the war" but as no papers were ready he was not able to show what was proposed. Then Tardieu read a long, and very inaccurate. Summary (of which I got a copy at 2 p.m.) of the Peace Terms. While this was going on, I went round and collected Venizelos, Bliss, Belin and Hope and we all went off to my room at the Astoria. There we arranged the steps to be taken to put one or two Greek divisions into Smyrna. I insisted on the fact that it was a Greek affair, under Greek command, and that there was danger of opposition both from the Italians and the Turks, and that both Governments ought to be warned. I drew up some notes to which all agreed. Of course, the whole thing is mad,

A telephone message from the War Office says that wires just received from India say the Afghans have declared a jehad against us I If true, this is grave. I dined with A.J.B. I told him about Smyrna. He was upset about Afghanistan. Then at 10 o'c. I went down to Lloyd George and told him what we had done about Smyrna, and also about the Afghan business. He saw no danger in either.

At midnight to-night the copies of the Peace Terms are not yet out, but we present them at 3 o'c. to-morrow. After I had left the Conference this afternoon Foch made his appeal for the line of the Rhine. A.J.B., Ian Malcolm and Lloyd George all said he did it clearly and with dignity.

On May 7 there is the entry:

Lloyd George went to Wilson's house at 10.50 and told me to be there at 11 o'c. I walked across, and just before 11 o'c. was greatly amused to see Orlando drive up and walk in, knowing he was not expected. Lloyd George came out to the room I was in and said Orlando's unexpected appearance was very awkward — we were going to thrash out the Greek occupation of Smyrna. And he said the three Frocks would meet at his house at 12 o'c., and I was to be there and to bring Venizelos. So I turned up, and there were Lloyd George, Tiger, Wilson, Venizelos, Hope, Hankey and me. They went through my notes of yesterday and approved them. They want the move of Greeks to Smyrna to be secretly done — I said this was quite impossible — and they are not going to tell either Italy or Turkey until the whole thing is well on the way. All this is wrong, and after the others had gone I told Lloyd George he was making a lot of trouble with the Turks and the Italians for nothing; but he would not have it. Up to midday the printers had not finished the Treaty, which is to be given to the Boches at 3 p.m.

The meeting with the Boches took place at Versailles at 3 o'c,, and the Peace terms were handed over *never having been read by any of us in their entirety*, Rantzau made a somewhat truculent speech. Foch telephoned to me when he got back, and told me all his impressions of our feebleness and Boches' truculence, and the ridiculous power we have given them of writing their objections. "*Soyez tranquille, Henri, c'est une affaire de wagons.*"* And, of course, he is right. He was in great form, now that his opinion as to the necessity of the Rhine front has been recorded in yesterday's *Procés*.

Next day Wilson wrote:

Bonar Law told me that the Boche speech at Versailles yesterday made him tingle with rage, and that my Cousin came up to him after the Boches had gone and said, "I see that speech has had the same effect on you as on me; you are quite flushed." What fools to think that Boches can be other than Boches. When I read Rantzau's speech this morning I found it both clever and a castigation of our poor Frocks.

I wrote this morning to Hankey to say that, now that the Boches had been given a copy of the Treaty, perhaps it might be safe to let the British Military Section have a copy. He replied that he had not

---

* "Don't worry, Henry, it's a matter of wagons."

yet been able to get a copy himself. At a quarter to 6 p.m. I got my copy — i.e. 27 hours after the Boches.

At 6.15 I went down to see Sonnino. I told him I was coming out of the Caucasus on June 15, and that he had better adjust himself, and also make arrangements for taking over the Caspian Fleet. And I told him I was so going to inform Denikin. This woke him up, but he still seems determined to go there. He told me that my Cousin was making things very difficult.

Sir Henry now found that the question of the strength of the different contingents in the occupied territories was being referred to the Military Representatives at Versailles, with the object, as it seemed to him, of cutting out Foch. as he remarked significantly in his diary: "Foch and I are much too strong and cunning to be beaten over such a manœuvre," They settled between them that it would be safe to effect considerable reductions in numbers as soon as peace was actually signed. A wire from the Admiralty had in the meantime come to hand which indicated that no tonnage was available for carrying Greeks to Smyrna; but the Hellenic authorities had managed to find transports for themselves, and they had already embarked some troops in the Ægean, although "the Frocks" had not yet informed the Italians that they had presented Smyrna to the Greeks. "What rotten behaviour to a friend and Ally," is Wilson's comment in his diary.

On Saturday, the 10th, he wrote:

> Lloyd George and I discussed the Greek expedition to Smyrna. It now appears that Venizelos is producing shipping for 14,000 men, and will be ready to push off his leading troops on Monday. I begged Lloyd George to tell the Italians. I told him that nobody could understand our not telling one of our greatest Allies, and that no one could defend the three Frocks having secret meetings to carry out this coup and not telling the Italians what they were doing. Lloyd George agreed, and said he would speak to the other two this morning.
>
> Then he discussed with me the three accursed Americans who have been travelling in Ireland and declaring that they had a mandate from Paris. Lloyd George told me that he had agreed to their going, because House had assured him it would be a great help to the President as regards the Irish vote in America. Lloyd George therefore, in order to help the President, agreed to these men going

over to study the situation on the spot, and said he would see them on the return. In view, however, of their scandalous speeches in Ireland, Lloyd George was writing this morning to House to say he would not see them on their return, and he had wired to the Viceroy (through Bonar Law) to deport the brutes. This is all tight.

At 3 o'c. we met in Lloyd George's house — Lloyd George, Cousin, Tiger, Venkzelos, Bliss, Admiral Le Bon, Admiral Fuller and self. Venizelos and Fuller agreed that the Greeks could sail from Kavalla on Tuesday morning, and, in spite of my protests and Bliss's, it was agreed that the Italians should not be told about this until Monday afternoon, that the Turks should be given 36 hours' notice before the Greek landing that they were to hand over the forts to French marines, that the Italians were not to land, that the Turks should be told 12 hours before the landing that the Greeks were coming. I also advised that Orlando should be asked to wire to his admiral at Smyrna to place himself under Calthorpe's orders, and told not to land. The whole thing is mad and bad, and I hope it won't lead to any massacres of our people in the interior. Venizelos is using the three Frocks for his own ends. After the three Frocks had gone, Bliss, Le Bon, Fuller and I had a talk, and we all agreed we were doing a stupid thing.

Of a meeting which had taken place in Lloyd George's absence at President Wilson's house on May 11, he remarked:

> The report of this meeting is a very disgraceful document. It shows positive hatred of Italy (an Ally) on the part of my Cousin, who threatened to come out in the Press again. A.J.B. pleaded very sanely for moderation and give and take, and the Tiger urged importance of telling the Italians, as I have all along. But Cousin was in an outrageous mood. He has ordered a second battleship over to the Mediterranean.

Admiral Calthorpe had been told to prevent the Greeks from sailing for another 48 hours. "Poor Calthorpe," wrote Sir Henry, "he gets contradictory orders every five minutes." For it had been decided by "the Frocks" later in the day to cancel the 48 hours' delay, and, in addition, to allow the Italians also to land at Smyrna. "Was ever such an exhibition of vacillation, weakness and duplicity" was Wilson's comment. Sir Henry also learnt that "the

Frocks" now proposed to divide up the whole of Turkey between the French, the Italians, the Americans and the Greeks. "This," he remarked in the diary, "will have a disastrous effect in our Mohammedan countries." Then, on the 14th, he had a conversation with Diaz in connexion with the question of the Caucasus, and he acquired the impression that the Italians were now thinking better of their intention of taking over that theatre of disturbance; so, to make sure that there should be no misunderstanding, he intimated to Diaz that he was going to begin shipping away our troops in the following month.

On the 15th the entry occurs in the diary:

> Across to Lloyd George, where I found that he had named me as his representative to discuss with Tardieu, who is Tiger's man, the zones of military occupation in Syria. When I asked why I was put on to do Foreign Office work, Lloyd George told me that Tiger had refused his first selection of Milner, because Milner shut his eyes like a lizard. The Tiger told me later that he thought also that Milner had too much German blood, whereas I had too much blood!
>
> We then went over to Cousin's house and, with four Frocks and military and naval experts, we discussed the military terms for Austria. We had given Austria a 40,000 voluntary army. The Frocks thought this was excessive, and Tiger thought 12 to 15,000 ample. The population of the new Austria is only 8 millions. Tiger said soldiers were always making wars, whereas the Frocks made peace. I here interjected the remark that there were 21 wars going on at this moment, which delighted Lloyd George but upset the Tiger and my Cousin! Finally settled that we soldiers should see how many troops the other small States should have, as I pointed out that it was manifestly unfair to cripple Austria and to allow Czechos, Yugos and Rumanians to have enormous armies.
>
> Montagu* turned up from London, and very angry with Lloyd George about cutting up Turkey, in which he is quite right. He says it means eternal war with the Mohammedan world.

The highly inconvenient quarrel with Afghanistan made the CJ.G.S. feel all the more anxious about the unfriendly attitude that

---

* Mr. Montagu was Secretary of State for India.

was being taken up by the Allies towards the Turks, and he observed in his diary:

> We are in for serious trouble with the Mohammedan world, and we don't want to increase our troubles by breaking up Turkey and dividing her amongst a lot of people — Greeks, Italians, French and Americans — who can't even govern themselves.

Foch, who had been for a tour of inspection on the Rhine, returned to Paris on the 19th, and he was at once instructed to be ready to march into Germany by the 27th, as it seemed very likely that the Germans would refuse to accept the Terms. Wilson had in the meantime held his first meeting with M. Tardieu about Syria; but they had made no progress, for Tardieu was found to possess no authority for discussing the question of the boundary that was to be established between the French and British spheres, the question upon which, in Sir Henry's opinion, the whole problem in reality hinged, and he wrote in his diary on the 21st:

> Lloyd George telephoned for me at 2.30 p.m. Winston was there. Lloyd George told me that he had shown the Tiger my map and my proposed boundary for Syria. On this the Tiger had exploded and accused us of bad and broken faith. On that Lloyd George had exploded and said that the Tiger would have that boundary or none, and that, if he did not accept, then not another soldier would be allowed into Syria. There was a first-class dog-fight, during which Tiger said Walter Long had promised the French half the Mesopotamian oil! Lloyd George asked me if I had ever heard of this. Of course, never. Whereupon Lloyd George wrote at once to Tiger and said that arrangement was cancelled. They met again at Cousin's at 4 o'c., but as Tardieu was not there I went away.
>
> I went twice to Cousin's later again, but each time the meeting was put off. The old Tiger pretending to be very angry with me, and Tardieu trying to get me to agree to a relief in Syria without first defining our boundaries, which is absurd.

This appears next day, May 22:

> Meeting at Lloyd George's at 11 a.m. on Syria. Lloyd George gave a long and rather discursive lecture on the Sykes-Picot and other

1919: April to June. The Peace Conference in Paris 235

arrangements and meetings of last winter, ending by stating that he stood firm on my proposed frontier. The Tiger answered and flatly refused that line. I then said that, as no agreement had been reached, Allenby remained in supreme command, and I asked Tiger not to send out any more troops unless Allenby asked for them. The Tiger did not answer, so I wrote him a letter to this effect, and sent Allenby two wires giving him full powers. I had long talks with Milner, and then A.J.B., and impressed on both the necessity for sending out a Mixed Commission. They agreed. I pressed this also upon Lloyd George, but he rather favoured Americans going alone. I think this is frankly stupid, but I met him at dinner and he told me he had changed and was now going to press for the Commission.

On the 23rd there is the entry:

> I went to see Foch. He does not think the Boches will sign, and he does not think my Cousin will agree to march into Germany. He thinks my Cousin will end as "arbitrator" between us and the Boches! This would be the devil, but I don't see how this can be done as the man is up to the neck in the Terms.
> At the Quai d'Orsay this afternoon I spoke to Tardieu about the necessity of sending out a Commission to Syria; and he agreed to reference to a Commission, but thought they ought to sit here in Paris.

Wilson heard on the 24th that the India Office had given permission to the Viceroy to move troops into Afghanistan so as to occupy Jellalabad. He had cabled to General Monro, the Commander-in-Chief, some days before for more information with regard to the matter; but no reply had as yet been received, and the India Office had taken this serious step without his having been consulted. He, moreover, ascertained that the War Office likewise had not been consulted, and he also learnt that Churchill had already pointed out to the Prime Minister that this new war was being embarked on without the Cabinet having given its sanction. Arrangements had been made by Sir Henry to send out some reinforcements to India on account of the Afghan imbroglio; but he had experienced great difficulty in finding the troops, owing to the depleted condition of the army and to the number of tasks oversea to which it was already committed. While recognizing that aggressive action on the part of the Ameer might render hostilities unavoidable, he was opposed to a campaign if it could possibly be avoided.

The German answer on the subject of the Peace Terms came to hand on May 29, and the document was discussed on the following afternoon at a special meeting of those of the Cabinet Ministers and Dominions Ministers who happened to be in Paris at the moment. Sir Henry refers to the discussion that took place in his diary, and we read:

> It was very clear that the feeling was that the Boches had made out a good case, and in several particulars an unanswerable case. The Frocks are in a beastly mess. The Boches have done exactly what I forecast — they have driven a coach and four through our Terms, and then have submitted a complete set of their own, based on the 14 points, which are much more coherent than ours.

He indeed speedily came to the conclusion that the Terms would have to undergo considerable modification. The Prime Minister gave a dinner that evening to the Cabinet, several members of which had come over on the last day of the month, and Wilson, who was a guest at this feast, recorded in his diary:

> For three hours after dinner we discussed the Peace Terms and the Boche answer, and it was amazing what unanimity there was in criticizing *all* the Terms. This will put Lloyd George in a very difficult position.

A Special meeting of the British Empire Delegation was, moreover, held in Paris on June 1, and here again Wilson found that the Terms were not finding approval. After the discussion was over. Sir Henry had a long talk with the Prime Minister, who was beginning to realize the awkwardness of the situation. As Sir Henry remarked in referring to the matter in his diary:

> If he goes contrary to the wishes of his Cabinet they won't sign; if, on the other hand, he tries to change the original terms and to modify them sensibly he will be in grips with Clemenceau.

The C.I.G.S. had never agreed to the occupation period of the

1919: April to June. The Peace Conference in Paris 237

Rhine Provinces lasting for so long as 15 years, he now proposed to reduce this period to two years, and on the 3rd, after his dining with Lloyd George, there appears in the diary:

> We had a long talk. To-day he had reopened the question of the Boche eastern front, and had insisted on a plebiscite for Silesia and Danzig. In this he was violently opposed by my Cousin, who realized that a plebiscite would go against the Poles, which did not suit him as he has two million Pole voters in the United States. Lloyd George had to be very rough with him, and to point out that self-determination was one of his own 14 points. To-morrow Lloyd George is going to tackle the 15 years occupation of the Rhine Provinces. This will be difficult also. Just before I left at 2 o'c. Lloyd George suddenly asked me whether I would rather have a Peerage or be a Field-Marshal. I replied that I did not want either, but, if he was determined to give me one or the other, I would infinitely prefer Field-Marshal.

On June 4 the entry appears:

> The Poles won't allow us to repatriate Russian prisoners through Poland, Paris gets more snubbed every day. The Frocks, without military assistance, feed on a strength of 30,000 for the Austrian Army. The poor Frocks still seem to think that someone is listening to them! It is pathetic!

Wilson wrote on the 9th:

> Orlando has gone to Italy to discuss the Frocks' final offer about putting Fiume under the League of Nations, and Hankey does not think they will accept. Then no *accord* has been reached as to reparations, or occupation, or even eastern frontiers. So Hankey is very sad, and I am very glad. We shall never do any good till Paris crashes.
> At 2 o'c. I went to meeting at Cousin's house. It was a depressing meeting. Different people abused different Small States, whereas the real blame lies with Paris. I whispered to Lloyd George: "It really is no use abusing this or that Small State. The root of evil is that the *Paris writ does not run*." Lloyd George came straight out with this, to the consternation of my Cousin, who, in order to prevent us soldiers seeing the depth to which he and the Frocks have fallen in incompetence and impotence, said he thought the soldiers could now

leave. And he and the other three Frocks moved off into another room. Yes, Paris is very near a crash this week. If Orlando comes back with a refusal as regards Flume, I think Paris will crash, and the Boches won't sign. What a business.

Dined with Lloyd George. During dinner we got Orlando's answer about Fiume. It is a flat refusal. This is a serious affair. It will go near to breaking up the Conference, and if the Boches hear of it — and they will — it wall stiffen them against signing. Personally I think the Italians are right in their refusal to give up Flume to a Yugo. The poor Frocks, who try and build on Small States and impotent Leagues of Nations! Poor things!

Wilson now paid another flying visit to London, as he was anxious to obtain the Cabinet's assent to the Allied forces at Archangel making a move south-eastwards for the purpose of joining hands with Kolchak. In this he was successful and the necessary instructions were sent to Ironside.

On returning to Paris he found the cosmopolitan horde of officials assembled there to be in considerable doubt as to whether the Germans would accept the Peace Terms, which, in a somewhat modified form, were to be represented to the Plenipotentiaries from Berlin on the 16th. "It is now seven months since the Armistice was signed, and practically nothing is settled in any theatre," he wrote in his diary. The Germans were, moreover, engaging in hostilities with the new Baltic States, and it looked as if the Allied forces on the Rhine would probably be called upon to advance farther into Germany by way of bringing pressure.

Wilson wrote in the diary on June 16:

> Lloyd George and I discussed the Italians going to the Caucasus and our attitude generally towards them, and I urged that we were foolish to quarrel with them just to please my Cousin. Lloyd George agreed, and sent for Sonnino to have a talk.
>
> At a quarter to 1 o'c. I was sent for to Cousin's house. As I walked in I met the Frocks coming downstairs. There was evidently trouble. Lloyd George and Clemenceau and Cousin brought me into a room. It appears that Foch, had been recalled from Luxembourg, had been summoned to Cousin's. On' arrival there he had been kept waiting, and this, after his recall from Luxembourg, seems to have been too much for him, and he went off. The Frocks wanted to know

1919: April to June. The Peace Conference in Paris 239

what this meant. I said I had not seen Foch so I did not know. I told them that, although Foch was quite ready to make his 90 kilometre jump to the Weser, I rather gathered that he did not like going to Berlin, and that he had several times told me that he had never been given clear directions by the Frocks, and therefore did not know what they wanted. At this, all three Frocks swore they had repeatedly told Foch what they wanted, and that this included going to Berlin. This was news to me, and I pointed out that this would require a good deal of consideration as the whole of the railways would be in Boche hands. After Lloyd George and Tiger had gone, I impressed this strongly on Cousin. He is hostile to Foch and says the old man won't understand the Frocks. The Frocks said that, if Foch would not carry out their wishes, they must get someone who would. They are going to summon Foch again at 3 o'c. I wonder. And what a way to get the Boches to sign — to unload Foch!

This appears next day:

Charlie Grant[*] in to see me early. He ran out yesterday afternoon to see Weygand at Versailles. Weygand, of course, exploded at the French treatment of Foch, and asked Charlie to thank me for my loyalty and friendship, and Charlie said his reference to me was most touching. I had told Charlie to take down a copy of my short note of yesterday afternoon to Lloyd George, and Weygand was much touched by this.

Lunch with A.J.B. I discussed with him what would happen, and what we should do, if Bele Kuhn[†] refused to withdraw his Hungarians from attacking Czechos, in accordance with Frocks' wire of a couple of days ago, when they ordered Czechos, Hungarians and Rumanians to withdraw to the frontiers defined by Paris. It is certain to me that no one will obey, and we have no way of enforcing obedience except to ask the Rumanians, who have six divisions along the Theiss, entirely against the orders of Paris, to march on Budapest — which, of course, they won't do without some *quid pro quo* which we can't give. Oh, what a mess Small States and Leagues of Nations with no power to enforce decrees has landed us in.

---

[*] Colonel C. J. C. Grant was on the staff in Paris.

[†] A Bolshevist Magyar who was now in control of Hungary.

Clemenceau sent for Wilson on June 18 and they had a prolonged conversation. Clemenceau had found that Pétain agreed with Foch and Wilson that an advance far into Germany would be most difficult to carry out, and Sir Henry now told the Tiger that our Navy could do nothing at Danzig or Wilhelmshaven, owing to guns and mines. "He was as nice as ever to me" appears in the diary, "but feels he is in a tight place and so turns to the soldiers, as Frocks always do" At a further interview on the following day the Tiger told Sir Henry the good news that he had had a most satisfactory discussion with Foch, and that the difficulties between the two were happily at an end. Doubt, in the meantime, still prevailed as to whether the Germans would sign the Treaty, and Wilson was inclined to hope that they would decline. He gives reasons for this view in his diary, the passage reading as follows:

> I don't think that the Boche signature, in the present discredited condition of Paris, is worth having. I am sure that, if he signs, he does so with no intention of carrying out his engagements, and I am equally sure that, after signature, the Allies will never agree to employ force again — so the whole thing would be a farce. After another display of force and decision and co-operation on the part of the Allies, not only would the Boche signature be more valuable, but all the Small States would come to heel also.

Robertson arrived from Cologne on the 20th on purpose to discuss various matters with the French and the C.I.G.S. in connexion with the contemplated advance beyond the Rhine, and that same afternoon news arrived in Paris of the fall of the Schiedmann Government in Berlin. A "sort of Council of War" was thereupon held at the French War Office at 5 o'clock, of which Wilson writes in his diary:

> Foch opened by describing his two bounds to the Weser, and then a halt, pending further reinforcements and separate armistices with Wurtemburg, Baden and Bavaria. He said he would be on the Weser in 15 days (200 kilometres from the Rhine). Robertson agreed with Foch, and said the Weser was the farthest he could go, and even to get there the Boches must help in the railways, telegraphs and telephones. He also

1919: April to June. The Peace Conference in Paris 241

pleaded that the Frocks should ponder whether they should go even that far, unless they were pretty certain that this advance would gain their end, i.e. signature of Peace Terms. Bliss followed, and in substance agreed that we could not go beyond the Weser, except Foch's conditions were fulfilled. Cavallero said that he had referred to *Commando Supremo* to know what assistance the Italians could give as against Bavaria, but in view of Italy's many commitments and dangers he was afraid it would be very slight, Pétain agreed that the Weser was as far as we could go, and added that it was now too late to co-ordinate combined operations of Poles, Czechos and Italians, and that this ought to have been done before.

Clemenceau summed up by saying that it was now clear that all military opinion was unanimous that we could not go beyond the Weser unless we made separate terms with Baden, Wurtemburg and Bavaria, or unless we were strengthened in force. A.J.B. agreed. So did Cousin. We finally decided that my Cousin should draft *une formule** for Foch, which he could present to Baden, Wurtemburg and Bavaria for a separate armistice and peace.

Tidings on the day following reached Paris of the outrage that had been committed by the naval personnel on board the German warships lying at Scapa Flow, in scuttling their vessels. Reports were also received by the War Office in London to the effect that Kolchak's advance had been checked by Bolshevist forces, and that he was now in retreat. Two days later, on the 22nd, the German answer was received with regard to the modified Peace Terms which had been transmitted to their representatives on the 16th. It raised various objections . But the reply of the Allies was couched in uncompromising language, and was to the effect that the matter had been fully considered, and that they had no intention of receding from the position they had taken up. The question therefore at once arose as to whether the troops on the Rhine should advance across the line of demarcation on the evening of

---

* "A plan."

242   *1919: April to June. The Peace Conference in Paris*

the 23rd, when the time limit that had been allowed would have expired. Sir Henry, as it happened, had made arrangements to cross the Channel to England on that evening, travelling via Havre. His record in the diary of the day's doings is of special interest, and it runs as follows:

> I was writing and working early, 6.30, and soon after 7 o'c. Hankey came to say another Boche wire had come in, asking for 48 hours. He had been round to see Clemenceau, who was firm in wanting the move in at 7 p.m. to-night, and Cousin, who was in favour of granting the 48 hours, and Lloyd George who was wobbly. A meeting to be held in Lloyd George's room at 9 a.m.
>
> At 8.15 Lloyd George telephoned for me to go over, and he and Hankey and I breakfasted alone. I was strongly in favour of not budging an inch, partly because Boche understands no other argument, partly because of the Scapa incident, partly because of the Small States, partly because of ourselves — we want a tonic. I think I persuaded Lloyd George.
>
> Just before I started at 12.20 for Havre, Winston told me the Frocks had refused the Boche request for an extension of 48 hours. Good. I got to Rouen at 4 o'c., had a short sleep, and then Asser[*] arrived to discuss what troops he could send up the Rhine. Then on to Havre. Dinner at 8.30. Just as P.T. and I were finishing, all the sirens and whistles went off, and we found that at last the Boches had agreed to sign unconditionally on Wednesday or Thursday.
>
> P.T. and I went for a walk in the town. Great crowds, but on the whole very quiet and orderly. We went into a Chapel which was lit up, crowds passing in and out and looking at a figure (lit up) of the Virgin Mary. So, after five years of war here comes peace at last. And yet I am as certain as I can be that the Boches have no intention of carrying out our Peace Terms, and in my judgment this ending is a disaster. Rough passage.

From Southampton Sir Henry proceeded by motor to Oxford; and he spent the night in that city in preparation for the ceremony that was to take place on the following day, when he was to receive the Honorary Degree of D.C.L. of the University. The company to share this distinction with him included General Joffre (he was not

---

[*] General Asser was commanding the British troops in France.

1919: April to June. The Peace Conference in Paris 243

yet a Marshal of France), Sir D. Haig, Sir D. Beatty and General Pershing, as well as some others. When the procession, headed by the Chancellor of the University, Lord Curzon, moved from the Hall of Trinity College to the Sheldonian Theatre, it passed through a dense mass of citizens and undergraduates, the soldiers and sailors being greeted with uproarious cheers. "A great honour," Wilson wrote of his experiences in his diary, "and a delightful day," He arrived back in Paris on June 28, just in time to drive out to Versailles to be present at the ceremony of the signing of the Peace Treaty. This historic event he describes as follows in his diary:

> We were sent round by front gate, and a very pretty sight it was driving up, with Lancers and Infantry lining the streets, and with their colours. Then into the Palace, and through some anteroom into the *Galerie des Glaces*.* About 1,000 people, of whom I daresay 150 were ladies — which I thought all wrong. Presently the Boches — four, of whom only two were signatories — were sort of half marched in by some six Allied officers.
> The moment they sat down, Clemenceau rose and said they would be asked to sign and then to carry out loyally. This was translated into Boche for the Boches. They said nothing, but rose and walked over to the table where the book was, and then straight back to their seats. Then some seventy Allied Frocks signed. Then Clemenceau declared the meeting closed, and the Boches walked out with the Allied officers. I have never seen a less impressive ceremony. The room was much too full, a crowd of smart ladies, a constant buzz of conversation, the whole thing unreal, shoddy, poor to a degree. The fountains played and some guns fired, and we went away. Considerable, but very undemonstrative, crowds. And the thing was over. It only took 45 minutes — from 3.10 to 3.55 p.m.
> I went up to Tit Willow's with him and I had tea there, and we discussed a number of problems put to Versailles by the Frocks. The real bald truth is that the Boche signatures represent nobody and nothing, that no peace has been made even with Germany, that the rest of Europe is in chaos, that the Frocks have proved their collective incompetence, as I always was sure they must seeing that they based themselves on small States, i.e. the curse of Europe, and on a League

---

* The Hall of Mirrors.

of Nations without power to enforce decree, i.e. a patent of impotency and incompetency.

On the following day the Prime Minister started from the French capital for home, and he was accompanied on his journey, which from the time of the steamer coming alongside the jetty at Folkestone became a triumphal progress, by General Botha, Mr. Hughes and Sir Henry. Great crowds had assembled about the pierhead in anticipation of Lloyd George's arrival, and when driving through the town he made Wilson sit beside hin, so that his military adviser during the past seventeen months should share the citizens' welcome. They proceeded to London by special train, and on arrival at Victoria the Prime Minister was met by the King, the Prince of Wales and several of the Cabinet Ministers, and he was moreover accorded an enthusiastic reception by the vast multitude that had gathered about the station. "I am so glad," Wilson entered in his diary, "and I wrote to him to-night and told him so."

Chapter XXIX – 1919: July to December

The Russian situation — Dinner to Wilson at the House of Commons — The "Lightning" Railway Strike — Problem of the Territorial Army — The question of Constantinople — Prospect of serious industrial unrest.

Many questions awaited investigation and decision at the War Office when Sir Henry returned from Paris, but, owing to his having arranged to receive the Honorary Degree of LL.D. at Trinity College in Dublin, he went over at once to stay for a couple of days with Lord French at the Viceregal Lodge. Degrees were duly conferred on the Lord-Lieutenant and himself, and they afterwards paid a visit of inspection to the Alexandra College. "Coming away in the motor, Johnnie got boohed and hissed by students in the National College opposite," Wilson noted in his diary, "a most disgraceful thing."

He makes particular reference in the diary to a conversation with the .Secretary of State, Mr. Churchill, on the subject of setting up a Minister of Defence; this project was also discussed exhaustively when he went with Churchill to stay for a few days with the Prime Minister at the latter's Welsh home, and of what passed at Criccieth he wrote in his diary:

> Winston and I warmly advocated. Lloyd George put up all the objections he could think of; but they were not very strong. One of the new S. of S.'s great difficulties will be to find three good Under-

Secretaries. Winston, who already sees himself Minister of Defence, suggested Hugh Cecil for War Office, Freddie Guest for Air, and no one as yet for Admiralty.

As we were finishing this discussion, a wire came from Balfour asking me to go over to Paris at once, as they were going to discuss war on Hungary, Versailles having reported that they were doubtful if the Allies could take Budapest. After some talk, during which I expressed strong views that, either Paris should force friend as well as foe to respect its decrees, or else should issue no decrees at all (I pointed out that Poland, Rumania, Czechos, Yugos and Greeks ignored Paris, just as much as did Russia or Hungary), a wire was sent in this sense to Balfour, and my immediate presence is not required.

The problems furnished by the existing situation in Russia and by the disturbed condition of Ireland were also debated, and Whson in his diary mentions the Prime Minister having consulted him on the subject of a scheme for Dominion Home Rule. Sir Henry poured ridicule on this project and, according to the diary, me Prime Minister remarked, "I absolutely agree that it is all pure nonsense." The C.I.G.S. was back in London in time to be invested with the G.C.B. by the King in private audience on July 15 and he was present next day at a pleasant little ceremony at the War Office, where General Pershing presented the American War Medal to the Secretary of State, to Lord Milner, and to certain other civilians who had been closely connected in prominent capacities with the department during the war.

The triumphal march of the army and of Allied contingents through the streets of the metropolis had been arranged to take place on the 19th, and Marshal Foch, who was to ride at the head of the French troops, arriving on the previous day in anticipation of the pageant, received an enthusiastic greeting from the crowds in the streets, as he drove with Haig, Wilson and Weygand from Victoria to the Carlton Hotel. Wilson was on the King's dais in front of Buckingham Palace during the procession next day, and a meeting was afterwards held at 10 Downing Street to consider Foch's proposals for occupying Budapest. It was, however, agreed that the decisions taken at Paris must be enforced on friend and foe alike, and that the Rumanians, who were still on the Theiss, must be compelled to go back to the frontier between Rumania and

1919: July to December 247

Hungary, decided upon at Paris — the line which Sir Henry had taken on the subject throughout. A great dinner took place at the Carlton Hotel on July 20, with the Prince of Wales in the chair; on the following morning Wilson accompanied Foch to Victoria on his departure for Paris, and this appears in the diary:

> He went off beaming, after a wonderfully successful visit; he told me of his visit to Englemere yesterday and of his enormous admiration for the Little Man [Lord Roberts].[*]

Somewhat serious news came to hand from Archangel immediately afterwards, for a proportion of the Russian troops serving under Ironside had mutinied and had joined the Bolshevists. All hope of a junction between the Allied forces assembled about the White Sea and Kolchak's tumultuary array was at an end, for the latter was in full retreat eastwards. So the C.I.G.S. hastened to make arrangements for the dispatch of transports to the White Sea to effect the withdrawal of the troops. Kolchak's tragic failure, synchronizing as it did with the disorders which had broken out amongst the Allied forces in North Russia, was the more disappointing, in that Denikin was making remarkable progress in the south just at this very time. That enterprising Russian commander had occupied the great industrial city of Kharkov at the beginning of the month, and he was now preparing to advance on Kiev. Wilson made up his mind that, apart from carrying out the withdrawal of the Allied forces in safety from the north, the wisest course would be henceforward to

---

[*] The practice, occasionally followed by Foch and Wilson, of exchanging their respective head-gear when in private, has been mentioned in an earlier chapter. One day, during the French Marshal's brief stay at the Carlton Hotel, he was sitting in his private room with Wilson, he with Wilson's "billy-cock" hat on and Wilson (who was in plain clothes) wearing Foch's képi. There was a knock at the door and in response to the summons to enter, a stalwart Grenadier marched in and presented a letter from Buckingham Palace to Foch. Foch, the billy-cock hat sitting low on his brow as it was too big for him, accepted the letter, and the Grenadier, with the imperturbable stolidity that was to be expected in a representative of the Brigade of Guards, saluted and marched out again. But he probably found something to tell his comrades in the barrack-room when he got back.

concentrate effort upon assisting Denikin with munitions and war material.

He motored down to Cambridge with Lady Wilson on the 23rd, to receive the Honorary Degree of LL.D. This distinction was conferred at the same time upon General Pershing, the four British Army commanders, Rawlinson, Birdwood, Home and Cavan, and Admirals Sturdee and Wemyss, besides some others, with the usual ceremonies. But Sir Henry was to be the recipient of what, in view of its unusual nature, amounted to an even higher compliment, for on the following evening he was entertained at dinner in the Guest Room of the House of Commons by some 200 Members of Parliament, including several Cabinet Ministers, with the Prime Minister in the chair.

Mr. Lloyd George proposed the health of the guest of the evening in one of his happiest speeches, making special reference to Wilson's transcendent services in connexion with ensuring that the Expeditionary Force should be capable of proceecHng to the Continent as a complete and fully equipped army at the shortest notice, to the unique influence that he had exerted in maintaining cordial relations between the French and British staffs during the progress of the great conflict, and to the pre-eminent part which he had played in the establishing of the Supreme War Council at Versailles. The Prime Minister spoke of Wilson as "never daunted, never dismayed, never despairing, never downhearted, calm, courageous, full of resolution, full of fortitude, and encouraging everybody to do his work" during the critical days of March and April, 1918. He concluded by intimating to the company present that he had His Majesty's authority for making known that Sir Henry had been created a Field-Marshal.

Wilson acknowledged the honour that had been done him in a speech which was at once witty and moving. Amongst playful references to past experiences, he told the tale (related in vol. I, page 19) of the telegraph boy in Victoria Barracks, Belfast. He spoke feelingly of his two great friends in the French Army, Marshal Foch and General Huguet, and of how much the British nation owed to those gallant soldiers. He acknowledged his indebtedness to the three War Ministers, Lord Derby, Lord Milner and Mr. Churchill, under whom he had been carrying on his duties since he attained his present position as C.I.G.S. He referred to the exceptional services of three British soldiers during the anxious war-time that was now at an end. Lord French, Sir D. Haig, and "Hanky Panky" (Sir M. Hankey) "without whom we might have won the War, but without whom we certainly should not have won the Peace." And he concluded with a warm tribute to what Mr. Lloyd George had accomplished as head of the British Government, under conditions for which there was no parallel in the country's history in the past.

Sir Henry, as was indeed his normal custom when honours were accorded him, only makes very brief reference to this dinner in his diary; but he was, not unnaturally, much gratified at so unmistakable a mark of respect and admiration being paid him at the hands of leading fellow-citizens, and also by the congratulations that were showered upon him by friends and acquaintances on his promotion to the highest rank in the British Army.* "An immense number of letters all day," he wrote in his diary on July 25. " It is very touching, and it all makes me feel I want to hide. The same in the War Office, and I *cannot* realize that I am a Field-Marshal."

But the many indications of esteem and popularity of which he was at this time finding himself the recipient did not prevent his passing long hours, day after day, in his office at Whitehall. He was at the moment much preoccupied with the position of affairs in Russia, and he now arranged that Rawlinson should proceed to Archangel so as to exercise a general supervision over the withdrawal of the Allied force. He mentions in his diary on the 29th attending a meeting of the Cabinet with regard to this subject:

> For the first time, we examined the Russian question as a whole and we came to certain decisions, notably to clear out of North Russia altogether, to restrict our efforts in Siberia to small missions, to help

---

* Sir Henry was the first officer brought up in the Rifle Brigade, not of Royal blood, to receive the baton. The great Duke of Wellington had, when already a Field-Marshal, become Colonel-in-Chief of the Rifle Brigade; but the Iron Duke's only previous association with the regiment lay in his having had battalions belonging to it under his orders during the Peninsular War and at Waterloo.

Denikin all we can.

That evening he proceeded to Victoria to meet Foch, for the Marshal had crossed the Channel again for the purpose of receiving his baton as British Field-Marshal at the hands of the King, and he wrote in his diary next day:

> Foch and I drove to the Palace alone at 10.30. The King made him a charming little speech, and then handed him the baton. Foch in reply recalled my first visit to see him in 1908, and said that neither General of Brigade Wilson nor General of Division Foch would then have believed that, at the end of the greatest war in the world, they would both stand in front of the King as Marshals of England. Then, later, Foch drove to the Guildhall in a King's carriage, getting a great reception. He made charming allusions to me in his speech. Then luncheon at the Mansion House.

A list of the peerages and baronetcies that were being conferred on our foremost sailors and soldiers for their services during the War appeared in the Press on August 6, and Wilson was awarded a baronetcy and a grant of £10,000.[*] Two days later he proceeded to Belfast to be present at a great march of Ulstermen who had taken part in the war, past the Lord-Lieutenant.

> Some 36,000 Ulstermen marched past in perfect order, all closed up, and I never saw a finer, more independent, well dressed lot of men. An enormous number of them had been wounded, and the whole of them were volunteers.

On returning to London, the Field-Marshal found the Cabinet somewhat exercised about the possibility of massacres taking place in Transcaucasia when the British troops should withdraw. The Italians had changed their minds about assuming charge of this disturbed region; but all preparations had nevertheless been made for the evacuation of Milne's force to begin on the 15th, and Wilson insisted that the arrangement should not be altered. He

---

[*] As supporters to his coat of arms Sir Henry chose a Rifleman, and a figure of Ulster holding a shield with the Red Hand emblazoned on it.

wrote on the subject in his diary:

> It is impossible for us to remain on. The cost, even of a brigade of one white and three native battalions, runs to 12 millions a year. A couple of divisions would be from £50-60,000,000 a year. Nor could we find the men, as we have not enough to garrison our own Empire.

While troubled as to possible eventualities in Circassia and Georgia, and disinclined to sanction complete withdrawal of Milne's troops, the Cabinet was importunately pressing for reduction of expenditure on the fighting Services, and the decision was come to to allow only a total of £75,000,000 to the War Office and the Air Ministry. So Sir Henry noted in the diary:

> I am preparing a paper — P. de B. gave me the draft last night — of what troops we require to keep our four storm-centres quiet — Ireland, Egypt, Mesopotamia, India. From these requirements we can build, and not from the allotment of an arbitrary sum.

On the following day he started for the Rhine with Churchill and the rest of the Army Council, to inspect the troops, barracks, establishments and so forth, and on the conclusion of this duty he motored through firom Cologne to Versailles in one day — 570 kilometres — driving his car him self. A number of questions required settlement, particularly the problem of what troops were to be told off to garrison the areas — Silesia, Schleswig and East Prussia — where it was proposed to hold plebiscites. The question of the repatriation, or otherwise, of German prisoners of war had also to be dealt with. Sir Henry spent several days in Paris and at Versailles discussing these questions. His view as regards the plebiscite areas was that these ought to be allotted to different Allies, so that the inconveniences and risks of an intermingling of contingents should be avoided, and this appears in the diary on August 25:

> We had another morning meeting in A.J.B.'s room at 11 a.m., and I got him to agree to bring up the Boche prisoners question at the conference. This he did at 3.30 at the Quai d'Orsay, when I was present; but no decision was reached, as the Tiger wanted much more

information.

On the 25th he wrote:

> Worked till 10.30. Then up to Paris to a meeting in A.J.B.'s room. There we discussed a note sent by President Wilson to the Sultan, threatening the Turks with all sorts of penalties if there are any more Armenian massacres. A piece of impotent impudence. The Americans are not even at war with the Turks.
> A meeting at Quai d'Orsay — Tiger, A.J.B., Polk,* Tittoni.† (Foch and Weygand both away). I pressed hard for solution of Boche prisoners, but got put off again, which maddened me. Also A.J.B. would not even bring up my proposal for allotment of plebiscite areas to countries. This also infuriated me.
> I went off with Tit Willow to Pershing, and luckily caught him and Bliss in his house. It is quite clear that in Pershing's and Bliss's opinions the Americans will not supply troops for any plebiscite area. Also it is quite clear that the Americans are as anxious as I am to repatriate their Boche prisoners. Pershing was very open in ridiculing the League of Peace, and he evidently looks forward to the President being unable to get a ratification.

Next day there is the entry:

> I went in to Paris and had a talk with A.J.B. before our 2 o'c. meeting, and he was primed up to force the pace about repatriating our Boches; and Polk, with whom I discussed, was equally determined — and the Tiger never came, and poor Pichon said he was unable to discuss the matter. Another 24 hours' delay. I lunched at A.J.B.'s and told him I was convinced that the Americans would not send a single man to the plebiscite countries. This shocked him very much. As the Italians say they can only find three battalions, it means — if the Frocks go on with their ridiculous plebiscites — that the French and ourselves may each have to find two divisions. I will put up a paper on this subject to the Cabinet.

---

* Mr. F.L. Polk was the U.S.A. Plenipotentiary after President Wilson's departure.

† Italian representative.

Sir Henry returned to London on August 27, some-what troubled by a racking cough, nothing whatever having in reality been settled while he was in France, in spite of his expostulations. He spent a day at Englemere before the end of the month, and during this visit to Ascot he saw a great deal of his little godson, Freddy Lewin. Delighting as he always did in children, he was particularly drawn to this one because of cherished associations of days past with the small boy's famous grandsire. Freddy warmly reciprocated the Field-Marshal's overtures of friendliness, and spent much time crawling about over him, babbling unceasingly the while about "Ze Long Job." But Sir Henry was after this seriously troubled by the cough during the whole of September, and as a result of the affliction, he spent great part of the month at the seaside, although a shorthand clerk came down almost daily from London with papers for him to deal with. On his return to Eaton Place on the 22nd he was little the better for his stay on the south coast, and it was not till the early days of October that his medical advisers came to the conclusion that their patient was in reality suffering from whooping-cough, which he had probably contracted when, having already a troublesome cough, he had been with his godson. For the little boy had developed the complaint shortly afterwards, and now, according to Wilson's diary, was "whooping like a hero."

Two matters had in the meantime been especially engaging his attention — a proposal of Clemenceau's to land 12,000 French troops at Alexandretta* and to dispatch them to Armenia from the

---

* The position of affairs in Syria at the beginning of September was that the country was still in occupation of British troops under Allenby, but that they were about to be gradually withdrawn. The Emir Feisul had been appointed by Allenby administrator of the greater part of Eastern Syria, with seat at Damascus. A treaty was signed during the month of September between the British and French Governments, which defined the limits respectively of Palestine and of Syria, and which laid down that the four important interior Syrian cities, Damascus, Homs, Hamah, and Aleppo, were to be under the jurisdiction of Feisul, that part of the country being mainly inhabited by Arabs, whereas the population of the rest of it was very mixed. In view of British responsibilities in connexion with the Arabs in general, and of the relations that existed with King Hussein of the Hejaz, it was very desirable from the point of view of the British Government that no hostilities

Gulf of Iskanderum to maintain order, and the question whether the Territorial Army should any longer be maintained under the transformed conditions consequent on the experiences and the results of the late war. The first matter was dealt with on the and at the only Cabinet meeting which he was able to attend during the month of September, and of what passed on that occasion he wrote in his diary:

> We discussed the coming massacres in Armenia, after we have withdrawn from the Caucasus, and Curzon favoured our leaving a brigade there. So did Milner; but Bonar Law, Montagu, Austen and I opposed this. We then discussed Clemenceau sending 12,000 men to Alesandretta to stop massacres in Armenia. Curzon and I both described the proposal as fantastic. I explained that it was not an operation of war for 12,000 Frenchmen to march, or to rail and march, from Alexandretta to Erzerum (450 miles). And I made the following proposal, to which the Cabinet agreed. I proposed that we should accept the French offer of 12,000 men, that we should open Batoum and the railway to these troops, that we should hand over dumps and transport and horses, etc., and should in every way facilitate the passage of the 12,000 to Erzerum. This was agreed to, and Curzon will wire in the sense to Balfour.

M. Clemenceau eventually sent an officer over to see him and to discuss the Alexandretta project. "I was quite open about it all," he wrote in his diary after their interview had taken place on September 11. From this it may be presumed that the Field-Marshal tactfully conveyed to M. Clemenceau's envoy that the proposal to send an expedition to Armenia via Alexandretta looked as if the troops involved might be intended for some nearer region, but that, if the force was really destined for Armenia, its proper jumping-off point was obviously Batoum. Be that as it may, the project was apparently forthwith abandoned. Sir Henry's view as regards the Territorial Army was that Home Defence need no longer be taken seriously into account, and that a Territorial Army intended for Home Defence was not, therefore, required. Of this

---

should take place between the French and Feisul, or Feisul's subordinates.

1919: July to December

question he wrote in his diary on September 26:

> Winston to see me at 10 a.m., and talked for an hour. He told me that, politically, it was absolutely necessary to rebuild the 14 Territorial Divisions. I said that I had nothing to say against that, but that I must put in my paper showing what, in my opinion, was absolutely necessary to keep the Empire safe — especially Ireland, Egypt, Mesopotamia and India. When their needs were satisfied we could go on with the Territorial Force. He said he proposed to make the Territorial Force available to maintain order at home. So much the better, but, of course, quite impossible in the present temper of the country. He was anxious to get me on his side about the Territorials; but I would not move out of my soldier view — which, as I told him, the Cabinet might overrule if they liked and might, politically, for all I knew, be wise in overruling.

The "lightning" strike of the railwaymen began that night at midnight, and Wilson shared to the full the general indignation of the community at the deliberate breach of their contracts of which the men, under the leadership of Mr. J. H. Thomas and others, had been guilty, and at their callous disregard of the convenience of passengers who had been left stranded all over the country in the middle of the night. There was a prospect of the transport workers and the miners also going on strike, and the C.I.G.S. rather hoped that they would do so, believing that something of the nature of a general strike was bound to come sooner or later, and that it would therefore be well to get it over. He wrote in his diary on October 5, when staying at Grove End, where he spent most of that month:

> This evening Mogg* telephoned to say the whole thing had collapsed. I am sorry, as I wanted this thing fought to a finish. I don't know what has made Thomas give in, but I hope that it is not weakness on the part of the Government.

On learning the facts of the case next day he wrote:

> Lloyd George has a genius for giving in at the wrong moment.

---

* Mr. H.W. Moggridge, his private secretary at the War Office.

Extending the present pay from next March to next September just allowed Thomas to save his face. Whew! We shall have the whole thing over again later on.

The evacuation of North Russia was in the meantime being carried out under Rawlinson's general superintendence, while Kolchak was being driven farther and farther eastwards in Siberia. Denikin, on the other hand, was making continuous progress in the south, and had occupied Kiev. General Yudenitch, with a force made up of Russians and Esthonians, was moreover advancing along the south of the Gulf of Finland, and was drawing near to Petrograd. So that Wilson was for the moment fairly well satisfied as regards the obstacles that were being set up to the advance of Bolshevism. But the Syrian question was causing the Government and him anxiety, and on the 13th he attended a Cabinet sub-committee, especially summoned to consider this subject, of which meeting he wrote in his diary:

> Lloyd George, Curzon, Bonar, Allenby, Feisul and self. It is quite dear that the French mean to occupy the four towns of Aleppo, Hamah, Homs and Damascus if we don't make it plain that we don't agree, and if Feisul has not troops ready to occupy and keep order when we move out. Feisul said he would want 15,000 men, and could get them. After 2 hours" talk we all agreed on Lloyd George wiring to Clemenceau asking him to send Gouraud (the new Commissioner, vice Picot) over to-morrow' to discuss with Feisul, Allenby and me the details of reliefs. Feisul insisted strongly on an American being present, so we wired Polk asking him to send Bliss over.
>
> After the Cabinet, Lloyd George said he wanted to have a talk with me (I had not seen him for eight weeks). We discussed many things over a cup of tea. He is not going to make any speeches in favour of the League of Nations, as he at last realizes what rubbish all that is. I asked him about his Home Rule Bill, and he said that he had to do something, as Asquith's rotten Home Rule Bill came automatically into force after peace, and no one would agree to that. So he had appointed this wonderful committee of Long, French, Macpherson, Auckland Geddes, Fisher, etc., to advise. He had no idea what would be the advice. Anything but union is suicidal.

Denikin was making such steady advance towards Central

1919: July to December 257

Russia that there appeared to be a prospect of his actually reaching Moscow. His days of triumph had, however, reached their zenith, although the collapse of his campaign was not foreseen at the moment. Yudenitch was also making satisfactory progress in his march on Petrograd, but that expedition was brought to a standstill actually after it had reached Gatchina; it never got farther, and it ultimately proved a complete failure.

Sir Henry was at this time watching with marked disapproval the efforts of the Greeks to make themselves masters of large portions of Anatolia at the expense of the Turks — one outcome of the action of President Wilson, M. Clemenceau and the British Prime Minister in sending the Greeks to Smyrna some months before. The C.I.G.S. was strongly opposed to such Hellenic adventures, and mention is made in his diary on October 28 of an interesting conversation on the subject with M. Venizelos at Eaton Place on that day:

> I told him straight out that he had ruined his country and himself by going to Smyrna; and the poor man agreed, but said the reason was because Paris had not finished off the Turk and had made peace with him. This, of course, is only partly so. Yenizelos very bitter against the Turk, and said the whole 12 divisions were available if we would finish the Turk off. He realizes that he is in a hopeless position, and is now trying to sell his 12 divisions. He begged me to tell Lloyd George that both he [Venizelos] and Greece were *done*. I said I would. The old boy is *done*.

He wrote in his diary a few days later, November 7:

> I am convinced that if our Foreign Office goes on backing Greece against Turkey we shall be in trouble all over the East. I told this to Curzon on Wednesday when I was at the Foreign Office.[*]

---

[*] Wilson bad been opposed from the outset to the descent upon Smyrna by Greek forces in the previous June (as has been shown in the last chapter), but it is somewhat singular that M. Venizelos should have expressed such pessimistic views on the occasion of the conversation between them of October 28. There had been serious trouble at Smyrna when the Greeks had landed, leading to some Turks being massacred and bringing grave discredit upon the Hellenic troops. But

A succession of distinguished visitors had been descending upon London during the last days of October and the first days of November — General Diaz, the Shah of Persia and President Poincaré — and Sir Henry had met each of them on the occasion of their arrival at Victoria. His Majesty's dinner to the French President at Buckingham Palace took place on November 10, the C.I.G.S. was amongst those commanded, and he mentions in his diary having had a long conversation with the Prime Minister about that statesman's "forthcoming misery of a Home Rule Bill." The first anniversary of the Armistice befell on the following day; and of the solemn ceremony which was then initiated in Whitehall, and which has been repeated yearly since, Wilson wrote in the diary:

> Two minutes of silence at 11 a.m. was a wonderful sight. I was at Cenotaph with Curzon and Winston, while some Frenchmen from Poincaré put flowers. Enormous crowds. Every head uncovered, and absolute silence. Lunch at Guildhall. Poincaré there.
> Cabinet Meeting about Russia, at which nothing was decided. They will not look at the picture as a whole. Cecil and I dined at the French Embassy. The King, Queen and Poincaré there.

His health was now almost completely restored, although he still stood in need of a real holiday, and he was very busy at the War Office at this time dealing with the future organization of Machine-gun Companies, the Tank Corps, the Signal Corps and other services that had been produced or affected by the experiences of the war. Plans were, moreover, on foot for making the Territorial Army liable for service abroad in time of war, a reform which Churchill and he were equally anxious to bring about. He was cheered by intelligence arriving from the other side of the Atlantic in the middle of the month to the effect that the Senate at Washington were making reservations in connexion with the ratification of the Peace Treaty, reservations which, if they should be adopted by Congress, would exclude the United States from the treaty and consequently from the League of Nations — to

---

at the time of the conversation the situation bad become fairly settled — at least for the moment.

both of which he felt strong objections. "There seems some chance now that the Americans will ratify the Peace Treaty," he wrote disappointedly in the diary on November 19, "what a pity." But on the following day there is the entry, "This evening's paper says the United States has finally killed the Peace Treaty. This is good." That the situation in Russia was becoming highly unsatisfactory is shown by another entry appearing in the diary on that same date: "Denikin is falling back, and, altogether, the Anti-Bolshevists are being pushed about; Yudenitch knocked out, and Kolchak has lost Omsk."

Two days later the Field-Marshal was handed his baton by the King at Buckingham Palace. He was becoming seriously troubled as to the general political and military situation, the more so as considerable doubt existed as to whether the German Government would sign an important Protocol in connexion with the Peace Treaty. The question was indeed arising as to what course was to be adopted should this doubt prove to be justified. Sir Henry was, moreover, being asked to provide eleven battalions for the Silesian plebiscite area, and he was finding great difficulty in doing so in view of the many other commitments that were tending to absorb troops. But, added to the various problems that were arising abroad, and the handling of which by the Prime Minister and the Coalition Government was by no means always to his taste, the Field-Marshal was regarding the attitude of Ministers towards Ireland with a growing suspicion and resentment.

Bitterly opposed to the principle of Home Rule as he was, he observed with concern the gradual acceptance of that principle by Unionist members of the Cabinet, who in former times had been utterly opposed to granting independent government to his native land. From this autumn dates the beginning of an estrangement from many of his best friends holding high positions in Whitehall, which grew more and more marked up to the time of his handing over the responsibilities of C.I.G.S. to his successor in February, 1922. He wrote in the diary at the end of the month:

> If England goes on like this she will lose the Empire. There is absolutely no grip anywhere. I propose, after the New Year and after I have had a holiday, to take a rather active part in matters — even in

some (like Ireland and Egypt) which are not solely military.

This appears on December 2:

> We had an Army Council meeting this morning on the final draft of our terms for the Territorial Force, which included an obligation for foreign service if, and when, the Regular Army was mobilized and the Reserve called up. We have been months at this, with Winston's knowledge and approval. This morning he suddenly and unexpectedly ran out. He said he would get no recruits, there would be a complete frost, etc., etc., and he wanted to revert to the Territorial Force of pre-war days. I said that I could not agree to 6-10 millions being spent on a sham. On the Cabinet's own ruling, there would not be an invasion for 10 years, and a force wholly devoted to repel invasion was therefore a farce. We had much argument, and nothing was decided except that Winston wants both schemes drawn out, and he will put both before the Cabinet. It is clear that somebody has frightened poor Winston. To add to our difficulties, it is suddenly found that we cannot enlist in Territorial Force with general-service obligation without a new Act of Parliament, and Winston said he could not get this before February. Here is a nice delay!
>
> This evening, Winston, Trenchard, Amery and I had a meeting about the coming campaign in Somaliland, to be conducted by the Colonial Office and Air Ministry. I had put in a strong objection; but this afternoon both Amery and Trenchard said that under no conceivable circumstances would they ask me for troops, so I withdrew my objection and gave my blessing.
>
> After Trenchard and Amery had gone, I had a talk with Winston, and I told him that I thought he was backing the wrong horse when he advocated the old form of Territorial Force. And I told him also about our great difficulties in finding troops for the Rhine, plebiscites, Egypt, etc., and I added that, if the Home Rule Bill was passed, we should lose all 16 Irish battalions. I then enlarged on the present political situation, which I described as one in which our statesmen (?) practically said they could not govern either in Ireland (or England) or Egypt or India, and that under various cloaks called devolution, federation, self-determination, democracy, and so forth, the Government said that they were unable to govern — and would these countries kindly govern for them! I so fired Winston that he said he would write a paper for the Cabinet.

1919: July to December 261

Foch had been sending Sir Henry messages begging him to go over to Paris for a consultation, so he crossed the Channel and they met on December 5. They agreed that there were not sufficient forces available for taking military action against Germany should the Berlin Government refuse to sign the Protocol. They also agreed that, although a threat would very likely have the effect of inducing the Germans to sign, there could be no certainty of this, and Wilson wrote in his diary:

> Foch points out that out present difficulties with the Boches are only the commencement of further troubles, and that the Boches, having got the Americans to run out, will become stronger each bout. There is no question but that the insensate haste of the Frocks to disarm has landed them into an impasse.

Later in the day he entered the fact that a message had come from London asking that Clemenceau should go over at once, and also that the Cabinet were much concerned at his having proceeded to Paris without their knowledge. He remarked in the diary

> The French newspapers have photographs of me, and large notices of my arrival in Paris to confer with Foch, and I expect the London papers have the same and that this has frightened the Cabinet.

This appears the next day:

> A long wire from Winston warning me not to mix myself up in politics, and saying Cabinet much upset at my going to Paris and a lot of rubbish of a like nature, and I answered in rather short vein.

After three days the Field-Marshal returned to London, and on the following morning he went to see Lloyd George and to inform the Prime Minister that Foch had not sufficient troops at his disposal for military action against Germany. A Note was being sent to the German Government with regard to the Protocol; its terms were discussed at a Cabinet meeting, at which Wilson was present, and were agreed to with, according to him, '"tremblings." A reply was received from Berlin a week later, as to which he remarked in his diary:

> The Boches have not signed. Though expressing their willingness, they start arguing. What will the Frocks do now?

The Protocol was, however, eventually signed, and this cause of misgiving disappeared, at least for the time being. But Wilson wrote on December 22:

> I am very anxious about future industrial unrest, and the part the Army will play. Last week I wrote in the strongest manner possible, about the Cabinet idea that we soldiers could help with lorries, drivers, wireless, etc., whereas we can't. Winston agrees to my putting in another paper to the Cabinet.
>
> Winston told me this evening that Macpherson had warned him to-day that Ireland might have to be seriously reinforced in the next fortnight. So best. This would save our sending troops to the plebiscite area.

This appears two days later:

> Office all morning, chiefly engaged in writing papers about the total lack of plans now in evidence as against strikes. We soldiers *cannot* help, as I have repeatedly pointed out, and Eric Geddes, the G.P.O. and the Home Office are doing nothing.

He moreover set a war-game on foot, dealing with the defence of Persia, now that Denikin was being driven back southwards by the Bolshevist forces, and assuming that these would probably reach the Black Sea and Sea of Azov, would overrun Transcaucasia and would gain command of the Caspian. He was asked by Mr. Montagu, who was unwell, to call at the India Office on the 30th, and of their conversation he wrote as follows in his diary:

> I had an hour with him in his room. He is very frightened about the state of affairs in India, Afghanistan and Turkey. He says he will resign if the Turk is kicked out of Constantinople. He defined Lloyd George's attitude, A.J.B.'s attitude and Curzon's attitude. Montagu said that every authority except these three men was in favour of keeping the Turk in Constantinople. We discussed India and the telegram from the Viceroy received yesterday in which he says that his military authorities advise strong course to be taken now with the

Ameer. But this action appears to consist in air-bombing on Kabul and Kandahar, which I said was childish. This baby-bombing has great limitations. The Viceroy is in favour of doing nothing until Feb. 6, when the six months is up with the Afghans and a new arrangement has to be made.

I told Montagu that in my opinion it was now too late to deal with Afghanistan as an isolated problem, and that the whole theatre of the Middle East, embracing Denikin — Caspian — Asia Minor — Mesopotanna — Egypt — Persia — Afghanistan must all be considered, and I told hm of my war-game now going on. He said that Curzon had decided with Berthelot to eject the Turk out of Constantinople, and that the Cabinet would agree, and that Lloyd George paid more attention to me than to anybody — and would I do all I could to stop this idiotic and calamitous proposal. I pointed out that, though Lloyd George paid attention to me as a soldier, he paid no attention to me in other matters. Witness his futile and childish proposals for Home Rule. At the same time, I would do all I could, and I might be able to influence matters by my war-game. And so we left it.

On the last day of the year he wrote:

> I walked over to Bonar and had an hour with him. I insisted that the Home Rule proposals are farcical, and that the only thing to do was to keep law and order, and that this ought to be done, not with soldiers but with police and the civil power. I said that the police ought to be doubled or trebled if necessary, but the soldiers kept out of it. I impressed Bonar a good deal, I could see. Then I turned to our arrangements, or rather want of arrangements, in case of serious strikes in England. I told Bonar that we soldiers had now no spare lorries, no technical experts, no telephonists, telegraphists nor wireless, and that we should be both immobile and blind in case of a Triple Alliance and Post Office strike. I told him that the Triple Alliance would undoubtedly beat us if we had no plans — and we had none — and I begged him to move in the matter. I certainly shook him up well on this also, and I was pleased with my morning's work.

He concluded:

> What a disappointing year. The Frocks have muddled everything — peace with our enemies, Ireland, Egypt, India, the Trades Unions,

everything. They seem incapable of governing. To me personally the year has been wonderful — Paris all through the Peace negotiations, dinner in the House of Commons, Lloyd George's speech at the dinner with announcement of my baton, then the thanks of the Houses, then a baronetcy and £10,000. But the coming year looks gloomy. We are certain to have serious trouble in Ireland, Egypt and India, possibly even with the Bolsheviks. At home, those who know best say we are going to have a strike of the Triple Alliance and the Post Office. This will be a direct threat and attack on the life of the nation. I am confident that, if it comes, we shall, provided the Cabinet wake up now, be victorious.

Chapter XXX – 1920: January to June

Wilson's contention that policy must have relation to fighting strength — Denikin's collapse — The C.I.G.S. at issue with the Cabinet over Batoum — The San Remo Conference — The troubles in Ireland — The case of General Dyer — Transcaucasia and Persia.

The opening of the year 1920 found public men of the United Kingdom in a state of anxiety for which there existed ample ground; and few, if any, of them realized more folly than did Wilson the perils that attended the existing international situation and the unsatisfactory conditions prevailing in the United Kingdom itself. Abroad, difficulties were springing up in connexion with many provisions of the Treaty of Versailles. Kolchak's position in Siberia had become hopeless, and Denikin's dwindling host seemed about to suffer irretrievable disaster. An accommodation with the Ottoman Empire had moreover still to be adjusted. At home, industrial disorder was assuming alarming proportions, the prospect of something of the nature of a general strike was causing the Civil Power grave concern, and the chaos in Ireland was becoming more and more acute from day to day. The Field-Marshal was losing all confidence in Mr. Lloyd George and his Coalition Government, owing to their palpable disinclination to grapple with the troubles that were besetting them on every side.

He felt convinced that it was imperative, in view of the comparative weakness of the military forces which he had at his disposal, to concentrate these in regions and in localities where the presence of British soldiers was indispensable for the security of the Empire. He saw that, were he to allot portions of those forces to undertakings in other directions, however worthy those undertakings might be in themselves, this must leave him insufficient numbers to safeguard vital points. He was prepared to insist upon the principle being accepted by the Cabinet that foreign policy and military policy alike must be governed by the question of available fighting resources. He was also disquieted at the unwillingness and the incapacity being manifested by the various civil departments of Government concerned, in respect to making appropriate arrangements for coping with unrest at home and to framing plans to meet that revolutionary upheaval, the possibility of which was coming to be admitted by those best qualified to judge.

On January 1 there appears in the Field-Marshal's diary:

> It is now clear by the wires that Denikin is going to give up Odessa, but hopes to hold the Crimea, and then a line covering Rostov and back to where he was in May last.

And next day he wrote:

> A long talk with the Q.M.G. this morning about strikes. He is in complete agreement with me in cursing the criminal folly of the Government for having no plan, and for making none, and indeed for refusing to realize the position. My paper to the Cabinet was dated November 6, and nothing practical has since been done.

Constantinople was, however, discussed at two successive Cabinet meetings, and the majority present, after hearing Wilson's views, decided that the city must remain in the Sultan's hands. He remarked in the diary:

> There is great trouble ahead, no matter what we do, but I think we have chosen the wisest course.

The question as to whether the Territorial Army was, or was not, to take general-service obligations remained undecided, in spite of the efforts of the rnilitary members of the Army Council; but Churchill at last, at the end of the month, gave way, and early in February he announced the new conditions under which these second-line troops would henceforward be serving. The defence of Transcaucasia had in the meantime caused a sharp disagreement in Cabinet circles, for Wilson wrote on the 12th:

> Curzon, who with Lloyd George is in Paris, sends a ridiculous wire about Georgia and Azerbaijan and the necessity for supporting them, just as I was writing to say that I wanted to withdraw our brigade from Batoum. We had a meeting at the Foreign Office, and I gave a lecture on a map showing the impossibility of standing on the forward lines in defence of India. I showed that Palestine — Mosul — Khanikin— Burujird was the only possible line, and that we should adjust our policy to that line. It was quite true that Georgia and Azerbaijan would go Bolshevik, in spite of the fact that those fools in Paris only yesterday agreed to acknowledge the "*de facto* governments" of those countries. It was also true that we should have to clear out of Persia, in spite of the treaty Curzon has just made with Persia without consulting the War Office. All this was agreed to by the Committee and wired to Curzon, and our wire will give Curzon and the Frocks in Paris something to think about.

Next day there is the entry:

> A long wire from Holman* which seems to indicate that Denikin is nearly done for. Holman seems to be organizing our mission of about 1,500 into a sort of rear-guard. A bad business. Now Mackinder seems to have guaranteed to embark Russian women and children, and neither we, nor Foreign Office, nor Admiralty know anything about it.
> The state of Ireland is really terrible. No one's life is safe, spies and murderers everywhere, the Cabinet absolutely apathetic. I urge with all my force the necessity for doubling the police and not employing the military.

This appears on January 14:

---

* Major-General H.C. Holman was our military representative with Denikin, and in charge of the various British detachments attached to that commander's forces.

> Winston sent for me to discuss Denikin. As a result of our talk I sent two telegrams, one to Holman telling him to collect at ports and stand ready for embarkation, and also to carry out the engagement that Mackinder had given, the other to Milne telling him to hold three battalions in readiness, and to go himself to Novorosisk and take charge if he reinforced.

On the 15th there is the entry:

> Transport Sub-Committee of Cabinet at 3 o'c. Eric Geddes (Chair), Walter Long, Winston, Munro (Scotland), Roberts (Food), Horne and others. An amazing meeting. One after another got up and said that we were going to have the Triple Red Revolution strike. One after another said there was nothing to be done, that the police were powerless, that the Citizen Guard had been forbidden by the Unions, and that now the Unions would not allow special constables to be sworn, and treated them as blacklegs. It is truly a terrifying state of affairs, and not one of them except Walter and Winston seem prepared to put up a fight.

Meetings of the Supreme War Council were about to be held in Paris, as a number of perplexing questions required consideration, especially so with regard to Russia and Bolshevism and to the Near East. The position of the Allies with reference to the Ottoman Empire was still merely that of a cessation of hostilities by agreement as between former belligerents, without terms of peace having been adjusted, or having indeed even been seriously considered. In response to a message ordering them over to Paris, the Field-Marshal crossed the Channel in company with Churchill, Long and Beatty on the night of January 15, and in his diary Sir Henry mentions their discussing affairs on the way over:

> I urged that in Paris we must try and prevent the 11 battalions going to plebiscite. As I kept saying, "We must secure our base first" before we go to plebiscites, or Caucasus, or anywhere. And who could defend 18 battalions on Rhine and plebiscite, and only 2 battalions in Scotland? We are undoubtedly coming to a very, very critical time.

The C.I.G.S. found on arrival:

There is complete chaos here. The Frocks have been at work for a week, and nothing done. Curzon now wants to hold Batoum — Baku, and Montagu backs him. Nothing settled about Constantinople. French Presidential elections to-morrow, and Clemenceau this evening in some preliminary canter beaten by Deschanel. Complete chaos there also.

The Field-Marshal had a prolonged discussion with Marshal Foch, and afterwards was present at a meeting of the Prime Minister with the British Cabinet Ministers then present in Paris. He had arranged with Hankey that the question of unrest in the United Kingdom should come first on the agenda, and he claimed in his diary to have made some impression with regard to this matter, although he failed to get a definite decision for revoking the project of sending battalions to plebiscite areas. The First Sea Lord proposed dispatching bluejackets to take over Denikin's ships in the Caspian, the crews of which could no longer be depended upon — but subject to the Batoum — Baku line being secured. Wilson, however, strongly opposed the idea of British troops having to undertake the latter duty, for which, he declared, there must be two whole divisions on the spot, with a third stationed in support at Constantinople. But he failed to get a decision, and he wrote in the diary:

> We broke up with nothing settled. We all dined with Lloyd George. I kept talking incessantly of securing our base (England), and did good work. We saw Pavlova dance; Carpentier was brought up to shake hands with me, and I wrote my name in his gold cigarette-case.

Further discussions took place on the two succeeding days, and when the Russian position was debated the Prime Minister "'specifically stated" that if Lenin were only left alone he would not "attack Georgia, or Azerbaijan, or Poland, or Rumania, or anyone." But Wilson entered in the diary:

> I pointed out that I could not see why Lenin should not attack all the Border states, since Paris had filched them from Russia, and Lenin might — and I thought ought to — claim them as part of Russia, and therefore ought to retake them. This was unanswerable.

No definite decision had, however, been come to with regard to any point in spite of all these confabulations (except that Lloyd George undertook to try to arrange that British battalions should not take part in the plebiscite work) when the Supreme War Council assembled on January 19. Of this meeting Sir Henry writes in the diary:

> Clemenceau in the Chair, Lloyd George, Curzon, Walter Long, Winston, Beatty, self, Foch, Nitti and others. We discussed Caucasus. I was asked my opinion about arming Georgia and Azerbaijan. I said I was wholly opposed to it unless we had command of the Caspian, and that, as command of the Caspian meant the employment of 2 divisions and was therefore impossible, I was opposed to arming these people, since, if Denikin fell down, die Bolsheviks would certainly take Baku, and all the arms would become presents to the Bolsheviks. Foch agreed. The Frocks then sent for the Georgian and Azerbaijanese representatives, who told the Frocks the same ridiculous cock-and-bull stories they had told me and Beatty, and, for Lloyd George's benefit and Winston's anger, they added that they feared and hated Denikin, who was a Tsarist.
>
> After these dagos had withdrawn, Foch laid out his plan for trying to get a combination of all the States from Finland to Odessa, which was my plan a year ago but which in my opinion is no longer practicable. We [military and naval gentlemen] were then dismissed, and the Frocks decided to arm, equip, and feed the Georgians, Azerbaijanese, and Armenians, and Foch and I are to advise on the amount, etc.
>
> I again asked Lloyd George if he realized what it meant for us to cancel our plebiscite battalions, and Winston was present, and neither of them thought anything of it.* Lloyd George said Clemenceau said he would try and find 5 others. Radcliffe dined; he is on his way back from Nice, and I told him all the story, and that I thought when Foch heard of this we might have to cancel. After dinner I again spoke to Lloyd George about the row there would be to-morrow, but he thought nothing of it. I am delighted to save those battalions, but I realize that it has grave consequences in France and Germany.

---

* Sir Henry had heard that the Prime Minister had told both Clemenceau and Nitti that he was unable to send battalions.

Next day there is the entry:

> Foch took the news like the great man he is, and he and Weygand were niceness itself. We at once set to work to readjust the forces left, but Foch is doubtful if he can carry on much longer with such Frocks, and so am I. "*Ils cassent tout, ils crévent tout,*"* said the old Marshal.
>
> To Quai d'Orsay, where Clemenceau presided for the last time, Millerand also being present.† We discussed plebiscites again, and I allowed Lloyd George to say we would find 2 battalions, one for Danzig and one for Marienwerder; and this greatly pleased Foch, which enchanted me. He is far the biggest man of the whole lot.

Lloyd George, with most of the Cabinet Ministers and Sir Henry, returned to London on the 21st, and two or three days later news arrived that a vessel carrying 450 Russian sick and wounded from Denikinas army had arrived at Malta with typhus on board, and that the authorities there had refused to permit any disembarkation; also that Constantinople had not doctors or nurses for dealing with the wounded arriving there from Denikin's army; also that preparations were being made to ship 25,000 refugees from the Crimea. Sir Henry brought these matters up at a Cabinet meeting, and he wrote in the diary:

> On this I asked for a decision, as I already had several times in Paris last week, as to what was to be done. Much talk and no decision. It is appalling.

The subject was brought up again at a Cabinet meeting on January 29, and of the proceedings on this occasion Sir Henry wrote:

> A very painful affair. De Robeck and Milne want to ship some 50,000 Russian wounded and women and children from Odessa, the Crimea and Novorosisk to save them from the Bolsheviks. But there

---

* "They break everything, they create everything."

† A change of government was taking place, M. Millerand becoming its head. M. Deschanel had just succeeded M. Poincaré as President.

is no place to ship them to. Then Milne recommends that we should land a battalion at Odessa, some troops to hold the Perekop peninsula and Crimea, and send two battalions to Novorosisk. Lloyd George asked me for my opinion on this, and I answered at once: "It is for the Cabinet to decide whether they want to go to war with the Bolsheviks or not. If yes, then I will draw up a complete plan of campaign from Finland to the Caucasus. If no, then no battalions should be landed." This killed the idea. Then we discussed taking away women and children, and in the end decided to transport them only to the Crimea.

It is all a most deplorable business. I tried hard in Paris to get the Frocks to decide on this question, but they would not I Now they must, that I suggested we should say that had two divisions there now and that these were required, but that after the Peace Treaty was concluded, and if all went well, we could gradually reduce to a brigade, or so, and some warships.

This recommendation was put forward, and on February 17, the conferences of the Supreme War Council being at an end, Foch and Weygand took their departure. Franchet d'Esperey's position remained unsettled; but certain other military problems had been to some extent dealt with, and the Supreme Council had arrived at one important decision — Constantinople was to remain Turkish. Of a Cabinet meeting that took place on the following day Wilson recorded in his diary:

We discussed the question of Batoum, and Curzon made a long speech, begging that our troops should remain there. I said that they must be withdrawn in order to strengthen Constantinople, that, even apart from the Turkish danger, there was the trouble and danger of Franchet d'Esperey. Curzon urged that they should remain until Batoum was taken over by the League of Nations. Arthur Balfour, who last week was President of the League of Nations meetings, said that this would mean "for ever" as the League had no army, nor police, and never would have. What nonsense it all is, and what a deception it all is on the people of this and other countries. In the end it was agreed that Curzon was to try and get an international force at Batoum, and that I was to stay there for a week or two to see if he could do this. Of course he can't. But what a hopeless muddle the Frocks are in. They can't get out of their difficulties by voting that the League of Nations should take over Danzig, Fiume, Constantinople, Batoum, and other parts, well knowing that the League can take over nothing.

He was watching the progress of events in Ireland closely, and was well satisfied with the plans which the local military authorities had elaborated, alike for meeting sporadic outbreaks and for dealing with a general rising. He anticipated an increase of outrages, but he did not believe that formidable rebellion would break out unless there should be a general strike in Great Britain. He had learnt that the Orange Clubs had been set on foot afresh in Ulster and that, if arms could be provided by the War Office, these clubs would furnish a force of some 50,000 to 60,000 men who could be put in the field very rapidly. Of a visit which M. Venizelos paid him on the 24th he wrote in his diary:

> I left him under no illusions as regards my views about Frocks and their League of Nations. He wants to take over all Thrace to Chatalja lines. He wants a large Allied force left to look after Constantinople and the Straits, the Turkish army to be reduced to 20,000, a Turkish gendarmerie under Allied officers, Armenia — strengthened and armed.

Lord Curzon had succeeded in inducing the French and Italian Governments to furnish troops temporarily for Batoum, so that Sir Henry was able to transfer all but two of the British battalions from that port to Constantinople, and by this means to strengthen the British position on the Golden Horn.

This appears in the diary on March 3:

> I was just off to Greenwich to lecture to the Naval Staff College when I was sent for to the Cabinet. We discussed the military terms I had proposed for the Turks. The Frocks thought my proposal to allow the Turks a military gendarmerie of 60,000 of all ranks absurdly high. Lloyd George quoted Canada with a police force of only 787, and I quoted Ireland with 10,000 police and 40,000 soldiers, and no order. The terms have been referred to Versailles again. A telegram from De Robeck shows that the Turks are getting uppish even in Constantinople.
>
> The Frocks, faced with a concrete and awkward situation, were as timid, ignorant, blustering and useless as ever. They are completely out of touch with realities. They seem to think that their writ runs in

Turkey in Asia. We have never, even directly after the Armistice, attempted to go into the backward parts.

The Field-Marshal and Lady Wilson travelled to Cologne on the 6th and they remained there until the 17th, spending two days at Wiesbaden, however, towards the end of the period. Foch and Weygand arrived while they were there, discussions took place as to what steps should be taken in the event of trouble with Germany; it was agreed that a war-game should be played at Mayence at which Foch and Wilson would command the German forces, and Wilson wrote in his diary on the 8th:

> I have never known Foch in better form. He ran round Morland's garden with me, he insisted upon our being photographed with each other's caps on, he talked and laughed and was absolutely happy with us.

A visit was paid to Coblentz on the 10th, and Sir Henry inspected American troops there on parade. He learnt, while he was on the Ehine, that the question as to who was in responsible charge at Constantinople had not been settled after all, so he wrote

> The Frocks appear to have looked at the question, and to have decided —out of pure funk — that we should command our troops in the town. the French theirs, the Italians theirs, and the Greeks theirs, I have sent a strong wire of protest.

The proposed war-game was played at Mayence, as arranged, on March 15 and 16, and some useful lessons were learnt from the exercise. News had arrived at Cologne on the 15th of a *coup d'état* in Berlin, and of the Government there having been overthrown; and the reports from various quarters during the next few days were to the effect that serious disorders had broken out in some of the towns, disorders which speedily spread to the Ruhr.

This appears in the diary on the 18th:

> There is no further news from Germany, but all looks like drifting to confusion unless some strong fellow catches hold. The mess our Frocks are in is indescribable. This Peace Treaty has resulted in war

everywhere.

Wilson wrote next day:

> Office at 11 a.m. and, Lloyd George shouting for me, I went over to 10 Downing Street. He and I discussed the German situation and Thrace and Turkish peace. We were joined by Curzon and Winston, and we discussed Feisul's latest move of proclaiming himself King of Arabia, Syria, Palestine and Mesopotamia, which, of course, is inadmissible though Lloyd George rather favours it. Curzon and I both pointed out that England could not really be asked to take a mandate from Feisul for Palestine and Mesopotamia.
>
> Winston and I had an hour with Venizelos this afternoon. We made it clear to him that neither in men nor in money, neither in Thrace nor in Smyrna, would we help the Greeks, as we already had taken on more than our small army could do. I told him that he was going to ruin his country, that he would be at war for years with Turkey and Bulgaria, and that the drain in men and money would be far too much for Greece. He said that he did not agree with a word I said.

On March 25 there is the entry:

> I found that the Frocks had decided to allow the Boches to send troops to the Ruhr, with Allied officers to go with them and see that they behaved themselves. I told Bill Thwaites to write at once to the Foreign Office and say I could not agree to send officers in that ridiculous position.

This appears on the 24th:

> Curzon telephoned to me this morning to ask my advice about Millerand's latest proposal to occupy Frankfurt and Darmstadt. I replied that the Frocks must really decide whether they were going to enforce the Treaty or not. If yes, then we must greatly strengthen the Rhine garrison; if no, then we ought to come away. I said that I would go and see him at 6.30 p.m. I gave Curzon a real good talking to, and told him that the Frocks must decide. I frightened Curzon.

This is noted on the 27th:

A long and most impudent wire from President Wilson, saying he disapproved of the Sultan being allowed to remain in Constantinople, he disapproved of the Allied terms as regards Armenia, Cilicia, etc. I would like the job of answering.

The news now arriving from Milne was to the effect that Denikin had withdrawn into the Crimea and that Holman's Mission had been safely shipped at Novorosisk. As to this Sir Henry remarked in his diary:

So ends in practical disaster another of Winston's military attempts — Antwerp, Dardanelles, Denikin. I feel rather disgusted with the present Government, and I am beginning to think that I had better get out. They very rarely take my advice when I give it; and now they seldom ask it, so I suppose they no longer value it. It is nearing time for me to go.

As an example of the extent to which the C.I.G.S. was being ignored by the Government it may be mentioned that General Macready had just been appointed to command the troops in Ireland, without Wilson having been consulted, or having even been informed until the appointment had been made. Although he approved of the arrangement, he justifiably felt slighted at having been so completely disregarded by the Secretary of State when the matter of an important military command was under consideration. He wrote in the diary on the 31st:

A ridiculous ruling of Winston's to say that no drafts were to go to Mesopotamia, on which I wrote that this would mean a large ration strength of inefficient, immobile, untrained men, and I reminded him of four things: Denikin's collapse and open Caspian; 2. Feisul's coronation and his brother's appointment as Governor of Mesopotamia; 3. Lloyd George's speech in the House saying we were going to hold the Mosul vilayet; 4. Foch's Versailles council having laid down that it would take 27 divisions to enforce the proposed Treaty upon Turkey. And in view of this, why should we court disaster by reducing out forces there to incompetency? I don't suppose that Winston will like this.

This appears next day (April 2):*

> I become increasingly suspicious of Lloyd George and whether he is not trying to shepherd England into class war. In the last 18 months (since the Armistice) he has not once stood out, *right out*, against the Unions, and as a consequence the forces of disorder are steadily strengthened, whilst the forces of order are weakening. There are three sorts of wars: 1. Wars between nations; 2. Religious wars; 3. Internal i.e. class wars. And it is into the last that we are drifting under Lloyd George's guidance.

He started for the north of Ireland on April 4 to stay for a few days with Lord Londonderry at Mount Stewart. He was being urged to send over additional troops from England, but was most unwilling to do so if it could possibly be helped, because the units available for the purpose in Great Britain were sadly in need of effective training, and this would become impracticable were they to cross St. George's Channel. While at Mount Stewart he received a letter from the Lord-Lieutenant "in which," according to the diary, "Johnnie says how sorry he was that he could not come up to-day, but he hoped to come to-morrow. But if he could not, owing to something deterring him, he would wire as 'Coulson' and say 'No.'" "A pretty pass we are in," was Sir Henry's acid comment "when the Viceroy has to wire like that. Johnnie *did* wire in the afternoon as 'Coulson' and said 'No.'" The Freedom of Belfast was conferred on him in the great City Hall on April 7. On the day following he visited Queen's College, where he was enthusiastically greeted by the students after delivering a stirring address to the O.T.C.; and during his brief stay in Ulster he met a number of the leading business men and land-owners of the loyal province.

This appears in his diary on the 11th, after his getting back:

> The Flocks are in a mess, the French having occupied Frankfurt and Darmstadt, and the English and Italians disagreeing. The whole

---

*Publisher's note: This appears to be an error, and is likely meant to refer to April 1.

question is simple enough, and, as I wrote to the Cabinet on March 17 from Cologne, resolves itself into this — do the Frocks mean to enforce the Treaty or not? But the Frocks are hopeless. Because the French are logical and want to enforce the Treaty, Lloyd George and Nitti cry out.

Gen. Weygand, Marshal Foch, Sir Henry Wilson at San Remo

Wilson wrote next day:

> Batoum is getting into a mess, and I have written to the Foreign Office for the 100th time saying that I want to get out of it, and also out of Danzig. Our interference in everybody's business is madness. The fools in the Cabinet are patching up their quarrel with the French.

An agreement had been come to for holding an Inter-Allied Conference at San Remo, so the Field-Marshal started for Italy with Lord Beatty on the 15th, and they travelled on from Paris with Millerand, Foch, Curzon and many others. On arrival, Foch, General Badoglio and Wilson discussed what action ought to be taken in reference to the Germans having sent a military force to the Ruhr of double the strength that the Allies had authorized, and to their now asking that it might remain where it was until July 10.

The trio's recommendation was that the Germans must be told to reduce numbers to the authorized figure by June 10, and that the military force must have been replaced by police by July 10. Sir Henry remarked that day in the diary:

> The Agenda for to-morrow is typical. We came down here to settle the Turkish Treaty, at least 12 months overdue, and the Agenda says: 1. Reply to President Wilson's Note about Constantinople; 2. Date to invite Turks to Paris; 3. As a matter of urgency. Lord Curzon to bring forward Labour Party's request for passports to go to Finland and Esthonia!

This appears on April 20:

> I breakfasted with Lloyd George. He is at last beginning to realize that he — and the Peace Conference — is in a hole. As regards the Ruhr, I told him that neither Foch nor I had been able to think of any other alternative. We had tried several, but had rejected them all. This did not suit Lloyd George at all, who was much concerned, finally saying that, if the Ruhr was occupied, we must put equal numbers with the French. I pointed out that this would be difficult, as we considered it would take 4 divisions to occupy the Ruhr, and we must have 4 more in reserve close by. Lloyd George has brains enough to see where this cursed Treaty is taking him.
> Then we discussed Turkey. I told him that I could not change my paper, which agreed with Foch's and worked out 25-30 divisions to enforce the Treaty, of which we had some 15-20 there already. This also upset him, for he is completely in Venizelos's pocket over this Treaty. I then told him I thought he was trying Ulster too high and might lose her loyalty, in which case England was ruined.
> At 4 o'clock we had a meeting of the full Conference. I think this was the most incompetent, impotent, cynical meeting of all the hundreds I have been present at. Subject — Turkey. Nitti opened, and then Lloyd George said it had been decided that morning that none of the three Powers would send a single battalion to Armenia; that they had decided to arm the Armenians and to let them fight it out with the Turks; if their cause was just, and if they were strong enough, they would win, and if not then they were not worth saving. (Note. — Not much mention here of protection of minorities, of Small States, of self-determination, of the brutality of the Turk, of poor Christians massacred by Mohammedans, etc.). This absolutely cynical avowal

was concurred in by Millerand. Then Nitti, Millerand and Lloyd George tried to shake Foch about our report, and, of course, failed. Then Venizelos said he had lots of troops and could work up to 12-13 divisions. He said it would be time to look after the minorities after he had established himself firmly in Thrace and Smyrna. The others agreed. Anything more cynical I have not heard.

Curzon spoke good sense when he asked how the boundary between Turkey and Armenia could be traced if, for example, Erzerum, now occupied by the Turks, was given to Armenians who were totally unable to take it away from the Turks, or if Armenia were given access to the sea and could not get there. I asked, "How do you expect Armenia to hold her own against a fully armed Turkey and a rearmed Azerbaijan, herself being unarmed?" These sort of questions proving too much for the Frocks, Nitti closed the Conference! Foch and I walked down the hill arm in arm, and we agreed that this was the most "*pitoyable*"[*] of any meeting we had been present at. "*La politique à deux sous*"[†] as the old Marshal said. It was a shocking exhibition.

Next day there is the entry:

At the 11 o'c. Conference the Frocks discussed Commissions at Constantinople, and in the end decided to refer certain things to us (the soldiers). We sat morning and afternoon and drew up our report on the demilitarized zones north and south of the Straits, and on the trouble of two Sovereign Powers (Turkey and Greece) having jurisdiction. As this did not suit Lloyd George because it was against the Greeks, he was rude to Foch. I was not in the room, as David Beatty and I had sneaked off at 8 o'clock to play tennis, but the others were furious with Lloyd George.

This appears in the diary on the 22nd:

Full Conference this morning about the Straits Commissions. Beatty and I got our way. I then asked if I might withdraw the two Batoum battalions. This led to an excited talk by the Frocks. Berthelot

---

[*] "Pathetic."

[†] "Two-penny politics."

said there was no danger from the Bolsheviks, and it would be a disaster to come away. I reminded him that two months ago he had promised a battalion and had not sent a man, and ditto the Italians. Curzon argued for staying. Nitti said he would send a battalion if the French did, but it was on no account to fight the Bolsheviks if the Bolsheviks marched on Batoum. He asked whether we were, or were not, going to war with the Bolsheviks. Curzon and Berthelot entirely ignored all danger of the Bolsheviks, and assumed a Friendly and martial and antiBolshevik Georgia. In the end the matter was referred to Foch and myself to report.

After a talk I got Foch and Badoglio to agree that we could not hold Batoum with less than two divisions, and this will, I hope, kill the whole of this ridiculous enterprise. We three then discussed the six solutions we were asked to find to coerce the Boches, and, having examined all sorts of ways, plumped for the occupation of the Ruhr with 4 divisions, and 4 more divisions in dose support. These two papers, i.e. on Batoum and on the Ruhr, will not please the Frocks.

On the 23rd, there is the entry:

A full conference on the question of whether Erzerum should be given to the Armenians or not. We soldiers plumped against it, saying the Armenians were quite unable either to take it or to keep it. Then we put in, and discussed, our paper about two divisions at Batoum. This was a complete knock-out for Curzon and Berthelot. Later in the day the Frocks again discussed Batoum and came to the wise conclusion, at last, to allow Milne and De Robeck to come away whenever they think it advisable. I wired this at once to Milne.

The Frocks engaged this afternoon in a battle-royal about Erzerum, which was broken off at 7 o'c., to be resumed in the morning 1 But as it does not make the slightest difference what the Frocks decide, I look on with amusement and the greatest contempt.

This appears next day:

The Frocks this morning, being unable to come to any agreement about Erzerum, at the suggestion of Millerand agreed to submit its allocation to President Wilson. This has the inestimable merit of losing some more weeks of time, and also, they fondly hope, of carting their great friend the President. My own opinion is that he will accept the task, and will then allot Erzerum to Armenia with an injunction to the Frocks to protect her, and to see she gets it.

Of the final meeting of the Conference which took place on April 26, Wilson wrote:

> The Frocks think they have done good work, we soldiers think they are all "rotters." Nothing is decided except that the Zionists get Palestine, France gets Syria, and Arabs get Arabia. The Turkish Treaty is still incomplete because the Armenian frontier has been referred to President Wilson, who will certainly cart the Frocks. The whole Boche question is in suspense owing to the coming Spa meeting on May 25. Nothing settled about Russia, or Caucasus, or Constantinople command, or plebiscite areas. In fact, the meeting demonstrated once more the total inability of the Frocks to take charge of events, and their cynicism throughout has been perfectly disgusting.

The Field-Marshal got back to London on the 28th, and he had a memorandum drawn up in which was laid down what were the minimum garrisons that he -was prepared to agree to in Palestine, Egypt and Mesopotamia. He wrote in his diary:

> This will queer the pitch which Winston has taken up while I was at San Remo, which consists in arbitrary reductions of garrisons for financial reasons, and wholly regardless of whether or not the residue are liable to be scuppered.

He was trying — in vain — to persuade a Cabinet, which was responsible for the safety of the nation and of the Empire, that policy must be governed by the resources available for enforcing the policy. That those resources should be reduced at a time when they were actually insufficient for enforcing the policy which the Cabinet was thinking fit to follow at Batoum, in Persia, and elsewhere, he regarded as unpardonable folly. ''My paper on our minimum needs in Egypt, Palestine and Mesopotamia will knock all this out," he wrote — somewhat optimistically — in his diary on May 1; "and it is high time."

At the first Cabinet meeting which he attended after his return from the Riviera, the Batoum question was discussed afresh, and the concise account in his diary of the result of the debate runs:

> To my disgust Curzon by a long-winded jaw persuaded the Cabinet to allow our two battalions to remain on for the present. Winston did not fight. I did, but was overruled.*

On taking up the command in Ireland, Macready had speedily come to the conclusion that eight further battalions, besides some technical personnel and a consignment of motor transport, were required to cope with the rapidly extending disorder in the country. A Cabinet meeting was consequently held (in the absence of the Prime Minister, who was ill) on May 11, to consider this new demand on available military resources, and of this meeting Sir Henry wrote in the diary:

> Before the meeting I had a walk on the terrace with Bonar. He was deploring the dreadful state of affairs — there were 4 more police killed yesterday — and I told him, as I have often told him before, that he had not begun his Irish troubles yet. Of course he said this was nonsense. Then we had the Cabinet.
>
> The Cabinet were frankly frightened, and agreed that all Macready's proposals must be acceded to. I pointed out that we now had only 36 Line battalions and 10 Guards battalions in Great Britain. Of these, 8 were Irish, and not available, so there were only 38 to draw upon. It was not wise to remove any Guards battalions, so we had only 28 from which to select. If 8 were sent to Ireland we should have very little for our own internal troubles, and nothing for India, Egypt, Constantinople, etc. It was for the Cabinet to decide if there was any danger of internal troubles. As far as I was concerned, I wanted to keep all infantry battalions where they were, so as to get on with discipline, training, musketry, etc.
>
> After much argument it was agreed that I was only to ear-mark 8 battalions, and that Macready would delay calling for them as long as possible. Meanwhile we were to try and get him all the transport and personnel he asked for, and money was no object! Bounties, for

---

* The Allies' Peace Terms had at last (eighteen months after cessation of hostilities) been handed to the Turkish representatives on May 5. They involved the cession of Eastern Thrace and a large area of Anatolia to the Greeks, besides the loss of Mesopotamia, Syria and Palestine.

which we have begged and begged for months, for wireless, etc., were granted at once! The Frocks are frightened. Winston suggested that a special force of 8,000 old soldiers be raised at once to reinforce the R.I.C. This, in principle, was also agreed to. Macready proposed that Bulfin[*] should be put at the head of the R.I.C. and Metropolitan Police and the new 8,000 men, and of an Intelligence and Secret Service. I sent for Bulfin later, and he flatly refused to take on the job, and he told Winston and Macready so.

Macready is not fighting Ireland; for in reality he is fighting New York and Cairo and Calcutta and Moscow, who are all using Ireland as a tool and lever against England, and nothing but determined shooting on our part is of any use. As usual I found the Cabinet hopeless. They are terrified about Ireland and, having lost all sense of proportion, thought only of that danger, and completely forgot England, Egypt, India, etc., in all of which we are going to have trouble — and serious trouble.

I met Austen and Eric Geddes on the Horse Guards Parade this afternoon and Austen said, on my suggestion that we must shoot by roster, that we [England] must have a very clear conscience before doing such a thing. I told him that it seemed to me to be an odd way of easing his conscience — by the murder of loyal Irish policemen; that, if he would state a figure of the number of policemen who must be murdered before his conscience was made easy, we might hurry up the process and get the lot murdered in a few days, instead of prolonging the agony. Marvellous people, the English.

The profound dissatisfaction which the Field-Marshal was beginning to feel at the manner in which H.M. Government was handling most questions, whether at home or abroad, was accentuated just at this time by the Cabinet's treatment of the case of General Dyer. This matter had been under consideration of Ministers for months past, and it was essentially one that admitted of sharp differences of opinion and that emphatically called for calm and deliberate examination. But the subject was brought up by the Secretary of State, without previous warning, at a meeting of the Army Council on May 14. The papers in connexion with the case had, as it happened, only reached the C.J.G.S. that very

---

[*] Lieutenant-General Sir E.S. Bulfin. Major-General H. Tudor took up the appointment shortly afterwards.

morning, he had not yet found time to read them, and, of what passed at the meeting in connexion with this highly controversial problem, he wrote in his diary:

> Winston made a long speech, prejudging the case and in effect saying that the Cabinet, and he, had decided to throw out Dyer, but that it was advisable for the Army Council to agree. It appeared to me, listening, that the story was a very simple one. The Frocks have got India (as they have Ireland) into a filthy mess. On that the soldiers are called in, and act. This is disapproved by all the disloyal elements, and the soldier is thrown to the winds. All quite simple.
>
> However at to-day's meeting I said I had not had time to read the papers and was therefore quite unable to express an opinion. The other Military Members took up the same stand, though Winston said the matter was pressing. The Frocks have sat on it for 18 months! After the Army Council, I had a short meeting of Military Members, at which I suggested that it was our duty to protect a brother officer until he had been proved in the wrong by a properly constituted Court of Inquiry. And we all agreed to read over the papers carefully and meet on Monday morning.

Next day there is the entry:

> Rawly came over to see me (I had telephoned to him) and I explained the Dyer situation to him, and how clear I was that in the near future we should have many Dyer cases both in India and in Ireland, and that if we did not stand by our own soldiers we should lose their confidence. Then they would not act, and then we should lose the Empire. Rawly cordially agreed — up to the point of saying that, if Dyer was jettisoned by the Frocks without a proper military Court of Inquiry, he [Rawly] would not go as C. in C. to India.

On the 17th Wilson wrote:

> Meeting of Military Members. We agreed that we would not agree to Dyer being thrown out on the evidence before us, and we therefore suggested that the precedent of the Mesopotamian Inquiry should be followed where the accused were given the report and were asked to answer it.
>
> Army Council Meeting. Winston tried again to rush a decision to remove Dyer from the Army, saying that it was only a matter of form.

I at once said that I could not agree, that we had not sufficient evidence on which to form a judgment, and that we must ask Dyer to state a case. This was a bomb for Winston; but when A.G., Q.M.G., and M.G.O. (the latter reading extracts from a speech of F.E.'s about Mesopotamia) joined in and agreed, Winston abruptly closed the subject by saying that he would consult the law officers, and would have an Army Council meeting later to discuss the subject further.

Later, Winston sent for me and said that he was much upset by this "pistol at his head by the Military Members" and that in future he would have to take precautions against these "ambushes." I said that he had only himself to thank. On Friday morning last we got a very incomplete file of the Hunter Commission, the Cabinet Committee on the Hunter Committee, and Dyer's defence, presented to us, and that same afternoon we were suddenly asked to agree to what *he* gave us to understand was a Cabinet decision to remove Dyer. I reminded Winston that at the Army Council he himself had made a strong pronouncement in favour of removing Dyer, and had tried to get us to agree. When we pointed out that we had neither time nor opportunity to examine the case, he had seen that he must postpone the case; but unfortunately for him he had already pronounced against Dyer. On examination, we Military Members were unanimously of opinion that we must have more evidence, and so and hence the deadlock. He tried to argue, but the more he argued the deeper I put him in the "muck heap." He gave it up at last, saying he would call a Cabinet meeting and report to the Cabinet, and then have another Army Council meeting. I finished by saying that nothing should be decided or done until we had another A.C. meeting, and to this he agreed.

We received this morning a letter from Dyer asking to be allowed to rebut the Hunter Report. Our [Military Members'] opinion was that we should reply by sending him a copy of the Report, *which he had not seen*, and asking him for his answer. This position was so strong that even Winston was not able to refuse our proposal, and to-night he agreed that he thought it was reasonable.

Sir Henry attended a special ceremonial that took place in Westminster Abbey on May 18 in honour of the Knights Grand Commander of the Bath, in which the King and the Duke of Connaught took part; he was on this occasion decked out in the full dress of a field-marshal. "Very quaint old customs in Henry VII Chapel, a procession round the Abbey and beautiful music," were, according to his diary, features of the pageant.

A telegram came to hand from Teheran on the following evening, the 19th, announcing that the garrison of Enzeli, a port on the southern shores of the Caspian Sea, had been surrounded by Bolsheviks and had been made prisoners. Something of this nature Wilson had been predicting for some time past, in view of the Bolsheviks having obtained command of the Caspian as soon as the flotilla (which had been frozen up in the Volga during the winter) recovered its mobility. The Cabinet had, however, persistently declined to accept his advice with regard to Persia and Mesopotamia, or to assent to his view that any line north of Mosul — Khanikin — Burujird was strategically indefensible with the forces that were available. "For months I have been begging the Cabinet to allow me to withdraw from Persia and from the Caucasus," he remarked bitterly in his diary; "now perhaps they will." He moreover admitted in the diary that he had been unable to resist writing privately to Curzon "I told you so." A meeting of the Cabinet consequently took place on the 21st, with the Prime Minister present, and of its proceedings the Field-Marshal wrote as follows in the diary:

> Curzon led off with a violent attack on me and the General Staff, quoting a wire that we agreed to on February 13, in which we said Enzeli was quite safe, whereas on May 13 we had said that Enzeli was in danger. As regards Batoum, he urged its retention, saying that our garrison (two battalions) was in no danger.
> I followed, and was able to show that there was no discrepancy between my opinion of February and May. But I began at January 12, when I had shown the Cabinet the result of a war-game I had played. At that time Denikin was very much in being, the Bolshevik fleet was frozen in the Volga, and Denikin's fleet commanded the Caspian. Moreover behind Denikin were (according to Curzon) the martial states of Georgia and Azerbaijan, who would die to the last man to defend their beloved countries from the Bolsheviks. Whereas on May 15 Denikin was a fugitive in London, the Caspian had passed to the Bolsheviks, and the martial states of Georgia and Azerbaijan not only had *not* fought the Bolsheviks, but had actually joined them (as I said they would). Therefore Enzeli was in danger, and *in fact* had been captured by the Bolsheviks 3 days ago. Therefore I urged in the strongest manner possible that we should now clear out of Batoum, before we had a disaster, and that we should first concentrate at

Kasvin — reinforcing Kasvin from the south — and then either: 1. Stand there and really fight, which meant a large increase of force; or 2, Clear out of Persia and go back to our rail-heads.

Winston supported me. Milner said that if we lost Persia we should lose Mesopotamia, and then India was in danger. Lloyd George said he thought we ought to get out of both Batoum and Persia. After much wrangling, it was agreed that I might wire to Mesopotamia to concentrate at Kasvin until further orders, i.e. until Lloyd George had had a talk with the Bolshevik, Krassin, who is coming here on the 30th, and that I could wire to Milne saying he could withdraw from Batoum if he considered it was in danger.

At 7 o'c. came in a very strong wire from Baghdad that, if we were not careful and strong, we should have chaos and disaster all over Mesopotamia in the autumn. I will write a short paper on all this to the Cabinet, pointing out that our small army is much too scattered, that in no single theatre are we strong enough — not in Ireland, nor England, nor on the Rhine, nor in Constantinople, nor Batoum, nor Egypt, nor Palestine, nor Mesopotamia, nor Persia, nor India.

Meanwhile nothing had been done with regard to raising eight garrison battalions for Ireland, although the matter had been agreed to provisionally on May 11. The dockers at Avonmouth, moreover, were refusing to load 150 lorries that were being sent over, the Sinn Feiners were burning the coastguard stations, the Irish railway men were refusing to carry more than 12 soldiers on any train, and the daily quota of outrages was increasing to an ominous extent.

Wilson wrote in the diary of the 28th:

I don't know where Macready is sending the Cameron Highlanders, who left Southampton yesterday and who ought to arrive at Queenstown to-night, but presumably they will walk. I rang up Austen to see if I could persuade him of the urgency of the case, but he was at East Grinstead. I rang up Milner, but he was at some meeting. I don't know what I can do to wake them up. I feel just like July, 1914.

After lunch A.G. came in to see me, to tell me he had seen Winston, who had told him that he and the Prime Minister had agreed that it was inadvisable to try to raise the 8 garrison battalions. So Lloyd George funks that also. He funks when labour won't load in Glasgow, or in Liverpool, or in Avonmouth. He funks when the Irish won't unload at any port. He funks to try to raise 8 garrison battalions. Now the Irish railways won't carry more than 10 [12?] soldiers on one train. Will he funk that? I think he has lost Ireland and the Empire. I have not seen Winston for a week.

On June 3 there is the entry:

> Thomas, Cramp, and some 30 N.U.R; came on a deputation this afternoon to Lloyd George to ask him to differentiate between munitions and other military stores. He and Hamar Greenwood and Macnamara and the Q.M.G. received the deputation. The Q.M.G. took up the stand that it was impossible to carry on his business if he had to differentiate, and that, if it was done for material, it would next be done for personnel — as in fact already had been done about the 12 men in a train and the refusal of the Great Southern to carry a Field Company of Royal Engineers. Lloyd George said the request of the deputation was a challenge to any Government. Thomas said it was only a challenge to this Government, but Lloyd George would not have it. The Q.M.G. was pleased with Lloyd George's attitude. But, after leaving the N.U.R. in the room to consider their next move, Lloyd George began to weaken and asked Q.M.G. if there was no way in which he could help the N.U.R. to save their faces! I am afraid that Lloyd George will send for Thomas and Cramp to 10 Downing Street thus evening and sell the pass to them. Since the Armistice he has never done anything except run away from everything.

This appears in the diary on the 8th:

> Winston told me of the Cabinet to-day about Dyer. He said the Cabinet were unanimous in their determination to fling Dyer out, that they told Winston he ought never to have referred the matter to the Army Council, that they would not hear of leaving Dyer on full pay, but that, on the other hand, they did not now feel in a position to refuse our request that Dyer should be given the chance of writing an answer to the Hunter Report, which would then be laid before us. Winston hinted, and more, at the difficulties which would arise if the Military Members differed from him and from the Cabinet. I said that it would be time enough to discuss the matter after we had read Dyer's explanations. And so the matter dropped for the moment.

Next day (June 9) there is the entry:

About 5 o'c. Edmund Talbot rang me up to ask when we would be ready with the Dyer case. I pointed out to him that our letter to Dyer, telling him that he might put in a statement about the Hunter Commission, had not yet gone out, as Winston said it was not to go out till after the debate. Dyer wrote to us on May 10 asking if he might put in a statement, and we have not answered him ! And all this is due to the Frocks. Talbot told me that Asquith is demanding an early decision — Asquith if you please — and that the debate, which was to-morrow, is put off till next week, and Asquith is clamouring for Monday or Tuesday,

I said some biting things about Asquith, and finished off by saying that, by Winston's orders, the letter to Dyer had not gone out yet, and that Winston could not be found. Later on, Montagu came over to see the A.G., and said it was imperative to get the letter off at once, and Bonar said it must be sent, so A.G. sent it.

Wilson sent in his memorandum, dated May 9, on British military liabilities to the Secretary of State on June 10. "It is a serious pronouncement," he wrote in the diary. 'Perhaps the most serious I have ever written." News from both Persia and Mesopotamia was becoming extremely disquieting, the urgent need of concentrating the available British forces dispersed throughout these remote territories was daily becoming more and more apparent, and the whole progress of events in the Near East was demonstrating how sound had been the advice which the Field-Marshal had been pressing upon a reluctant Cabinet for months past. That he was proving to have been right, and that Ministers in refusing to follow his sensible counsel were proving to have been wrong, may peradventure have been one cause of a movement having apparently been started in Downing Street circles for displacing him from his position as CI.G.S. "Mogg writes this morning" is entered in the diary on the 13th, "that there is talk of my removal by the Cabinet! So the Foreign Office and Curzon are at work."

Sir Henry was apprised about the same time that the Cabinet had decided to keep the British battalions at Batoum for yet another month, this in spite of the earnest representations that he had been making as to the risks involved in their remaining, and as to the need of their presence at Constantinople, where the situation

1920: January to June 291

was presenting all manner of difficulties. The position of affairs on the Golden Horn and about the Straits was rendered particularly delicate and awkward by the fact that the Turkish civil population, and the fighting forces of what was left of the Ottoman Empire, were, alike, split into two separate camps. A minority were loyal to the Sultan. The majority — the "Nationalists" — acknowledged the leadership of Mustapha Kemal. The official Government, that of the Sultan, had sent a reply some time before this as to the Terms of Peace which the Allies had proffered in the month of May. But no answer to this communication from the Sublime Porte had been vouchsafed, owing to the Allied Governments being unable — as usual — to agree upon what they were to say.

The Field-Marshal wrote in the diary on June 15:

> A long talk with Winston, who told me that he had circulated my paper of the 9th to a few selected members of the Cabinet! He had had a talk with Lloyd George last night, and he told me Lloyd George's proposals. Lloyd George is in favour of coming out of Persia, of fighting for Mosul, of getting Samuel to keep order in Palestine with Jew and Arab police — save the mark — of occupying Constantinople with British and Greeks if the French and Italians turn crusty.
>
> Lloyd George is persuaded that the Greeks are the coming Power in the Mediterranean both on land and on the sea, and wants to befriend them. The whole of Lloyd George's foreign policy is chaotic, and based on totally fallacious values of men and affairs. He thinks I am pro-Turk, and therefore I am suspect and my opinion not worth having, just as it is not worth having about Ireland — and so I am no longer consulted. I am all the more glad that I have given my opinion, and very fully, in my Note sent in on June 9.

Next day the entry occurs (he was staying at Grove End for a few days):

> A dispatch-rider with telegrams sent down by Mogg, and a of them from Milne saying that the Turkish Government troops had been defeated by the Nationalists and in consequence had withdrawn, and now the Nationalists under Kemal were attacking us on the Ismid line; and Milne says he has not sufficient force to hold Constantinople and Ismid and he asks for orders what to do, and also to withdraw from

Batoum! So now all my warnings are coming true, and I don't know what the Frocks will do next.

On the morrow, the 17th, he wrote:

> I told Winston that in my opinion we were heading straight for disaster in Constantinople, Dardanelles, Mesopotamia, and Persia. As I had over and over again pointed out, our policy had no relation to the forces at our disposal, and we were incapable of carrying out our commitments. Even now, although Milne has begged for the battalions from Batoum, the Cabinet cannot make up its mind to let them go. I have ordered a cavalry regiment from Palestine and a battalion from Malta to Constantinople, but when I see the Cabinet I mean to tell them that we shall want far more forces than that. I will urge that the Greeks be allowed to take Eastern Thrace and to threaten from Smyrna towards Panderma. But I will point out that all this means war with Turkey and Russia, and will end in our being kicked out of Constantinople. I saw Venizelos, who is sketchy to a degree. He promises Lloyd George everything, and Lloyd George believes everything he is told; but when I come to pin Venizelos down, he knows nothing and can promise nothing.

Of a Cabinet meeting held next day, Wilson wrote:

> I made, for me, a long and full statement, amounting to this. That I had not enough troops to carry out the Cabinet policy in Ireland, Constantinople, Palestine, Mesopotamia and Persia, not to mention England, Egypt and India, I said I must have at least another division in Constantinople and another in Mesopotamia, I proposed a Greek division for Constantinople, since I gathered that neither France nor Italy would help, and I proposed to withdraw the whole 9 battalions from Persia and thus secure Mesopotamia for the present. But I warned the Cabinet that all this meant war with Turkey and possibly Russia, and with Arabs, Kurds, etc. — a very serious war, for which I could not give an estimate of troops. I begged once more for the Batoum battalions. As I was speaking, a telegram came in from Milne calling for a division, two cavalry regiments, etc., and a lot of guns. This fitted in exactly with what I had said, and was most opportune.
> Venizelos was sent for and asked if he could give a division. He said I could have one of the three divisions lining up on the Maritza, and he would postpone his advance into Eastern Thrace. At 5 o'c. he

came to my room and we discussed details. Meanwhile, at the Cabinet, my paper to withdraw from Persia brought Curzon and Milner to their feet, and it was quite clear they would resign if it was done. Lloyd George therefore temporized, and said he would wait for Percy Cox, now at Baghdad, to get home, i.e. at least a month!

The Field-Marshal motored down to Hythe on June 19, as a meeting with Millerand and Foch had been arranged. He gave Foch details of the statement he had made to the Cabinet on the previous day, and he found that French military opinion entirely coincided with his own as regards the Near East. He wrote next day:

> A talk early with Lloyd George, who is as much convinced as ever that the Greeks are splendid soldiers and that the Turks are perfectly useless. It is a most dangerous obsession.

Sir Henry was nevertheless in favour of making full use of the Greeks in the present emergency — the more so as news now arrived that Kemalists were threatening the Dardanelles. So, after prolonged discussion between Lloyd George, Millerand, Venizelos and the military representatives present at Hythe, Venizelos cabled to Smyrna, directing the Greek troops to move on Panderma, while Wilson arranged for a message to be sent to Milne authorizing him to call for a Greek division to move from Dedeagach to Ismid.

A large party of British Ministers, with Millerand, Foch and Wilson crossed the Channel to Bordogne on the 21st for a more formal conference. This was held next day, when a paper that had been drawn up by Foch and Wilson on the subject of disarming the Germans was passed as it stood. The British representatives returned home in the afternoon, and Sir Henry had a talk with Venizelos while crossing the Channel, of which the C.I.G.S. wrote in his diary:

> He says that the Greeks like Milne and believe in him, and he says that he is perfectly willing to hand over the whole Greek army to us if we are going to make a serious effort, but that otherwise he won't. We agreed between ourselves that, before anything was decided, we would wait for the result of the move of the Greeks to Panderma and the arrival of the Greek division at Ismid.

The C.I.G.S. believed that the Hellenic forces were capable of carrying out a relatively speaking modest programme such as this; but he was not unduly confident, for he wrote two days later:

> Venizelos says he can overrun Eastern Thrace with 2 divisions. The general on the spot says he wants 5 divisions. Yet Lloyd George is gambling upon the Greeks turning out trumps. My own opinion is that they won't, and then we shall be in the soup.

The situation in Ireland was, in the meantime, growing steadily worse, and the troops, who now were scattered in detachments all over the country, were experiencing a most trying time. As the Field-Marshal expressed it, the Sinn Feiners were at war with the troops, but the troops -were not allowed to be at war with the Sinn Feiners. Although Macready had been reinforced by six battalions and four cavalry regiments from England, there manifestly were not soldiers enough in the country to restore order, unless far sterner measures than had hitherto been employed were to be adopted so as to cope drastically with the situation. "I am very unhappy about Ireland," Sir Henry wrote in his diary on June 28, "I don't see any determination or driving power in the Cabinet and I really believe we shall be kicked out."

Chapter XXXI – 1920: July to December

The Spa Conference — The Allies and Turkey — The situation in Ireland growing graver — The struggle between Poland and Bolshevik Russia — Lloyd George's relations with Krassin and Kameneff — Question of reprisals in Ireland — Possibility of a Triple Strike — The Unknown Warrior — Sinn Fein outrages in Ireland — The Cabinet's volte-face *about Persia and Mesopotamia — Wilson's disgust at the Cabinet's proceedings.*

Arrangements had been made for a conference to be held early in July at Spa, at which German plenipotentiaries should meet the plenipotentiaries of the Allies, who would then bring forward the subject of German failures to carry out the terms of the Treaty of Versailles. But the Spa Conference was to be preceded by one at Brussels, at which only representatives of the Allies would be present, so as to prepare the ground. A somewhat anxious situation had arisen with regard to Poland, for that reconstituted state stood in danger of being overrun by Russian Bolshevik forces. The position of affairs at Constantinople and about the Straits was also pre-occupying the British Cabinet, in view of the Greek advance on Panderma and of the transfer of a Greek division from Thrace to Ismid. The British representatives at the two conferences were to be Lloyd George, Curzon and Worthington-Evans, and Sir Henry proceeded with them to Brussels on July 1.

The C.I.G.S. wrote in his diary:

> We got here at 7 o'c. Guards of Honour, flags, crowds, but more curiosity than acclamation. Tit Willow down from Paris. He and I dined with Lloyd George, Curzon and Evans, but nothing but political

talk and of the possibility of Bob Cecil forming a party from disgruntled Unionists, Wee Frees, and Leaguers of Nations. We discussed Ireland, and Lloyd George is under the ridiculous belief that for every one of our people who was murdered, two Sinn Feiners were murdered! And Lloyd George was gloating over this and hugging it to his heart as a remedy for the present disgraceful state of Ireland. An amazing frame of mind to be in.

On the following day a plenary meeting took place at which the question of German disarmament was discussed; Foch and Wilson were requested to draw up a paper on the subject. Sir Henry found Foch to be much disquieted at the Polish situation, and he wrote in the diary:

> I pointed out to him that 18 months ago I had begged the Frocks to define the eastern frontiers of Finland, Baltic States, Poland, etc., but they never would do it, and now no one can say what is the frontier between Poland and Russia.

Bad news came to hand from that quarter that same night, and again on the following morning. The Field-Marshal's view was that "the Frocks" ought forthwith to define the eastern frontier of the country, ought to bid the Poles get behind that frontier, and ought to forbid the Russian Bolshevik forces to cross the line. But he recognized the extreme difficulty of enforcing such injunctions at a moment when the Polish troops were apparently giving way at all points before victorious antagonists. He moreover pointed out that the Poles appeared to be occupying a line some 200 kilometres beyond their proper ethnographical frontier, that this must tend to accentuate Russian hostility, and that they ought to be called upon to retire. To Foch's contention that such a retirement would ruin the morale of the Polish army. Sir Henry rejoined that their morale must be risked for the sake of getting them out of Russian territory, where they had no business to be. The conferences in the Belgian capital completed, the various delegations motored on to Spa on July 4, and that day there is entered in the diary:

> It will only be when the French really feel safe in their own homes that we shall be able to get them reasonable as regards the

1920: July to December

Boches, or Poles, or Constantinople, or Syria, or reparations, or coal. Therefore all these conferences are waste of time, and we are all so many mines, bumping — sometimes out friends, sometimes our enemies.

I had a long interview with Venizelos about the question of command. Now that the Greeks from Smyrna, who are not under Milne, are in Panderma as well as Greeks by sea, who are under Milne, the question has become even more complicated. Venizelos showed his hand quite plainly and frankly. He thinks that the whole country, roughly west of a line Brussa — Smyrna, ought to be handed over to the Greeks. He thinks that he will next occupy Eastern Thrace up to the Chatalja lines. Then, later, he thinks he ought to have Constantinople. He was very insistent that the demilitarized zone arranged last February, without more troops than we could keep there, was no protection to the Straits. I agree, at any rate for the present.

A wire from the War Office saying that an Army Council meeting to-morrow to consider Dyer's case, and asking for my observations, I am replying that I have no observations, as I have not had time even to read the papers. What a disgraceful rush the whole thing is, and purely political.

The Field-Marshal eventually arranged that Milne should hold the command at Constantinople, on the Ismid front and on the Asiatic side of the Dardanelles, while the Greeks were to have control in the region between Ismid and the Dardanelles and were to occupy Eastern Thrace.

The first meeting of the Conference, with the German delegates present, was held on the 6th at a villa about a mile outside Spa. The German delegates were the Chancellor, Fahrenbach, the Foreign Secretary, von Simon, the War Secretary, Gissler, and the Chief of the Staff, General von Seckt, and Wilson gives his impressions of what passed, as follows, in his diary:

> The room was small and packed. Gissler spoke first. He made a long rambling statement of the difficulties the Boches were in. Lloyd George very restless, and continually talking to me, or Curzon, or Evans, and at last broke in to know whether Gissler was going to say when he could reduce from 200,000 to 100,000. Gissler said this was impossible, etc. Was that the final word, asked Lloyd George, No, said Gissler — and so on.

Then the meeting was adjourned and de la Croix and Hymans [the Belgian representatives], Lloyd George, Curzon, Evans and self, Millerand, Foch, Weygand, Sforza and Japanese Ambassador assembled in a small room, Lloyd George asked Foch whether there was anything in the demand for 200,000. Foch said there was nothing; if you gave 200,000 they would ask for 300,000; moreover they themselves fomented trouble in order to prove their case, notably rows now at Hamburg, all got up for Spa. Lloyd George not quite satisfied, nor I, so he asked me. I repeated what I have often said, viz. that nobody knows the right figure. The Boches may be right. We may be right. Nobody knows, but what we *do* know is that the Boches have never yet employed 100,000, so how can they claim the necessity for 200,000? We now give them 100.000 soldiers, 150,000 police, 17,000 gendarmerie, and all this outside the Occupied Territory. This argument clinched the matter and the meeting reassembled.

Lloyd George then gave a *résumé* of where we would have been had the Treaty been carried out, and where we actually are. It was not very well done, rather halting, rather theatrical, not convincing — but he wound up by asking whether the Boches would come here to-morrow with a clear proposal of dates for reduction to 100,000 and dates for handing over all material.

Simon followed, full of excuses. Then the Chancellor. Fahrenbach is a faded person. He made a long and well delivered speech. He described revolutions, strikes, riots, etc. Said everything would be done that could be done, but the impossible must not be asked; and he wound up by saying that he was an old man who was soon going before the Almighty, and he pledged his honour that ever3rthing would be done. It was rather pathetic.

Then, a pause. Lloyd George asked again his definite question, as also did de la Croix. Simon said they would try, and a meeting is arranged for to-morrow. My impression of the meeting is very clear. There is no personality, no vitality, no magnetism, no power in those three Boches, and so it does not really matter what they say, because those men can enforce nothing. It is a desperately serious situation. I personally doubt if they will fix a date, but it makes no matter whether they do or not.

The British, French and Italian plenipotentiaries met on the folio-wing morning, with M. Venizelos present, to decide upon the reply that should be sent to the Sultan's Government, in answer to representations begging for certain substantial modifications in the Terms of Peace which the Allies were imposing. The Terms had been presented in May, the question had already been left in suspense for several weeks since receipt of the Ottoman protest, and the matter had consequently become pressing. The plenipotentiaries, however, decided that, but for one trifling alteration, the Treaty must be accepted intact by the Turks; and, having come to this conclusion, they proceeded to draft a sternly worded Note intimating that the Treaty must be signed within ten days of receipt of the Note. But the plenipotentiaries were perfectly well aware that the Sultan's Government no longer exercised effective control within Turkish dominions outside of Constantinople, and that acceptance of the Treaty by the Sublime Porte would not bind Mustapha Kemal and the Nationalists (who dominated all Turkey-in-Asia that was not occupied by the Allies) in the slightest degree.

That accomplished, the Plenary Conference met afresh in the afternoon, when General von Seckt set forth his plans for handing over armament to the Allies, and for reducing the German military forces to a total of 100,000, which latter process, he intimated, would be completed within fifteen months. Lloyd George at once challenged the disarmament figures; he said, further, that to allow the length of time proposed for effecting the reduction was quite out of the question, and Wilson wrote in the diary:

> He elaborated a stupid argument that if the Boche Government really meant to disarm the three million peasants who have arms, they could do so at once; and he got the answer that he deserved from Simon, who said that even victorious England could not disarm Ireland.

What period should be allowed the Germans to reduce their military forces to 100,000 was referred to the Allies' military representatives, and these agreed on insisting that the operation must be concluded by September 1.

Wilson wrote in his diary:

> On the return to the hotel I found a telegram from Tim Harington saying that Macready has asked for another three battalions and a

brigade head-quarters, and asking if I approved. I at once wired approval, but added that I hoped the S. of S. realized that these incessant demands would make us impotent in all other theatres, and that we should be faced with grave difficulties in Ireland when winter set in as to barrack accommodation. I told Lloyd George about this further call for troops, and that in my opinion not only Macready, but all the authorities, were gravely miscalculating the situation. But he reverted to his amazing theory that someone was murdering 2 Sinn Feiners to every loyalist the Sinn Feiners murdered. I told him that, of course, this was absolutely not so, but he seemed to be satisfied that a counter-murder association was the best answer to Sinn Fein murders. A crude idea of statesmanship, and he will have a rude awakening.

Two days later (July 9), Wilson wrote in the diary:

At 10.30 we met the Boches again, but this time only the Chancellor and Simon, as Gissler refused to sign and had resigned and gone off. The Chancellor and Simon signed, but Simon made it quite clear that it meant nothing — nor does it. But our amazing Frocks were quite satisfied. We then passed on to the "Coupables"; but F.E. and Cambon and other Frocks who have been considering the Coupables for 18 months asked for another ¼ of an hour! Typical Frock work. The whole of this Conference is a farce and waste of time. Not much other news, except that the Frocks saw the Poles, Patek and Grabski, and told them to behave and under certain conditions they would support. How the Frocks are going to support I do not know, nor does Foch.

This appears next day:

I went across and had a long talk with Venizelos. He scouted the idea that it was not safe to withdraw 2 divisions from the Smyrna command; he hopes to have Thrace occupied in a month from now. Then if that is not a sufficient lesson to the Turks, he thinks we ought to occupy Brussa, Eski Shehr and Afium Kara-Hissar. I said that this might prove a rather serious operation, and I proposed that all operations based on Constantinople should be under Milne, and all operations based on Smyrna under the C. in C. Greeks. To this he agreed. For this operation Venizelos said he would call out three more divisions. He also told me quite frankly that he meant to chase the

1920: July to December 301

Turks out of Constantinople and also occupy Trebizond.

At 2.30 p.m. Venizelos came to my room in a state of excitement and anger, to show me a telegram he had just received from C. in C. Smyrna that the Greeks, against all Venizelos's orders, had occupied Brussa. We did not want this just now, and Brussa is a holy place to the Mahommedans.

Sir Henry returned to London on July 11. He had a discussion with Churchill on the subject of Ireland on the following day, and, according to his diary, he spoke his mind to his superior with a refreshing candour:

> I told him that the present policy was suicidal, that it would lead to our being put out of Ireland, that we must take strong measures or retire, that if we retired we lost our Empire, that before taking strong measures we must convince England that they are necessary. I told him that Foch was more anxious about Ireland than he was about Poland; that Venizelos, the King of the Belgians, three Belgian Cabinet Ministers, Foch and many others saw more clearly where things were drifting than did our Cabinet. But I did not make much impression.

The Field-Marshal was strongly opposed to the carrying out of reprisals in haphazard fashion by more or less irresponsible policemen or soldiers, as a reply to the Sinn Fein outrages; but he was quite prepared to acquiesce in reprisals if these were to be carried out openly under proper authority and were directed against rebel leaders — "shooting by roster," as he expressed it. He was, however, recalled to Spa within three days, for the Germans were showing themselves recalcitrant over coal. The question of occupying the Ruhr was consequently discussed there between Foch, General Degoutte, himself and others, and they agreed that such an operation could be carried out by a force of seven divisions. But an understanding was in the end arrived at with the Germans, although Sir Henry doubted its being loyally carried out. Bad news arrived from Mesopotamia while he was at Spa, for General Haldane, who was in command in that theatre, was asking for a brigade and was also warning the War Office that a whole division might have to be sent from India

Wilson wrote in his diary:

> I told Lloyd George that this is what I have been prophesying and that what is essential is *concentration* of forces in theatres vital to us, viz. England, Ireland, Egypt, India, Mesopotamia, in that order. I asked if I might withdraw from Persia, but he said Curzon would not stand it. At midnight, just before going to bed, I wired to Winston that in view of reports from Mesopotamia I urged the dispatch of a whole division from India and not only a brigade, for it was essential to give these Arabs on the lower Euphrates a good lesson.

Next day (the 16th) there is the entry:

> Lloyd George told me he had heard — I don't know how — that the Bolsheviks were going to completely overrun Poland and come up against Germany. We had a meeting of Lloyd George, Millerand, Foch and me. Foch and I said that it was no use pouring in more arms into Poland, unless, and until, the Poles had a good national government, fully representative of a united people determined to stand against invasion. Lloyd George asked if Foch would go out to Poland and steady the situation. He replied that that was a matter for M. Millerand. Millerand said he could not agree, unless the conditions put forward by the two Marshals were fulfilled, and I said it would never do to risk the priceless asset of Foch's name in a wild scheme of this sort.

Wilson returned to London with Lloyd George on July 17, and he occasionally spent a day or two sailing in a yacht, the *White Heather* which he had bought, during the succeeding weeks. But there were too many pressing matters to attend to in London, for him to be able to enjoy a real holiday. Aproposal that the Bolshevik forces which were threatening Poland should enter into an armistice had been submitted to Russia by the Allies; but the reply to this suggestion was by no means favourable, and Sir Henry wrote in his diary in reference thereto:

> A Cabinet this morning, Lloyd George presiding, of some 20. We spent three hours discussing -what last night's telegram from the Bolsheviks meant, when it is as plain as a pikestaff — an impudent refusal of all Frock demands. The Gadarene swine never galloped as

fast as these Frocks.

He also mentions in the diary a conversation with Lord Duncannon on the subject of Ireland, whom he told that, if he were in the House of Commons, he would

> march down to Lloyd George and say: "You have two courses open to you. One is to clear out of Ireland and the other is to knock Sinn Fein on the head. But, before you do this latter, you must have England on your side, and therefore you must go stumping the country explaining what Sinn Fein means. If you get England on your side — and you can — there is nothing you can't do. If you don't, then there is nothing that you can do."

For the ferment in Ireland was spreading, outrages were becoming more frequent, the campaign of murder was being carried on with ever-increasing ferocity and daring, and the Executive was showing itself more and more incapable of suppressing the disorders. Very serious riots had broken out in Belfast. There were some signs of the Cabinet awakening to the gravity of the situation, but no signs of that body being prepared to take adequate steps to cope with the peril, and this appears in the diary on July 28:

> Long Military Members' meeting this morning. We discussed at length the parlous situation we are drifting into for want of a policy. We have 28 battalions in England and 40 in Ireland. When we have drafted from Ireland for India we shall be 4,500 men down on our present effectives. Macready will then ask for another 8-10 battalions. Then, if we go to martial law, Macready says he will want another 9 battalions. This will leave 10 battalions (and of these 3 are for India and 5 are Irish and very weak), besides 10 Guards battalions, to look after England. Altogether we are now pretty near our disaster. I rubbed all this into Winston to-night with the utmost vehemence, but had no effect. I told him I was putting up a paper about the state of our military affairs for the Cabinet to read and chew, and I am going to make this paper pretty strong stuff. He asked me if I would put up a proposal to hand over Ulster to the Ulstermen, and withdraw our 5 or 6 battalions from there. I said I would think over it.

Next day there is the entry:

> I had a long talk with Winston, I told him we were getting a bad name for business, and I quoted a number of cases — Rawly for India, this has been going on for months; dress for the army; abolition of brigadiers; formation of T.F.; recasting of T.F. office in the War Office, etc., etc. Winston had nothing to say, but he did not like my attack. We then discussed the general situation, and I told him we were heading straight for disaster. The news from Ireland, from England of coming strikes, from Palestine where Samuel wants to annex Trans-Jordania, from Mesopotamia where the Euphrates L. of C. is still cut, from Persia where Kurds and Bolsheviks are attacking, is all bad. But it would not matter a button if we had any reserves *anywhere*. But we are all out before the blow falls. A most dangerous situation.

On the following day (the 30th) Wilson wrote:

> I got Winston to agree at last to the dispatch of the whole division from India to Mesopotamia. I urged this from Spa a fortnight ago and only get a decision now! Marvellous. The news from Ireland continues even worse. The Sinn Feins are steadily getting the upper hand, and unless this Cabinet act soon all this will spread to this country and become wholly unmanageable. Basil Thomson's secret report for this week is the gravest I have read yet and forecasts revolutionary strikes for the end of September. And we have practically no troops to meet this.

Sir Henry was able to pay some flying visits to his yacht at Cowes during the first week of August. He had been elected a member of the Royal Yacht Squadron, and he sailed on friends' yachts in some of the races. But he was recalled to London before the end of the week, owing to the situation in Mesopotamia having become worse. A small British column had been destroyed, and the C.I.G.S. felt more than ever convinced that it was necessary to withdraw the troops from Persia and to concentrate them in Iraq. He wrote in his diary:

> I had two long talks with Winston and rubbed this in once more, and I am drafting a telegram to Haldane on these lines, to lay before

the Cabinet to-morrow.

Winston told me that when he went over to see Lloyd George he found him closeted with Krassin and Kameneff, and he sent out a note to Winston to say, have told them that if they don't stop their advance in Poland I shall order the British fleet into the Baltic at once." So he is thinking of declaring war on the Bolsheviks, having thrown away every card in the pack.

Lord Riddell came to see me. He is very seriously concerned about the future, and asked me what he was to say to his 3,500,000 readers, I replied, "Let the Cabinet give up whispering in 10 Downing Street and come out into the open. Let them hoist the flag of England and rally England round them. With the English behind us there is nothing we can't do, and without England there is nothing we can do." Riddell was much struck with this and said he would play on it in his newspapers. I hope he will, for we are sadly in need of a *positive* lead. I told Riddell that I had seen no sign of government since the Armistice, and that I was afraid that Lloyd George and all his gang would go right under. Riddell repeated that no one he had ever met had "so clear a grasp of essentials, so wide an outlook, so far-seeing a gaze into the future." I asked him for a cigarette!

This appeals in the diary next day (August 5):

Winston and Lloyd George pressing me hard to write a paper on Mesopotamia. I have written a short paper, showing our dispersion and once again advising concentration and a withdrawal of 16 battalions from Constantinople and the whole of the troops from Persia. I showed this to Winston, who said it was not a bit what he and the Cabinet wanted. What they wanted was a tactical paper on the situation on the Lower Euphrates. I told him that I had not sufficient local knowledge to write this, and I refused to do it. Winston had, therefore, to accept my paper, which he circulated at once to the Cabinet.

He told me that Lloyd George was now considering the question of helping Wrangel in the Crimea.* Either even at this late hour, we go to war with the Bolsheviks and mobilize all possible forces among the Allies and along the Border states from Murmansk to the Caucasus, or we clear out. What was a perfectly easy operation last

---

* General Wrangel was in command of an anti-Bolshevik force in the Crimea, operating in conjunction with Don Cossacks.

January year is now a forlorn hope. The real fact is that this Government is going under and is dragging the country with it. The miserable Versailles Treaty has gone long ago — built on the three false bases of: 1. Great Empires are a danger and therefore Balkanize Europe; 2. All "Peoples" love each other, therefore have a League of Nations; 3. My Cousin represents America, therefore let him lead us by the nose. The Peace Treaty was bound to crash. But *what* a mess.

Next day there is the entry:

Cabinet in Lloyd George's room in House of Commons. We discussed Persia and Mesopotamia. No decision, except to send Sir Percy Cox back to report. He has just come home to report — now he is going out to report. I spoke very strongly in the sense of my paper of last night; but it was no use. Milner and Curzon made it clear that they would resign if we came out of Persia, and Lloyd George funked. So, although Winston spoke up, no decision was reached.

At 4 o'c. Lloyd George sent for me, and I remained till to to 9. First of all drawing up terms of a truce between Bolsheviks and Poles, and then, with Lloyd George and Bonar Law, discussing these with Kameneff and Krassin. I was horrified at the almost servile way in which Lloyd George looked after Russian interests and was hostile to the Poles. Also the way in which he told the Bolsheviks what he would do with our fleet at "Helsingfors and in the Black Sea" if he had to take action, making it quite clear that his only action would be naval. The whole tone of Lloyd George shocked me very much. He was with friends in Kameneff and Krassin, and together they discussed the French and the Poles.

In fixing a date for an answer to our truce proposals, Lloyd George fixed, as latest, 10 a.m. Sunday (i.e. the day after to-morrow). I pointed out that it was quite impossible to get an answer by then from Moscow. But neither Lloyd George nor Kameneff took any notice. In fixing a date for the truce and "cease fire" they fixed midnight Monday-Tuesday. Again I pointed out that this, of course, was impossible, so this date was fixed as the date when orders for the "cease fire" should be issued from Moscow and from Warsaw. When I said that I thought we ought to put "from G.H.Q. Russian Army and G.H.Q. Polish Army" as very possibly the Poles would no longer be in Warsaw, the two Bolsheviks and Lloyd George burst out laughing, Kameneff having to stuff his handkerchief into his mouth. It was quite clear to me that all three knew, and that Lloyd George approved, of

1920: July to December 307

the occupation of Warsaw by the Bolsheviks.

It was an amazing 5 hours meeting. It left me with a clear sense that Lloyd George is in company with friends and kindred spirits when with the Bolsheviks. All through the meeting, the Bolsheviks, assisted by Lloyd George, were driving a wedge between the English and the French, and Lloyd George went so far as to say that if the French did not agree to the truce terms, then he would not support Poland nor make war on the Bolsheviks. WHEW!

A conference took place at Lympne on August 8,[*] Millerand, Foch and Berthelot having come over to England for the purpose, and Lloyd George read out the proposed terms of truce between the Bolshevists and Poland. Wilson wrote in his diary:

> Millerand followed with a clear statement that he would not deal with the Bolsheviks, that their word and signature were worth nothing, and that they had neither honour nor laws.

This created an impasse; but messages were received just then which solved it. For these indicated that the Bolsheviks for all practical purposes declined to accept the Lympne truce terms and proposed, as a condition of granting Poland an armistice, to insist upon that country adopting Soviet government and its disarming and demobilizing. This intelligence obliged the conference to discuss how pressure could be brought upon the Bolsheviks. But all that Foch, Wilson and Beatty could suggest was blockade in the Baltic and Black Sea, efforts to induce the Baltic States to help Poland, and the sending of some assistance to Wrangel and the Don Cossacks. So Wilson wrote in deep dejection in his diary:

> All this will inevitably lead to the French occupation of the Ruhr and this again will lead to the break up of the Alliance. I have no doubt at all in my own mind that our only way out of all these troubles is in a new and firm alliance with France. Foch agrees. He is very anxious at my accounts of Ireland — and well he may be. I don't

---

[*] The Treaty of Sèvres, a treaty of peace between the Allies and the Sultan's Government, was signed this day. But the Nationalists — the Kemalists — always repudiated many of its provisions.

believe that we can now keep the Bolsheviks apart from the Boches. This will mean that we shall lose Danzig; and Beatty says that, if he has not got Danzig or Helsingfors, he cannot blockade. A wire from Haking tonight says he won't be able to hold Danzig without 4 more battalions and some guns, etc. Of course, we have not got 4 battalions. And so the whole Versailles Treaty continues to crash, and even these idiotic and self-satisfied Frocks are beginning to see this.

Next day there is the entry:

> At the meeting to-day Lloyd George and Millerand differed heavily about Lloyd George's absolutely indefensible decision to allow Kameneff and Krassin to remain on in London, after the Soviet's refusal to agree to our truce terms. Lloyd George's attitude is incomprehensible. Millerand and Foch were very angry. Nor could Millerand extract from Lloyd George what Kameneff and Krassin were doing, for Lloyd George said they were not discussing trade! Then what *are* they doing? I wrote on a slip to Beatty, "I agree with every word that Millerand has said; Lloyd George's attitude of political funk is disastrous."
>
> In the end it was decided to wire to the Poles and say that, if they appointed a C. in C. and kept their 22 divisions in being, and were determined to fight this thing out, we would help all we could; and after an hour's wrangling we got a form of words to which both Prime Ministers agreed. But Millerand and Foch were both profoundly dissatisfied and alarmed and suspicious. I drove in with Foch to Folkestone, where he got a great reception.

Two days later (August 11), Wilson learnt that the Foreign Office had telegraphed to Warsaw, repeating the message to Paris, and had recommended the Poles to agree to the Bolshevik terms for an armistice. This recommendation the French Government, as it had not been consulted, straightway repudiated. The Field-Marshal was therefore summoned to a Cabinet meeting at the House of Commons in the evening, and there he

> found the Frocks in a great state of excitement, abusing the French, rushing off into the House to answer Labour members about the Wrangel affair, and in short a Cabinet of perfectly useless old men.

1920: July to December 309

The French had acknowledged Wrangel, and this Wilson considered unwise. But he fully sympathized with their annoyance at the action of the British Government in advising the Poles to accept the Bolshevik terms without first communicating with Paris.* At a Cabinet meeting held on the following day (the 12th) a Note, about to be sent the French to point out the danger of divergence of opinion between the two countries, was discussed, and according to the Field-Marshal, the Ministers present seemed "blissfully ignorant of the fact that they were the party to blame" The situation in Mesopotamia and Persia was then considered, but Churchill and the C.I.G.S. were, as usual, unable to persuade the Cabinet to withdraw from Persia.

Wilson wrote in the diary on the 15th:

> We are in a regular pie everywhere. News from Mesopotamia increasingly uneasy, the same from Ireland. Then, the Unions, with their "Committee of Action," are challenging the Government and threatening Triple Alliance strikes nest month; as usual, the Government are not governing.

He was, moreover, seriously concerned on seeing secret correspondence which showed unmistakably that Kameneff was carrying out mischievous propaganda in this country, was plotting to create discord with France, and was in close touch with the "Committee of Action." This appears in the diary on August 18:

> I sent for Sir Basil Thomson, he told me some curious things. He was publishing this morning in America and this afternoon in the *Temps* certain wireless messages which showed the connexion between the *Daily Herald* and the Bolsheviks. One of these had an allusion to Kameneff, which was cut out by the Cabinet because Lloyd George said that, if published, there would be an immediate

---

* The Bolshevik forces had for several days been sweeping forward towards the Vistula, and the prospects of Poland appeared to be most gloomy; but the situation was about to be transformed. On the 14th the Polish forces gained important successes, the Bolshevik troops broke into disarray, many guns and swarms of prisoners were captured, and the Poles within a very few days had chased the invaders back into Russia, a vanquished host.

call from the country for Kameneff's removal. At a Cabinet meeting it was decided that Curzon should write to Kameneff and say that it appeared now that he -was carrying on a propaganda, and asking for his reasons. After the Cabinet had gone away Lloyd George sent for Curzon, and put so many conditions on to the letter that finally Curzon said he would not write the letter — and did not!

I had two long talks with Winston; he enumerated the different steps from Prinkipo to to-day when, although pretending to uphold the integrity of Poland, we did nothing to ensure it and even prevented arms and stores passing through Danzig. The whole thing is most perplexing and worse, and my often recurring suspicions of Lloyd George crowd in on me to-night.

Next day there is the entry:

I drafted my Note to Winston before breakfast. I based the whole thing upon military grounds. I showed that the "Council of Action" were challenging the Government, and at the same time were in close touch and collaboration with the Bolsheviks, whose avowed intention, purpose and action are the ruin of England. And I then said that if it was the Government's intention to fight the "Council of Action," it was a military necessity to uncover the whole of this nefarious plot and explain to the troops what it was they were going to be called to fight upon, otherwise I could not guarantee what would happen. I discussed my Note at length with Tim and Bill Thwaites and they agreed to all I said. I would not be surprised if my Note to Winston led to my resignation, and I said this to Tim and to Bill.

Churchill wrote a Minute of uncompromising character on Wilson's Note; he urged the expulsion of Kameneff and Krassin, and, after a conversation with the C.I.G.S., he sent on the whole correspondence for certain members of the Cabinet to see. The Field-Marshal wrote in his diary that day:

I told Winston it was the chance of his life to come out as an Englishman, and that in one bound he would recover his lost position and be hailed as saviour by all that is best in England. Winston and I also discussed the ridiculous position of Danaig, where the Labour leaders absolutely refuse to allow any arms, ammunition, etc., to pass through to Poland, Danzig being a Free city under the League of Nations.

1920: July to December 311

While they were talking, a telegram, sent by Radcliffe* from Warsaw, was handed in which dissipated any doubts that might have remained as to the extent of the Polish successes over the Bolshevik forces.

Milne had come home on leave from Constantinople. He was anxious to be replaced after his long spell of active service in the Near East, and, in the course of this conversation with the C.I.G.S., Churchill put forward the suggestion that Harington should be selected to act as Milne's successor. Sir Henry was delighted at this proposal, although the departure of the deputy, who had acted for him for weeks on end during the protracted confabulations of the Peace Conference, would be a serious loss to the General Staff in Whitehall; and that evening he wrote in his diary:

> I asked Tim later, and he liked the idea. Nothing is good enough for Tim.

The good news that was arriving from Poland was counterbalanced just at this time by a telegram from Haldane, who stated that the troubles in Mesopotamia were growing worse, and who was asking for very substantial reinforcements from India. A letter written by the C.I.G.S. to General Sir H.F.M. Wilson, who was commanding at Constantinople during Milne's absence, shows how the unbalanced policy of the Cabinet was straining the resources in troops that the War Office had at its disposal. The Field-Marshal wrote:

> I think you know that during the month of August we sent 10 Native battalions from India to Basrah, and in this month of September we are sending 6 more Native battalions and 3 British battalions from India, making a total reinforcement from India for Mesopotamia of 19 battalions, plus a few guns, sappers, etc. On the top of this comes a telegram from Haldane asking for yet another two divisions and two cavalry brigades. These, of course, we cannot

---

* Radcliffe was in Poland as British Military Representative on a Franco-British Mission, on which Weygand was French Military Representative and was acting as principal Military Adviser to the Poles.

supply, because India has warned us in the most solemn manner that she has reached the limit of her possibilities. In looking round the dish, the only bit of food I see is your three battalions at Constantinople. There is nothing worth talking about either in Palestine or Egypt. There is obviously nothing on the Rhine or in Ireland, and we have not nearly enough troops here in England in view of the danger of this miners' strike which is now hanging over us. I write you all this gossip so that you may know that I am not going to call on you for troops unless the matter is vitally urgent. The fact, of course, is that the Cabinet policy has completely outrun their military power, and although we have repeatedly told the Cabinet that this course of action is bound to lead to disaster, I have never been able to change their headlong course.

At the request of Churchill, and in concert with the Director of Naval Intelligence and Sir B. Thomson, Sir Henry had drawn up a memorandum indicating the connexion between Kameneff and some extremist members of the British Labour party, and urging that the so-called Russian Trading Mission should be expelled from the country. Several of the Cabinet Ministers were in favour of this step, but the Prime Minister had betaken himself to Lucerne, he did not wish action in the matter to be taken until he should return, and there was yet further delay after his return to England on September 7. Wilson wrote in his diary on the 9th:

> It seems from a note of Mogg's, that Lloyd George has not taken action against Kameneff, that the Cabinet is angry, that Winston and Walter Long from Copenhagen in the *Enchantress*, and others, are all summoned for a Cabinet on the 13th; and meanwhile Lloyd George has gone away again. I thought that he would act like this.

But the Prime Minister had apparently remained in, or near, London on this occasion, for on the 10th the Field-Marshal entered in the diary:

> There was a scratch Cabinet this morning, with Lloyd George present, to discuss Kameneff and expulsion. I was told to stand by, but was not sent for. Then, this afternoon, Kameneff and Krassin were with Lloyd George at Downing Street, but to-night I have not heard the result. I was all along afraid that Lloyd George would not take

1920: July to December 313

action, and I said so to Horne. It was on the 18th of last month that I wrote to Winston about Kameneff, and nothing has been done. The Miseries who are in the Cabinet talk and do nothing. Horne, Eric Geddes and Winston a week ago were as strong as I am, but have done nothing. Austen, Curzon, Balfour and Milner all wrote to Winston in the same strain, and nothing done.

My case is pretty clear. I am told to get ready for war with the Triple Alliance and Council of Action. I find there is collusion with Kameneff. Propaganda amongst the troops by the *Daily Herald*, In my plans I propose to withdraw 4 battalions from the Rhine and 10 from Ireland. Macready told me last Monday that if I take 10 battalions from Ireland the whole of the R.I.C. would go, and he would have to "put up the shutters." And this is the position I am in.

Sir Henry, however, learnt next day that Kameneff had taken his departure, and that this Bolshevik agent furthermore had been told by Lloyd George that he was not to come back. He wrote in the diary:

> This is something, but why have Krassin and any of his vile brood? In the report of yesterday's Cabinet Krassin and his fellows are described as the "more honourable" members of the delegation. Ye Gods!

The situation in Ireland was in the meantime going from bad to worse, and Wilson and Macready were in agreement in disapproving strongly of unauthorized reprisals to which, so far as could be judged, the Prime Minister and the Secretary of State for War saw no objection. A brigade commander in Ireland had called to see him on September 10, and of their conversation Sir Henry wrote in his diary:

> He gives a shocking account of the state of affairs, and sees no remedy except martial law and real stern justice, which, he says, would stamp out all murders in a week.

On September 13 the entry occurs in the diary:

> I put in a note to the Cabinet to say that my plans for the strike in England consisted, among other things, in bringing back 4 battalions

from the Rhine and 10 battalions from Ireland, and that Macready had told me that if I withdrew 10 battalions from Ireland he would have to put up his shutters, for the R.I.C. would resign. I asked the Cabinet which theatre they wished to gamble in. Not an easy paper to answer.

On the 15th Wilson wrote:

> I went over to Downing Street at 11.15 a.m. and had ¾ hour with Lloyd George alone, and then attended for a part of a Cabinet. Lloyd George began about Repington's book, which has just come out and which I have skimmed. In one part of the book (which I have missed) Repington says that Robertson told him that Lloyd George had been rude to Foch. This has infuriated Lloyd George, who claims never to have been rude to Foch.[*]
> Then Lloyd George discussed the coming coal strike, which he thinks is really coming, and, according to Horne, may be complicated by a railway strike. Lloyd George wanted to know if the army was sound. I said it was. I told him the steps I had already taken as precautions. This pleased him very much. Then we discussed Persia and Mesopotamia at the Cabinet.

On the 20th there is the entry:

> I lunched with d'Abernon alone at the Ritz. He was very interesting about his Polish trip, and about the future of Poland, Russia, Germany and France. He thinks the Poles will be able to hold their own all this winter, and he has real hopes that the Bolsheviks will crack before spring. He was more inclined to agree with me now than he was at Spa, that we shall never do any good in Europe until we make the Frenchmen happy about France by a regular alliance, and that this alliance should carry with it conditions about Germany, the Near East, etc. I am sure that this is the foundation of our foreign policy, but we shall never do this so long as Curzon is at the Foreign Office.

On the 29th there is a long entry in the diary with regard to Ireland:

---

[*] Vide p. 280 in this connexion.

I had 1½ hours this evening with Lloyd George and Bonar Law. 1 told them what I thought of reprisals by the "Black and Tans," and how this must lead to chaos and ruin. Lloyd George danced about and was angry, but I never budged. I pointed out that these reprisals were carried out without anyone being responsible; men were murdered, houses burnt, villages wrecked (such as Balbriggan, Ermistymon, Trim, etc.). I said that this was due to want of discipline,* and this *must* be stopped. It was the business of the Government to govern. If these men ought to be murdered, then the Government ought to murder them. Lloyd George danced at all this, said no Government could possibly take this responsibility. After much wrangling, I still sticking to it that either these things ought to be done or ought not, and if they ought then it was the business of the Government to do them, and if they ought not then they ought to be stopped, I got some sense into their heads, and Lloyd George wired for Hamar Greenwood, Macready, Tudor and others to come over to-morrow night.

I warned Lloyd George that, although up to now the army had remained disciplined and quiet, it was quite possible that they might break out any minute if one of their officers were murdered by Sinn Feiners, and that the report to-night that Mallow had been sacked after the murder of one of the sergeants of the 17th Lancers may well prove to be that the 17th Lancers had sacked the town. All this was terribly dangerous. What was quite evident to me after this long talk was that neither Lloyd George nor Bonar Law had the faintest idea of what to do.

We discussed also the possibilities of the strike coming off, and they were both so much inclined to think that it might, that I telephoned across to War Office and told them to wire round to Commands to postpone all sailings of troops to the East for yet another week. These postponements cost us £1,000 a day in ships, and I told Lloyd George. But, of course, he did not mind in the least. It is only Government [public?] money.

---

* In a sense, this no doubt was so. But discipline of a very high standard indeed would have been required to ensure absolutely that individual members of the R.I.C. and of the "Black and Tans," or even that parties of these severely tested agents of the law, would not occasionally take the law into their own hands in face of what they had to put up with. Scattered about the country in very small detachments, as most of them were, the maintenance of a rigid discipline would have been difficult even in far less trying circumstances.

> All this is profoundly disquieting. Lloyd George has never shown a sign of the power to govern since the Armistice, and this Irish affair is typical of his ideas of governing. It is a hopeless and heart-breaking affair. I am glad I am in no way responsible, and that I have protested for months against this method of out-terrorizing the terrorists by irresponsible persons. We drift from bad to worse, and always under the guidance of Lloyd George. Anyhow, neither Lloyd George nor Bonar can ever say that I have not warned them and very plainly spoken my mind.

During the whole of September the question of a coal strike, with the possible corollary of a sympathetic strike on the part of the railwaymen and the transport workers, had remained in suspense, negotiations being carried on continuously between Sir Robert Horne and the miners' leaders. The War Office had taken various precautionary steps, and Wilson had his plans all ready for a number of military moves to take place should the strike actually be declared. But the upshot still remained in doubt at the beginning of October, and it remained in doubt for the whole of that month.

The situation in Mesopotamia was easier, and General Monro had agreed to send another division thither from India. Wilson had moreover dispatched a trusted commander to Persia to take charge of the troops there, and he was able to note in his diary on October 7; "Tiny Ironside has got up to Kasvin." "Lloyd George made a fine fighting speech about Ireland at Carnarvon," he wrote in gratified surprise, on the 10th, "at long last he has come out into the open." But next day an entry appears, pitched in a very different key:

> Lloyd George in his Carnarvon speech accused the War Office of "stupidity" in their treatment of Ireland. At Victoria this morning I tackled him on the subject, and he had nothing to say. It strikes me that he will try and father reprisals on the soldiers. He had better be careful.

The Lord Mayor of Cork had been nominally on hunger strike in Brixton Prison since the middle of August, and interesting references to this matter, and to others, appear in the diary under date October 13:

J.T. Davies read me out yesterday's report on McSwinney, the Lord Mayor of Cork, by the Home Office doctor. He said that he and another doctor had walked suddenly into the cell, and had seen McSwinney munching something and swallowing it. Later on the nurse found some substance in the basin after he had washed his teeth, and this had been sent to the analyst. The other doctor said that, if he had been called in to a case such as he found in McSwinney, he would have ordered gentle exercise! It was the 61st day of starvation.

A long talk with Winston, just back from 3 weeks in the south of France. He was full of admiration for Lloyd George's speech at Carnarvon and for its bravery. Winston said, "You have been right all along, C.I.G.S., and the Government must shoulder the responsibility of reprisals." So at last there is some hope that the Cabinet will stop whispering in the back-parlour and will come out into the open.

Winston is going to repeat at Dundee all that Lloyd George said, and go still farther towards responsibility. As I said to him, once the Government shoulder responsibility the reprisals can start in mild form and go on *crescendo* if necessary.

Next day there is the entry:

I had a long talk with Lloyd George about Ireland. He told me he was going to shoulder the responsibility for reprisals, but wanted to wait till the American elections are over, as it would give such an election cry to Cox against England. The cursed elections take place next month. He told me the Cabinet this morning discussed Ireland, and many of them wanted to give way on Ireland. Lloyd George said he never would. A most disgusting thing, for, as I said to Lloyd George, every member of the Cabinet ought now to hop on to his individual whisky barrel and help Lloyd George to shoulder the situation.

There had been a noteworthy entry in Wilson's diary on October 4, dealing with an entirely different question. He had then written:

Dean Ryle (Westminster Abbey) came to see me with a proposal which greatly pleased me. He wants to exhume the body of a private soldier (not identified) in France, and to bury it with full honours in Westminster Abbey, putting a plain stone over it, saying something to the effect "Here lies the body of an unknown British soldier who died for his King and Country" I suggested some other word being used than "soldier," as then this would cover the Navy and the Air Force, and he agreed. I told him he must ask the King, who returns from Balmoral on Friday.

A further reference to the same subject appears in the diary on the 15th:

> Lloyd George then asked the Cabinet's opinion about the Dean of Westminster's idea of the burial of a private in the Abbey. Lloyd George, Horne and Arthur Lee were in favour, all the rest were against. Lloyd George then asked me. I said that no words could tell how proud we officers and men would be to have one of our simple soldiers buried in Westminster Abbey, and that I had suggested to the Dean that we should use the words "British Warrior," which would include soldiers, sailors and airmen, as we would love them to come in with us. I said that if the funeral took place, I would ask to be a pall bearer, and I suggested that the coffin and gun-carriage, after moving from Victoria, by Grosvenor Place, Constitution Hill, Admiralty Arch and Whitehall, should halt at the Cenotaph, for the unveiling and the two minutes silence, and then that the King and Cabinet should follow the coffin from there to the Abbey. My little speech completely turned the Cabinet, who became unanimously in favour, and Curzon was made chairman of a committee to draw up the programme. I am very glad.

The industrial situation had meanwhile become so strained, and the prospects of a coal strike, followed by a triple strike, appeared to be so imminent that Wilson obtained leave from Lloyd George to carry out a number of moves of troops, including bringing back two battalions from the Rhine; and he issued the necessary orders. Some of the moves were, however, cancelled next day as the position of affairs became more hopeful again. Several meetings between members of the Cabinet and leaders of the Trades Unions concerned took place during the following few days, and eventually it was arranged that certain proposals should be submitted to the miners for ballot on November 2. Sir Henry was inclined to hope that the triple strike would take place, for he felt convinced that the struggle must come and he doubted whether its postponement would in the end prove of advantage to the nation.

He was much gratified just at this time by the Duke of Connaught asking him to succeed his old commanding officer of the early 'nineties. Sir L.V. Swaine, as Colonel Commandant of the 3rd Battalion of the Rifle Brigade, and to that position Sir Henry was gazetted in due course. Sir H. Rumbold, just appointed Ambassador at Constantinople, came to see him on one of the last days of October before proceeding to take up the post, and he wrote in the diary:

> He was lamentably ignorant of the Turkish and Greek situation, and said that he had learnt more in our half-hour's talk than in all the Foreign Office palavers and papers. That Foreign Office and Curzon are hopeless. They have not even got maps.

The Lord Mayor of Cork had died, apparently of scurvy, on October 25, and on the 28th the Field-Marshal wrote in his diary:

> I telephoned to Macready and told him that Hamar Greenwood told me last night that the Government could not prevent the Lord Mayor's body being taken through Dublin, so all precautions must be taken. I then went to Winston, and I stormed about it to such an extent that he raced over to see the Prime Minister, with result that the body will not be sent through Dublin, but will be shipped straight to Cork. This is good. I telephoned to Macready and told him of the change.

Harington had definitely accepted the Constantinople command, and Sir Henry had arranged that Sir P. Chetwode, then holding the position of Military Secretary, should take over Harington's duties as D.C.I.G.S. As Rawlinson was leaving England to take up the appointment of Commander-in-Chief in India just at the same time, the Army Council invited him and Harington to a farewell dinner, at which the Secretary of State presided. Sir Henry was asked to make the final speech of the evening and of this he noted in his diary: "I touched lightly on the characters and careers of Rawly, Tim and Winston, and Winston said after I sat down, 'Thank God that man is not in the House of Commons.'" He was somewhat disturbed a day or two later by receiving a letter from Macready, who declared in it that more drastic action was imperative if reprisals on the part of the troops in Ireland were to be prevented. The rank and file had been behaving admirably hitherto; but the strain to which they were being subjected was beginning to tell, and a few isolated cases had already occurred where soldiers had taken the law into their own hands. The Field-Marshal told Churchill of this letter on November 2, and wrote in his diary:

> I told him that Macready was going to take more severe disciplinary action, even to removing C.O.s if the men took reprisals on their own. Winston wants me to go on shouldering the onus of reprisals for some time longer. Now that the American elections will be over to-day or to-morrow it will be easier for Lloyd George to take the responsibility. But I told Winston to hurry up, as it was not fair on the soldiers, and if the present regime was continued much longer the Prime Minister would have the army against him, or else have a mob instead of an army. I asked Winston to remember that in the end the authority of the Cabinet rested on the bayonets of the soldiers.
>
> Winston told me that Lloyd George was displeased with my minute, written a fortnight ago, on Macready's letter saying that discipline must be upheld, and that Lloyd George said that I had always been for drastic action and then, when it was taken, I criticized it. I said that of course this accusation had no relation to truth, and that, although I was in favour of strong action, it must be by responsible authority.

He wrote on the 6th:

> More murders in Ireland yesterday, and more reprisals. How the Cabinet can agree to all this and not take the responsibility absolutely beats me, or how they think this class of work will solve the Irish question passes my comprehension.

On the 10th there is the entry:

> A Cabinet on Ireland. I was not sent for, but they thought that everything was going on so well in Ireland, i.e. government by "Black and Tans," that they would leave it at that and not take over reprisals by Government action.
>
> Foch sent me a fine wire about our Unknown Dead, and he was

1920: July to December 321

at Boulogne when we shipped the coffin on the destroyer *Verdun*. I went to the dinner and dance given by the Pembrokes to the King and Queen of Spain. As I got back at 11.30, the telephone was ringing, and the Orderly Officer at the War Office read me a wire just received from Tim, telling me that Wrangel had lost the Perekop and that news from the Crimea was bad, and we might expect a lot of refugees at Constantinople. The French will hate this, as they have been backing Wrangel.

The Field-Marshal acted as one of the pall-bearers at the procession of the Unknown Warrior on the following day. He was deeply impressed and moved by the solemn pageant, by the scene at the unveiling of the Cenotaph, by the Silence, and by the further progress of the funeral cortege to Westminster Abbey and the service at the grave. He wrote in his diary:

> I don't think that even the old Abbey ever held so wonderful a ceremony, and I don't think that even London, even the world, ever saw so marvellous a procession, so beautiful a conception, so perfect a setting in such lovely weather.

News received from Constantinople within the next two or three days left no doubt as to the collapse of Wrangel. Moreover, a few days later, a fresh problem arose in the Near East owing to the elections held in Greece ending in Venizelos being decisively defeated — political transformation which pointed to an early return of ex-King Constantine to the Hellenic throne. "Lloyd George will find that he has backed the wrong horse," Sir Henry remarked in his diary on receipt of the news, and again, "The fall of Venizelos is a great defeat for Lloyd George, as he had put his shirt on the old Greek." The Field-Marshal foresaw that this event would be likely to complicate the position as between the United Kingdom and the Turkish Kemalists, and he arrived at the conclusion that the right British policy would be to make friends with Mustapha Kemal. He wrote in the diary on November 15:

> Great fuss going on about League of Nations' wish that we should send two companies to Vilna for a plebiscite. Ridiculous nonsense. I keep on refusing, at any rate until I know who is to

command, where they are going, what are their duties, and how long they will be wanted.

With regard to this matter there is the further entry on the 26th:

> The Cabinet have sided with me now about Vilna, and have so wired to Balfour at Geneva, I have won the first round!

News had reached London on the 22nd of the murder of fourteen officers in Dublin that morning — a deliberately plarmed atrocity on the part of the rebels, remorselessly carried out, which aroused the utmost indignation amongst the general public in England. Wilson bitterly resented the callous attitude of indifference that was displayed by the Cabinet in face of this shocking outrage, and he expressed himself with warmth on the subject in his diary:

> To-night Winston insinuated that the murdered officers were careless fellows and ought to have taken precautions- This fairly roused me, and I let fly about the Cabinet being cowards and not governing, but leaving it to "Black and Tans," etc. No Cabinet meeting, as the Cabinet do not seem to think that anything out of the way has happened! I urged on Winston, for the 100th time, that the Government should govern, should proclaim their fidelity to the Union and declare martial law. But this had no effect. I told him that I had not intended to speak about Ireland, as it was useless. But I was angry at the Ministerial attitude about these poor murdered officers, and I frightened Winston.

On the 24th he wrote:

> Another 3 murders in Ireland yesterday. Nothing having happened in Ireland in the last 2 days of any importance, there was again no Cabinet to-day! It is all simply past belief; a matter of 17 murders in 48 hours is considered of no importance by Lloyd George and his amazing Cabinet.

On the 26th there is the entry:

> Cecil and I to Westminster Abbey to the service for the [6]

murdered officers in Ireland. A most pitiful sight. Just as our service in the old Abbey on November 11 was the most glorious I ever saw or ever shall see, so the service this morning was the most pitiful, and, in a sense shameful, that I ever saw, and Lloyd George, Winston and Hamar Greenwood walked up the aisle behind the coffins. I wonder they did not hide their heads in shame.

I had a long talk with Jeudwine,* who came over this morning from Dublin and goes back to-night. He is in command while Macready is away on a month's holiday. He thinks that, in the war in Ireland, we have now got to the same position as in the war with the Boches in 1915. A stalemate, with rising morale on our side and dropping morale on the rebel side. What a business. He agrees absolutely with me that the Government must take over reprisals and government.

On the 28th, when Wilson spent some hours at Grove End, there is the note:

There were 4 policemen at Grove End when I got down, the Scotland Yard orders being that I was to be looked after; and the Inspector told me that two were to sleep in the house whenever I stayed there.

I see by the papers that all approaches to Downing Street have been boarded up! What a scandalous state to have brought the country to, and, even so, the miserable politicians are not safe. We must stamp out these murderous pests or we shall be ruined.

Next day Sir Henry wrote:

The papers this morning report a number [15] of incendiary fires in Liverpool, and at least one murder there. So the Sinn Feiners are beginning in England at last. Perhaps this will wake up the Cabinet. I saw Winston. I asked him if the Cabinet were going to declare martial law in Ireland. He replied, no. I told him that if the Government did not govern we should lose everything, that apparently Downing Street's answer to outrage was to build a fortification round the place, whereas they ought to arrest the Council of Action, kick out Krassin and his vile brood, declare martial law in

---

* Lieutenant-General Sir H.S. Jeudwine.

Ireland and stamp the vermin out. I asked him what Lloyd George was doing, what it all meant, what was going on about Tino and the Turks, and I advised Winston to clear out of the Cabinet before it was too late.

On the 30th Wilson learnt that the Prime Minister, M. Leygues and Count Sforza,[*] who had come over to discuss the problem that had arisen in Greece and a number of other matters, had agreed to offer 300,000 Silesian out-voters the right to proceed to Cologne to record their votes on the plebiscite question in that city. "The Frocks are in good form to-day," he remarked in his diary: and he hastened to remonstrate at such an arrangement having been made without consulting the War Office. He pointed out that 300,000 men would require from 600 to 1,000 trains to bring them to Cologne and to remove them, that they would require 300,000 beds and about a million meals, and he contrived to get the precipitate decision reversed until the matter had been examined into by the War Office, in consultation with the Army of Occupation on the Rhine. These various plebiscites, and the problem of maintaining order while they were being conducted, the Field-Marshal found a constant source of vexation and difficulty. They provided the Government with some sort of excuse for employing British troops, whose presence was sorely needed elsewhere, on tasks that were of very secondary interest to the welfare of the nation; he could at least congratulate himself on having prevented such misappropriation of the country's military resources in the case of Vilna. He was, however, somewhat encouraged on the last day of the month by a meeting with Churchill and Hamar Greenwood, at which trying the effect of martial law in Cork County and Cork City was debated, and he wrote in his diary:

> I pointed out that it will be no use trying it in a small area, unless you are prepared to enforce it at least in Munster, Connaught and Leinster. They did not agree. I pointed out that we must have a clean-

---

[*] M. Leygues was now Prime Minister in France, having succeeded M. Millerand on that statesman being elected President in the summer. Count Sforza was the Italian representative.

cut policy about carrying arms, murders carried out by men in plain clothes, shooting by roster, watching the coast, organized reprisals, "pinching" Sinn Fein funds, priests to be treated like ordinary civilians, press censors, and other things, and that it will be impracticable to confine martial law to a small area. However the others thought differently. And so, at long last, Lloyd George and his miserable Cabinet are coming down to earth again.

This is entered next day (December 1):

> Winston in full blast for martial law, and because I wanted to get Macready back, and also wanted to proceed with care and discretion, he said I was obstructive. I gave him the rough side of my tongue, pointing out the complete *volte-face* of Lloyd George and himself; for it was only two nights ago that he said all was going well and that the Cabinet would *not* put on martial law!

On the 2nd there is the note:

> I got an excellent letter from Jeudwine, written after his interview with Hamar Greenwood. Judy said the same as I did, viz., that you must apply martial law to the whole of Ireland, and then work it differently in different parts. He was calling his generals together to discuss what reinforcements he will want. Meanwhile he wired for two battalions, of which one at once.
>
> The Frocks [Lloyd George and Leygues and Sforza] have decided to do all they can to prevent the Greeks from "self-determining" in favour of Tino!

This appears on the 6th:

> I attacked the Prime Minister before dinner. He said that he did not agree, for political reasons, with me about applying martial law to the whole of Ireland, but he was all for beginning with Cork, Kerry and Limerick and then extending its operations. After dinner Hamar came in, and from a talk I had with him I am afraid he is weakening and thinks he is so nearly through with the business that it will be unnecessary to apply martial law. It is hopeless. There is not a single thing that Lloyd George and his wretched Cabinet do with which I agree.

Next day Wilson wrote:

> Macready back from south of France to see me. While we were talking, Boyd* came with a letter from Jeudwine which he, Boyd, amplified. Mr. Dumont, the American Consul in Dublin, said to Boyd a couple of days ago that he [Dumont] knew that the rebel army wanted to get into touch with our army with a view to arranging terms of peace. Dumont told Boyd he could put him in touch with a responsible Sinn Feiner who Dumont would guarantee was not one of the murder gang. Boyd agreed to meet this man, and accordingly Dumont arranged a meeting. The man was a shopkeeper called Keating.
>
> Keating said he could answer for the rebel army (including Michael Collins). The rebel army were profoundly distrustful of their own politicians and equally distrustful of Lloyd George, and they therefore wanted to come to an arrangement with our soldiers. After some talk, Boyd said that it must be clearly understood that he undertook no engagements, except that he would report to the C. in C. Macready, Boyd and I had a long discussion and were agreed that it was out of the question to hold parley with rebel murderers, and that the thing to do was to clap on martial law at once, as it was evident that the murderers were getting rattled and now was the time to push on.

This appears next day (December 8):

> Macready summoned to Cabinet. He told me that, after endless talk, the Cabinet agreed to put martial law on Cork, Kerry, Limerick and Tipperary only, and this from about Wednesday week, so as to have two Sundays during which the priests are to be exhorted to get the rebels to hand over their arms to them [the priests], to be passed to the military authorities. At long last it is a beginning of the Government governing.

On the 13th the diary gives an interesting account of a Cabinet meeting with regard to Mesopotamia and Persia:

> I never saw the Cabinet in a worse plight. They had decided to

---

* Major-General Sir G. Boyd was commanding in Dublin.

remain in Mesopotamia and Persia against every advice and remonstrance on my part. Now they find that the House of Commons and the public will not stand the sinful waste of life and money; and so now they must come out. They have promised Persia that they would stay till April, and in any case we probably can't move before, owing to snow. They have accepted the mandate for Mesopotamia. Both of these engagements must go by the board, and they were searching for a form of words which would cover their ignorance. I pointed out that we could not, in all probability, leave Kasvin before April, that it would take two months to roll back to Khanikin, that we could only then begin to fall back from Mosul, and that the whole operation of clearing out of Persia and Mesopotamia and down to Ahwaz-Amara-Nasiriyeh would take at least six, and probably eight, months, and that we should require all the 4½ divisions now there to conduct the operation. The Frocks were beneath contempt.

The Press of almost all shades of political opinion was at this time enlarging upon the urgent need of financial retrenchment, and the Cabinet were at their wits' end as to how to effect savings — the more so in that any substantial reduction of expenditure in respect to the military forces was manifestly rendered almost impossible by the numerous commitments abroad for which H.M. Government had made itself responsible. The Prime Minister and his colleagues had deliberately scouted military opinion. They were now reaping their reward. It is not surprising in the circumstances that the War Minister should have been much disconcerted on December 22 on receiving a cable message from Haldane on the Tigris which declared that a withdrawal from Mesopotamia to the Basrah line could not be completed before March, 1922. He promptly, and without consulting the C.I.G.S., cabled back expressing grave disappointment and intimating that the Cabinet would never agree. "I will take this matter up to-morrow. Sir Henry wrote in his diary on becoming aware of what had passed, "for the Cabinet will have to deal with me, and not Haldane."

An appeal moreover reached the Foreign Office from Silesia a few days later, begging that some British troops from the Rhine should be transferred thither, seeing that grave troubles were apprehended during the forthcoming plebiscite. But the Field-

Marshal insisted that the appeal could not possibly be complied with. The Rhine battalions were, he declared, the only reserve available in case further troops were required for Ireland — as was likely to occur, seeing that the Royal Assent had been given to the Home Rule Bill on the 23rd. Under the provisions of that measure separate Parliaments were to be set up in Ulster and in the rest of the distracted country, and, so far from anybody competent to judge believing that the passing of the Act would procure pacification, the general opinion in Ireland was that it would merely aggravate the existing troubles. Sir Henry makes mention in his diary of an important Cabinet meeting on December 29, at which, besides himself, Macready, Tudor, General Strickland (commanding at Cork) and Boyd were present:

> There a long talk about behaviour of "Black and Tans," and the burning of Cork, and Strickland's report thereon, and then Lloyd George advanced the proposal of 1 or 2 months' truce. He was backed by Winston, to my disgust. Fisher and Austen also in favour. Shortt against. Hamar gave no opinion. Tudor, Strickland and Boyd very good. I finished up with a strong statement against so fatuous and fatal a policy, which would immeasurably strengthen the enemy, and would incalculably weaken our friends, as also that great central body of peasants who always side with the stronger man. I asked for martial law for all Ireland. Macready wants to add Clare, Tipperary, Wexford and Waterford to Cork, Kerry, Limerick and Kilkenny, which are already under martial law. But I gathered that even Macready's request is too strong meat for the Cabinet. They *are* a miserable crowd. My contempt for their brains, knowledge, pluck and character deepens every day. They will ruin England and the Empire. The suggestion to-night was that by having a truce of 2 months the rebels would be pacified and would never give any further trouble! Whew! I think that we have scotched the plan of making a truce with rebels and murderers.

The Government, a day or two later, consented to the extension of the area over which martial law was already in force, so that it should henceforward include the whole of Munster and also the county of Clare. Sir Henry was strongly of opinion that the area ought to embrace the whole of Ireland. Nor was his reason for holding this view merely due to there being disturbed districts in

1920: July to December 329

all parts of the country. He realised what practical difficulties a patchwork arrangement such as the Cabinet had sanctioned was bound to create in the administration of martial law, and to what an extent the Prime Minister's ramshackle policy would hamper the military and the police in the carrying out of their onerous duties. He had lost all confidence in the Government, and that he had been thoroughly disillusioned by their infirmity of purpose alike at home and abroad is shown by the summary with which on December 31 he closed his diary for the past twelve months.

He wrote:

> What a miserable and disappointing year. Lloyd George and his Cabinet have lamentably failed, whether in England where Lloyd George has given in every time to the Trades Unions and has tolerated the formation of a Council of Action, or in Ireland, where ever since the spring he has handed over the Government to the "Black and Tans" until public opinion and the logic of facts have driven the Government to martial law for Munster, or in Egypt where Milner frankly proposes to hand over to the Egyptian Government, or in Mesopotamia where Percy Cox is trying to form an Arab Government while lack of £ s. d. is driving us out of the country, or in India where Montagu favours the rebels against the loyalists. No matter where we look, we find Lloyd George totally unable to govern. And when I remember all the speeches of Lloyd George and others two years ago about England being a land of heroes, etc., it makes me all the more contemptuous. The League of Nations has already proved itself incompetent and imbecile. Lloyd George's foreign policy has been beneath contempt. He has tried, luckily with little success, to make love to Kameneff and Krassin and the Bolsheviks. He fairly carted the Poles during the Bolshevik advance on Warsaw. He has nearly quarrelled with the French. He has backed the Greeks against Turks. He has made enemies of all countries and friends of none.

Chapter XXXII – 1921: January to June

Visits to the Rhine, Paris and Madrid — The Greek offensive in Anatolia — Steps taken to meet a General Strike — The Government and Ireland — Wilson's advice as to distribution of troops ignored by the Cabinet — He realizes impossibility of strong measures in Ireland while England is kept in ignorance of the state of affairs.

Early in January, the Field-Marshal, accompanied by Lady Wilson (who had recently been seriously ill), proceeded to the Rhine. He had attended a Cabinet meeting before leaving, at which it had at last been definitely decided to withdraw from Persia in the following April. He had also heard that Churchill was to cross Whitehall to the Colonial Office, and that his place was to be taken by Sir L. Worthington-Evans. While at Cologne, Sir Henry carried out a number of inspections, and he also delivered a lecture to the officers, of which he wrote in his diary:

> Hall packed to the limit; I got a great reception at the end, and Robertson, the High Commissioner from Coblentz, was most enthusiastic.

A ceremonial parade was also held in the Cathedral Square, at which Wilson invested General Degoutte with the K.C.B. He also carried out an investiture on behalf of the King. He wrote in the diary on January 11:

> At 5 o'clock I got a SOS from Philip Chetwode, who reported a

1921: January to June 331

wire just received from Rawly to me, which said that, in spite of his most strenuous opposition, the Viceroy in Council had ordered a reduction of British troops by 4 battalions and 2 cavalry regiments. Rawly says this is "madness" and asks for my help.

I have wired to Philip to go to Montagu and to find out whether I am, or am not, his military adviser; and I told Philip not to be put off by being told that this was a matter of internal economy to be decided by the Viceroy in Council, because the internal security in India, the protection of her frontiers, the power to send troops to countries outside her frontiers such as Mesopotamia, Burma, Singapore and Hong Kong, and finally the obligation on the Home Government to reinforce India in case of necessity, were all matters interwoven in Imperial strategy and therefore come under me.

I wonder what Philip will get as an answer. As I said a week ago when writing to Rawly — Montagu and Chelmsford have set up a Council with a lot of natives on it and have lost control, and now they dare not impose the extra taxation necessary. This same Council will before long refuse to allow Indian native troops to serve outside of India! And then!

On arrival at Coblentz the party were met by General Allen, and were escorted by two squadrons of American cavalry to Mr. (now Sir Malcolm) Robertson's house. The party proceeded to Mayence and back one day, and while there Sir Henry inspected a mixed brigade of French troops. General Allen also held a special parade for him of all the U.S. troops in garrison at Coblentz — "a fine, hard-bitten, savage-looking lot," he described them in his diary. Lady Wilson and he went on to Paris, she continuing her journey to Biarritz, while the Field-Marshal remained as a meeting of the Supreme War Council was about to take place. General Gouraud, back from Syria, came to see him, and the following appears in the diary:

> He says it is essential that we should make our peace with Kemal Pasha. I, of course, agreed. He said that the whole trouble began with the Greek occupation of Smyrna. I said this from the beginning.

General Pelle (who had been Chief of Staff to Joffre in the early days of the War, and who was going out to Constantinople as Ambassador) also came to see him, and Wilson wrote in the diary:

> I told him that I was at the Quai d'Orsay on the day that the Big Four gave Smyrna to Venizelos, and that I drove Venizelos up to my office in the Astoria and told him that this would ruin Greece and himself, and would box up the whole of the Middle East.

King Constantine, it should be mentioned, was back on the Hellenic throne; but, although entirely opposed to Venizelos politically, he was showing himself quite prepared to carry on the old Cretan statesman's ambitious projects as directed against the Turks.

The conference was carried on intermittently in Paris from January 24 to 29, on which latter day, according to Wilson's diary:

> The papers of the Financial Experts and our military paper were brought up and, after some wrangling (in which Lloyd George was at his worst, hectoring and blustering against the French, and insisting on taking out of our military paper all semblance of threat of action against the Boches), we all got *d'accord*[*] and broke up.

The Field-Marshal then hastened to Biarritz. He remained there until February 19 and he then travelled on with Lady Wilson to Madrid, where they remained a few days, getting back to London at the end of the month for a meeting of the Supreme Council there, and also so as to meet Foch. While at Madrid the Wilsons lunched with the King and Queen at the Palace one day, and of this Sir Henry wrote in his diary:

> I sat between the Queen and Princess Patsy, and we had a very enjoyable lunch- After lunch the King took me aside into a big window in the dining-room, with no one else in the room, and he spoke with the utmost frankness about the situation.[†] A very interesting conversation. He credits me with more power than I have, perhaps not more than I may have.

---

[*] "Agreement."

[†] The Field-Marshal gives a full account of what the King said, but this obviously cannot be quoted.

The following, entered at 36 Eaton Place on the 28th, appears in the diary:

> Foch telephoned to me to come and see him. He recounted his visit to Chequers yesterday. He was most amusing. He arrived (with Weygand) at 1 o'clock. Then came *le lunch*. There were a lot of ladies, etc.! Then, after lunch, they all went out on the terrace. There were 15 photographers and cinema men. Innumerable photographs. Then a walk to the top of the hill, followed by the photographers, hard at work. Then a lecture by Lloyd George on the Roman encampment, the cinema going all the time. Then walk down to the old church, followed by the cinemas. Then back, exhausted, for tea at 5 o'c — *le 5 o'c*. Then a scratch conference of Lloyd George, D'Abernon, Foch, and one or two others, nothing seriously discussed; and then Foch and Weygand, refusing dinner and bed, came straight back to dine at the hotel (Carlton), after a futile day which, the old Marshal said, had done nothing except to show of Lloyd George the fact that *son sac est vide*.*

Sir Henry was much put out at learning that the four battalions from the Rhine, that had been asked for by the Foreign Office for work in Silesia during the plebiscite, were to proceed thither after all; the plebiscite was to take place in three weeks' time. But the Prime Minister paid no heed to the Field-Marshal's remonstrances on the subject. That additional troops might shortly be required in Ireland was forcibly brought home to Wilson by a very depressing account of the situation which Macready brought over. Macready was eloquent in his praise of the troops, pronouncing their morale to be wonderful in spite of the extraordinarily disagreeable conditions in which they fotmd themselves. No fewer than six unarmed soldiers had been murdered in the streets of Cork on the last day of February, and ten others had been wounded; the Government, however, appeared to accept these episodes with comparative equanimity.

The Supreme War Coxmcil opened its sittings in St. James's Palace on March 1; but neither Foch nor Wilson was called upon to be present on that first day. They learnt, however, that the

---

* "His bag is empty."

discussions had not proceeded altogether smoothly. The German representatives had been present at this opening meeting; but they were not invited to be present at the second day's conference. This Foch and Sir Henry did attend, and the Field-Marshal gives the following account of the proceedings in his diary:

> The Jurists told us in what particulars the Boches had broken the Treaty. Austen told us that a committee, of which he was chairman, had examined the possibilities of administering the occupied territories, and were rather opposed to the idea. Then Foch was asked, and confined to, the question of the occupation of Duisburg, which he said he could easily do with the troops at his disposal. I was asked if I agreed. I did. Foch tried to enlarge the subject, but was not allowed; and then we broke up, nothing having been settled.
> The Greeks have refused Lloyd George's proposal for a Commission to sit at Smyrna to decide who the place belongs to! They very wisely stand pat on the fact that the Frocks gave it to them.

That evening the Wilsons gave a dinner party in honour of Foch, Gouraud and Weygand. Lady Edwina Lewin was one of the guests, and Foch spoke most feelingly of her father, Wilson writing in the diary:

> His love and admiration for Lord Bobs is very touching and very curious, since they knew each other very little and always spoke through an interpreter, and generally through me. The placards to-night have "Foch and Wilson." What an honour to be coupled with the great Marshal.

The soldiers were present at the conference on the following day, and at this meeting Lloyd George warned the German representatives that, unless the Allies' terms were accepted by the 7th, Duisburg, Ruhrort and Dusseldorf would be occupied — this although on the previous day Foch had only been asked as to Duisburg. So the soldiers met later, and they worked out plans for occupying all three towns, should this prove necessary. The meetings that took place on March 7 Wilson describes as follows in his diary:

There were 10 Boches facing us to-day, as General von Seckt, in uniform, was present. It became very clear early in Dr. Simon's speech that the Boches were not going to agree to our terms. He tried to show that Germany was doing everything possible, that no case had arisen for "sanctions," that the League of Nations ought to intervene, etc., etc. At the end Lloyd George said the conference would reassemble at 4.30, when the final answer of the Allies would be given.

At the afternoon conference Lloyd George intoned another sort of sanctimonious answer to the Boches; but in the end, after considerable pressure by Briand and Jaspar (Belgian), he made it clear that Simon's terms were rejected. We adjourned for tea, and after tea Simon made a short reply, accepting the Allies' "sanctions," but once more making it clear that in his opinion these would lead nowhere. The Boches then bowed and went out. They have been quiet and dignified throughout.

Then Lloyd George summoned a small meeting to discuss our next moves. The Frocks were astonished to learn that we soldiers had everything cut and dried and only awaited permission to "go" — which, was given. Foch wired to Degoutte, and I to Morland; whereas Foch and I were amused to find that the Frocks had made *no* plans nor arrangements for the customs and other sanctions. And not only that, but it appears that Robertson from Coblentz has wired that, without occupying the Ruhr, the customs cannot be imposed. The Frocks really are the limit.

Wilson wrote on the 11th:

Amazing *volte-face* on the part of the Frocks at 10.30 last night in regard to Turkey. They then agreed to withdraw the Allied troops from Constantinople, to withdraw the Greek troops from everywhere in Asia Minor except Smyrna town, to allow the Turks to have troops in Constantinople, etc., etc. All this is at last in the right direction, but why it was done I cannot imagine. An amazing performance. I suppose the Frocks think it quite natural. Perhaps they hope that by keeping Greeks in Smyrna the Turks will refuse the whole thing, and so they will throw the whole blame on Turkey.*

---

* The Supreme Council formulated its proposals for revision of the Treaty of Sèvres on March 12.

> To Sandown for the Grand Military. I saw Bainbridge* from Belfast and Caviare† from Longford, both equally unable to see daylight under the present regime of neither civil nor martial law authority. Lloyd George will neither run a show himself nor allow us to run a show. The result is hopeless.

There appears on March 14:

> No further news of Turks and Greeks agreeing to the last proposals, but several indications that the Greeks are going to attack the Turks at Afium Kara Hissar and Eskishehr. If this is done at Lloyd George's instigation it will be pretty hot stuff. The Turks meanwhile have occupied Batoum. What a rotten peace (?) the Frocks made.

The Field-Marshal mentions in his diary having a long talk with the Secretary of State (Worthington-Evans) on getting back, with regard to the folly of scattering troops all over the world, when there was a crying necessity for more troops in Ireland. Fourteen soldiers and R.I.C. had been killed on the previous day in that country, and he wrote in the diary:

> We must either clear out or govern — by which I mean much more drastic steps than we have yet taken. Sweep up all motors, bicycles and horses, and make the rebels immobile, then close the Post Offices and banks, and then "drive." A foul job for any soldier.

He attended a Cabinet meeting on the 22nd, and succeeded in securing a decision that Trans-Jordania was not to be occupied — as Churchill (who in his capacity of S. of S. for the Colonies was at the time in Cairo) was recommending. Of what followed at the meeting he wrote in the diary:

> Then we discussed the Greek attacks on the Turks at Eskishehr and Afium Kara Hissar. I whispered to Fisher and Addison, between whom I sat, "Surely the League of Nations would not agree." On this

---

* Major-General Sir G. Bainbridge.

† Colonel F.W.L. Cavendish.

Fisher put up a feeble protest. But Lloyd George said there was "a great concentration" of Turkish troops in front of the Greeks and that it was "impossible to prevent the Greeks attacking in self-defence." So far as our (and Greek) information goes, there is no concentration of Turks on that railway, and therefore this coming attack is entirely uncalled for and wholly unprovoked. And Lloyd George knows this. The whole thing is a ramp, and a disgusting ramp. Because the Turks are at this moment considering the terms offered to them a fortnight ago here in London, the Greeks, with the full knowledge of Lloyd George, attack the Turks.

He says the Greeks must attack in self-defence. Yet when the Poles said the same thing as against the Bolsheviks, he said it was a scandalous thing, not to be tolerated for a moment. But he launches the Greek attack just at the moment when the Turks are engaged in heavy fighting with the Bolsheviks at Batoum, thus helping the Bolsheviks — as he always does. He signed the Trade Treaty with Krassin last week.

The Greek Chargé d'Affaires came to see me about the Manissa Division. They wanted it left under Tim's command — this, of course, to embroil us. But I took a strong, clear line, "If the Manissa Division remained under Tim's command, then they would not move and the Greeks could not use Ismid as a base for any troops. In my opinion Ismid port and railway were essential to the whole of the Greek operations, but they could only get them by taking back their division, in which case we would hand over Ismid also. In short, it was the division and Ismid, or neither the division nor Ismid." I told them this was really a political matter and that they must get our Cabinet's sanction.

The whole thing is disgusting. In my opinion the end of this will be the total ruin of the Greeks — the friends of Lloyd George. And all this at a moment when the Bolshevik attack on the Turks at Batoum really throws the Turks into our arms. At that moment Lloyd George flings the Greeks against the Turks. Who is paying for Greek mobilization, etc.?

Next day there is the entry:

I sent off several wires to Tim to make clear that I wanted him to get rid of all the Greeks from under his command, handing them back to the Greek C. in C., and also the town and port of Ismid, and that none of our personnel should help to feed or victual the Greeks, nor should the Greeks be allowed to draw from our dumps.

A letter which the Field-Marshal wrote on March 30, in reply to one from Lord Ventry concerning Ireland, deserves to be quoted here:

> You ask whether it is more dangerous to have Ireland inside or outside the United Kingdom system. The answer is very simple. If there was anything in Irish history for the last 500 years to show that a concession, like independence, would make her friendly to England, I would say without a moment's hesitation — grant her the concession. But if my reading of history for the last 500 years is correct, and I see it is the same as yours, a concession of that sort would only be used by Ireland still further to embarrass and endanger the position of England and the British Empire; and what is certain is this — that a hostile Ireland, lying geographically as Ireland lies to England, is just as fatal to the continued existence of the British Empire as a hostile England was, is, and will be, to the growth and existence of a German Empire.
> Therefore, if my reading of history is right, if my military diagnosis of a hostile Ireland is right, the answer to your question is quite simple. It is that Ireland must be incorporated into the system of the United Kingdom and the British Empire. As I always say to those who do me the honour to listen to me — and they are not many — there are two courses, and only two, in regard to Ireland. One is to come away, which as I have just said in my opinion would be fatal; and the other is to govern Ireland. Where our politicians fall into the mess in which they are always floundering over Irish affairs is that they will neither come away nor will they govern. They are always attempting some middle course, which is fatal to the continued prosperity of Ireland herself and the safety of the Empire.

A strike of the miners had been threatened for months past, and at midnight on March 31 — the last day of Government control of the mines, which under that control were being administered on an uneconomic basis — the strike was declared. In this action the miners enjoyed the moral support of the railwaymen and the transport workers, but the question of these associations declaring a sympathetic strike remained in suspense for the moment. The C.I.G.S. nevertheless decided to carry out some minor movements of troops at once in view of possible eventualities, and, in consequence of the numerical weakness of the military forces in the United Kingdom, he was anxious to bring some battalions home from abroad. But, on his asking for permission to warn the French that he might have to withdraw the four battalions from Silesia (where the result of the plebiscite had favoured the Germans), the Prime Minister, who was staying at Chequers, asked him to come there and explain his views. Sir Henry therefore motored down, and of what passed he wrote in his diary:

> Lloyd George and I walked up and down on the terrace, talking, for three-quarters of an hour. I pressed on him the necessity for bringing back the four battalions from Silesia. I said they might get mixed up in some rotten internal rows, and then it would be difficult to get them away. I urged that, even if the Triple Alliance did not come out, we should still want them for Ireland, which I wanted to reinforce by 12--16 battalions and 3 cavalry regiments at the end of next month. I told him that if he would allow me to bring back 4 battalions from Silesia, possibly the remaining 3 from the Rhine, 3 from Malta, 1 from Egypt, and if possible 2 from Constantinople, we ought to be able to hold both England and Ireland in the event of a triple strike — failing which, i.e. the return of the above battalions, I would only be able to hold England at the cost of losing Ireland, and I had already arranged a plan with Macready to take 10 battalions from him. I asked Lloyd George if he wanted to be Prime Minister of England or of Silesia, and I did my best to put my case before him, which is the *dangerously* weak and narrow margin of troops on which we are running the Empire.
>
> Lloyd George was most unsatisfactory. He was scattered in his talk. He wanted to discuss Turkey and Greece, said there was great danger in Silesia, said Macready ought to have carried out "drives" before now owing to fine weather, said the question was "whether Democracy could govern," said that the Romans tried it and that Cæsar found it would not work and took charge, and he thought that "our Cæsar would come from the Lenin class." He seemed resigned, and for all I know, pleased with this prospect. In short, I got no good out of him, no decision, nothing but scattered talk. He said he would have a meeting Monday morning. He thinks the Triple Alliance is coming out. It is a rum game. Got back at 9 p.m.

This was on a Saturday. During the Sunday and the Monday

morning the Field-Marshal saw several Cabinet Ministers privately, and he attended the Cabinet meeting at 1 o'clock on the Monday, of which he wrote in his diary:

> Shortt (Home Secretary), Eric Geddes and Horne were all very clear that we were up against the big thing. I made it clear that, if we were, then we must scrape up troops from Silesia, Rhine, Mediterranean and Ireland, call up the Reserve, embody the Territorial Force, and call upon all loyal citizens to enrol. After a good deal of argument this view prevailed, and I was given a free hand to carry out the necessary moves.

Inspection of the 1st Royal Ulster Rifles

Sir Henry thereupon sent orders to Silesia and to Malta, and he also arranged for several battalions at Aldershot and in out-stations in England to move up to London. He also dispatched instructions for two battalions from Ireland to proceed to Liverpool, as well as for certain movements of tanks to big towns to take place, and he reported what he had done to a Cabinet meeting which assembled at the House of Lords that same, evening. There appears in the diary:

1921: January to June 341

Lloyd George told us at this meeting that Thomas had just been to him to tell him that "Jesus Christ could not now stop this revolutionary movement," and also that our troops were not to be trusted. I told Lloyd George that I did not believe this about the troops, and later on the A.G. endorsed what I said. Lloyd George said that Thomas, Bevin and Gosling would try and stop the triple strike and revolution.

I telephoned to Tit Willow in Paris, telling him of the situation, and asked him to go and explain it all to Foch, and how sorry I was to have to withdraw from Silesia and possibly from the Rhine, Tit Willow went up at once to the old Marshal, who said that as "Henri was in danger" he was to withdraw everyone he wanted, and he [the Marshal] would hold the gate until I was able to send him back troops again. And he added that any mortal thing he could do to help me he would, and I only had to ask him. What a splendid old man he is, and what a loyal comrade.

After further consideration at the War Office, arrangements were made to raise a special Defence Force forthwith. One battalion was moreover ordered home from the Rhine. Kensington Gardens had been taken over by the military for the encampment of the additional troops that were arriving in London.* By the morning of April 6 the military arrangements, in so far as the regulars were concerned, were in a very forward state, although time must naturally elapse before the battalions ordered home from the Silesia and the Mediterranean could reach their destinations in the United Kingdom, and on that day Wilson wrote in his diary:

> There was great trouble about Jeffreys.† Lloyd George sent for him last night, and after 5 minutes' interview, came to the conclusion that he was no use, and ordered "Worthy" to remove him, and even wrote this order again this morning. Worthy sent for me and asked what he was to do. I said that I really could not agree, that I had complete confidence in Jeffreys, that, to put it bluntly, the Prime Minister was in a funk, that I personally, as C.I.G.S. and C. in C. must

---

* One of the battalions brought up was the 1st Royal Ulster Rifles. The illustration facing this page shows Sir Henry taking its salute at the march past.

† Major-General Sir P.D. Jeffreys, commanding the Home District.

be considered, that the Prime Minister had no business to send for a general like that and cross-examine him — and, incidentally, ask him d—— stupid questions — and finally that on his [Prime Minister's] own showing at our Cabinets of the day before yesterday, the only thing standing between the Prime Minister and red ruin was the army, and that if he went on like this he would lose the army, and then he was done.

Worthy understood. In the end we agreed that, to meet the Prime Minister and at the same time to maintain discipline and good feeling, I should appoint Cavan — who now has neither infantry nor cavalry at Aldershot — to command Jeffreys and the two T.F. Divisions in London (both of whose G.O.C.s happen to be senior to Jeffreys), and on the other hand Jeffreys should continue to command all the regulars in the London district. I telephoned for Cavan to come up and see me, and I also had Jeffreys there and I explained the situation, and all was arranged. I also told Worthy that he must tell Lloyd George that he was not to interfere with us again, otherwise there would be real trouble.

Jeffreys described to me his interview last night with Lloyd George and the silly questions Lloyd George asked him about the danger of Red trench mortars on the roof of the Ritz, of crowds collecting in twos and threes, of guarding Whitehall, etc., and also of his [Jeffreys'] question to Lloyd George as to whether our officers would be supported in any action they might think it necessary to take, as they had not forgotten the Dyer case. This was the culminating point, and Lloyd George bounced out of the room.

My news to-night is that all direct action by Reds is postponed for 14 hours to allow of more talking, and I am certain that Lloyd George is going to capitulate, and I suppose will carry his Cabinet with him. Oh, Lord!

This morning I telephoned to Tit Willow to ask him to go up and see Foch, and ask the old Marshal whether, in the event of my having to withdraw the whole 8 battalions* and their being replaced by 8 French battalions, he would allow Morland to remain in command. And the old Marshal said that if I so wished it he would certainly agree. He is a real loyal comrade.

At a meeting of a Cabinet Sub-Committee next day, telegrams were read out showing signs of serious trouble in South Wales and

---

* That is to say, from the Rhine.

in parts of Scotland. The local civil authorities were clamouring for troops to be sent, and Sir Henry remarked in the diary:

> I had to explain that we could not guard Silesia and South Wales at the same time. The Frocks hate this.

Three more battalions were, however, coming home from the Rhine. The safety men had been to a large extent withdrawn from the mines, and these were in some cases becoming flooded in spite of the labours of clerks, officials and volunteers. The Field-Marshal attended two Cabinet meetings on April 9, and he now came to the conclusion that the triple strike was not going to take place after all. The truth was that the rapid movement of troops had shown the Trade Union leaders that, the authorities were prepared. Wilson noted in the diary that day:

> I was curious to see what Lloyd George would say to me to-day, but he never dared to challenge me and, beyond some sneering remarks about Jeffreys, De Lisle, and soldiers generally, he did nothing.

The reservists were pouring in, the new Defence Force was filling up fairly satisfactorily, and battalions from abroad were arriving, so that the military situation was becoming more favourable from hour to hour, while, as Wilson put it in his diary on the 11th:

> the Frocks of all descriptions are talking and talking and talking, at conferences, out of conferences, in the House of Commons, outside the House of Commons, so they are all extremely happy.

He wrote in his diary on April 14:

> After the Army Council meeting, Austen, Shortt and Munro came over to express the concern of the Cabinet about the inefficiency of protection, and the wrong distribution of the troops. It was a veiled attack upon me, and all because I had said that I could not guard Silesia and Fife at the same time — which Austen quoted. I challenged Austen to produce a case where the responsible civil

authority had asked for military help and had not received it. Austen was unable to quote such a case.

I then passed to the attack. I said that it was only because I had said that about Silesia that we had now got those 4 battalions, that without Frock permission I had ordered home 3 battalions from Malta and the first two had arrived in Plymouth Sound this morning, that without Frock knowledge there were 4 battalions from Ireland in Liverpool, and that, far from lagging, we had been in front all the time. Austen's attack failed completely, and Shortt later on told me in the House of Commons that he had warned Austen that I was an awkward fellow to take on, and that Austen thought so now.

Next day there appears:

A real Frock day. Up to 11 p.m. last night it was certain that we were going to have a Triple. After some speeches in the House of Commons at that hour it was certain we were not. Then at 10.30 a.m. this morning it again became certain we were, and at 3.30 Lloyd George made a statement in the House that there was no escape. At 3.40 all idea of Triple was over, and Hodges had resigned, and Thomas was asking for military protection for railwaymen as against miners — he, who warned us a few days ago that we could not trust our soldiers!

Although the situation that day appeared to be fairly satisfactory, the fact remained that the miners' strike was continuing. So, as there still remained a possibility of the railwaymen and transport workers coming out. Sir Henry recommended the Government not to dismiss the Reservists for the present, and also to retain the Defence Force a little longer, although both measures presented a difficulty in that, in view of the obviously altered situation, the men might become discontented. The regular troops were, however, for the most part sent back to the stations they had come away from, and by the end of the month the situation in Great Britain had so greatly improved that the C.I.G.S. was beginning to hope that he would shortly be in a position to send substantial reinforcements over to Ireland, where they were badly needed.

While the threats and the action of certain of the Labour leaders had, as narrated above, been compelling the Government, in obedience to Wilson's advice, to agree to somewhat extreme measures so as to ensure troops being available to maintain older, the Greek forces had in the latter days of March sustained a heavy reverse in Anatolia, at the hands of the Turks. Enjoying at the outset a decided advantage in respect to numbers, the Hellenic troops had penetrated far outside of the area which they had been in occupation of hitherto since the descent upon Smyrna of 1919. Ottoman reinforcements had, however, been hurried to the scene. These had within a few days partially restored the balance in strength. The Kemallst levies had fought with grit. Yet further Osmanli contingents had appeared, and the Greeks had eventually been compelled to fall back, discomfited, after suffering heavy losses. This development of the situation rendered a conciliatory policy towards Mustapha Kemal, such as Sir Henry had been advocating for months past, highly expedient, the more so in that the position of the Allied contingents stationed about Constantinople might well become precarious were the Turkish successes to be driven determinedly home. The C.I.G.S. was indeed in favour of the Allies withdrawing from Turkey altogether, for he was desirous of bringing home the British troops so as to swell the forces available in the United Kingdom. He was also becoming perturbed at reports suggesting that the Reservists were discontented; so he spent two days at Dover, visiting the battalions quartered there and conducting investigations as to the alleged unrest. He found, however, that the reports had been much exaggerated, and he wrote in his diary:

> In each case I addressed all the officers in their mess-rooms — some 30 in each mess — and explained our present position and why they were being pushed about. All these 3 battalions belong to the Rhine, and I brought them back from Silesia. I hope that I did some good, for in each case I gave great praise to the regimental officer for being able to produce a contented army — the only contented body of men in the United Kingdom at the present moment. I impressed on them the enormous importance at this moment of a happy and thoroughly contented and efficient army, and that this could only be secured by the personal touch. All the officers I spoke to gave me good reports of the men and of the Reservists, and I spoke to a number of serving men and Reservists also.

In the meantime M. Briand and Lloyd George were holding a palaver at Lympne, in anticipation of a fresh meeting of the Supreme War Council, which was advertised to take place in London shortly in view of the failure of the Germans to pay the portion of indemnity that was now due. M. Briand proposed that the Royal Navy should undertake operations of some kind or other against Hamburg and Bremen, and he offered the loan of a division to help; but Wilson and Beatty agreed that such a venture was quite out of the question, and they reported to that effect. Foch, with Weygand, arrived in London on April 30, and they, together with Wilson and Beatty, attended a meeting of the Supreme War Council on May 3. At this, Foch laid out his scheme for occupying the Ruhr if ordered to do so. It was agreed that no British troops could assist, owing to the disturbed situation at home, and the Supreme War Council dispatched an ultimatum to Berlin, requiring acceptance of the terms now laid down by the 12th. Wilson wrote in his diary on May 6:

> There are some interesting wires to-day from Auckland Geddes. They have collected a large sum of money for Irish women and children who are starving in Ireland! And they now propose to set up machinery in Ireland for its distribution! Whew! And all this comes from the fact that Lloyd George and his Miseries are not governing, and so other people barge in! It is the old story, that either you govern other people or they govern you, and if you don't take charge of events they take charge of you.

The miners were showing little disposition to return to work, and there again appeared to be some likelihood of the railwaymen and the transport workers coming out. Just at this time, news also reached the War Office of somewhat serious trouble in connexion with the Reservists at Aldershot and at some other stations. The Army Council decided in these circumstances that, in the event of the triple strike actually materializing, the wisest course would be to reopen recruiting for the Defence Force. And they, furthermore, decided that leave should in the meantime be granted liberally to Reservists and to men of the Defence Force, by way of keeping them contented. The Field-Marshal was nevertheless about to send several battalions from England over to Ireland. He was indignant at hearing from Worthington-Evans on May 11 that the Prime Minister had sent a summons for Macready to come over to discuss the adjusting of a truce while the elections (which were about to take place both in the north and in the south of the country) should be in progress, and he wrote in the diary:

> I said that I was wholly opposed to this as we are having more success than usual in killing rebels, and now is the time to reinforce and not to parley.

That evening he replied for the Army at a dinner of the Newspaper Society, and he delivered a speech at Cambridge on the following night on the subject of Toc H. The Japanese Crown Prince was in London on a State visit just at this time, the Field-Marshal attended a reception held at the Japanese Embassy in the Prince's honour on the 13th, and, of a conversation that he took part in while there he, wrote in his diary:

> On walking into the room, Austen signalled to me, and I had a long talk with him. He at once referred to my recent two speeches. He said, or I gathered, that Prime Minister and Cabinet were angry with me, that what I said would be excellent propaganda for Asquith, and he hinted that it might be necessary for me to resign. Evidently he and the Cabinet are displeased and frightened.
> I answered very openly, and I told him that, as far as I could judge, the Cabinet had hopelessly miscalculated every element in every problem, whether in Poland, or Silesia, or Turkey, or Greece, or Egypt, or India, or England, or Ireland. So far as I could see, Austen had no answer. I rubbed in that the Cabinet had been angry with me for wanting to come away from Silesia* and yet was not I right? That even I could not have made a bigger mess of Ireland, and that our foreign policy had been so laid that I've had not a single friend in the world. And now, to-night, in the House of Commons, Lloyd George had advocated that the Boches should be let loose on the Poles in Silesia. As I said to Austen, the Boches should be invited to carry out and execute the Treaty of Versailles.

---

* The Poles had created disturbances in Silesia, and the French troops had been obliged to fire on them. This had been after the British battalions had left.

Austen was quite unable to defend a policy of interference in everybody's business, with no force to carry it out, resulting in our asking our enemy, the Boches, to enforce our Treaty against our own Allies I Was there ever such a mad policy, with such a mad remedy. From what Austen said, I think it is quite possible that Lloyd George and his Cabinet may try and "mat" me. I shall have some fun before I resign. But there was one thing that I made clear to Austen, which was that it was, to say the least, unwise for the Frocks to try the army too high. I told him that owing to Cabinet policy we soldiers and sailors were being set a task which with the troops at our disposal we were unable to carry out, that we strongly objected to the relations with Krassin and Lenin, that we strongly objected to the Cabinet Greek policy, that we strongly objected to the Irish policy, to the Egyptian policy, to the Indian policy, and that owing to the fact that the Government never told us, and England, what was going on about this labour unrest, we ourselves were in doubt as to the real state of affairs. As I said to Austen, I knew what the inside story really was. I knew that Lloyd George was in favour of Krassin. I knew that when the Poles had said they wished to attack the Bolsheviks last autumn because they declared that the Bolsheviks were concentrating against them, Lloyd George was furious; whereas when the Greeks said they wished to attack the Turks because they said the Turks were concentrating against them, Lloyd George positively egged them on — and at a time when the Turks were being attacked by the Bolsheviks (see my diary). I made all this clear to Austen, who was rather taken aback.

The military authorities were about this time becoming seriously disturbed at the activities of the Communists, who were distributing leaflets and were employing other sinister methods of propaganda in the army, and the Field-Marshal made strong representations on the subject to the Secretary of State. The news from Ireland was also particularly bad, for thirty-seven soldiers, police and civilians had been murdered within the space of a single week. "I will have another try to wake up the Cabinet to the necessity of stopping their puerile game of talking peace, and of clapping on martial law everywhere," he wrote in his diary on May 17. He moreover expressed himself forcibly in his diary concerning a speech which the Prime Minister had delivered in the House on the 13th approving of the Germans being allowed to restore order

in Silesia, a speech which had, not unnaturally, raised a storm in Paris.
The following appears on the 18th:

> At 1.30 Curzon rang me up. He gave me a long sermon about the state of affairs in Silesia, ending by saying that Prime Minister and he had decided that 5 battalions should go to Silesia. I at once attacked. I said that, directly England was safe, every available man should go to Ireland, that even the 4 battalions now on the Rhine ought also to go to Ireland. I said that the troops and the measures taken up to now had been quite inadequate, that I was terrified at the state of that country, and that, in my opinion, unless we crushed out the murder-gang this summer we should lose Ireland and the Empire. I spoke in the strongest manner and I frightened Curzon, who said he must refer it all to the Prime Minister.
>
> At 4.30 Curzon rang me up to say Prime Minister agreed to 4 Rhine battalions going to Silesia if the French asked for our help, and if I could arrange it with Foch. But Curzon not so pompous.
>
> Nothing further settled about coal strike. Lloyd George has issued another rotten statement about Silesia, accusing the French Press of creating trouble and making out that the world is on his side.

On May 23 there is the entry:

> Tim from Constantinople to see me. He agrees with everything I say, viz. that, no matter what happens between Turkey and Greece, our 2 white and 4 black battalions are no solution, and, therefore, we ought to come away.[*]
>
> Then Macready in, and a long talk, and I brought him in to the S. of S. Macready absolutely backs up my contention that we must knock out, or at least knock under, the Sinn Feiners this summer or we shall lose Ireland, and he told S. of S. so in good round terms, and that it was not wise nor safe to ask the troops now in Ireland to go on

---

[*] In forwarding Appreciations by the General Staff and by Harington on the Turco-Greek situation officially on May 26, the C.I.G.S. wrote: "I think the chances are that the Turks will drive the Greeks back on to Smyrna, and quite likely out of Smyrna too, and that our troops in Constantinople will be in danger. Nor in such a case can I see any possibility of holding the Dardanelles. In short, I think we ought now to take the necessary steps to withdraw, and to withdraw completely, both from the Bosporus and the Dardanelles."

as they are now for another winter. As there were no troops with which to relieve them, we must make our effort now, or else, tacitly and in fact, agree that we were beaten. S. of S. is really impressed and frightened.

Not only four battalions from the Rhine, but also two battalions from home, were dispatched to Silesia in spite of the Field-Marshal's protests. This dispersion of force at a time when the situation in Ireland demanded the presence of every infantryman who could possibly be spared from other regions, he regarded as wholly indefensible. He possessed the faculty of drafting remarkably incisive State papers, and he now prepared a memorandum (which was in due course laid before the Cabinet) in which he pointed out in unmistakable terms the false strategical position in which these British units planted down in Silesia were placed, isolated as they were and depending upon a line of communications that was entirely in German hands. Their existence was, in fact, entirely dependent on German goodwill. He did not succeed in persuading the Cabinet that they were acting wrongly in this matter, but he was more successful in regard to another pressing question. This was his contention that the Reserve ought to be demobilized, as the Defence Force was now capable of doing all that was required; for, although the coal strike continued, there now appeared to be small prospect of movements sympathetic with the miners taking place. His representations on this subject were agreed to at a Cabinet meeting on May 24, and it was decided at the same time to reinforce Ireland to the utmost possible extent. "I take credit for all this" Wilson wrote in his diary, "although at the Cabinet I was not asked for an opinion and never uttered one." A Cabinet Committee met two days later to consider his detailed proposals, and of this he recorded:

> Hamar excellent, as he advocated a clear plan of martial law in the 3 Provinces on July 12 if the southerners had not started their Parliament, and a clear pronouncement now to that effect. After a good deal of discussion this was agreed to and will be submitted to the Cabinet. Austen irritable with me because I said that I would pour every man, including Silesia, into Ireland, and he said that I "always wanted to do something that the Cabinet did not want to do" — which

I am afraid is very generally true. However at long last, after 2 years of sticking to it, I believe the Cabinet are going to agree. Whether can now do the job I don't know. But I am certain that we ought to try.

Two days later Wilson wrote:

> The newspapers this morning blurt out that we are going heavily to reinforce Ireland. This, I am afraid, will have the effect of the extremists in the coal strike putting up a show and making a settlement impossible, and therefore making the dispatch of troops to Ireland impossible also.

Of a Cabinet meeting held on May 31 to consider the proposal of the C.I.G.S. to evacuate Constantinople, he wrote in his diary:

> Tim explained situation. I showed how it affected Mesopotamia, Palestine, Egypt, etc. Curzon made a long statement which advocated entering into negotiations with the Greeks to find out what they were going to do, what Venizelos thought of things, what the French were going to do. Winston urged some arrangement with Kemal. Mond urged large reinforcements for Constantinople. Montagu backed my proposal and wrote me a slip, saying, "At what stage are you going to say with a chuckle — I told you so." Lloyd George is prepared to come out of Constantinople, but only on condition of holding Dardanelles, which is impossible. Fisher said it was far more important to hold Constantinople than Ireland, and we ought to send troops from Ireland to Constantinople. No decision taken. A truly amazing Cabinet. A more hopeless, ignorant, useless lot of men I have never seen.
>
> We met again in House of Commons at 5.30, and for two hours went over the ground. And, of course, no decision. We meet again tomorrow. Winston, Worthy and I had a long talk at C.O. in Winston's room. I repeated what I have already said, viz. that Lloyd George has backed the wrong horse from the beginning and is going on doing so now, and will lose the race. It is quite simple. Winston and Worthy were in complete agreement with me, I still urge coming completely away and trying to come to terms with Kemal, which I believe we can still do, bargaining with Mesopotamia, and a loan, and officers for his gendarmerie, etc.

On June 1 there is the entry:

Cabinet Committee at 4.30 in Lloyd George's room in House of Commons. Immense amount of talk (2½ hours) and nothing settled. Winston wanted to reinforce Constantinople and make a "posture," and than try to come to terms with Kemal. Curzon wanted to open negotiations with the Greeks and Turks, and Lloyd George did not know what he wanted. I said that the positions out there and in Ireland were substantially the same, and the choice of solutions the same, i.e. either knock the gentleman on the head — or — come out. In Ireland we must knock the gentleman on the head so we *can't* come out. In Turkey we can't knock the gentleman on the head and so we *must* come out — but come out and make love to Kemal.* Nothing was decided and we meet again to-morrow.

Of the meeting next day Wilson wrote:

I pleaded once more for making love to the Turks, and I showed that we could offer them more than could the Bolsheviks. Much talk by Winston, Lloyd George, Mond, Worthy, Fisher, Montagu and Curzon; and in the end, on Lloyd George's proposal, it was agreed that Venizelos, who is coming to Paris to-morrow, should be asked to come straight on, that I should see him and have a talk with him and then report to the Cabinet. Lloyd George said that I was the man Venizelos trusted. They are amazing, these Frocks. Montagu wrote on a slip of paper and passed to me, "It looks to me as if the peace of the East and India is in your hands to-morrow." And so it is. A curious game.

M. Venizelos did not arrive in London until June 6, but the Field-Marshal had a prolonged conversation with him on that day, Venizelos held the view that unless King Constantine restored the Venizelist officers to their positions in the army — they had been ejected wholesale after the usual fashion when one party upsets another in modern Greece — the Hellenic forces would soon cease to exist as a fighting machine. But he expressed the opinion that, if the Venizelist officers were restored, and if the British Government would give money and guns and munitions and aeroplanes, the Greek army might yet retrieve its morale, recover

---

* A typical example of Sir Henry's method — metaphorical and terse — of summing up a complicated situation.

its efficiency and gain the upper hand over the Osmanli. From what he had learnt in this discussion, the Field-Marshal came to the conclusion that the only prospect of that army coming to be of any use whatever rested on the substitution of a Venizelist for a Constantinist regime. He so reported to Worthington-Evans, to the Foreign Office and to Lloyd George, who was at Chequers. It was thereupon arranged that a meeting of the Cabinet Committee should take place at the mansion in the Chilterns on the 9th, and of its proceedings Wilson recorded in his diary:

> We discussed what was to be done, and in the end it was agreed, more or less, that certain terms should be offered to the Turks, viz., an autonomous Smyrna, return of Constantinople and Dardanelles to Turkey, and no interference in finance. That, before offering these things to the Turks, they should first be shown to Greece and she should be asked to accept. If she accepts and Turkey refuses, then we support her with money, munitions, aeroplanes, etc., and we blockade Turkey. I gave it as my opinion that it was impossible to bolster up the Greek army, and that the only thing of real importance was to make Turkey friendly; for with a hostile Turkey I did not think that we should ever have peace and quiet in Egypt, or Mesopotamia, or India. However, no one agreed, so I was alone.

Although the Cabinet had consented to martial law being proclaimed in Munster, Leinster and Connaught on July 14, in the event of the Southern Parliament (which had now been elected) failing to assemble. Sir Henry was beginning to feel grave doubts as to whether such a proclamation would now be expedient, except on the clear understanding that Macready was allowed a free hand in carrying out its provisions. That the Commander-in-Chief in Ireland would be granted such liberty of action appeared to the C.I.G.S. to be in the highest degree unlikely. The Cabinet, never having taken any steps to make England acquainted with the true state of affairs on the farther side of St. George's Channel, were only too well aware that, were they to approve the prosecution of a vigorous punitive policy in southern and western Ireland, they would not have the predominant partner in the United Kingdom whole-heartedly at their back. "I am having a lovely Ascot of 12 hours a day at the W.O.," the Field-Marshal wrote to Colonel E.

Dillon, who was on the staff in Silesia. Some of those hours were being devoted to urging on the Secretary of State the paramount importance of securing the support of public opinion in England before an uncompromising form of in martial law was imposed on the sister island, as we find recorded in the diary:

> I told him that, unless we had England entirely on our side, I would strongly advise that we should not attempt martial law in all its severity, because I was sure it would not succeed, and failure meant disaster. If the soldiers knew that England was solid behind them they would go on till they won out; if on the other hand they found that this was not the case then we should have disaster. I have developed this thesis over and over again to Lloyd George, Bonar, Austen, Winston and others, and I never made so much impression on anybody as I did to-night on Worthy.

The situation in respect to the miners had been looking decidedly more hopeful for some days past, as certain proposals, which they seemed likely to accept, had been placed before them, and as these proposals, if accepted, were calculated to form the basis for a satisfactory settlement. The miners, however, rejected the terms, and the continuance of the strike was attended by some unrest in industrial districts. The question in consequence arose as to whether in such circumstances the transfer (for which the Field-Marshal was arranging) of a number of military units from England to Ireland ought not to be deferred. Sir Henry, however, urged that his programme should not be interfered with, and he carried his point, although not without some difficulty. But even allowing for the garrison of Ireland being swelled by these reinforcements, he was growing more and more doubtful as to the wisdom of enforcing martial law with real vigour, so long as the question was not fully understood in Great Britain, and he wrote in his diary on June 22:

> A long talk with S. of S. I referred to F.E.'s speech in the House of Lords last night, where he said that the Government were going to continue and to increase coercion, and the vote which followed and which gave Government a narrow majority. I said that this was another sign that the country was not whole-heartedly in favour of

flattening out the rebels. I said that my own personal opinion was that England was sound and could be roused, but what I wanted to make clear was that unless England was on our side we would fail, and if we failed we would break the army. *Therefore, unless England was on our side, I was wholly opposed to trying to increase coercion.* Worthy said England was not on our side and could not be got on it, and I repeated that it would be madness to try and flatten out the rebels.[*]

De Valera having been invited by the Prime Minister to come to London and discuss matters, Wilson wrote on the 27th:

> I told S. of S. this morning that in my opinion inviting Valera over was pure cowardice, that if a man committed a sufficient number of murders he was qualified to be asked to breakfast at 10 Downing Street. Worthy was rather shocked and said it was done to get England on our side. My answer was that the way to get England on our side was to expose the murderers and not to breakfast with them.

De Valera had, as a matter of fact, been captured a few days before; but the Cabinet had ordered his release — an order which had naturally exercised a very bad effect upon the troops in Ireland, to whom such conduct on the part of those set over them appeared wholly unintelligible. Many officers were raising objections to remaining in Ireland, and to going to Ireland, owing to the impression, which was gathering strength in the army, that the Government was not affording it the support that it was justly entitled to. On the last day of June, Wilson, moreover, wrote in his diary,"I had two long talks with Macready. He and I are coming somewhere near the limit of patience."

---

[*] The Field-Marshal makes no mention in his diary of an important factor bearing upon this question. The vast majority of the more powerful journals in Great Britain were at this time supporters of Mr. Lloyd George's Coalition Government, and it is scarcely an exaggeration to say that the Press in England deliberately suppressed much of the information at its disposal as to the outrages that were being committed by the Sinn Feiners, and as to the terrorism to which Loyalists were being subjected in Ireland. No previous British Government had established such close relations with successful newspapers of large circulation as had this one.

Chapter XXXIII – 1921-22: The Field-Marshal's Last Eight Months as C.I.G.S.

Wilson's strong line as to meeting representatives of Sinn Fein — Narrow escape from drowning at Cowes — His attitude with respect to Turkey — The Irish negotiations — The Geddes "Axe" Committee — Wilson elected M.P. — Close of his military career.

The Dominions Premiers had assembled in London during the closing days of June, and Sir Henry attended two meetings of the Imperial Conference. The subject under discussion on July 4 was naval, and was mainly concerned with the position in the Pacific. The Field-Marshal observed in his diary:

> Apparently one of the Frocks is leaking badly to *The Times*, and Lloyd George said it was really impossible to carry on secret conversations if they were always given away. They all protested the danger and their horror, and all mistrusted each other. What a crowd.

The subject on the 5th being the general military situation, the Field-Marshal made a statement; but before entering upon this he had enjoyed a sharp passage of arms with the Prime Minister — as appears from his diary:

> Lloyd George told me this morning at Downing Street that Valera was coming over and that I would have a "chance of talking to him." I replied that "I did not speak to murderers." He said, "You have

often done so," to which I replied, "Never, and if I met Valera I would hand him over to the police." All this made Lloyd George angry.

The room then filled up and the Imperial Conference sat, and I made a statement. I said Navy had a two-power standard and a one-power standard. We soldiers had no standard. A voluntary army answered no military war problem. War could not be considered in the abstract, an enemy must be named and plans prepared. Then I gave my three lines of defence for India, then showed importance of a friendly Turkey — at this Lloyd George plunged in and said it was an *ex parte* statement, and generally was grumpy and disagreeable. This was all Valera, Then I pleaded for a General Staff meeting with the Dominions. Then Lloyd George and others once again deplored the fact that it was impossible for them to talk secrets because they were at once given away to the Press! What beauties!

This afternoon S. of S., A.G., Macready and I had a long talk about what we were to do with officers and men who applied not to be sent to Ireland when ordered there. These cases are becoming more and more numerous. I said I thought that officers and men should be ordered over to Ireland and treated as on active service, provided that the fathers and mothers of these men (living in Ireland) were brought over to England, if they so wished, and were looked after by England, and their houses and property were insured by the Government. Worthy agreed to the equity of this, but doubted its practicability. Seeing that the Government has just given the miners a dole of 10 millions, I see no difficulty in forcing the Government to do their manifest duty.

This appears in the diary next day:

> Macready to see me in the afternoon. He had been at a Cabinet meeting this morning on Ireland. He gathered that they were going to come to a "gentlemanly undertaking" (as they called it) with Valera for a month's truce. Valera has done well; a month's delay makes it impossible to take on the murder-gang seriously this summer, as the weather breaks in September-October. Valera knows this well enough.

It was announced in the newspapers on July 9 that the Republican leader was coming over to London for a conference in the following week, and that a truce in Ireland had been arranged which was to begin at midday on the 11th, Wilson's comments on Lloyd George and the Cabinet in his diary on hearing this were of a vitriolic character. He had an opportunity of expressing his views to Mr. Chamberlain at 11 Downing Street on the day that the truce was supposed to commence, and he recorded the substance of their conversation in the diary as follows:

> He said that Lloyd George was cross with me, from gossip repeated to him. I told him that there were other people who could get cross besides Lloyd George, and that I was one of them, that the army was being tried too high, that we were never given a chance, that we were continually interfered with, that we *hated* being beaten by murderers, that it was only on November 9 last that Lloyd George had the murderers by the throat, that now he was shaking hands with them, that the Cabinet had done nothing to wake up England and get her on our side, etc., etc. To all of which Austen really had no reply at all, and I honestly think I turned him inside out.

A day or two after this the Army Council were suddenly ordered to reduce Army Estimates by three millions, and the General Staff came to the conclusion that the saving must be effected on the Territorial Forces. This view was pressed by the C.I.G.S., who pointed out that these non-permanent troops could not be employed in industrial troubles, that they could not be sent abroad in peace time, that they were no longer required for stopping invasion, and that great wars had been ruled by the Cabinet to be out of the question for ten years. During a discussion which Sir Henry had on the subject with the Secretary of State on the 20th the latter "said the Government could not do it, and at any rate he would not attempt it," so runs the diary. "And then I said, 'If I were you I would skip now.'"

The Field-Marshal had been expressing himself freely to the S. of S. on the subject of de Valera and Lloyd George, and he had offered to make a calculation as to the number of murders that would be necessary in Egypt and in India for those countries to achieve independence. As regards the reduction to be effected on the estimates, the Army Council came unwillingly to the conclusion that, as the Territorial Army was to be left intact, the three millions could only be saved by disbanding some battalions, some cavalry and some batteries.

The Greek forces in Anatolia embarked upon a fresh offensive in this month and at first they made good progress, the Turks retiring before them; and an important action was fought at Kutahia on July 18 in which the Ottoman troops were overborne. But, seeing that information was derived almost entirely from Greek sources, Wilson was not prepared to accept all tidings that came to hand at their full face value, and he questioned whether King Constantine's forces would prove ultimately the victors.

Owing to the coal strike having come to an end on July 4, the industrial situation in Great Britain was, however, no longer a cause, of anxiety to the War Office. On receiving a copy of the terms which Lloyd George had handed to de Valera (which were not made public till the middle of August) Sir Henry wrote in his diary:

> These terms are called a "Treaty"; there was some talk of calling them a "Pact" at the Cabinet, but this was dropped. The Treaty is an abject surrender to murderers. It gives complete independence under the guise of Dominion Home Rule. It gives army, police, judiciary, fiscal autonomy, taxation, no war debt, agriculture, education, etc. It begs leave to recruit in Ireland, it does not deny a fleet, and so on, and so on; in short, Ireland is gone. There is not one word about the loyal people of the south and west. So Lloyd George is getting on fast with the ruin of the Empire. We shall, incidentally, lose our 16 Irish battalions and have to withdraw altogether from Ireland. It is quite impossible to see what all this means.

The difficulties under which the military in Ireland were stiffering had by no means disappeared with the signature of the truce. A very awkward situation also arose at the end of the month owing to a ruling by the Master of the Rolls in Dublin that court-martial convictions of civilians were illegal. A number of rebels were under sentence of death by court-martial, while others had been awarded terms of penal servitude and imprisonment. Soldiers hold martial law to signify government by military tribunals, and the suspension of ordinary law except in so far as the responsible military authority permits it to function. In their view, the action of the Master of the Rolls rendered martial law an absurdity. The Law

Lords in England were moreover just at this time supposed to be considering the question whether martial law was in itself legal or not — as if it had never been put in force before within British Dominions. But they carefully refrained from pronouncing judgment. The Field-Marshal was disposed to attribute the very inconvenient attitude that was being assumed by the judiciary on both sides of St. George's Channel to die influence of the Prime Minister. But the very fact that martial law had not been, as Sir Henry had urged months before, extended all over Ireland gravely complicated the whole problem, and this appears in the diary on July 28:

> He [Lloyd George] has now got into the position — at the muzzle of Valera's pistol — that he can say it is illegal and impossible to govern Ireland by the military; and, as the police are disappearing and are quite useless without soldiers, it follows that Ireland cannot be governed by civilians either.

The Master of the Rolls on the 30th issued a writ for contempt of Court against Macready and Strickland for not releasing the prisoners who, according to him, had been illegally tried by military Courts.

Sir Henry spent the first week of August on board his yacht at Cowes for the annual week of the Royal Yacht Squadron, a week which turned out to be one of unusually boisterous winds and rough seas for the season of the year. On different days he sailed on board the *Britannia* and the *Joyette* while racing, and on the 3rd he met with an adventure which went very near to having a fatal termination. He had run across to Stokes Bay in the forenoon in the *White Heather*, with the intention of picking up his niece, Mrs. Coote, and her two little children — small girls who were special favourites of his — and of bringing them back to Cowes, where Lady Wilson was staying on shore. The sea had, however, proved too rough for landing, he had been obliged to anchor, and he was only able to get the party off in the afternoon when the wind had abated to some extent. Besides the skipper. Pope, the *White Heather* had a crew of two deck hands; and the Field-Marshal's servant also happened to be on board. What followed can best be

1921-22: The Field-Marshal's Last Eight Months... 361

told in his own words, taken from the diary:

> It, at once, came on to blow strong. We had a fine beat back to Cowes. Lowered sail in Osborne Bay and got under ketch; but headwind so strong and so rough, made slow way. Pope had not taken in all the slack of the main sheet, so it was banging about, and somehow it knocked me overboard. I had a mackintosh and long gum-boots on. I had a long struggle in the water, about 20 minutes, and Pope got to me at last with the dinghy, and held me up. Dudley Carleton[*] came up directly after in a small racing yacht belonging to Sir Arthur Cope, and after several tries (in a rough sea and a 5-knot tide) jumped into the dinghy and he and Pope were able to drag me in. I was rather tired, but luckily had not swallowed any water,[†] although at the end I was only just above water and the sea slapping me hard. One boot came off; but I could not get the other off and it dragged me down. No one threw the life-buoy. It was an unpleasant, but a valuable, experience.

He goes on to say that, after getting back to Cowes he took Mrs. Coote and the children to the R.Y.S. lawn, where Lady Wilson was awaiting him in great anxiety, and where he received many congratulations on his remarkable escape — an escape partly to be attributed to his powers as a swimmer and his hard condition, but partly due also to Mr. Carleton's skilful seamanship in reaching the dinghy. On the folio-wing day Sir Henry gave an account of his adventure to the King and the Duke of Connaught on board the Britannia. He was overwhelmed with telegrams and letters when accounts of the accident appeared in the newspapers, and one significant entry appears in his diary in this connexion:

> I am much amused by the fact that, with the exception of Curzon who wrote me a charming letter, not a single member of the Cabinet wrote or telegraphed to me about my being nearly drowned. Probably

---

[*] Now Lord Dorchester.

[†] His father had impressed on Sir Henry and his brothers when they were boys the importance of always keeping the mouth shut when bathing. That his mishap in Osborne Bay did not have a fatal termination, the Field-Marshal was wont to attribute largely to that teaching of long ago.

too busy running away from Valera's pistol.

He had particularly appreciated, amongst the many messages of congratulation received on his escape, letters from Huguet and Weygand and a cable from Rawlinson from Simla. This appears in the diary, written at Cowes on August 5:

> A lot of papers and letters, notably one from Macready relating his interview with Lloyd George at Criccieth, during which Lloyd George laid the blame on Ulster for "delay in peace," and proposed a monstrous plan of withdrawal and blockade if hostilities were renewed.

His Majesty the King, Sir Henry Wilson, the Duke of Connaught on board the "Britannia"

Back in London, he wrote on the 8th:

> I had a long talk with Worthy, principally about Ireland. I told him frankly what I thought. Only on Saturday last the Cabinet decided to let out all Members of Valera's House of Commons, except McKeon, the Ballinalee murderer, convicted as such. I told him that, of course, Lloyd George would let him out, as Valera's pistol had

1921-22: The Field-Marshal's Last Eight Months... 363

already come round. It appeared that this morning the Cabinet decided to let him out, and telephoned to Lloyd George in Paris yesterday, where he is for the Silesian Conference, for his decision. We can take this as granted. I told Worthy that Lloyd George would obey any order of Valera's right up to putting Ulster under Valera, but that he [Valera] would be brought up with a round turn by Ulster. I said that, on that, Lloyd George would start a Press campaign against Ulster, and that I had absolute signs of this.

On the 13th there is the entry:

Macready to see me at 10 a.m. He told me that he came over last night with Fitzalan,* who read him Valera's terms. They were quite uncompromising and were simply total independence. Macready thought that this would settle the matter and that we should go straight back to operations, but I told him that he did not understand Lloyd George.

The Cabinet met again after lunch and sat till 4 o'clock, when Worthy sent for me and told me the answer had been handed to Valera's man. It was to the effect "thus far and no farther," with a lot of "verbiage" as a "golden bridge" at the end of it. Macready came to see me. I told him I thought officers and men ought to be confined to barracks, as Valera might claim that the Cabinet answer broke off negotiations and might start in with a lot of brutal murders. I reminded him that Valera's experience was that the more murders he committed and the more brutal, the better terms he got from Lloyd George. This impressed Macready. He would see to it directly he goes back to-morrow morning.

Although feeling no confidence that the Prime Minister and the Cabinet would not give in to the pretensions of the Irish Republican leader, the Field-Marshal now examined the problem of how an adequate military force could be ensured for Ireland if a rupture of negotiations were to occur, and if the truce should come to an end. Thirteen thousand five hundred men would have to be withdrawn from the existing garrison in the winter, as drafts for India, and these men would naturally represent the more experienced soldiers in the force. He decided to ask for a special

---

* Lord Fitzalan had recently succeeded Lord French as Viceroy.

enlistment of 40,000 men for the infantry, to undergo one year of service within the United Kingdom, and his paper on the subject was in due course sent by the S. of S. to the Cabinet. Serious riots had broken out in Belfast, and they continued for several days, for the Civil Power hesitated to make use of the military owing to the existence of the truce. Wilson realized only too clearly that the time taken up in negotiations between the Cabinet and de Valera must prejudice the prospects of the troops in the south and west should active operations be resumed, but he was beginning to feel certain that the Cabinet would ultimately give way and that no such operations would take place.

The Prime Minister had repaired to the north of Scotland, and on September 6 Sir Henry wrote in his diary that a Cabinet of 17 were "gathering at Inverness to surrender once more to Valera." General Holman, home from India, declared that there was no sign of governing in that country either, and he told the C.I.G.S. an interesting story, which the latter wrote down in his diary and which deserves to be quoted:

> The other day Holman was talking to a friend of his — a native — who spoke as follows: "Why have the British Raj given up governing? They used to govern, and all was peace, prosperity and contentment. Now they have ceased governing and all is chaos. A few days ago Christ was walking in the bazaar, and there he met the Devil. Christ said to the Devil: 'Devil you are behaving badly, and if you don't mend your ways I must punish you!' The Devil replied, 'Christ, far from behaving badly, I have never been so good.' And as he said this he picked up a sweet off the counter in the bazaar and rubbed it on the wall. A fly saw the sugary morsel and settled on it. A lizard saw the fly and gobbled it. A cat saw the lizard and killed it. A British private with his dog was passing, and the dog killed the cat. The owner of the cat killed the dog. The British private killed the native. In half an hour there was chaos and the rattle of machine guns. The Devil turned to Christ and said; 'Do you hear that awful tapping of machine guns — and I did nothing to bring it about!'"
>
> The native said to Holman, "Ghandi is putting the sugar on the wall."

On September 11 the entry occurs in Wilson's diary:

Valera is now firmly established, thanks to Lloyd George, and has a Government, and Ministers, and Judges, and Magistrates, and Police, and Army, and money. I think that we shall want 100,000 to 200,000 men, and one or two years, to stamp out the murder-gang and re-establish law and order and the King's writ.

The evening papers say that Valera has sent his answer to Lloyd George and that he accepts the Conference at Inverness on condition that the question of loyalty to the Crown is open to discussion. If this be true he has cornered Lloyd George, who will, of course, agree to this, i.e, Valera now dictates terms — as I said he would.

The following appears on the 13th:

I had a long talk, and lunched, with Worthy, he was just back from Scotland and told me about Lloyd George and the Inverness Cabinet, I attacked vigorously. His one plea and justification was that Lloyd George now had the country behind him. I told him I doubted this, and that, if Lloyd George not only would not rouse the country on two years of filthy murders, but took every precaution to make sure that the country knew *nothing* about them, I begged leave to doubt his *bona fides* on the question of loyalty to the Crown. I told him that Lloyd George had played exactly the same game about conscripting Ireland in 1918, and that this Note, being delivered from Valera now, would be agreed to no matter what terms Valera imposed for the Conference on the 20th.

I also pressed strongly for a reversal of the Cabinet's decision not to send drafts to India, as I said, if hostilities were renewed in Ireland we should want 100,000 to 200,000 men in Ireland, and therefore 8,000 drafts were quite immaterial, whilst on the other hand they were vital to India.

Wilson wrote in his diary next day:

A delightful comedy at Gairloch, when McGrath and Boland brought Valera s answer to Lloyd George's note of September 7. In that Note was prepared to enter a conference with the murderers "to ascertain how the association of Ireland with the Community of Nations known as the British Empire can best be reconciled with Irish national aspirations." Valera's reply, as telephoned down to Worthy, was that "the Irish Republic would be glad to discuss this question with the Community of Nations known as the British Empire." Lloyd

George realized that this was rather strong meat even for his Cabinet, so he set to work to redraft Valera's reply in such a form that it would be agreeable both to Valera and the Cabinet.

This appears on the following day:

> Worthington's private secretary told Mogg this morning that Lloyd George had wired up last night to say that the report previously sent of Valera's answer was wholly unauthorized, and the members of the Cabinet were told to burn their copies! This is hot. But at midday Charlie[*] heard from Dublin that Valera had heard of Lloyd George's manœuvre and said at once that he would show whether it was authorized or not, by publishing his letter in the evening papers! And sure enough, he did. At 10 o'c. I telephoned to Worthy, who is down at his cottage in Surrey, and I told him that Valera had published his letter in the evening papers, and I read him extracts, which he checked with the "unauthorized" copy that he got last night, and which, he said, tallied and was therefore the real original. I am afraid Worthy has not burnt his copy.

The Prime Minister now informed de Valera that the proposed conference was cancelled, adding that he must consult his Ministers; but further messages continued to pass between the pair, and Wilson remarked in the diary on September 19:

> We have had 9 of these letters and telegrams since Lloyd George on September 7 wrote that the correspondence had lasted long enough and asked for a definite reply!

The Field-Marshal was much put out a few days later, on hearing that he was to go to Washington in connexion with a conference that was shortly to assemble about disarmament; he had no wish to cross the Atlantic at this time and he furthermore questioned the advantage of discussing such a subject. News was coming to hand from Asia Minor to the effect that the Greeks were now in full retreat — as Sir Henry had expected, and had predicted would prove to be the case from the outset. But the full measure of

---

[*] Colonel C.N. French.

the mischief caused by insensate Hellenic ambitions, stimulated as these ambitions had been by the British Prime Minister's encouragement and approval, was not to become manifest for some months to come. Nor was the Field-Marshal destined to see proved the correctness of his appreciations on this subject, appreciations which dated back to when President Wilson, Mr. Lloyd George and M. Clemenceau had banded themselves together, behind the back of their Italian colleague, to invite M. Venizelos to occupy Smyrna.

Sir Henry did not object to the proceedings of the Greek Government, merely on military grounds and because he foresaw that the offensive campaign of the Hellenic troops was bound to end in disaster. He disapproved also because his sympathies were with the Turkish Nationalists, who were in Asia Minor defending genuinely Ottoman territory peopled in the main by Osmanlis, and because he was strongly of pinion that the old friendship between the British and the Lurks ought to be revived. He had been much impressed with what he had learnt in Constantinople at the time of his visit in 1913 (recorded in Chapter VIII) as to the loss of that time-honoured friendship, and as to its cause. He believed in succouring and supporting one's friends, and in this connexion it may be mentioned that he was a convinced advocate of maintaining the most cordial relations with the Japanese. He had deplored the attitude of President Wilson at the time when British, French and Italians had in 1918 favoured active intervention by the Japanese against Bolshevism in Siberia, and he had foreseen what disastrous consequences must result from the President's opposition. One of the last General Staff appointments to be in the Field-Marshal's gift was that of Military Attaché at Tokio, which fell vacant a few weeks after this; and Lieutenant-Colonel (now Colonel) F.S.G. Piggott, chosen to fill the post, writes of a farewell interview with Sir Henry:

> The C.I.G.S. had already decided that I should be a member of the Military Section of the British Empire Delegation at the Washington Conference, due to assemble in the following month, and he spoke freely both of the forthcoming conference and of my future work in Japan.
> The gist of Sir Henry's remarks may be summed up in his reply to my definite inquiry as to whether he had any special instructions

for me to follow during the next four years. The Field-Marshal said, "You ask me to give you a general line, or policy, to pursue in Tokio. Well, I cannot do better than recommend to you my own motto, which I have always tried to live up to. *Stick to your friends and kill your enemies.* You will know how to interpret this in Japan. I have always hoped and believed that the Japanese are our friends, and that it is of vital importance to keep this friendship. I hope that your association with their army will result in your being able to report that they and we can still stand together, representatives of law and order. Tell my successor when you come home. I shall not be here then, but I hope you will come and tell me too.

Macready used to forward detailed weekly reports to the War Office concerning events in Ireland, and these the Field-Marshal was in the habit of passing on to the Secretary of State to see, generally adding some brief comments of his own. These documents were week after week indicating that the truce was not being loyally observed by Sinn Fein, and so, when forwarding the report dated September 20, the C.I.G.S. noted on it that he was "unable to understand how these breaches of the truce were allowed with the full knowledge of the Cabinet." In forwarding the next week's report, the Field-Marshal put the point still more strongly by appending a note to say that it passed his understanding how such things were allowed to go on "with the full knowledge and therefore, presumably, the approval of the Cabinet." An invitation was sent to de Velera (who had nowise receded from his position at the end of September) to attend a conference on October 11, and the Field-Marshal, who had gone over to the north of Ireland on a visit to Lord Dufferin at Clandeboye, noted in his diary:"Valera accepts Lloyd George's invitation, in a letter which completely dishes him." Of a conversation which he had with Sir J. Craig at Clandeboye he wrote:

> He thinks that, if the conference breaks down, Ulster ought to be under martial law like the rest of Ireland, but administered somewhat differently and scarcely under Dublin. This seems rather difficult. I explained to him the plans I have drawn up in case of resumption of hostilities — of martial law on the 26 counties. Press and passport arrangements, taking over railways, telegraphs, telephone and post, shipping to only two ports (Dublin and Cork), no clearing of ships to

and from foreign ports, etc. And, alternatively, the arrangements that I have made in case of agreement — how troops will be withdrawn from the 26 counties, and how I proposed to pack as many troops as possible into Ulster, which much pleased him.

I must review this Ulster position after this talk. He told me that he has 6,000 Class A of the R.I.C., and 16,000 Class B of Special Constables. But this small Parliament, with very little money and still less power, is a hopeless proposition, and they all think so.

The rebel Press is delighted at the coming conference. And even I will have a sort of grim satisfaction, watching Valera, who has a halter round Lloyd George, running Lloyd George up and down and then selling him. Valera will show his power. He probably won't attend the conference himself, he will order Lloyd George to let out the 5,000 internees, he won't agree to the conference being held at 10 Downing Street, etc.*

On his getting back to London Sir Henry was visited by General (now F.M. Sir Claud) Jacob, Chief of the General Staff in India, who expressed a very gloomy view of the state of things in that country, and who reported that numbers of the older soldiers and civilians were disposed to throw up their appointments in view of the regime that was being introduced. But, with a wire from the Indian Viceroy which was received on the following day and which begged the Cabinet to make friends with the Turks, the Field-Marshal was in cordial agreement. He informed Worthington-Evans that, as Foch was not going to attend the conference at Washington, he did not think that he ought to go either, and that he moreover did not wish to go; the arrangement was in consequence cancelled and Cavan went instead. In the course of their conversation on this occasion, the S. of S. remarked that he understood that the C.I.G.S. did not wish for an extension of his appointment, and Wilson assented. "He wanted to know what I was going to do, but I was not to be drawn," appears in the diary. Then, on October 8 the entry occurs:

> David Beatty rang me up. He wanted to know about the medal which Congress had voted for the grave of our Unknown Warrior, and

---

* The first two of these forecasts proved correct.

which Pershing was sent over to lay. Pershing has just performed this ceremony in Paris and was now hanging about, waiting for permission to come over here. David said there was a full kettle of fish, etc., and no one knew anything about it. I told him I knew all about it. That some 3 weeks ago Foreign Office sent over a paper asking for my opinion. I wrote S. of S. strongly advising refusal, on the ground that our Unknown Warrior was a strictly family and jealously personal affair, that at the funeral no representatives of foreign countries were allowed to take part, that if we accepted a medal from America we should have to accept from France, Belgium, Italy, Portugal, Japan, etc. We would have to return the compliment by giving a V.C. I went on to say that during the last 3 weeks I had several times jogged Foreign Office, but, of course, with no result. And I advised David to jog Foreign Office again, which he said he would do.

Of a conversation with the S. of S. on the 10th he wrote:

I told him about the Congress medal and how necessary it was to get something settled. David had told me in the morning that Curzon and Lloyd George had agreed to accept. The Americans are so angry with us, because no one wants to go over to their beastly conference, that they are quite in a mood to say, "The 30 millions you are going to spend on four battleships is ours, so hand it over and stop building." All the Cabinet are urging Lloyd George to go over. I hope he does, as he will do less harm there than here. I think he will go as a *beau geste*,* and also because he is in a filthy mess there.

Next day there is the entry:

The conference met at 10 Downing Street at 11 o'c. I do not know what happened, but at 12 o'c. Lloyd George sent over for my map of the world. I suppose that Lloyd George was going to give one of his fantastic naval and military strategical lectures — to the murderers.

A few days later the Field-Marshal went over to Paris, and he had a long conversation with Foch, who was shortly going to America, but was not attending the Washington Conference

---

* "Kind gesture."

although he was to visit every state in the Union. They discussed India, Mesopotamia, Egypt, Palestine, Syria and Constantinople, and Wilson wrote in his diary:

> I told him of Winston's medicine for Mesopotamia, of hot air, aeroplanes and Arabs, and for Palestine of hot air, aeroplanes and Jews — and he simply threw up his hands. He agreed with me that the Greeks would have to retire to Smyrna, and possibly even to clear out of that, but he was not so certain as I am that they would also have to clear out of Thrace and Adrianople! *"Pauvre Angleterre, pauvre Angleterre,"** he kept on repeating, and then he said a thing to me that he would not have said to any other Englishman, "You break your written word. You cower under the assassin and the Jew. Your friendship is no longer worth seeking. We must go elsewhere." The old Marshal thinks that France will pull through, partly because of her peasant proprietors, and partly because, as no one pays taxes and as everyone has saved in the War, so everyone invested in *rentes*† and so no one wants a revolution.

Wilson crossed the Channel on the return journey in the same vessel as General Pershing, and wrote:

> I told him of our Irish situation, of the foul murders, and of Lloyd George's capitulation. He knew nothing of all this and was terribly upset. I thought it good that he, a friendly and loyal comrade, should know the real truth.

This appears in the diary on October 17:

> Cecil and I were present at the Abbey when Pershing laid the Congress medal on the Unknown Warrior. A horrible service, with political speeches by American Ambassador and Lloyd George. A few more such ceremonies and the sanctity of the Abbey will be gone for me. Then Pershing laid a wreath on the Cenotaph. No Frocks there. So we were happy, and he whispered to me, "This is my first happy moment."

---

* "Poor England, poor England."

† "Annuities."

> Duke of Connaught gave Pershing lunch. Lloyd George there, but I did not speak to him.
> The Army Council gave Pershing a dinner. The Duke of Connaught there, but not Lloyd George or other Frocks except X.* I sat between Trenchard and X, and had a row with X. I trailed my coat by saying that I was looking out for a yacht, in which to escape from England or Ireland and sail for Ulster when Collins had taken over the United Kingdom. X said that Collins was a better general than any of the English generals, to which I replied that he had certainly done a thing that none of us had done *yet* — that was that he had taken the "Prime Minister and the Cabinet by the throat and cowed them." To which X replied. "It was the British Army he cowed." To this I replied, "That is a lie, and you know it is a lie, and you will apologize." And he at once apologized. These matters amicably settled, X set to work and cursed Lloyd George in a way that did me good to hear. X said that Lloyd George knew nothing, cared nothing except for himself, interfered with everybody, and made chaos of everything he touched!

Next day there is the entry:

> This morning Worthy sent for me, George Stanley† being present, and said that he understood that I did not wish to go to these murderers' meetings, nor did any officers. I said that was so, and that I thought he would be wise not to press the matter. He agreed not to, but said he would consult me about things before going to the meetings. He wanted to know what I thought about recruiting in Ireland, and Irish battalions and Irish depots. I told him he might make his mind easy about such matters, as Valera would have none of them. He said that he was not hopeful of coming to terms, and I replied that the only way he could come to terms was by unconditional surrender to the murderers.
> Another pathetic wire from Reading, begging the Government to tell Turkey that they might retake Smyrna and Thrace. This is what I have been urging for 2½ years.
> To-night's papers say that the Ulster Volunteers were being called up. If this is true it will probably lead to trouble. Curiously

---

* A Cabinet Minister. The name is, of course, in the diary.

† Lieutenant-Colonel Hon. G.F. Stanley. He was Financial Secretary at the W.O.

enough only in speaking to Worthy this morning, and this evening to George Stanley, I had gravely warned them of the danger of allowing the rebels to break the truce in Ulster.

This appears next day:

> Long talk with Worthy this morning. He said the conference must break down, but I demurred saying that Lloyd George would give in. I reminded Worthy of all Lloyd George's letters to Valera, and of the episode of his ordering the Cabinet to burn "unauthorized copy" of one of Valera's letters.

The Field-Marshal mentions in his diary giving evidence before the Geddes Committee (the "Axe" Committee) on October 25, and he relates how, after an hour and a half of "niggling" questions, he gave that body a lecture on the larger aspects of the military problem. He explained that, with troops scattered all over the world, with 69 battalions in Ireland at one-third of their proper strength, and with only four battalions in Great Britain, there was absolutely no reserve anywhere, that if there were trouble in Egypt or India no assistance could be sent except by withdrawing troops from places where, owing to the Government's policy, their presence at the time was virtually indispensable. He gave evidence again on the following day; but on this occasion he dealt with the question of a separate Air Ministry, to which he was strongly opposed. Sir J. Craig and Macready were both at this time pressing for 12,000 rifles and 3,000,000 rounds of small-arms ammunition to be sent to Carrickfergus, but the Secretary of State and Lloyd George agreed that "it would be provocative" to comply with their request. "Have we reached this stage," the Field-Marshal said to Worthington-Evans, "that we dare not send arms to Ulster even when the C. in C. and Prime Minister of Ulster ask us and say it is urgent?"

He had bought another yacht, a yawl called the *Pleiad*; but he had no intention of fitting her out until the spring, when he would be a free man and able to indulge his love of sailing to an extent that he had found to be quite impossible during the past two seasons in the *White Heather*.

Negotiations had been in progress for some little time past, it was known in England, between M. Franklin Bouillon, acting in the capacity of French plenipotentiary, and the Turkish Nationalist leader, Kemal Pasha. The Cabinet were nevertheless somewhat taken aback on learning early in November that an agreement had been arrived at with Kemal on behalf of the French Government, without the British Government having been consulted. One result of the pact seemed likely to be that the French troops would be withdrawn from Constantinople, which might make the position of Harington (who happened to be on leave in England at the moment) more difficult than it was already; and on the Secretary of State asking the C.I.G.S. for his views as to what ought to be done in this pass, he received the following reply:

> Write to the French and say that this separate action on their part completely frees our hands, and then inform Kemal that, so far as we are concerned, he was welcome to take over Smyrna, the Straits, Constantinople, Thrace and Adrianople, and that we would clear out of Turkey altogether and resume our old rôle of Friend. Then tell the Greeks that they had tried expansion under the direction of Venizelos, Tino and Lloyd George, to their own ruin and to everybody's danger, and therefore they must contract again. In short — reverse our policy absolutely and make friends with the Turks instead of with the Greeks.
>
> Worthy said that Lloyd George would never do this. Nor would Curzon, "whose honour was pledged." I can well believe all this, but, as I said to Worthy, the only difference will be that we shall be kicked out of Constantinople instead of retiring gracefully.

The conference between Lloyd George and certain members of his Cabinet on the one hand, and the representatives of Sinn Fein on the other hand, had been in progress since October 11, and the negotiations were to continue for several weeks longer. But one result of this traffic, and of the uncertainty that prevailed as to its issue, was to create considerable unrest amongst the people of Ulster, and especially amongst the citizens of Belfast. The recently established Government of Northern Ireland was consequently confronted with a two-fold problem. Order had to be maintained throughout the six counties. Preparations had at the same time to be made for meeting the eventuality of attack from the south. On being consulted by Sir J. Craig, the Field-Marshal recommended that the duty of guarding the frontier should devolve upon the troops stationed in Ulster — which would save them from being called upon to suppress riots — and that the prevention of civil disturbances should be effected by police forces, advice which was, at least in principle, accepted by Craig.

Wilson wrote in the diary on November 9:

> I had two hours with Spender,* he says Craig and his Cabinet absolutely refuse to budge an inch, that Craig asked Lloyd George to reduce all his proposals to writing, that Lloyd George promised this by last night, that nothing came, that Craig telephoned to-day and was told the paper would be ready in a couple of days! In short, Lloyd George can't get the permission of the murderers to put the matter in writing. Spender tells me that Craig has at last fully realized the blackguardism of the whole thing. Spender told me that the Ulster Cabinet were not going to budge *one inch*. This is good, as it will force Lloyd George out into the open, and we shall see who are our friends and who are our enemies.

A day of two later the Field-Marshal learnt from Spender that the Prime Minister would not agree to certain letters that had been passing between him and Craig being published, and this appears in the diary:

> I reminded him that if in 1915 we had not answered the Boche employment of gas by counter-gas, the Boche would have won the war, and so with Lloyd George and his tricks.

A large party representing Ulster, including the Field-Marshal, proceeded to Amiens on November 18 (Sir J. Craig and Lord Carson unfortunately being ill and unable to travel), for the unveiling of the memorial to the 36th (Ulster) Division at Thiepval. Sir Henry described the ceremony as follows in the diary:

> I went out with Weygand, who got down from Paris at 9 a.m. It was a wonderful ceremony. A beautiful building. I opened the door,

---

* Lieutenant-Colonel W.B. Spender, He was Secretary of the N.I. Cabinet.

and made a speech in French of welcome; then Weygand unveiled the Memorial; then dedication of the building by the Primate, and Moderator and the President of the Methodists; then Duchess of Abercorn hoisted the Jack and the Tricolor; then we planted trees from Ulster; then lunch at Albert and more speeches; then back to Amiens and got back here to No. 36 at 11 p.m.

Coming over in the boat. Spender gave me the 4 letters which have passed between Lloyd George and Craig. Having read all this, I told Spender that two things stood out: (*a*) That Lloyd George carefully avoided all mention of allegiance; (*b*) That Craig had agreed to meet Lloyd George. I made the following observations to Spender: "The thing for us to smash the conference on is the question of allegiance, therefore I think that Craig should now write to Lloyd George and ask whether the Sinn Feiners have signed allegiance or not, and say that on receipt of reply, or at the latest in four days, he will publish all the correspondence." I rubbed this in for all I was worth into Spender.

Wilson entered in his diary on the 25th:

Morland writes asking for two battalions to be sent back to him from Silesia as he was expecting strikes, etc. He has only 2 squadrons 14th Hussars and some police at Cologne now. The distribution of our army is wonderful.

The Cabinet had some weeks before this, as we have seen, insisted on Morland's battalions going to Silesia, where the Germans and the Poles were at daggers drawn and whither the French were sending additional troops. The C.I.G.S. had protested against this transfer of troops, and he had made more than one unsuccessful attempt to secure the return of the battalions to the Rhine since their departure. Now Macready was begging that the two battalions first for foreign service should be sent over from England to Belfast; but these two were already under orders for Gibraltar and Constantinople, their heavy baggage was already embarked, and Wilson did not see how he could alter their destination at the last moment. There were no other battalions, other than Guards battalions, available to send. "I have still got three companies of M.I. of R.F.A.," he noted in his diary (artillery were being converted temporarily into Mounted Infantry in the emergency existing), "and they can go to Ireland, and that is our last effort until we especially recruit." The Cabinet's fatuous persistence in framing their policy without any consideration whatever of the resources at their disposal for enforcing it was continuing to make the task of the War Office almost an impossible one.

This appears in the diary on December 3:

> I wrote S. of S., who is still sick, that we must give Craig the 26,000 rifles and 5,000,000 S. A.A. which he asks for, because the Imperial Cabinet had handed over to him on November 22 the responsibility of keeping law and order, and it was impossible to refuse to give him the means of carrying out his responsibilities.
>
> Later I was called on for a paper about the state of affairs about the arms for Ulster, and I drew up a short Note on the same lines and sent it in at 6.30 for a Cabinet at 7 o'clock. I am never asked to a Cabinet now on any subject — and a good job too, for I have such a contempt for the whole of them that I could not well conceal it.

An agreement was at last reached between the Cabinet and the Sinn Fein representatives in the small hours of the morning of December 6. Sir Henry heard details of its terms late that night, and he wrote in his diary:

> The agreement is a complete surrender, 1. A farcical oath of allegiance; 2. Withdrawal of our troops; 3. A rebel army, etc., etc. The British Empire is doomed.

The question, however, now arose as to whether the treaty would be ratified by Dail Eireane in Dublin or not, and it remained in suspense for the whole of December, de Valera holding out against an agreement which did not grant total independence, Michael Collins prepared to accept the terms as they stood. But the War Office could get no definite instructions in the meantime as to whether the troops were to begin withdrawing from the country. Although well aware of the perplexities and dangers that were likely to arise before evacuation was completed, the military authorities were anxious to begin the movement as soon as possible. This appears in Wilson's diary on the 8th:

After Selection Board, Macready and I went to see the S. of S. We put before him the picture that we saw. At the present moment the 26 Counties are under London, so all goes as usual. When (and if) the Dail Eireane ratify, then a kind of Colonial Government, with the Dail as Executive, will be set up till Easter, when the Dail take over completely. In this intervening period of 3 or 4 months it would be open to the Dail to call upon our troops in aid of the civil power, or, as I put it, it would be open to the Dail to call on our troops to shoot another set of murderers, or to shoot loyalists. I said that this was an intolerable state of affairs, and therefore, when (and if) the Dail ratified, we must get all the troops away as fast as we possibly could.

To complicate matters, Winston has no money for Mesopotamia, so we shall have to withdraw our last two white battalions. And Winston has just written a paper about Palestine in which he says our army there is much too expensive, and he wants us to withdraw our 3 cavalry regiments and 2 battalions. And as there are no barracks for these 4 battalions and 3 cavalry regiments, they will no doubt be abolished.

McCalmont (Irish Guards)[*] to see me about his Sergeant Roche. He told me that he had ascertained that the Attorney General and the Home Secretary had given orders not to let the fact out that Roche was acting under Michael Collins's orders, and he told me also that he had spoken to Worthy who had told him that on no account was this to get out.[†]

Next day there is the entry:

Winston says he cannot afford to run Palestine with our troops, so proposes to do so with Jew levies and 700 Black and Tans! The real fact is that Winston is between a cheap and fatal tenure of Mesopotamia and a real occupation with security and peace which he

---

[*] Colonel R.C.A. McCalmont.

[†] Roche was implicated in a raid, by Sinn Feiners (who secured machine guns and rifles), upon the barracks at Windsor on November 23. Further references to the incident appear in the diary. That, during a period of truce and at a time when Michael Collins was engaged in negotiations with the Cabinet in Downing Street, that Irish leader should have been arranging for raids to be conducted on military barracks in England for the purpose of securing arms, would not have sounded well had the truth been allowed to leak out.

can't pay for. In short, his "hot air, aeroplanes and Arabs" is leading him to disaster, and he is beginning to realize it. To-night he sent over to beg for 3 Armoured Car Companies for Mesopotamia from Ireland. I sent him word to say that the Armoured Cars would be the last thing to leave Ireland, and so he would not have them before next hot weather, i.e. not till October.

This appears on the 10th:

> About 1.15 p.m. Macready came racing back into my room very excited and angry. It appears that some internees, let out yesterday from Ballykinlar [Lloyd George had ordered the release of all the internees], when arriving by train were bombed at Thurles. On this, Lloyd George, being determined to put the soldiers in the wrong, and totally ignoring the War Office as usual, and Macready (who he thought was at Salisbury with his son), drafted and sent (with the aid of Hamar) a wire to Wroughton (Macready's A.G.) to take most severe disciplinary action at once, and to "suspend" all soldiers in the neighbourhood on suspicion. Macready luckily heard of this and at once went to the Irish Office; Hamar at first pretended to know nothing about it, then, when Macready began to get to work on him, Hamar said it was Lloyd George (and this was no doubt true). Macready got on the telephone to Wroughton in front of Hamar, and ordered Wroughton to put the telegram in the safe, tell no one and take no action beyond ascertaining the facts of the case. And then Macready, with Fitzalan present, gave Hamar the length and breadth of his tongue, and Hamar completely crumpled up. This is another dirty business.*

One of the difficulties that the War Office was faced with was that of finding the necessary barrack accommodation for the troops apparently about to be withdrawn from Ireland. In this connexion the C.I.G.S. wrote in his diary on December 16:

---

* Sir N. Macready refers to this incident in his "Annals of an Active Life." "On investigation it was found," he writes, "that what actually happened was that some Sinn Feiners, to celebrate the releases, placed fog signals on the line, and as the train passed, in order to still further emphasize their Hibernian delight and make more noise, threw a few bombs which of course they had handy in their pockets. The bombs were not thrown at the train, nor was anybody injured."

A.G. came in for a talk and told me that he and the Q.M.G. had been for 1½ hours with Worthy, who now said that the Cabinet would not tolerate any battalions from Ireland going to the Rhine, as the French would probably go into the Ruhr and we might have to follow them. Lloyd George was even contemplating withdrawing all troops from the Rhine, i.e. quarrelling with the French. So poor A.G. and Q.M.G. have to remake all their plans about battalions, married families, barracks, etc. A.G. said he was in despair about everything, and that he never made a plan which was not immediately upset by the Frocks.

The Report of the Geddes Committee reached the War Office a day or two later, and Sir Henry learnt to his consternation that this body proposed to demand a saving of £20,000,000 from the army. The question whether this could possibly be accomplished, and if so how, had to be considered; and the Field-Marshal arrived at certain broad conclusions on the subject, which were to be examined in detail by his staff, before proceeding to Wynyard to spend Christmas with Lord and Lady Londonderry. It had been almost an invariable custom on his part in the past to sum up on December 31 in his diary the leading events of the past twelve months, and the fact that he refrained from doing so on this occasion, when he must have had the necessary leisure, is not without significance. The year 1921 had, in his view, been a year of humiliation for England. He bitterly resented the surrender of the Prime Minister and his colleagues to the forces of disorder in Ireland, and he regarded the gross betrayal of the loyalists, which the Cabinet's sudden capitulation to Sinn Fein of necessity involved, with abhorrence. The frigid indifference which the Government were displaying with regard to the insults of which the military were constantly victims at the hands of rebels, as also with regard to the actual losses which the army and the police had suffered from the activities of the murder-gang, revolted him.[*] He

---

[*] "The history of every country, England included, has its dark and shameful chapters. But I doubt if that of any civilized community in modern times can show anything which for cowardice, wickedness, stupidity and meanness can equal the handling by the British Government of the situation created for them by a couple of thousand Irish peasants and shop-boys," — "History of Ireland. 1798—1924,"

was now rarely, if ever, consulted by the Cabinet in connexion with questions of policy involving strategical considerations, and, if he was by any chance so consulted, his advice was not taken. Only a day or two before going down to Wynyard he had been much hurt on hearing for the first time from Lord Cavan himself that Cavan was going to succeed him in February; he rightly thought that he ought at least to have been formally consulted, and that he ought to have been informed of the decision by the Secretary of State, and not by his chosen successor who had naturally supposed that he knew all about it. His personal relations with many Ministers, which had in the past been cordial and even intimate, had moreover become so strained that he was scarcely on speaking terms with some of those who had been the most prominently concerned in yielding to de Valera and Michael Collins. Nor did the fact that he had been proved to be in the right in a number of cases where he had found himself at issue with the Cabinet — in respect of the Turko-Greek question, for instance, and in respect to Persia — provide much consolation to a man so jealous of his country's honour and so eager for its prosperity as was Henry Wilson. He wrote in his diary on January 3, after getting back to London:

> Two long Military Members' meetings, with George Stanley and Charlie Harris[*] in addition. We discussed Geddes' proposals. Charlie told us that the abolition of 28 battalions[†] and 8 cavalry regiments and guns, etc., to match, only meant a saving of 8 millions. And Geddes wants at least 20 millions. We spent 6 hours trying to get further reductions in schools, education, R.M.A., R.M.C., barracks, commands, staff; but we only scraped up a few 100 thousands. Geddes leaves Volunteers and Yeomanry practically intact, whilst all the money has to come off Regulars. C.O.s come to see me, and write from all over the world, asking that their units may be spared. Cavan

---

By the Right Hon. Sir James O'Connor.

[*] Sir C. Harris, Director of Finance at the W.O.

[†] 16 Irish battalions, and 12 from the existing 6 regiments comprising 4 battalions each.

has an awful job in front of him.

P. de B. told me this afternoon that Panouse had just been to see him, to tell him that the French Government were going to give me a present when my time as C.I.G.S. was up next month. This is without precedent, and I am much touched.

This appears in the diary next day:

I am very hostile to Worthy's and A.G.'s proposal to abolish the 3 Ulster regiments (Inniskilling Fusiliers, Irish Fusiliers, Royal Ulster Rifles), as though they were on all fours with the other 3 regiments (Royal Irish, Connaughts, Leinsters, Munsters and Dublins).

The Dail Eireane at last, on January 7, ratified the treaty agreed upon by the Cabinet and the Sinn Fein delegates in the middle of December. A special committee, under Churchill's chairmanship, had been sitting to deal with the problems that would arise in handing over the government, and he held a meeting on the 9th. Of what passed, Sir Henry wrote in his diary:

He told A.G. (who told me) that, as it now appeared most likely that there would be rows in Ireland, all orders for withdrawing the troops must be held up, although it had been previously decided that, the moment the Dail ratified, the troops were to be instantly withdrawn. I won't let this new ruling go for long without making a row.

The C.I.G.S. also learnt that Lloyd George was going to hand draft articles for an alliance between Great Britain and France to Briand at Cannes. A day or two later he received an offer of the seat of St, George's, Hanover Square, if there were to be a General Election; but he was not prepared to give a decision at the moment.

This appears in the diary on the 11th:

Harris now says that the cuts proposed will only amount to 14 or 15 millions . How are we going to work up to 20 millions? I have no idea.

I went over to Colonial Office and had a talk with Winston. We have had several assaults on officers and men in Ireland the last few days, and I told him we would not stand it, and we must take over or come out. He agreed and hoped we might begin on Monday. He anticipates peace under Collins, but said he would use troops to bolster up Collins. I differed, and pointed out that no troops could be sent to Canada to take part in a party war. He had no answer. He agreed with me that the Ulster regiments must not be abolished.

Then a meeting of Austen's C.I.D. on India. It is quite clear that the Indian situation has got completely out of Montagu's grip, and he knows it. When sitting at this committee about 6.30 J.T. Davies (who I thought was at Cannes) brought in a slip for Austen, who read it and tossed it across to me. This was to announce that Briand had resigned. I threw it back without comment. So Lloyd George's fish-wife's bargaining has not succeeded.* I suppose that Cannes will break up, and that Lloyd George will soon come home to ponder about a General Election. I can't help thinking that Lloyd George is near the end of his rope. But I am afraid the Empire is gone. Ireland Free State is gone, and India (on Montagu's showing) is in a very dangerous state.

The Field-Marshal wrote on January 14:

I lunched at Londonderry House, only Lord and Lady Londonderry there, and we discussed the possibility, necessity and probability of forming a real Conservative Party. Lady Londonderry is working hard to this end with Salisbury, Northumberland, Carson, Ronald McNeill, and I am sure this is the right thing to aim for. And I believe if they could get a fine leader it is a real possibility.

On the 16th the entry appears:

A wire from Curzon at Cannes to Cabinet, proposing a military convention with Belgium, which he had discussed with the Belgians and which he would lay before the Cabinet on Wednesday. Another case of policy ignoring strategy.

A.G. came to tell me that Winston had this morning told him to start withdrawing troops. Winston has been so incredibly brave as to give this order without getting Michael Collins's permission.

I am delighted with the papers' reports of Poincaré's interview

---

* It was apparently the Prime Minister's golf rather than his fish-wife's bargaining that upset Briand.

with Lloyd George. He seems to have said that these ridiculous meetings of Prime Ministers and their circuses must cease, and diplomacy and Foreign Office and Ambassadors resume their proper work. This is a slap in the face to Lloyd George. At Cannes there was even no agenda. Johnnie Du Cane, back from Mentone, says the Frenchmen won't stand any more of these expensive farces.

Then, later. Worthy sent for me. He talked a lot about Cannes and the coming meeting at Genoa with Boches and Bolsheviks, which he says will take place whether the French agree to it or not! I told him something of our work on the Geddes Committee. I explained my paper on the reductions. He said that he had not seen it, but professed to be anxious not to ruffle Lloyd George, which, from what he had heard of it, he was afraid my final paragraph might do. I told him I thought it was high time somebody told Lloyd George the truth, and that I could think of no one in a better position to do so than myself.

The Field-Marshal proceeded to Dublin on the evening of January 17, *en route* to Belfast, and he spent a day in the Irish capital with Macready at the Royal Hospital. Sir Henry saw the Lord-Lieutenant, from whom he learnt that the police barracks at Cookstown had that very morning been attacked, and that three of the police were missing, so he wrote in his diary:

I said to Fitzalan, how in the world any sane man can imagine that Collins and Co., who none of them have ever administered 2 type-writers, can be expected to keep law and order over 3 millions of people who have now no sense of either, and this without either any army or police, simply passes my comprehension.

He went on to Belfast on the 19th, and he met many of the leading men of Ulster during a two-days' visit to the north. He got a great reception in Belfast, and again on the following day at Lisburn, where he unveiled a statue of John Nicholson in the market square. Before pulling the cords he delivered an address in which a noble tribute was paid to that great soldier, and the crowds gathered round the plinth were told how, even yet, more than sixty years after his death at Delhi, the wild tribesmen of the North-West Frontier still teach their children to salaam at the mention of his name. The Field-Marshal concluded:

I would say to you men and women of Lisburn, treat that statue as something to be not only exceedingly proud of, but as something sacred, arid teach your children the story of the life of John Nicholson of Lisburn.

Later in the day he unveiled a Roll of Honour in the drill hall of Queen's University in Belfast, and Sir J. Craig, in moving a vote of thanks to Sir Henry, declared that there was no better Ulsterman than the distinguished soldier who had honoured them with his presence, and that there was no more prepared to aid Ulster in her difficulties. "A very successful and interesting three days in Dublin and Belfast," Wilson wrote on getting back to London on the 20th, and this also appears in the diary that day:

> Began with a talk with Worthy about my Note. He tried to get me to cut out my final paragraph. He said that everyone was agreed that I was "one of the outstanding figures in England, and one of the most brilliant intellects." I replied that it was very nice of him to say so, and that I never would have thought it by the way the Cabinet had ignored my advice for the last 3 years. I said that I did not know who could write the final paragraph except myself, and that I felt sure it ought to be written. But I would think over it as he pressed me so much. Curiously enough, this afternoon several telegrams came in showing that Curzon had concluded a Military Convention with the Belgians, again without any warning or consultation with us. So I strengthened my final paragraph by a reference to this, and sent it in to Worthy.

Matters in Egypt had come to a head, for the situation as between the Cabinet and the Egyptian authorities had been at a deadlock for some weeks; the Egyptian Cabinet had resigned, the Nile Delta was in a condition of suppressed rebellion against British domination, and on January 26 an alarming telegram came to hand from Allenby, of which Wilson wrote in his diary:

> He takes the line that we have missed the train, and he tenders his formal resignation and humble duty to the King. I don't know what the Cabinet will do now. I suppose a number of meetings and discussions, and more drift. It is a very serious position, and it is entirely due to the miserable weakness and ignorance of Lloyd

George and his Miseries.*

This appears next day:

> Worthy tells me to-night that the Cabinet have ordered Allenby home to report. It is a proper mess, and I suppose Lloyd George will now put in someone else in Allenby's place, and then work behind his back as he did in the Irish business. I asked Worthy whether the Cabinet were prepared for the odium of governiag Egypt by force, if no Egyptian Cabinet can be formed except on the platform of complete independence and full sovereign rights. I expressed grave doubts in view of Lloyd George's Irish record. I am certain that Lloyd George will cart us again.

The Field-Marshal spent a couple of days in Paris at the end of January, and while there he enjoyed long conversations with both Foch and Weygand. Foch had much to tell of the United States, after his having toured the whole country under auspices of the different States of the Union. Sir Henry on getting back was apprised that the Prime Minister had decided to release a number of men of the Connaught Rangers who had mutinied in India in 1920, and who had received life sentences by court-martial. "This is, of course, on the orders of Collins," he commented, "and is bringing cowardice and politics into the army with a vengeance." He found moreover that far more Yeomanry were to be allowed to remain Yeomanry than the General Staff thought desirable, and this appears in the diary:

> This is, of course, to save Winston's Oxford Hussars. In

---

* Lord Milner's Commission had in the summer of 1920 recommended granting Egypt what amounted to almost complete independence. But H.M. Government had been unable to decide how far to fall in with this recommendation. Negotiations had been proceeding with the Egyptian Government ever since, and the delay in arriving at a settlement had given rise to much unrest in the Nile Delta and had made the position of the High Commissioner a very difficult one. Sir Henry was not enamoured of Lord Milner's recommendations, and during the year 1921 he made occasional references to the matter in his diary. But he was still less enamoured of the vacillation displayed by the Cabinet concerning a question that called insistently for a definite decision.

consequence, several T.F. divisions will go without R.A., R.E., etc. I told S. of S. that such action was unpardonable — but it will surely be done.

On February 1 Wilson wrote in the diary:

> I had an Army Council on our final paper to be presented to the Cabinet on Geddes. In this we show that we can only produce one division and one cavalry division in 15 days; the other divisions much later, i.e. 2nd Division in 2 months and 3rd and 4th Divisions in 4 months, with no date for the 5th Division, and with no 6th Division at all. Compare with 1914, when I had 1½ cavalry divisions and 6 divisions ready, complete, in 10 days.

On the 3rd there is the entry:

> A.G. showed me a Note he had written, which Worthy was signing for the Cabinet, condemning in the strongest manner the release of the Connaught Rangers mutineers. It is an excellent Note. But I don't believe it will weigh one moment with Lloyd George as against Michael Collins's *orders* for their release, and I said to A.G. and to Philip Chetwode that, if Lloyd George ignored this warning and insisted on release, we would seriously have to consider our resignations.
> A long wire from Cox (Baghdad) saying that affairs in Mesopotamia were getting into a dangerous state, principally because we had not made friends with the Turks, which was essential.

A vacancy had occurred in the representation of North Down in the House of Commons, and Captain Charles Craig arrived in London on February 4 to offer the seat to the Field-Marshal. There appeared to be no likelihood of a contest, so, after giving the matter due consideration. Sir Henry decided to accept the proposal, but on the clear understanding that he would only offer himself if there would be no opposition. "It is curious," he remarked in his diary, "this offer coming in the nick of time." Ulster was at the moment attracting much attention in and around Whitehall, for Sir J. Craig had informed the Prime Minister that the boundary between Northern Ireland and the Irish Free State must stand as it had been laid down in the Home Rule Bill of 1920. That affrays would probably occur on the frontier, when this decision became known, was obvious to all acquainted with the situation; and such affrays, in fact, began to take place within a very few days.

Macready had been summoned to London just at this time, and the Field-Marshal and he found themselves in complete agreement as to the importance of withdrawing the troops from the Irish Free State as soon as possible, even if Collins should ask for some of them to be left to maintain order. Under the arrangements that had already been made there would still be thirteen battalions and three cavalry regiments left in the country (besides eleven battalions in Ulster) on April 1, and four of the battalions would, moreover, be stationed at Cork — the worst possible place for them to be. Associates for several years past in war and in peace, a thorough understanding existed between the C.I.G.S. and the C. in C. in Ireland, and, even if they occasionally differed on points of detail, their co-operation in endeavouring to maintain law and order during 1920 and 1921 had been cordial and complete. The handsome tribute which is paid by Macready to Sir Henry in "Annals of an Active Life" may therefore appropriately be quoted here — its reference to the attitude maintained by the Field-Marshal in respect to Ulster is of special significance:

> Henry Wilson gave me unfailing and vigorous support, even at the expense of other calls upon the army which from a professional standpoint he considered of even greater urgency; and when affairs became troublesome he maintained a judgment as clear and unbiased as if he had no connexion with the "Black North," as he used to call it, in any shape or form. Being in almost daily correspondence with Henry Wilson, seeing him also at frequent intervals when I came to London, there was never an occasion when he did not use every means at his disposal, first to strengthen and assist the troops in Ireland in their difficult task up to the time of the truce of 1921, and afterwards to alleviate the invidious and impossible position in which they found themselves. To me personally his support, and his cheery optimism in everything except the political future of his native land, was one of the few bright spots in a trying and anxious experience.

The following appears in the Field-Marshal's diary on February 8:

> James Craig came to see me in the office before lunch. He and I discussed at length what his refusal to take part in the Boundary Commission would mean, and we are both agreed that it would be the right course.
>
> Worthy sent for me at 5 o'c. and told me that Craig had just rung him up and told him that the I.R.A. had raided over the boundary of Tyrone and Derry and captured some 40 Orangemen and taken them off, burnt houses, wounded men, blown up bridges, etc. I could not help smiling. I telephoned at once to Macready, who had not heard about this, and told him to take the necessary steps, which, of course, he will do. I told Worthy that the Cabinet would no doubt take action with Collins. Lloyd George must be pleased.

On the 10th there is the entry:

> I met Allenby at Victoria Station, 10.15 Philip Chetwode also there. No high Foreign Office official and no car to meet the Bull. It was a scandal.
>
> I held a Military Members meeting about our evacuation of Ireland. Everything is in chaos. But we are coming away all right, and if the Frocks will agree to it, we can be completely clear by April 10, except, of course, for 11 battalions for Ulster.
>
> I went to a Cabinet at 5 o'c. — the first I have been to since July 5 last year.[*] Lloyd George did not nod at me nor take notice of me, nor I of him. The subject was the Indianization of the Indian Army. Lloyd George was angry and made quite a long speech that the British people were not going to be intimidated by the Indians, etc., etc., and I wrote on a slip, "I have heard these exact same words used about the Irish, and they mean nothing but abject surrender."

Sir Henry heard on the following day that he had been unanimously selected as candidate for North Down, but he learnt a few days later that there might be opposition after all. He decided to stand even so, although the expense of a contested election would be a serious inconvenience for him; but on the 18th, his last day in the War Office as it happened, he received a telephone message that his opponent not only had withdrawn but had become

---

[*] The occasion on which Wilson had informed the Prime Minister that he declined to speak to murderers.

one of his nominators. "An amazing people," he remarked in his diary, "but a great relief to me." He was consequently elected unopposed on February 21. On the 12th the entry had appeared in his diary:

> Worthy telephoned to say he wanted me at the W.O. at ¼ to 11. We (Worthy, A.G., Q.M.G., self) assembled and discussed the last atrocity of Sinn Feiners, having shot 4 police, wounded others, and made capture of 16 on Clones station platform. Worthy had great plans of piqueting the whole frontier, which I demolished at once, both from point of view of uselessness and of impossibility as regards accommodation, water-supply, etc., and also because we had not got enough troops.
>
> Then we went over to the Colonial Office, where, till 2 o'c., we discussed with Winston, Montagu, Hamar and Anderson.* Winston (and Lloyd George who is at Chequers and with whom Winston had spoken on the telephone) had a wonderful plan for making a No Man's Land, 15 miles broad (7½ miles off each side of the present boundary), to be cleared of inhabitants and occupied by troops. This really was a fine effort! There was no difficulty in tearing it to bits. In the course of doing so, I said that there were only two courses open to us, viz., reconquer Ireland or lose the Empire, and Winston jumped in with "the way I gloated about reconquest." To which I replied that this was untrue, but that my feelings were those of intense and burning shame for the scandalous state the Government had got Ireland into. Winston curled up. I suggested that the only straight course now was to call Collins to account, and to reinforce Ulster up to her full accommodation possibilities. Winston's and Lloyd George's fantastic proposals having been demolished and my proposals approved, we broke up.
>
> Then, at 5 o'c., over to the Colonial Office again, with the same lot as this morning, less Montagu. I told them all my news, and then we considered drafts of telegrams to Craig and Collins. Put shortly, we promised Craig reinforcements and we called on Collins to keep order.

The North of Ireland Government was complaining that troops had not been placed south of the boundary line, but Wilson, when

---

* Sir John Anderson, then Under-Secretary to the Lord-Lieutenant.

appealed to by Churchill, pronounced such an arrangement to be impracticable without declaring martial law. He moreover pointed out that a declaration of martial law would in the circumstances be equivalent to a declaration of war upon the Irish Free State. The only thing that could be done, in fact, was to reinforce Ulster to the full. But this would not, as he took care to add, solve the problem. In the meantime he arranged that some armoured cars, machine-guns, etc., should be sent over at once to Belfast.

An interesting entry appears in the diary on February 16, reading as follows:

> To lunch with Leo Maxse, where were also Northumberland and Esher. It is clear that they have no plan and no leader, and that they rather look to me.
> Then Hankey came to see me to say good-bye. He was very nice. He told me that he had never read a better nor more interesting paper than mine on Geddes, and that, when he came to my last page of warning and advice, he could not believe his eyes; he was completely knocked out.

This appears next day:

> By the King's Command I went to see him at 11.30. I told him quite definitely what I thought about Ireland, Egypt and India, also about Geddes' cuts. He finished by thanking me for my 4 years work, and I walked out.
> I had a trying day of good-byes. Philip, Johnnie Du Cane and the A.G. were very much upset. I managed in my own mind to slip out tomorrow and not go to the office, but Philip said the G.S. would never get over this, so I consented to meet them all and say good-bye. I dread it.

The Field-Marshal went to the War Office during the forenoon of his last day as C.I.G.S., and gave the General Staff who had been serving under him, some 50 or 60 of them, a short farewell address. After touching briefly on his own career he thanked them heartily for their help, their untiring zeal, and their unfailing loyalty to himself. He, according to the diary, depicted his own feelings on laying down his task as those of a sentinel who has tarried long on his post and who at length hears his relief approaching. Then, having shaken hands with all present. Sir Henry quietly passed out of the War Office, his career as a soldier at an end.

Chapter XXXIV – 1922: In the House of Commons

Experiences as a legislator — Presentation to the Field-Marshal by the French Government — Visits to Ulster — Last speech in the House.

The ceremony of introducing the new member for North Down into the House of Commons took place on February 23. Captain Craig and Colonel F.B. Mildmay (now Lord Mildmay of Fleet) officiated as the Field-Marshal's sponsors. "The Treasury Bench was full," he remarked in his diary, "but Lloyd George slipped out just before I walked up. Winston, Horne and others chaffed me as I went by." He afterwards attended a meeting of the Ulster Party in a Committee room.

> It is a curious feeling, being an M.P. at 57, after 40 years of soldiering. I was much struck with my reception everywhere. Everyone seems to think that I am going to do something in the House of Commons. I wonder; am I?

— so he summed up his first experiences of the place, which would not seem to have impressed him signally.

His first speech after becoming a legislator was an address which he delivered to the 200 members of the 1900 Club on the last day of February; he expressed himself very openly on the political situation on this occasion and his hearers were deeply interested in what he found to say. A strong feeling was springing up in the Conservative party at this time that the coalition with Lloyd George and those Liberals who fought under the Prime Minister's standard ought to be brought to an end. With the movement for giving effect to this Sir Henry was in cordial sympathy. He attended daily in the House, during the fortnight following his first taking his seat, with the object of learning the routine of the institution, and, as was indeed only to be expected, he became at once the foremost figure at the meetings of the military members of the House. The Irish Agreement Bill was being debated in Committee of the House at this time, and the Field-Marshal was indignant at the manner in which the Government was supported in the division lobbies by members who were ready enough to criticize the provisions of the Bill unofficially in strong terms. That he should have been incensed at such an attitude suggests that he was not, perhaps, cast in nature's special mould for filling the rôle of typical politician. He wrote in his diary on March 8:

> We Ulster men took no part in the Report stage and Third Reading, except that Charles Craig said that, owing to our treatment, we would do nothing but vote — which we did, after a miserable speech of Winston's. And we only got 52 votes. In the afternoon I joined a curious group at tea in the Smoking Room of about ten Ulster members and Joe Devlin, all telling stories!
>
> The Irish Agreement Bill is through the House of Commons and goes to the Lords next week. At this present minute Limerick is in the hands of Valera, and I think within three months we shall have a Republic declared in Ireland. And what will Lloyd George and his crew do then?

He proceeded to Paris on the 9th, to receive the present that the French Government had decided to give him, and while there he heard of Mr, Montagu's resignation, owing to the publication of a dispatch that had come from Simla advocating the handing back of Constantinople, Adrianople and Smyrna to the Turks. The publication had taken place without Cabinet sanction; but the Field-Marshal earnestly hoped that the effect of the dispatch's appearance would be to compel the Government to adopt the policy which was being urged from India — as he had been urging himself ever since the Sublime Porte had craved an armistice in October, 1918, He gives the following account in his diary of the presentation:

> At 11.30, Tit Willow, Reggie, and I (in *chapeau de forme*)* arrived at the old Marshal's office in the Invalides. I went first alone into his room, where he told me how delighted he was about the present; and then we went into another room where the Marshal's staff — Weygand, Desticker, Pagazy, L'Hôpital, and others — and Buat and civilians representing the President, the Prime Minister and the War Minister were present.
>
> The old Marshal at once made a speech. He recalled our old friendship and all our work before, during, and since the war. He was very flattering, but obviously he meant every word. Then I answered as best I could, referring to the help of Huguet and Panouse, and of course to the old Marshal as one who held all my admiration and all my friendship, and for whom I entertained a reverence.
>
> Then we inspected the 5 pieces of Sèvres. They are beautiful, and each one stands on a blue Sèvres base. They are a complete hunting set — hounds held in leash by one man, a man with the long coil hunting-bugle, a man with a gun, a bear fighting hounds. A really wonderful present.
>
> Then we went to lunch with Marshal and Madame Foch. Then I paid the War Minister (Maginot) a visit. Then I went back to the old Marshal and had another talk. Then called on the President (M. Millerand) and had a long talk with him. I found him, as always, not only charming to me but also shrewd, logical, clear-headed. Then I paid a long visit to Poincaré at the Quai d'Orsay, who was also delightful and very sensible, and neither he nor Millerand are under any illusions about Lloyd George or his total inability to govern.

On getting back to London, Sir Henry found a letter awaiting him from Sir J. Craig, begging him to cross over to Belfast to advise the Executive as to what was to be done in Ulster, promising that whatever he should recommend would be carried out, and stating that the Ulster Cabinet wanted to be able to

---

* "Shaped hat."

announce the advent of the Field-Marshal in the Northern Parliament. Wilson promised to go over; but he found that he would not be able to do so until after the 15th, on which day the Army Estimates were going to be laid on the table of the House of Commons and on which he proposed to deliver his maiden speech in that assembly. He was able in the meantime to discuss what he intended to propose for Ulster with General A.R. Cameron, who commanded the troops in the north of Ireland but who happened to be over in London. The following appears in the diary on March 15:

> Craig announced in the Northern Parliament yesterday that I was coming over to advise how to crush out the murder-gang, and that he had put 2 millions aside to carry out my plan. This morning's papers are full of this.

That afternoon he made his maiden speech in the House. Worthington-Evans having brought in the Army Estimates and having been followed by Sir D. Maclean, acting as leader of the Opposition, the Speaker called upon the Field-Marshal, whereupon the benches filled up at once. He was cordially received and was listened to with rapt attention.

Speaking for only about twenty minutes, he conifined his observations to the question of the great reductions in the army which the Secretary of State had just announced, reductions that followed the recommendations of the Geddes Committee. Those recommendations, he pointed out, had been made on two hypotheses, viz.: that, the German peril being at an end, an army was not needed to face it, and that modern inventions made a given force automatically more formidable than it would have been in times past. He maintained that this country had never possessed an army in peace time to face the German peril when it had existed, he reminded the House that foreign armies enjoyed the advantage of modern inventions as well as the British, so that the inventions did not in reality affect the question of numbers, and he moreover added that experience had proved these inventions to favour irregular as against regular forces. He declared that British liabilities in 1922 were far greater than they had been in 1914,

1922: In the House of Commons

thanks to the policy which the Government had thought fit to pursue in various parts of the world, quoting in support the commitments of the Rhine, Silesia, Constantinople, Palestine and Mesopotamia, as also the pacts which had recently been entered into with France and with Belgium. He concluded by contending that an army which ensured peace to its country served a useful purpose, and that the same thing held good in respect to an army which, if war broke out, would win that war, but that an army which neither ensured peace nor yet ensured victory if the peace was broken served no purpose at all. Many compliments were paid him during the debate, he was warmly felicitated in the lobbies by friends and opponents,* and he received a number of letters of congratulation. *The Times* devoted part of its leading article to his maiden speech. Of the letters which he received none gave him greater pleasure than the one from the veteran parliamentarian. Lord Chaplin, who wrote:

> In my humble judgment it is the best military thing that has been done in the H. of C. in my time, and for which you deserve the fullest credit. I am not the least surprised, for I felt very sure that I had taken your measure pretty correctly when at Wynyard, and fortunate indeed the country is in having a military man of your experience, position, and ability in the H. of C. What the future may have in store for us — God knows. But we shall at least have one man of competence and resource to meet it.
>
> It reads to me as if it got an excellent reception, and I hope it is only the beginning of a successful career in a direction which is sadly needed. Now that you have started it in the H. of C. it ought to be taken up in the H. of Lords. But who is the right man in that House?

The Times leading article declared:

> Everything that he has to say on the subject of the army and its ability to secure the defence of these islands and meet our liabilities in other parts of the world must command the deepest respect. His closely reasoned speech on the Army Estimates, which consisted of

---

* "All the evening, during the washing of the Montagu dirty linen, members kept congratulating me," he wrote in his diary.

a grave warning as to the perilous condition in which the country would be placed if the contemplated reductions in the strength of the Army take place, was received in that spirit by the House of Commons.

He left London for Belfast on the following evening and spent two days there, returning on the night of March 18. The situation at this time was most unsatisfactory in the north, as well as in most other parts, of Ireland. Many districts of the Free State were virtually in a condition of civil war; for the Republican bands which acknowledged the leadership of de Valera were committing outrages of all kinds, and these the forces of Collins's Government were only coping with most ineffectually. Sinn Fein outbreaks were moreover occurring even within the confines of Northern Ireland, raids were taking place across the boundary line, and Belfast itself, so often the scene of riots in the past, was in a highly disturbed state as a result of the religious animosity which the tension throughout the land had stirred up. Wilson was by no means favourably impressed by what he learnt of the measures being taken to maintain order, and he particularly disapproved of the severe strain, physical and mental, that was being thrown upon the troops. He noted in his diary:

> It is quite clear that the soldiers are being nightly called on not "in aid" of Civil Power but in substitution; this is all wrong and points to reorganization and increase of Constabulary.

He discussed the situation on the first day with several of the Northern Cabinet Ministers and with Spender, as also with Cameron and the officer commanding the troops on the spot, and this appears in the diary next day (a Saturday):

> Up at 6.30 a.m., and got my mind cleared and all my thoughts recorded by breakfast. I registered my opinion and advice to Craig in the shape of a letter which does not mince matters about Lloyd George and the state he has got Ireland and Ulster into, and then I went on with my advice, Craig later in the day, with my full approval, decided to publish this letter. I think it will make a stir when it comes out.

The letter began:

> You have asked me for my opinion and advice on the present and the future. Here they are.
> Owing to the action of Mr. Lloyd George and his Government, the 26 counties of South and West Ireland are reduced to a welter of chaos and murder, difficult to believe, impossible to describe. A further consequence of the course pursued by Mr. Lloyd George is seen by the state of unrest, suspicion and lawlessness winch has spread over the frontier into the six counties of Ulster.
> The dangerous condition which obtains in the 26 counties will increase and spread unless: (1) A man in those counties rises who can crush out murder and anarchy, and re-establish law and order. With a thousand years of Irish history to guide us, it is safe to predict that this will not happen. (2) Great Britain re-establishes law and order in Ireland. Under Mr. Lloyd George and his Government this is frankly and laughably impossible, because men who are obviously incapable of holding the Empire, are still more incapable of regaining it.

Definite recommendations were then made. The most noteworthy of these recommendations were that a general and staff should be secured to superintend the constabulary, that the R.I.C. at present existing in Northern Ireland should be disbanded, that a force of 3,000 Royal Ulster Constabulary, with 5 regular officers to each 1,000, should be raised to take their place, that stringent regxilations should be introduced and enforced in respect to the carrying of arms and that the law should be strengthened in various ways for dealing with men found guilty of outrage. These proposals received the full approval of Macready, who had come to Belfast on purpose to meet the Field-Marshal, and who arranged to increase Cameron's thirteen battalions by two from the south.

Wilson's letter to Craig duly appeared in the newspapers on the morning of March 20, and it attracted much attention. On the following afternoon he spoke in the House of Commons during the debate on the Air Estimates, and he strongly condemned the existence of an Air Ministry — a subject with which he was thoroughly familiar, as he had drawn up a formidable indictment against that institution some months before, when C.I.G.S., for the information of the Cabinet. Churchill, who addressed the House later, devoted most of his speech to answering the Field-Marshal's attack, and this appears in the diary:

> I made him drive me up to Londonderry House at 10.30, after his speech, and told him what I thought of his defence — and he quite agreed.

"The word co-operation, translated into action, is the way to lose war," was one of the striking phrases which Sir Henry had made use of on this second occasion of his being called on by the Speaker. The Army Estimates came up for further debate in the House on the 22nd, and a passage from the speech delivered by the Field-Marshal on this occasion deserves to be quoted. It illustrates that lucidity of expression combined with the employment of effective imagery which used to bring members flocking in to fill the empty benches when news had flown round the lobbies that Wilson was "up":

> It is said that, if we reduce 22 or 24 battalions, 5 or 9 cavalry regiments, 47 batteries of artillery and a good number of Army Service Corps and other units, we shall save some £16,000,000. That is so! But there is another way of reducing — of saving money — and that is (I have been advocating it ever since the Armistice) to come out of places that do not belong to us, and to hold on to the places that do. The greatest Chancellor of the Exchequer that I ever heard of was Mr. Micawber, and Hon. Members will remember what he said: "Income, £20; expenditure, £19 19s. 6d. Result — happiness. Income, £20; expenditure, £20 0s. 6d. Result — misery." It is the £20 0s. 6d. policy that the Government have been pursuing for the last few years.
>
> We can make economies, we can make large economies on the army, but I think it is not only unwise but very dangerous to make economies in the fighting troops. Under the conditions of the world as it is, and supposing that the Government decline absolutely — as they appear to be going to do — to change their policy, if they decline absolutely to come out of places that do not belong to us and to hold places that do, then, to reduce the numbers of your fighting troops is, in my judgment, absolute madness.

He had arranged that Major-General A. Solly-Flood should take up command of the Ulster Constabulary, and he was very anxious that the organization of this force should be taken up at once, seeing that the situation both in Belfast and along me North Ireland boundary was growing more disquieting. Conferences took place at the end of the month between Churchill, Sir J. Craig, the representatives of the official Free State Government (Griffiths and Collins) and others. But Sir Henry had no belief in such meetings affecting an improvement in the situation, in view of the fact that the official Free State Government appeared to be losing authority daily, and on March 31 the following entry occurs in his diary:

> Last night at 11 p.m., in the House of Commons, Winston read out the terms of an agreement signed by Craig, Collins and Winston. The opening sentence reads that "peace is declared." Then what have we been doing since December 6 last, when Lloyd George declared peace? What rubbish it all is. But I don't like some of the points of agreement, because Craig has agreed to Collins's interference in arrangements in Ulster. After breakfast I got on the telephone to Spender and then Craig, both at Londonderry House. Luckily all those fantastic arrangements will mean nothing, because Collins is a back number and the extremists under Valera are rapidly taking over — as daily Press shows.

This appears on April 4:

> Valera still forging ahead with a big meeting at Dundalk. I ask every M.P. to say what he proposes to do if a republic is declared. And none of them know; but the general opinion is that England, i.e. the Government, will agree.

Next day there is the entry:

> A number of questions about the poor disbanded R.I.C., who will undoubtedly be murdered when they go home, especially the Roman Catholics. I spoke to Hamar after Questions, but he threw up his hands in despair. I tried to see Winston but failed. These poor R.I.C. must be brought back to this country, and accommodated in barracks until they get restarted or they sail for the Colonies. Joynson Hicks brought forward a vote of want of confidence at 8.15, and I meant to speak, and had quite a nice little speech ready; but the first time I jumped up Austen also rose, and the second time Hugh Cecil rose, so

I did not get the chance. The House was rather excited, and I would have given worlds to have followed Austen. We only got 98 in our lobby, to 288.

The Field-Marshal wrote on the 12th:

> At 3 o'clock, on the adjournment of the House for Easter holidays, Page Croft raised the Irish question, and I followed with a plea for camps and quarters for R.I.C., who are crowding over here to escape being murdered in Ireland — this Winston afterwards agreed to do. And then I went on to urge Winston to state *now* what the Government will do when Valera declares a republic. Winston refused to do this. Then I suggested that Winston and other Cabinet Ministers should go over to Ireland, north, south, east and west, and see for themselves the state of the country. This Winston did not refer to in his speech, and I went and sat behind him after he had finished and asked him why he did not accept my challenge, and he said he couldn't. Quite true, although I pointed out that Belfast was not so far as Gairloch, nor Cork so far as Genoa.*

The Field-Marshal had arranged to make some speeches to his constituents in the middle of the month, and he arrived at Mount Stewart with Lady Wilson on the morning of April 14, where they stayed with Lord and Lady Londonderry until the 22nd. He found that Solly-Flood had already made some progress with the organization of his force; but he was not by any means satisfied that the local Government was acting with the energy and firmness that the critical situation demanded. "I am determined to wake up this place," he wrote in his diary, and he regarded it as unfortunate that Sir J. Craig was away from Ulster for some weeks at such a critical time. He was, moreover, particularly angry to find that the recruitment of 3,000 "A" Specials had been stopped because of the agreement arrived at with Collins. He discussed these and a number of other matters at a meeting which he had at Mount Stewart with several members of the Government, and he wrote of this in this diary:

---

* A conference was in progress at Genoa, which the Prime Minister was attending.

1922: In the House of Commons 403

I bit the meeting a couple of times by asking, " Who is governing Ulster, you or Collins?" and by announcing that the Northern Parliament could not act on "my advice and the orders of Collins at the same time."

The Republican army had seized the Four Courts in Dublin on the 15th, and nothing was being done by the official Government of the Free State to eject the intruders.

The Field-Marshal delivered the first of his series of speeches to his constituents at Newtownards on the 18th, and he delighted his hearers there by his powerful indictment of the Coalition Government for its conduct, alike in respect to Ireland and to foreign affairs in general. Next evening he spoke in similar strain at Bangor, where he was accorded a most enthusiastic reception by great crowds, and where his address was punctuated with the cheers of an excited audience. This was followed by a speech at Comber on the 20th, and by another and final one at Donaghadee on the 21st, where he declared that Mr. Lloyd George had proved himself to be totally unfit to govern. He concluded this, his last speech of the series, with:

> It is for Ulster men and women to prepare themselves for what may be coming, and, above all, to put themselves in a position to stand on their own feet.

He had in the meantime attended a Cabinet Meeting of the North Ireland Government, at which all his proposals with regard to the R.I.C. and "Specials" had been agreed to, as well as various matters of detail concerning these services which he had previously discussed fully with Solly-Flood. That vertebrate and energetic government was urgently needed in Ulster for the repression of lawlessness, and that the organization of an adequate and an efficient police force would brook no delay, had been very apparent during his brief stay at Mount Stewart. For a number of murders had taken place in Belfast within the week. Sir Henry at the same time insisted upon the importance of the Executive acting impartially in any steps taken by it to maintain order within the She Counties. "In London," as an intimate friend of his has written, "he was a black Ulsterman and anti-papist, in Belfast he preached moderation."

Lady Wilson and the Field-Marshal got back to Eaton Place on April 23, and they paid a visit to Lancashire at the end of the month. Sir Henry spoke on several occasions in that county, and he was brought into contact with some of the most prominent men concerned in local industries. He also on the Sunday unveiled a window in the church at Todmorden, where he and the Dean of Manchester delivered addresses; and he was afterwards present at the cathedral in Manchester to hear the Dean preach. He remarked in his diary on May 1:

> My speech at Shaw on Saturday night was fully reported in the *Manchester Guardian*, was garbled in the *Yorkshire Post*, *Morning Post*, and *Daily Mail*, and was not mentioned in others in spite of the efforts made to get publicity. It shows how difficult it is to get a hearing when speaking against Lloyd George.

This appears in the diary on the 2nd:

> Mr. Curnock (?) came to see me at 2.30, sent by Northcliffe to discuss Palestine. I asked him if I could do a deal about Ireland, to which he replied that he wished Northcliffe would. Mr. Curnock (?) and I had an interesting talk, and he asked me if he might embody the views I expressed in his paper — whether *Times* or *Daily Mail*, I don't know.

Wilson wrote next day:

> No mistaking my interview yesterday with Northcliffe's man. It is out with flaming headlines and photo on the front page of the *Daily Mail*, and a leader on the facing page. I had no idea that the play-boy was going to put some of my chaffing remarks in so baldly, but it won't do any harm.
> There is considerable excitement and big posters, of praise and blame in the evening Press about my D.M. interview, and I confess that I would have preferred that the *Daily Mail* man had not interpolated some of his own stuff, although substantially he has reported well.

He took patt in a "Die-hard" meeting at Caxton Hall on the 9th, where he spoke for three-quarters of an hour, and where he was well received by a great crowd while delivering a strong attack upon the Government. During the course of this address he said:

> I worked for years during the war with the Prime Minister and the present Cabinet most cordially and in closest agreement, and we were working at that time together against the King's enemies. But since the peace I have noticed that both the Prime Minister and his colleagues have been increasingly inclined to work with the King's enemies, so that it is really not I who have changed my outlook. It is the Prime Minister and his colleagues.

And on the following evening he spoke in the House, when the adjournment was moved on the question of three officers who had been kidnapped in County Cork three weeks before, and of whom no news had been received.* This speech of his, lasting only a few minutes, was one of his most remarkable utterances, and it greatly impressed supporters and opponents alike, who flocked into the Chamber from the lobbies on hearing that he was on his feet. He wound up:

> Have the Government not yet learnt their lesson about Ireland? Can they not see that a Provisional Government, which is not able to eject a small handful of men from the Four Courts in Dublin and Kilmainham Gaol, is totally unfit to govern 3,500,000 souls in the 26 counties? Have the Government not yet learnt their lesson in Ireland? How many more murders must be committed in Ireland before the Government realize the true situation in the country? We are dealing to-night with the question of officers and men. May I suggest that some Cabinet Minister should go over to Ireland, and, if necessary, beseech the Provisional Government to grant the lives of our soldiers in that country.
>
> If, as may be the case — and God forbid! — these three officers have already been murdered, on what body of men lies the responsibility for their lives? As I see it, the whole world is looking on at the present moment at a manifestation of incompetence, and, if I may be allowed in this House to say so, of cowardice, which will

---

* It was learnt later that they had been murdered by the Republicans.

surely bear fruit in all the other parts of our great Empire. Therefore, I would ask the Government, as they are responsible for the lives of these poor men who are ordered to remain in Ireland, not at the request of Mr. Collins, not for purposes of law and order, not at the beseechings of the War Office — I would ask the Government, who are responsible for their lives, to take some action which will insure their lives.

He noted in his diary next day:

> I got much praise for my short speech last night, and the general opinion seems to be that I hit Austen very hard — which, indeed, was easy to do. I wrote Cavan this morning to say I hoped that my speech did not embarrass him, but that the treatment of our men in Ireland made my blood boil. He wrote back to say that, on the contrary, I had done good, and he added that, for the fourth time, he had written to Winston begging to be allowed to come out of Cork

Although the Government could at this time still reckon with certainty upon a majority when matters were pressed to a division in the House of Commons, the feeling was growing up amongst Conservatives, even outside of the Die-hard group, that the days were nearly over when they could be expected to continue to support Lloyd George and the Coalition. Wilson had been approached on the subject of assuming definite leadership of the malcontents, with whom he was in sympathy; but he considered that such action on his part would as yet be premature. Their triumph was not to become an accomplished fact for another five months, and Sir Henry was not destined to witness its fulfilment.

This appears in the diary on May 15:

> James Craig now writes that Winston agrees to our employing active officers in Ulster [i.e. with the Constabulary], I wonder? I wrote to him to say that I doubted this, as I had seen Cavan, Chetwode and Macdonogh, and none of them had heard of it. I also said to him that I was very dissatisfied with our want of good propaganda — in fact, we have none.
>
> Partly because of my attack on Government on Wednesday last, partly because Cavan stood up well, the four battalions now in Cork are to be withdrawn and sent to Ulster. Cavan told me that Winston

was adamant till Friday last. I can well believe that Austen told Winston he must withdraw the troops after the shaking he [Austen] got last Wednesday. Philip told me that Cope had come over from Collins with a request for rifles, for trench mortars, for armoured cars, etc., which even Winston thought hot stuff! Philip said to Winston that Collins only had a few men he could trust, and so the whole of these arms, etc., would be used against Ulster. Apparently Winston refused Collins's outrageous demand.

This appears in the diary on the 18th:

After questions, Butcher* moved the adjournment of the House on an Irish question which Hamar had not answered. The Speaker ruled against Butcher, whereupon he was tackled by many members, and, in his anxiety to save the Government, he gave a drastic ruling against asking questions about the business of the Provisional Government. If carried out, this would really bar almost all questions about Ireland. So a Die-hard meeting was called at once and I was asked to attend, and Banbury drew up a petition to Austen asking that, by Standing Order or by other way, we should be allowed to ask questions about the lives and property of British citizens in all parts of the world.

The question of allowing officers on the active list to take service under Solly-Flood was not settled, however, till nearly the end of the month owing to the procrastination of the Cabinet. But even before their arrival, the R.U.C. unexpectedly arrested large numbers of Sinn Feiners in Ulster and interned them, a step which had an excellent effect, and which before long reduced the number of outrages that had been occurring in Belfast and in the country districts. Sir Henry now paid another visit to the North, arriving at Mount Stewart on May 26, to find that fair progress had been made since he had been there last in respect of establishing a reliable force of constabulary. Much, however, still remained to be done, and after discussing matters with Cameron and with Solly-Flood,

---

* Now Lord Danesford.

he came to the conclusion that some of the fourteen battalions that were being kept in Dublin ought to be brought up to Ulster to reinforce the nineteen battalions already there under Cameron's orders. He also wrote in his diary:

> It is a disgrace keeping battalions in Dublin where they are insulted, useless, and almost in danger. My last attack in the House on May 10th got all the troops away from Cork, and now I will try to get them away from Dublin. The R.U.C. have now only about 1,300, instead of 3,000. The Specials are now all Protestants. The whole of this miserable affair will go straight not only into civil war but into religious war. It is heart-breaking.

He was very angry at learning that tents, rifles, Stokes mortars, etc., which had been promised by Churchill to the R.U.C. had not yet come to hand. "Solly showed me a wire from Winston to Craig," appears in the diary on the 27th, "in which Winston puts off handing over the arms once again." He left Ulster that evening to return to London.

Wilson's dejected reference in his diary to the development of an untoward form of religious warfare in Ireland, which is quoted above, is highly significant. His lament was indeed most fully warranted by the condition of affairs that had arisen in Ulster, and especially within the city of Belfast — a condition of affairs that was growing more and more alarming as the tale of acts of violence mounted up. Outrages of all kinds were being perpetrated as a direct result of acute sectarian differences, differences that were being stimulated by the state of uncertainty which hung over the political situation like a pall. If the activities of Roman Catholics of pronounced Sinn Fein sympathies were at the root of the grave unrest that prevailed, those activities were being countered by uncompromising reprisals on the part of Orangemen. This condition of affairs had one very unfortunate consequence. It served as a basis for the promotion of a sedulous propaganda, on the part of certain organs of the Press and of fomentors of disorders in the Free State. These depicted the Roman Catholics within the confines of the six counties of Northern Ireland as being in process of extermination at the hands of representatives of the opposing faith, with the full approval of the local executive.

1922: In the House of Commons

An impression moreover undoubtedly existed — and this not only in Ireland as a whole, but also amongst those of the public in Great Britain who interested themselves in Irish affairs — that the Field-Marshal himself was taking a far more prominent part in the carrying out of the executive functions of the North Ireland Government than was actually the case. He had, it is true, given certain advice with regard to the organization of the constabulary, and this had been accepted. He had urged the vital importance of effectual steps being taken to preserve law and order impartially in the six counties. But he was not responsible for the manner in which the constabulary performed their duties, nor was he concerned in the executive measures that were actually being taken in hand by Sir J. Craig and his colleagues to repress disorder and to stamp out crime.

The two rivals, Collins and de Valera, had in the meantime arrived at a working agreement, in view of the General Election which was to take place in the Free State in July. The general opinion in England, an opinion which was concurred in by the Law Officers of the Crown, was that this pact amounted to an infraction of the "treaty" of December 6. So it had come about that the Cabinet, in accordance with the wonted practice of such political bodies when they find themselves in a difficulty, were endeavouring to find a "formula," a "form of words," by which the situation could, at least in appearance, be restored. The Field-Marshal wrote in his diary on May 31:

> Winston made his statement about Ireland and the Valera-Collins pact. It was exceedingly unsatisfactory. He admitted that the pact broke the treaty, but pleaded for patience and conciliation. In other words, he agreed to this flagrant breach of the treaty. The House was decidedly sceptical. Several spoke against him, including myself, and I extracted from him that the troops were being kept in Dublin in case a Republic was declared. Collins and Griffiths were in the Distinguished Strangers' Gallery. In ten days from now, when we come back from the Whitsun holiday, things will be much worse, and the Government in a still more ghastly hole.

The Whitsuntide recess commenced next day, and this was in fact the last time that the Field-Marshal was to address an assembly in which he had made his mark to so unusual an extent within a period of three months from his first taking his seat. It seems, therefore, a not inappropriate occasion for quoting the following appreciation of this great servant of the State written by a friend of his of very old standing, the late Sir Henry Craik.

> Anything I can say represents only the estimate of an outside and non-professional observer, who happened, for considerable although widely separated periods, to be thrown into contact with Sir Henry Wilson.
>
> My first opportunity was as a member of the Educational Advisory Board, established in 1902, which has continued under different names and with varying functions to exist from that time to this. But, in spite of these alterations, it has had a continuous and connected existence. I happen to be the only member who has belonged to the Board from its start. That fact has given me the great privilege of coming into fairly close contact with all our foremost military leaders for the last 25 years, and it has given me the chance of comparing their standard of intellectual and moral qualities, and of learning how favourably that standard may compare with that of any other class of professional men. A certain proneness to follow routine may show itself. But in public spirit, in punctilious honour, and in the power of carrying a keen controversy on while at the same time maintaining it on the highest plane of courtesy, I have never known any body of men to excel them.
>
> I am certain that those laymen — who were very few in number — who had the same opportunities of forming an estimate as I had, would agree with me in saying that Sir Henry's intellectual force and guidance in regard to difficult questions compelled recognition from us from the very first. If I remember rightly, he was only our Secretary;[*] but he very soon became a dominating influence. His advice and his initiative weighed with all. His methods, as I recall them, were not always smooth nor conciliatory; but, none the less, they had the supreme quality of avoiding acrimonious controversy; and this was perhaps of particular merit when dealing with laymen who were accustomed to a different habit of mind.
>
> Then suddenly, after some years of intercourse, I was entirely parted from him, meeting him only at rare intervals. Our friendship

---

[*] Vide Volume I, Chapter IV, p. 62.

was renewed after he entered the House of Commons. It must have been a strangely novel experience for him, and yet I never knew anyone who accepted so quietly, so modestly, and yet with such a sense of mastery, the new sphere upon which he had entered. As a rule, a soldier who after a long and notable military career, enters into the muddy waters and the often unintelligible and apparently irrational methods of the House of Commons, finds it very difficult to reconcile such diverging methods with those of his past experience. But what was most remarkable in Sir Henry Wilson's short parliamentary career was the ease with which he entered upon it, the rapidity with which he learnt to dominate the House, and the ready recognition which was accorded by all to his natural gift of taking a leading part in the proceedings of the assembly. I do not think that he ever spoke for more than 15 or 20 minutes. But on each occasion he had, when he sat down, made a definite impression which no subsequent speaker could hope to remove. This was not by means of eloquence, certainly not by means of studied and carefully prepared argument. It was due to the irresistible conviction forced upon us, that we had listened to the words of a master of his subject, and of one whose judgment was based upon an absolutely unselfish patriotism.

Wilson spent the Whitsuntide recess on board his new yacht, the *Pleiad*, and he returned to Eaton Place on Sunday, June 11. The House reassembled on the following day, and on the 13th an interesting debate took place on the Cabinet Secretariat, regarding which he noted in the diary:

> I could have knocked Lloyd George and his quibbles with ease, but not without using my inside knowledge, which I did not think was fair. The truth, of course, being that Hankey and his Secretariat are essential, whereas Philip Kerr, Ned Grigg, etc., are poisonous.*

He had been asked to go to Glasgow and speak there; but, the place being known to be full of disaffected Irishmen, certain brother M.P.s of his tried to dissuade him from going. "They might

---

* The Field-Marshal was not, of course, speaking in a personal sense. What he objected to — and what has since been stopped — was the Prime Minister's plan of maintaining a staff of a departmental nature, tacked on to the Secretariat and doing the work that is properly performed by various Departments of State.

shoot you, Henry," said they. "Well, anyhow, it would be nicer to be shot at by them than to have to shake hands with them," was his reply, and he decided to accept the invitation. The entry in his diary narrating the events of the day on the aist closes as follows:

> Gretton persuaded me to go and speak in Glasgow on July 4. It's rather a turbulent place. Cecil came up from Grove End. I dined with the Army Chaplains at the Trocadero. The Prince of Wales got a great reception on his return from India. A lovely day.

These few sentences were to close a record which for a period of twenty-nine and a half years had been entered daily — the story of his life, as told by himself, dating from that early stage in his career as a soldier, when he had, while still a subaltern, commenced his two years' course as a student at the Camberley Staff College.

Chapter XXXV – The Death of the Field-Marshal

June 22 — At Liverpool Street Station — The assassination — The burial in. St. Paul's — A brief appreciation.

Sir Henry Wilson had been approached in April by the Chairman of the Great Eastern Railway Company (Lord Claud Hamilton), with an invitation to unveil the War Memorial which was being set up by the company in the great booking-hall at the entrance to Liverpool Street Station. The Field-Marshal had consented to do so, and it had then been arranged that the ceremony was to take place on June 22. On that date therefore he proceeded to the City to be the guest of the directors at luncheon, prior to the unveiling taking place. Numbers of relatives of the fallen, as well as a contingent of ex-service men on the staff of the railway, had assembled to take part in the ceremony, and Sir Henry reviewed the latter and spoke to several of them while passing along the ranks. Owing to the site of the memorial being in a busy section of the great terminus, the ritual was necessarily of a summary character, and it consisted only of a brief service of dedication. Then, before carrying out the actual unveiling, the Field-Marshal delivered a speech, and he ended with the words:

> It is always a proud duty for one soldier to speak of others. I like to think that, all over the face of our country, there are to be found

memorials to those who carried out their duty in the Great War. We soldiers count as out gains— our losses. Those men we love most to honour are those who died in a great cause. This tablet commemorates some twelve or thirteen hundred men who fell doing their duty. In doing what they thought right, they paid the penalty.

> "The tumult and the shouting dies;
>   The Captains and the Kings depart;
> Still stands thine ancient sacrifice.
>   An humble and a contrite heart.
> Lord God of Hosts be with us yet.
> Lest we forget — lest we forget!"

> "The wind sublime eternal soars.
> And scorning human haunts and earthly shores.
> To those whom godlike deeds forbid to die.
> Unbars the gates of immortality."*

Then, after admiring the imposing memorial and conversing for a few minutes with some of those present. Sir Henry repaired to the Underground Station hard by, and he proceeded as far as Charing Cross Underground Station, where he took a taxi in which he drove to the Travellers' Club. Remaining a few minutes in the dub while the cab waited outside, he came out again and directed the driver to take him to 36 Eaton Place. This is a corner house with its hall door in Belgrave Place. The driver was not sure of its exact position and, as it happened, some road-repairing was in progress at the corner; but, when close by. Sir Henry called out directions, the cab pulled up near the steps, and he alighted. He paid the driver his fare and the cab at once moved off, while the Field-Marshal walked towards the steps. Just as he mounted them, one of two young men who had been loitering at the street corner, a point where they commanded the approaches to the house from all sides, fired a revolver at him, but apparently missed. The Field-Marshal turned and drew his sword. Both men at once opened fire

---

* The last two of these lines from Horace are inscribed on the Field-Marshal's tomb in St. Paul's, and also on the memorial to him in the R.M.C, Chapel at Sandhurst.

and their victim fell, mortally wounded. A servant down in the basement, hearing the shots and looking up through the window, saw something of what had occurred, and rushed up and out of the house to where the dying man was lying. He tried to speak, but could not. Lady Wilson, who had heard a commotion and the hall-door being thrown open, hurried out, and the Field-Marshal was borne tenderly into the house by willing hands, but within a very few moments all was over. Two bullets had passed through his chest, each of them inflicting a mortal wound, and he was also found to have been hit in other places although these latter injuries were not vital. The crime had been skilfully planned, and it had been carried out with ruthless determination.

The two assassins in the meantime, one a man of powerful build, the other a cripple with a wooden leg, had made off towards Chesham Place, pursued by workmen who had actually witnessed the deed. The alarm had been promptly given, and the fugitives were kept in sight by a growing crowd of citizens aware that an atrocious outrage of some kind had been committed, while policemen from neighbouring beats joined in the chase and took the lead. The murderers, in the course of their flight, endeavoured to make use of vehicles that they passed, and they eventually turned southwards, their route taking them near to Gerald Road Police Station, from which other members of the police force turned out in haste on hearing the blowing of the whistles. The two miscreants kept their pursuers at bay for a time, and they wounded two policemen and a civilian; but they were eventually disarmed and captured, and the resolution displayed by those who hunted them down provided the one bright spot in connexion with what in all other respects must be accounted as one of the most terrible tragedies of our time. After giving false names to start with, the two prisoners were in due course identified as R. Dunn and J. O'Sullivan, Irishmen and Roman Catholics, both of them connected to some extent with the Irish Republican Army, and found to be armed with service revolvers and service ammunition.

The news of the event created a tremendous sensation in London and throughout the Empire. Cowardly butchery of individuals had been only too common in Ireland of late years, so common indeed that those in high places responsible for the maintenance of law and order and for the repression of crime in the United Kingdom had seemingly come to regard such incidents almost with indifference when they occurred outside of Great Britain. But, for one of the foremost men of the day to be struck down in broad daylight in the heart of the Metropolis and actually within sight of some of its citizens, was viewed in a more serious light. Tidings of what had taken place startled the House of Commons on its assembling that afternoon, and business was suspended after a few words of heart-felt regret from Mr. Asquith as leader of the Opposition and from Mr. Austen Chamberlain, who moved its adjournment as leader of the House. A resolution expressing horror at the crime and deep sympathy with Lady Wilson was at once agreed to in the House of Lords, the Bishop of Norwich, who had taken part in the ceremony at Liverpool Street only a very few hours before, being amongst those who paid moving tributes to the memory of the great soldier whose career had been brought so suddenly to a close. Messages from the Dominions, from France, from the United States and elsewhere, testified to the high esteem in which the name of the murdered man was held in territories far outside the confines of the British Isles.

The Government proposed that, subject to the approval of the Field-Marshal's widow, the crypt of St. Paul's Cathedral should be chosen for his last resting-place, and so. Lady Wilson's assent having been obtained, the necessary steps were taken in hand for a great public military funeral. This was accompanied by all the solemn and imposing pageantry which some few years before had attended the burials of Lord Wolseley and Lord Roberts, a pageantry which had at the time greatly impressed Sir Henry himself. So it came about that on June 26, a dark and grey and rainy day, his coffin was borne on a gun-carriage behind an immense cortege of troops from his house in Eaton Place to the steps of the great temple in the city of London, and was carried thence up to the catafalque beneath the dome. Vast crowds of fellow-citizens had mustered in the streets to see the passing of the funeral procession. Within the cathedral was gathered a notable assemblage of men and women, prominent in every walk of life — Cabinet Ministers, the Diplomatic Corps, the Lord Mayor and Sheriffs, present in state, and all the most distinguished British sailors and soldiers of the day who could attend. Mourners — representatives of the King and of Queen Alexandra, the Duke of Connaught, Marshal Foch, relatives, and officers bearing his many decorations — followed the coffin on foot though the streets, also a solitary carriage in which sat the widow of Sir Henry. His mother had proceeded to the cathedral in advance. The singing of "Oh God our help in ages past" — the hymn of the Lowland Covenanters of old which has served to inspire the loyalists of Ulster on countless occasions in more recent times — was an impressive feature in a noble service. When all was over and the coffin had been lowered into the crypt, it was the Field-Marshal's old friend and comrade-in-arms, Foch, who escorted the widow out of the church.

The funeral

At their trial a few weeks later the assassins made no defence beyond declaring that they were justified in taking Sir Henry's life. Their crime would appear to have been due to some extent to political motives, but it had no doubt been provoked mainly by a conviction that their victim was concerned indirectly in massacres of their fellow religionists in Ireland, of which lying reports were being deliberately propagated for the purpose of creating a hatred of England amongst Irish Roman Catholics. They paid the penalty in Wandsworth Jail on August 16. But the fact that Lady Wilson received a number of threatening letters after the Field-Marshal's assassination, and that she stood in need of police protection for the following two years, goes far to prove that the murder was not merely the act of two unbalanced fanatics, but was the outcome of an organized conspiracy of murder.

Henry Wilson rests appropriately between two other famous Irish warriors in the crypt of St. Paul's Cathedral. The grave fills the space between those of Lord Wolseley and of Lord Roberts, and is situated in an alcove which opens off the circular space emplaced immediately beneath the dome. In the centre of that circular space is erected the sarcophagus in which are enclosed the ashes of Lord Nelson. Hard by towers the tomb of Wellington. Lord Napier of Magdala lies buried in the antipodal alcove. All around within the confines of that sombre vaulted cemetery are to be seen memorials set up to great dignitaries of the Church, to eminent men of letters, to painters of renown, and to British commanders who in days gone by have upheld the nation's honour by sea and ashore and whose names have added an abiding lustre to the annals of their native land.

To sum up in a few fines the qualities and characteristics of a man so versatile as was Henry Wilson is no easy task. The story of his actual career bears surest witness to his fitness for filling those high positions in the service of his country which, during the last dozen years of his strenuous life, he came so signally to adorn. Endowed with abilities quite out of the common, the possessor of a temperament that if ardent was also calculating, if kindly was also masterful, if eminently sympathetic was also inflexibly resolute, the illustrious Irishman who became principal military adviser to the British Government during the closing months of the greatest war that the world has seen, ranks beyond question as one of the foremost figures of his day.

To casual acquaintances, even to keen observers practised in the reading of character, he was apt at the first blush to prove an enigma. The sunny disposition, the flamboyant personality and the exuberance of the man would conceal the keen analytical faculties, the sound judgment, the fervent zeal for the interests of the State,

The Death of the Field-Marshal

that underlay his sometimes boisterous demeanour. Even that enviable talent of his for explicit statement, coupled as it was with a singular capacity for making a perplexing problem appear to be simpler than it in reality was, would sometimes mislead those who were brought into contact with him for the first time. His infectious gaiety, his unflagging optimism and his strong sense of humour were at once noticeable. The acuteness of his intellect, the amplitude of his knowledge and that instinctive faculty of his for probing to the very bottom any question that might come up for consideration, only after closer association became apparent to those brought into contact with him.

Nimble wits, a bent for the whimsical, and exceedingly unconventional methods of expression are not generally found in combination with a methodical disposition and an orderly mind. And yet, in much that he. did. Sir Henry showed himself meticulous, painstaking and systematic to a degree. As Commandant of the Staff College, and at a later date as designer of an efficient method of employing the war material that was being poured into Russia in 1917 by way of Archangel and Murmansk, he displayed gifts only to be found in the born administrator. Even in the case of his invaluable work while Director of Military Operations in connexion with the Expeditionary Force, the splendid results attained were as much the outcome of a rigid attention to questions of detail as they were the product of a mastery of the art of war. Considering the pressure under which incidents and conversations were often entered, his diaries are remarkable for their almost invariable precision. The manifold documents that he prepared in the War Office, and that he in due course tendered — to the Secretary of State for War or to the Cabinet during the closing years of his life, are almost as noteworthy for their perfection of arrangement as they are for the candour with which their author was wont to express his opinions, and as they are for the uncompromising character of the counsel which the papers conveyed. No man knew better than he did how to marshal his facts, how to develop his arguments step by step, and how to produce a memorandum which was readily intelligible to the comparatively uninitiated, was convincing to the unprejudiced, and was ample in the sense of covering the whole of the subject that was actually at issue. Passages of an unorthodox type, such as Sir Henry occasionally interpolated into written statements of this kind, were rendered all the more effective by the symmetry and formalism of the document as a whole.

References have appeared in foregoing pages to the Field-Marshal's fondness of children and his delight in their company. But he was a welcome figure wherever he went, in barracks, in camp, in the council chamber and in society. Nor was this popularity that he enjoyed to be attributed solely to his high spirits, to his originality of thought and of expression, and to the inexhaustible supply of laughter-provoking anecdotes that he had at command — many of them the output of his own fertile brain. For he also possessed to a tare extent the gift of sympathy. And that gift of sympathy, owed to some extent to the land of his birth and beyond the compass of the normal Anglo-Saxon, proved a priceless asset to the army of which he was so conspicuous an ornament during the progress of its great adventure from August of 1914 to the final triumph of the Allies on Armistice Day It enabled him to allay misunderstandings and to ensure goodwill between the British and French staffs during the anxious days when Sir John French was at the head of our Expeditionary Force. It enabled him to harmonize divergences of opinion between associates who differed in temperament and in race, when he was acting as connecting link between General Nivelle and Sir Douglas Haig in the year 1917. It enabled him to appease discord amongst the associated military authorities of three nations, at a time when the alarming situation in Italy after Caporetto demanded above all things that there should be cordial co-operation and mutual confidence in that theatre of war.

Those who knew him intimately were well aware that optimism and strength of purpose were the two outstanding features in his character. An excessive buoyancy of spirit might — as was the case during the opening phases of the contest on the Western Front — lead him astray. But even at that time the possession by the Sub-Chief of the General Staff of the quality of hopeful confidence in such rich measure was of incalculable service to General Head-quarters. When the great German offensive in the St. Quentin region of March, 1918, thrust the

British Fifth Army back in disarray, the refusal of the Chief of the Imperial General Staff to despond sustained and emboldened a Cabinet shaken sore by the magnitude of the disaster. "He was the most unyielding man I have ever met," a brother subaltern of his wrote in a passage which has been quoted in an early chapter, and many others who were associated with him during his career would say the same. By sheer determination he compassed the creation of the General Staff, transforming mere good intentions on the part of those set in authority over him into actual deeds. By sheer determination he completed the organization of the Expeditionary Force for service in the field, in time for the great emergency when it came. By sheer determination he brought about the setting up of the Supreme War Council at Versailles, in default of which victory would never have crowned the Allies' efforts so early as the autumn of 1918.

Some may reprobate his uncompromising views and actions in respect to Ireland in the year 1914 and again in 1919 and the two succeeding years. Others peradventure may call in question the conclusions that he arrived at on different occasions during the Great War as to what strategical course was the right one to pursue. Subjects of keen controversy, it would be out of place to debate such questions here. But in what Sir Henry said, and what he wrote, and what he did in connexion with these grave matters he was ever ruled by sturdy sense of duty to his country. Just as his attitude when the Supreme War Council sided with him in contentions between Westernism and Easternism in January, 1918, was instrumental in raising him to the position of Chief of the Imperial General Staff, so was the position which he assumed regarding Ireland at a later date to rob him of what every public official particularly prizes — the confidence of his Government. In the one case he won authority and power, in the other he sacrificed both without hesitation; in either case he adopted what he believed to be the right course in the nation's interest, without consideration of his own career. Posterity may be disposed to regard him merely as a brilliant soldier. But he was more than that. A profound thinker and single-minded patriot, upright, resolute and unafraid, his name is one to be handed down as that of an illustrious servant of the State.

Index

Americans ... 18, 40, 41, 61, 83, 99, 103, 122, 125, 128, 136, 142, 150, 153-155, 164, 166, 171, 172, 183, 188, 190, 198, 206, 217, 218, 227, 231, 233-235, 252, 259, 261, 370
Antoine, General 18
Antwerp. 276
Archangel . 119, 125, 132, 144, 151, 188, 192, 202, 207, 209, 216, 223, 225, 238, 247, 249, 419
Armenia. 45, 62, 198, 213, 227, 253, 254, 273, 276, 279-281
Armistice Day 420
Arras 82, 107, 124, 128
Arthur, Sir George. . . . 73, 109, 119, 272, 318, 361
Ascot. 253, 353
Asquith, Rt. Hon. H. H.. . . . . . 25, 26, 73, 118, 290, 347, 416
Asset, Lt.-Gen. Sir J . 168, 302, 420
Athens 161
Austria. . 22, 60, 135, 143, 147, 157, 161, 162, 166, 168, 169, 174-179, 193, 210, 222, 233
Austrians 59, 85, 133, 157, 158, 162, 169, 176, 177, 219, 222, 225, 226
Bailleul 108, 110
Bainbridge, Major-General Sir G. 336
Baird, Sir J. 24, 47
Baku . 144, 151, 202, 203, 227, 269, 270
Balfour, Rt. Hon. A.J. . . 39, 42, 73, 109, 124, 153, 155, 191, 197, 246, 254, 272, 313, 322
Balkans . 5, 137, 149, 158-160, 170, 177, 189, 226, 227
Baltic. 119, 192, 220, 238, 296, 305, 307
Bangor, Ireland 403
Barisis 55, 63, 69, 79
Barnes, Rt. Hon. G.N. . . . 10, 72, 98,

Index

99, 105, 138, 152, 164, 169, 180, 196, 200, 227
barrack accommodation... 300, 379
Barthou., M. 27
Batoum ... 178, 187, 198, 202, 203, 227, 254, 265, 267, 269, 272, 273, 278, 280-282, 287, 288, 290, 292, 336, 337
Beatty, Admiral Earl 122, 168, 169, 179, 243, 268, 270, 278, 280, 307, 308, 346, 369
Beauvais .. 102, 103, 106, 117, 136, 139
Beersheba 45
Bele Kuhn 239
Belfast .. 8, 248, 250, 277, 303, 336, 364, 374, 376, 384, 385, 391, 395, 398, 399, 401-403, 407, 408
Belgian Army 46, 137
Belgium... 162, 168, 177, 186, 187, 370, 383, 397
Belin, Gen 177, 229
Benson, Admiral 227
Berthelot, Gen. . 154, 159, 160, 263, 280, 281, 307
Bertie, Sir F. 64
Bessarabia................. 223
Biarritz 331, 332
Birdwood, F.-M. Sir W.R.. 184, 248
"Black and Tans"............ 329
Black Sea.... 57, 58, 152, 158-160, 169, 170, 179, 198, 217, 262, 307
Bliss, Gen. .. 39-41, 43, 46, 47, 60, 64-70, 82-86, 103, 104, 108, 117, 125, 175-178, 212, 218, 224, 227, 229, 232, 241, 252, 256
Blondecques 3, 110, 111
Bolshevism 56, 136, 166, 180, 191, 193, 197, 198, 200, 205, 208, 213, 214, 217, 256, 268, 367
Borden, Sir R. ... 131, 143, 147, 188, 192, 201, 202, 226-228

Botha, Gen. Louis ... 203, 227, 244
Bottomley, Horatio 196
Bouillon, Franklin..... 27, 28, 374
Boulogne.. 3, 78, 95, 103, 111-114, 321
Boundary Commission 389
Boyd Maj.-Gen. Sir G. ... 326, 328
Boyle, Colonel.............. 191
Briand, M...... 335, 346, 382, 383
Bridges, Maj.-Gen. Sir Tom . 31, 99, 104, 389
British Empire Delegates.. 227, 228
Brussa 297, 300, 301
Brussels....... 153, 182, 184, 295
Budapest .. 169, 216, 219, 239, 246
Bulfin, Lt.-Gen. Sir E.S. 284
Bulgaria. 9, 22, 147, 153, 154, 156-158, 160-162, 176-178, 193, 226, 275
Byng, F.-M. Lord . 87, 94, 147, 156
C.I.G.S..... 6, 14, 25, 43, 48, 61, 68, 70-75, 77, 78, 87, 88, 90, 99, 103, 109, 111, 114, 115, 117, 118, 121, 127, 132, 134, 138, 147, 151, 153, 168, 170, 172, 179, 182, 189-191, 193, 194, 197, 198, 201, 205, 212, 236, 240, 246, 247, 249, 255, 257-259, 265, 268, 276, 293-295, 304, 309-311, 317, 319, 327, 338, 341, 344, 345, 349, 351, 353, 356, 358, 364, 367-369, 374, 376, 379, 382, 388, 391, 399
Cabinet . 3-5, 7, 9-11, 15, 17, 20-22, 25, 29, 36, 44, 50, 57, 58, 62, 64, 69, 73, 74, 77, 79, 81, 82, 86-90, 94, 96-100, 102, 105, 106, 109, 112, 113, 118, 119, 127, 128, 131, 132, 138, 140, 146-152, 157, 164, 166, 170, 172, 173, 179, 180, 183-189, 191, 192, 195-197, 199-201, 203, 205, 207,

424 *Index*

208, 235, 236, 244, 248-252, 254-256, 258-269, 271-273, 278, 282-295, 301-306, 308-314, 317, 318, 320, 322-330, 336, 340, 342, 343, 347, 348, 350-353, 355, 357-359, 361-366, 368-370, 372-378, 380-383, 385-387, 389, 394, 395, 398, 399, 402, 403, 405, 407, 409, 411, 416, 419, 421
Cabinet Secretariat 74, 411
Cadorna, Gen. . . . 18, 24, 25, 27, 30, 31, 34, 40, 46, 47, 55, 67, 69, 70
Calais.......... 78, 111-114, 124
Callwell, Maj.-Gen. Sir C. E. 3, 438
Calthorpe, Ad. Sir S. . 169, 170, 173, 175, 180, 232
Camberley................. 412
Cambon, M............. 170, 300
Cambrai......... 54, 63, 153, 164
Cambridge, Duke of 248, 347
Cameron, Gen. A.R. . 288, 396, 398, 407
Cannes............ 197, 382-384
Capel............. 110, 119, 133
Caporetto disaster 17, 27
Carson, Lord . . . 5, 9, 10, 15, 21, 57, 64, 375, 383
Caspian . . . 132, 231, 262, 263, 269, 270, 276, 287
Cassel 149
Cavan, Gen. Earl . 31, 32, 34, 69, 81, 89, 126, 133, 151, 160, 171, 176, 248, 342, 369, 381, 406
Cavendish, Col. F.W.L........ 336
Cecil, Lord Robert. . . . 10, 140, 188, 197, 222, 228, 246, 258, 296, 322, 371, 401, 412
Cenotaph, the .. 258, 318, 321, 371
Central Powers 12, 55
Chamberlain, Rt. Hon. A. . 209, 358, 416
Champagne . 27, 138, 153, 164, 168

Channel ports 45, 53, 113, 117
Chaplin, Visc............... 397
Chatalja............... 273, 297
Chelmsford, Lord 331
Chemin des Dames .. 122, 128, 153
Chequers...... 333, 339, 353, 390
Chetwode, Gen. Sir P..... 319, 330, 387, 389, 406
Churchill, Rt. Hon. W. . . 24, 25, 81, 82, 89, 92, 95-98, 103, 118, 164, 170, 180, 184, 189, 191, 196, 197, 199-202, 203, 205-206, 234-235, 242, 245-246, 248, 251, 255, 258, 260-262, 267, 268, 270, 275, 276, 282-286, 288-292, 301-306, 309-313, 317, 319-320, 322-325, 328, 330, 336, 390-391, 351, 352, 354, 378, 382, 383, 393, 399, 401-402, 406-409
Clemenceau, M... 17, 36-41, 45-47, 50, 54, 59-61, 63, 66-68, 78, 80-82, 84-86, 92-96, 98, 103, 104, 107, 109, 113-115, 117, 125, 127-130, 133, 136, 138, 139, 142, 145, 150, 152, 159-161, 163, 168, 170-174, 182, 185-187, 193, 206, 207, 210, 213, 216, 219, 221, 224, 227, 236, 238, 240-243, 254, 256, 257, 261, 269-271, 367
Clerk, G. 253
Clive, Col. S................ 19
Close, Lieut.-Col. F.M. . . . 16, 40, 50, 155, 182, 279, 309, 310, 336, 355, 356, 410, 412, 414, 416
Coalition Government.... 259, 265, 355, 403
Coblentz .. 221, 274, 330, 331, 335
Collins, Michael 326, 372, 377, 378, 381, 383, 384, 386, 388-390, 401-403, 406, 407, 409

Index

Comber 403
Communists................ 348
Connaught..... 185, 187, 286, 319, 324, 353, 361, 362, 372, 386, 387, 417
Connaught Rangers...... 386, 387
Conscription . 9, 11, 60, 89, 91, 96-99, 102, 105, 116, 118, 142, 150, 152, 157, 158, 164-167, 170, 171, 186, 210
Constantinople . 147, 152, 157, 159, 160, 168, 187, 192, 194, 201, 203, 204, 207, 213, 217, 227, 245, 262, 263, 266, 269, 271-274, 276, 279, 280, 282, 283, 288, 290-292, 295, 297, 299-301, 305, 311, 312, 319, 321, 331, 335, 339, 345, 349, 351-353, 367, 371, 374, 376, 394, 397
Cookstown................. 384
Coote, Mrs............. 360, 361
Cork.. 316, 317, 319, 324-326, 328, 333, 368, 388, 402, 405, 406, 408
Cowan, Ad. Sir H............ 220
Cowans, Gen. Sir J........... 149
Cowes 304, 356, 360-362
Craig, Captain .. 368, 373, 375-377, 385, 387, 389, 390, 393-396, 399, 401, 402, 408, 409
Craig, Sir James......... 389, 406
Creedy, Sir J.H............ 72, 75
Crimea.... 266, 271, 272, 276, 305, 321
Crossfield, Major............ 204
Crowe, Sir Eyre............. 214
Currygrane.................. 8
Curzon, Marq. 5, 10, 18, 72, 89, 138, 164, 165, 169, 173, 185, 189, 192, 196, 201, 203, 207, 243, 254, 256-258, 263, 267, 269, 270, 272, 273, 275, 278-281, 283, 287, 290, 293, 295, 297, 298, 302, 306, 310, 313, 314, 318, 319, 349, 351, 352, 361, 370, 374, 383, 385
Czech Republic............. 167
D'Abernon, Lord........ 314, 333
D'Aosta, Duc.............. 27, 32
D'Esperey, Gen. Franchet . 123, 149, 158, 161, 207, 272
Dail Eireane........ 377, 378, 382
Daily Herald 309, 313
Daily Mail.............. 64, 404
Damascus .. 56, 156, 204, 253, 256
Danesford, Lord 407
Danzig.... 211, 212, 214, 218, 237, 240, 271, 272, 278, 308, 310
Dardanelles 68, 160, 170, 175, 176, 276, 292, 293, 297, 349, 351, 353
Darmstadt 275, 277
Davies, Gen, Sir F.J. . 69, 72, 73, 96, 317, 383
de la Croix, M. 298
Debeney, Gen............... 178
Degoutte, Gen....... 301, 330, 335
Demobilization 176, 180, 182, 183, 187, 194-196, 199
Denikin, Gen. .. 188, 205, 207, 208, 219, 223, 231, 247, 248, 250, 256, 262, 263, 266-268, 270, 276, 287
Derby, Earl of .. 15, 24, 38, 47, 71-75, 96, 106, 112, 133, 160, 172-174, 189, 207, 248
Deschanel, M........... 269, 271
Diaz, Gen. ... 30, 31, 33-35, 80, 81, 133, 151, 167, 176, 214, 218, 233, 258
Dillon, Col. E........... 107, 354
Dominion Home Rule 246, 359
Donaghadee................ 403
Dorchester................. 361
Doullens 77, 79, 93-95, 97, 98, 100, 101, 103, 104, 106, 108, 136
Dover................. 124, 345

426 Index

Downing Street 5, 7, 10, 12, 25,
72-74, 84, 89, 91, 92, 95,
100, 112, 118, 128, 143,
167, 169, 179, 180, 183,
186, 191, 196, 246, 275,
289, 290, 305, 312, 314,
323, 355, 356, 358, 369,
370, 378
Du Cane, Lt.-Gen. Sir J.P. . 105, 107,
110, 115, 119, 124, 125,
128, 129, 133, 137, 140,
141, 145, 150, 151, 158,
171, 174, 384, 391
Dublin 96, 113, 245, 319, 322,
323, 326, 359, 366, 368,
377, 384, 385, 403, 405,
408, 409
Duchesne, Gen. 30
Dufferin, Lord 368
Duisburg 334
Dumont, Mr. 326
Duncannon, Viscount 9, 26, 30,
38, 184, 223, 303
Dunn, R 415
Dyer, Gen. . 265, 284-286, 289, 290,
342
Eastern Command 3, 13, 17, 75
Eastern Front 237
Edward, H.M. King 438
Egypt . . 6, 10, 11, 13, 15, 19, 22, 32,
59, 74, 80, 81, 216, 220,
251, 255, 260, 263, 264,
282-284, 288, 292, 302,
312, 329, 339, 347, 351,
353, 358, 371, 373, 385,
386, 391
Englemere 247, 253
Enzeli 287
Es Sault 152
Esher, Visc 59, 74, 391
Executive Board . 68-70, 76, 79-81,
84, 85, 101, 117
Feisul, Emir 191, 204, 253, 254,
256, 275
Fifth Army 89, 90, 95, 105, 167,
172, 421
Fisher, Ad. Lord 118, 256, 328,
336, 337, 351, 352
Fitzalan, Lord 363, 379, 384
Fiume 178, 184, 216, 220, 222,
237, 238, 272
Flanders . . . 3, 11, 12, 16, 19, 21, 22,
45, 54, 70, 79, 110, 112,
114, 123, 127, 132, 156,
167
Foch, Marshal . 2, 12, 13, 17, 18, 22,
23, 27-37, 39-41, 43, 46, 47, 49,
55, 61, 63-65, 67-70, 79-
82, 84, 85, 87, 88, 91-98,
100, 102-108, 110, 111,
114-117, 119, 121, 123-
130, 133-142, 144-146,
149-152, 154, 155, 158-
164, 170-180, 182, 185-
187, 190, 198, 201, 202,
204, 208, 210-219, 221,
222, 224, 225, 227-231,
234, 235, 238-241, 246-
248, 250, 252, 261, 269-
272, 274, 278-281, 293,
296, 298, 300-302, 307,
308, 314, 320, 332-335,
341, 342, 346, 349, 369,
370, 386, 395, 417
Fontainebleau 194, 212, 216
Foreign Office 6, 81, 153, 197,
198, 201-203, 233, 257,
267, 275, 278, 290, 308,
314, 319, 327, 333, 353,
370, 384, 389
Fourth Army 32, 94, 107, 131
France 4, 5, 7, 8, 12, 13, 19, 23,
25, 29, 32, 33, 35, 36, 41,
48, 59, 62, 65, 81, 83, 84,
86, 90, 91, 95, 96, 103,
107, 109-111, 114, 117,
118, 121, 125, 127, 130-
133, 136-138, 143, 145,
149, 151, 153, 158, 162,
168, 172, 186, 187, 192,
195, 196, 200, 202, 210,
211, 213, 219, 223, 225,
242, 243, 253, 270, 282,
292, 307, 309, 314, 317,

Index 427

324, 326, 370, 371, 382, 397, 416
Frankfurt 275, 277
Frazier, Mr. 47, 55, 60, 117, 163
French . 3, 4, 6-8, 10-14, 16-18, 20-23, 25-31, 33-37, 39-41, 44-47, 49, 50, 53, 57, 60, 61, 64, 69, 75, 79, 82-87, 89-92, 95-100, 103-108, 110-119, 121-123, 125-131, 133, 134, 136-140, 142-144, 150, 152-155, 158-160, 162, 164, 166, 168, 170-172, 175, 186, 188, 190, 198, 203, 204, 206-209, 211, 213, 215-217, 221, 223, 225, 227, 232-234, 239, 240, 244-249, 252-254, 256, 258, 261, 269, 273, 274, 277-279, 281, 291, 293, 296, 298, 306-309, 311, 321, 329, 331, 332, 339, 342, 347, 349, 351, 363, 366, 367, 374, 376, 380, 382, 384, 393, 394, 420
French, Col. C.N. 366
French, Sir John . 14, 15, 20, 22-24, 26, 47, 82, 96-98, 107, 118, 119, 122, 124, 137, 141, 158, 170, 183, 245, 277, 384, 391
Gairloch. 365, 402
Gallipoli 159, 160
Galway 8
gas attack. 12
Gatchina 257
Gathorne-Hardy, Maj.-Gen. Hon. G.F. 36
Gaza. 45
Geddes, Sir Auckland 125, 158, 183, 196, 256, 341
Geddes, Sir E. 9, 19, 39, 41, 82, 96, 97, 124, 180, 183, 218, 262, 268, 284, 313, 340, 346, 356, 373, 380, 381, 384, 387, 391, 396

Geddes Committee . . 356, 373, 380, 384, 396
General Reserve . 46, 61, 66, 68-70, 74, 76-85, 87, 88, 93, 101, 105
General Staff 75, 134, 149, 287, 311, 349, 357, 358, 367, 369, 386, 391, 420, 421
George V, H.M. King . . 8, 96, 120-122, 145, 152, 180, 183, 189, 244, 246, 250, 251, 259, 286, 318, 320, 361, 362, 385, 417
Germany . 22, 58, 59, 161, 162, 168, 169, 175, 177, 178, 180, 184, 187, 192, 197, 202, 206, 208-210, 213, 215, 218, 219, 234, 235, 238, 240, 243, 261, 270, 274, 302, 314, 335
Gissler, Gen. 297, 300
Glasgow. 204, 288, 411, 412
Golden Horn 273, 291
Gough, Col. J, E. 87, 94, 103
Gouraud, General 40, 256, 331, 334
Granet, Sir Guy 83, 85
Grant, Col. C.J.C. 204, 239, 250, 338, 377, 405
Great Britain 29, 273, 277, 283, 344, 354, 355, 359, 373, 382, 399, 409, 416
Great War 157, 414, 421, 438
Greece 12, 49, 50, 56, 177, 216, 257, 275, 280, 321, 324, 332, 339, 347, 349, 352, 353
Greenwood, Hamar . . 289, 315, 319, 323-325, 328, 350, 379, 390, 401, 407
Grey, Sir E. 416
Grigg, E. 411
Griscom, Lt.-Col. L.C.. 165
Grove End . . 16, 255, 291, 323, 412
Guest, Hon. F. 19, 236, 246, 248, 413
Guillaumat, Gen. . . . 49, 55, 117, 149, 158-160

Guise 359
Gwynne, H.A. 75
Haifa 152
Haig, Field-Marshal Earl 4-6,
  11, 14, 17, 18, 20-27, 48,
  50, 51, 54, 55, 61, 63, 64,
  66, 67, 70, 74, 78-85, 87-
  95, 103-108, 110, 111, 114-
  119, 121, 122, 125, 127-
  131, 134, 135, 138-142,
  144-146, 149-156, 164,
  167, 168, 171-175, 178,
  185, 189, 192, 199-202,
  243, 246, 249, 420
Haking, Gen. Sir F. 224, 308
Haldane, Gen. Sir A. . 301, 304, 311, 327
Hall, Admiral Sir R. . . . 11, 104, 243, 277, 330, 385, 404, 413-415
Haller, General 211
Hamilton, Lord Claud 122, 126, 413
Hamilton, Lieut.-Col. P.D. 32
Hamilton-Gordon, Lt.-Gen. Sir A. 122, 126
Hankey, Lt.-Col. Sir Maurice . . . 24,
  26, 46, 47, 57, 68, 73,
  74, 83, 84, 92, 95, 103,
  144, 158, 160, 163, 164,
  175, 177, 186, 191, 212,
  214, 217, 221, 222, 226,
  228, 230, 237, 242, 249,
  269, 391, 411
Hardinge, Lord 8
Harington, Gen. Sir C. H. . . . 36, 118, 299, 311, 319, 349, 374
Harris, Sir C. 381, 382
Havre 242
Hazebrouck 108, 112, 114, 129, 145
Heath, Maj.-Gen. Sir C. . 57, 74, 166
Henderson, Rt. Hon. A. . . . 5, 10, 11
Hicks, Rt. Hon. Joynson 401
Hindenburg Line 147-150, 153, 156, 164, 175
Holland, Lieut.-Gen, Sir A. . . . 6, 41, 180, 205, 208, 225

Home Rule 106, 113, 118, 246,
  256, 258-260, 263, 328,
  359, 387
Home Rule Bill 113, 118, 256,
  258, 260, 328, 387
Hope, Admiral 160, 217, 219
Horne, Sir Robert 94, 154, 178,
  179, 192, 268, 313, 314,
  316, 318, 340, 393
House, Col. . . . 39, 43, 46, 176, 206
House of Lords 340, 354, 416
Houthoulst Forest 153
Hughes, Mr. 132, 143, 144, 147,
  152, 188, 189, 192, 227,
  244
Huguet, Gen. 248, 362, 395
Hunding Line 168
Hungary . . . 135, 157, 168, 174, 176,
  178, 179, 193, 213, 222,
  223, 239, 246, 247
Hunter, Sir Charles . . 286, 289, 290
Hussein, King of the Hejaz 253
Hutchison, Col. Sir R. 104
Hymans, M. 298
Hythe 293
Imperial Conference . 131, 356, 357
Indemnity 346
India . . . 58, 63, 121, 125, 151, 179,
  196, 200, 216, 220, 229,
  233, 235, 251, 255, 260,
  262-264, 267, 283-285,
  288, 292, 301-304, 311,
  312, 316, 319, 329, 331,
  347, 352, 353, 357, 358,
  363-365, 369, 371, 373,
  383, 386, 391, 395, 412
Inverness 364, 365
Ireland . . . 3, 7-9, 11, 60, 64, 77, 78,
  82, 89, 91, 92, 96-99, 102,
  103, 105, 113, 116, 118,
  119, 142, 150, 152, 157,
  158, 164-168, 170, 171,
  190, 193, 199, 200, 202,
  218, 220, 231, 232, 246,
  251, 255, 259, 260, 262-
  265, 267, 273, 276, 277,
  283-285, 288, 289, 291,

Index

292, 294-296, 299-304, 307, 309, 312-314, 316, 317, 320, 322-325, 328-330, 333, 336, 338-340, 344, 346-355, 357, 359, 360, 362, 363, 365, 368, 372-374, 377, 379, 380, 382, 383, 387-391, 394, 396, 398, 399, 401-409, 415, 417, 421
Ironside, Major-Gen. Sir E..... 223, 224, 238, 247, 316
Ismid 291, 293, 295, 297, 337
Italy . . 13, 15, 17, 22, 24-30, 32, 34, 35, 37, 41, 45, 46, 54-56, 58, 62, 69, 73, 78, 80, 81, 83-85, 87, 96, 117, 125, 126, 133, 136, 143, 158, 162, 165-168, 177, 183, 207, 213, 222, 225, 226, 229, 230, 232, 237, 278, 292, 370, 420
Jacob, F.-M. Sir Claud 369
Jaffa...................... 45
Japan . . . 86, 88, 190, 367, 368, 370
Jeffreys, Maj.-Gen. Sir P.D. 341-343
Jellicoe, Admiral Visc. 126
Jerusalem................ 45, 56
Jeudwine, Lieut.-Gen. H.S..... 323, 325, 326
Kameneff. . 295, 305, 306, 308-310, 312, 313, 329
Karl, Emperor of Austria...... 176
Kemal, Mustapha . . . 291, 299, 321, 331, 345, 351, 352, 374
Kemmel Hill 114
Kerr,, Philip. . 14, 57, 97, 158, 164, 177, 206, 228, 411
Keyes, Ad. Sir Roger. 184
Kharkov................... 247
Kiev................... 247, 256
Kiggell, Sir L. . . 3-4, 18, 26, 50-51, 62
Kitchener, Lord.............. 73
Klotz, M................ 27, 145
Knox, Maj.-Gen. Sir W.A. 132, 140, 200

Kolchak, General. . . . 205, 207, 208, 212, 222, 225, 238, 256, 259
Krassin . . . 288, 295, 305, 306, 308, 310, 312, 313, 323, 329, 337, 348
Kutahia 359
labour unrest 348
Lake Garda 33, 36
Langemarck................ 153
Law, Rt. Hon. A. Bonar. . 4-7, 9-11, 14, 15, 18, 38, 59, 69, 72, 73, 88, 89, 91, 92, 95-98, 105, 118, 148, 152-154, 162-164, 167, 168, 173, 180, 185, 186, 188, 196, 197, 199-202, 213, 218, 224, 226-228, 230, 232, 254, 256, 263, 283, 286, 290, 303, 306, 313, 315-316, 320, 322-326, 328, 329, 336, 348, 350, 353, 354, 359, 360, 365, 368, 377, 384, 388, 391, 399, 406, 409, 416
Lawrence, Gen. Sir H. . . . 62, 66, 78, 89, 90, 93-95, 103, 106, 110, 114, 115, 117, 122, 125, 128, 129, 131, 142, 145, 150, 173, 191, 199
Le Cateau 164, 171
League of Nations . . . 165, 190-192, 197, 203-205, 209-211, 213, 221, 222, 225, 228, 237, 244, 256, 258, 272, 273, 306, 310, 329, 335, 336
Lemberg 211, 212, 218
Lenin 269, 339, 348
Lewin, Lady Edwina 334
Lewin, Freddy (Wilson's godson) 253
Leygues, M............. 324, 325
Liddell, Sir Robert............. 9
Lille........... 4, 145, 163, 167
Lisburn 384, 385
Liverpool. . 204, 288, 323, 340, 344,

430 *Index*

413, 416
Lloyd George, Rt. Hon.. 5, 6, 9, 12-14, 17, 18, 20-30, 35, 37-43, 46-50, 54, 57-60, 62-64, 66-68, 70-74, 78, 81, 83, 84, 86, 89, 91, 92, 95-99, 102-104, 106, 108, 109, 112, 113, 117-119, 122, 124-128, 132, 135-140, 142, 143, 148-152, 154, 158-171, 173, 175-180, 184-189, 191-193, 195-200, 203, 206, 208-214, 216-222, 224-239, 242, 245, 248, 249, 255-257, 261, 263, 265, 267, 269-273, 275, 277-280, 288, 289, 291-300, 302, 303, 305-310, 312-318, 320-326, 328, 329, 332-337, 339, 341-344, 346-349, 351-354, 356-359, 362, 363, 365-367, 369-376, 379, 380, 382-384, 386, 387, 389, 390, 393-395, 398, 399, 401, 403, 404, 406, 411
London . 4-6, 12, 17, 18, 20, 22, 25, 39, 50-52, 54, 55, 57, 59, 68, 70, 75, 81, 82, 85-88, 90, 91, 104, 108, 109, 115, 122, 131, 138, 142, 147, 163, 164, 176, 179, 182, 185, 189-191, 201, 203-205, 208, 212, 220, 221, 227, 233, 238, 241, 244, 246, 250, 253, 258, 261, 271, 282, 287, 301, 302, 304, 308, 312, 321, 322, 332, 337, 340-342, 346, 347, 352, 355-357, 362, 369, 378, 381, 385, 387, 388, 395, 396, 398, 403, 408, 415, 416
Londonderry .. 277, 380, 383, 400-402
Loos. 63

Ludendorff, Gen.. . . . 11, 21, 98, 144, 153, 174
Lympne 307, 346
Lys. 102, 116, 171
Macdonald, Rt. Hon. R. 10, 11
Macdonogh, Gen. Sir G. 24, 148, 149, 158, 187, 406
Maclean, Sir D. 396
Macpherson, Ian 166, 256, 262
Macready., Gen. Sir N. 148, 355, 363
Madrid. 330, 332
Mangin, General 139-141, 153
Man-Power Bill (1918). 102
Marne 102, 116, 123, 124, 129, 140, 142
Martello towers 124
Mary, H.M. Queen 152, 242
massacres. . 232, 250, 252, 254, 417
Maurice, Maj;-Gen. Sir F. . . 26-28, 66, 97, 105, 118
Maxse, L. 59, 391
Mayence 221, 274, 331
McCalmont, Col. R.C.A. 378
McSwinney, Lord Mayor of Cork 317
Mediterranean 62, 63, 116, 119, 126, 232, 291, 340, 341
Mesopotamia. . 8, 19, 22, 45, 58, 59, 62, 63, 78, 81, 125, 147, 166, 213, 251, 255, 275, 276, 282, 283, 286-288, 290, 292, 295, 301, 302, 304-306, 309, 311, 314, 316, 326, 327, 329, 331, 351, 353, 371, 378, 379, 387, 397
Mesopotamia Report 8
Metz 145, 163, 167, 223
Mildmay of Fleet, Lord 393
Millerand, M. . . 271, 278, 280, 281, 293, 298, 302, 307, 308, 324, 395
Millet, M. 217
Milne, Gen. Sir George . . . 152, 154, 162, 170, 189, 268, 271, 272, 276, 281, 288, 291-

Index

293, 297, 300, 311
Milner. Visc... 5, 13-15, 18, 21, 29, 38, 39, 42, 46, 56-58, 60, 62, 66, 67, 70-75, 78, 79, 84, 86, 89-99, 101, 110, 112-117, 119, 121, 123-130, 132, 136-140, 143, 148-152, 158, 164, 165, 167-176, 178-180, 183, 187-189, 191, 192, 195, 196, 205, 208, 233, 235, 246, 248, 254, 288, 293, 306, 313, 329
miners' strike........... 312, 344
Moggridge, F....... 255, 291, 366
Moir, Sir E................ 122
Monash, Lt.-Gen. Sir J........ 146
Money, Maj.-Gen. Sir A..... 6, 176, 275, 283, 315, 327, 346, 352, 353, 365, 369, 378, 381, 400
Monro, General Sir C. 121, 235, 316
Montagu, Rt. Hon. E.... 212, 233, 254, 262, 263, 269, 290, 329, 331, 351, 352, 390, 397
Montagu of Beaulieu, Lord..... 18
Montdidier.. 97, 106, 125, 128, 131, 142, 144
Montreuil... 50, 78, 90, 93, 94, 103, 114, 128, 185
Morland, Gen. Sir T.. 335, 342, 376
Moscow........... 257, 284, 306
Mount Stewart.. 277, 402, 403, 407
munitions.. 136, 163, 171, 202, 248, 289, 352, 353
Murmansk..... 119, 131, 132, 188, 192, 202, 209, 216, 217, 305, 419
Murray, Gen. Sir A............ 17
Naval Liaison Committee 52
Near East.. 137, 268, 290, 293, 311, 314, 321
newspapers . 75, 168, 174, 203, 261, 305, 351, 355, 357, 361, 399
Newtownards.............. 403

Nicholson, John......... 384, 385
Nieuport 11, 14, 41
Nish..................... 159
Nivelle, Gen.......... 16, 48, 420
North Russia 247, 249, 256
North Sea.................. 39
Northcliffe, Visc....... 15, 47, 404
Northumberland 383, 391
Norwich................... 416
Noyon 106, 125, 126, 128, 142
Occupation, Army of... 17, 30, 160, 163, 167, 168, 176, 185, 187-189, 196, 199, 204, 221, 222, 224, 230, 233, 236, 237, 253, 281, 307, 324, 331, 334, 345, 378
Odessa.... 57, 217, 219, 266, 270-272
Ollivant, Lieut.-Col. A.H....... 61
Omsk......... 192, 200, 202, 259
Orange Clubs............... 273
Orangemen 389, 408
Orlando .. 27, 28, 36, 46, 66, 67, 82, 86, 117, 158, 160, 161, 177, 178, 185-187, 216, 220-222, 224, 226, 230, 232, 237, 238
Orpen, Sir W. 208
Ostend........ 4, 16, 21, 167, 184
Ottoman Empire 170, 265, 268, 291
Oxford................ 242, 386
O'Connor, Sir James......... 381
Padua....... 30-32, 34, 36, 37, 67
Painlevé, M. .. 3, 12, 14, 22, 23, 25, 27, 28
Palestine .. 9, 10, 19-21, 58, 59, 61-63, 78, 81, 125, 132, 136, 147, 151, 152, 160, 161, 166, 213, 227, 253, 267, 275, 282, 283, 288, 291, 292, 304, 312, 351, 371, 378, 397, 404
Panouse, Gen. Vicomte de la... 382, 395
Paris.... 9-11, 23, 26-29, 36-39, 41, 47, 51, 54, 59, 61, 62, 64,

432 Index

65, 68, 78, 80, 91-93, 95-97, 100, 103, 105, 107, 112, 116, 123, 141, 142, 158, 159, 166, 170-172, 186, 187, 189, 192, 194, 197, 199, 200, 203, 205, 207-213, 215-219, 221-224, 226, 227, 231, 234-241, 243, 245-247, 251, 252, 257, 261, 264, 267-269, 271, 272, 278, 279, 295, 308, 309, 330-332, 341, 349, 352, 363, 370, 375, 386, 394
Peace Congress 186, 204
Peace Treaty ... 243, 258, 259, 272, 274, 306
Pelle, Gen. 331
Percy 293, 306, 329
Pershing, Gen. ... 26, 27, 60, 61, 63, 65, 66, 91, 95, 103, 104, 115, 117, 126, 131, 147, 164, 170- 173, 177, 178, 243, 246, 248, 252, 370-372
Persia 147, 258, 262, 263, 265, 267, 282, 287, 288, 290-293, 295, 302, 304-306, 309, 314, 316, 326, 327, 330, 381
Persia, Shah of. 258
Peschiera 30
Pétain, Marshal .. 18, 25, 26, 39, 45, 50, 51, 54, 60, 61, 63, 67, 78, 80-82, 84, 85, 87, 88, 91-94, 103-105, 117, 121, 123, 125, 141, 171, 173, 228, 240, 241
Petrograd.. 223, 225, 226, 256, 257
Piave line. 32, 35, 36, 41
Piggott, Col. F.S.G. 367
Plebiscite question. 324
Pleiad, Wilson's yacht. ... 373, 411
Plumer, Field-Marshal Lord 29, 31, 36, 70, 73, 81, 94, 108, 110, 111, 121, 149, 153, 192
Poincaré, M. . 92, 94, 258, 271, 395

Polecappele 153
police strike (1918) 135, 148
Polk, F.L. 252, 256
Poole, Maj.-Gen. Sir F.C. . 131, 132, 144
Porro, Gen. 27, 28, 33-35
Portuguese.......... 10, 106, 108
Price-Davies, Col. 69
Prilep.................... 152
Prime Ministers.. 14, 29, 44, 65, 67, 131, 132, 143, 160, 162, 163, 188, 197, 198, 210, 308, 384
Prinkipo... 202, 205, 206, 218, 310
Quartermaster-General 62
Quatre-bis (French War Office).. 40
Radcliffe, Maj.-Gen. Sir P. de B.
  .. 118, 148, 160, 200, 270, 311
railway strike... 152, 187, 204, 245, 314
Ramsay, Lieut. Burnet...... 10, 11
Rantzau, Herr 230
Rapallo .. 17, 27, 29, 30, 39, 40, 44
Rawlinson, Gen. Lord .. 75, 78, 80-82, 84, 85-87, 92, 107, 131, 141, 142, 146, 147, 153, 154, 156, 248, 249, 319, 178, 179, 192, 285, 304, 319, 331, 362
Reading, Earl.. 60, 89, 97, 102, 144, 147, 164, 169, 170, 186, 228, 240, 286, 338, 372, 391, 394, 418
recruiting... 20, 141, 183, 346, 372
repatriation of German prisoners of war 177, 251
Repington, Lt.-Col. 314
Reservists 343-346
Rethondes 179
Rheims. 50, 87, 123, 124, 127, 139-141, 154
Rhenish Provinces... 175, 186, 208, 222
Rhine..... 161-163, 165, 167, 175, 178, 185, 186, 189, 190, 199-202, 205, 208, 215,

219, 222, 228-230, 234, 237, 238, 240-242, 251, 260, 268, 275, 288, 312-314, 318, 324, 327, 328, 330, 333, 339-343, 345, 349, 350, 376, 380, 397
Ribot, M............ 3, 12, 36, 48
Riddell, Lord........... 158, 305
Rifle Brigades.......... 249, 319
Roberts, F.-M. Earl.. 268, 416, 418
Robertson, F.-M. Sir William
. 6, 13, 14, 17, 18, 20, 22-25, 27-30, 39, 40, 42, 43, 46-50, 54, 55, 57-59, 61, 63-75, 80, 87, 93, 121, 180, 196, 203, 240, 314, 330, 335
Roche, Sergeant............. 378
Roman Catholics.... 401, 408, 415, 417
Rosetti, Col................ 159
Roullers............... 153, 154
Ruhr.. 274, 275, 278, 279, 281, 301, 307, 335, 346, 380
Rumania ... 25, 27, 28, 41, 46, 112, 154, 158-160, 162, 168, 169, 178, 179, 191, 246, 269
Rumbold, Sir H............. 319
Rupprecht, Prince .. 125, 138, 140-142
Russia .. 4, 6, 13, 15, 22, 25, 26, 28, 41, 45, 48, 58, 88, 112, 119, 131, 164, 177, 179, 188, 191, 192, 197, 198, 202, 205-207, 211-213, 220, 223, 224, 246, 247, 249, 256-259, 268, 269, 282, 292, 295, 296, 302, 309, 314, 419
Ryle..................... 317
Sackville-West, Maj.-Gen. the Hon. Sir C. ("Tit Willow")
.... 26, 36, 38, 40, 46, 82, 107, 116, 117, 119, 133, 138, 142, 158, 159, 163, 177, 178, 252, 295, 341, 342, 395
Salonika.... 6, 9, 10, 12, 13, 32, 41, 46, 49, 50, 55, 81, 115, 117, 125, 136, 137, 149, 152, 161, 166, 183
San Remo 265, 278, 282
Sandhurst.................. 414
Sarrail, Gen...... 5, 10, 12, 49, 50
Scapa Flow 241
Scarpe 88, 98
Schiedmann government...... 240
Seckt, General von .. 297, 299, 335
Second Army... 19, 32, 34, 81, 108, 149, 171, 173, 174
Selle River................. 168
Serbia 160-162, 177, 178
Sèvres, Treaty of 307, 335, 395
Sforza, Count........... 298, 324
Sharman-Crawford, Col....... 142
Shortt, Rt. Hon. E.... 142, 158, 328, 340, 343, 344
Siberia .. 82, 86, 125, 132, 135, 136, 140, 144, 179, 190, 205, 212, 223, 249, 256, 265, 367
Silesia ... 237, 251, 327, 333, 339-341, 343-345, 347, 349, 350, 354, 376, 397
Simon, Dr. von .. 89, 297-300, 335
Sinn Fein..... 8, 96, 295, 300, 301, 303, 325, 356, 368, 374, 377, 380, 382, 398, 408
Smyrna ... 216, 226, 227, 229-232, 257, 275, 280, 292, 293, 297, 300, 301, 331, 332, 334, 335, 345, 349, 353, 367, 371, 372, 374, 394
Snow, Lieut.-Gen. Sir T.D.O. 15, 327
Sofia 159, 162, 219
Soissons.. 55, 63, 69, 124, 126, 139
Solly-Flood, Maj.-Gen. A...... 402, 403, 407
Somaliland................. 260
Somme... 89, 95, 98-100, 105, 107, 108, 113, 114, 116, 117, 127, 129, 141, 146, 155

South Africa 220
Spa.. 214, 215, 217, 224, 282, 295-298, 301, 304, 314
Spa Conference 295
Spender, Lt.-Col. W.B. ... 375, 376, 398, 401
St. James's Palace 333
St. Omer 108, 111, 124
St. Paul's Cathedral 416, 418
St. Quentin 77, 88, 159, 420
Staff College 273, 412, 419
Stanley, Lt.-Col. Hon. G.F. 372, 373, 381
Stephanik 211
Stockholm 10
Strickland, Lieut.-Gen. Sir E. ... 328, 360
strikes 135, 148, 152, 167, 187, 204, 205, 245, 255, 262-266, 268, 273, 295, 298, 304, 309, 312-316, 318, 330, 338, 339, 341, 343, 344, 346, 349-351, 354, 359, 376
Studd, Col. H. W. ... 51, 57, 62, 64, 133
Sturdee, Admiral Sir D. 248
Supreme War Council ... 15, 17, 22, 29, 34, 37, 39-41, 43, 44, 46, 49, 52, 53, 55, 59, 60, 65, 66, 71, 75, 76, 82, 84-87, 101, 102, 115, 117, 131, 133, 135, 137, 138, 150, 163, 177, 178, 217, 248, 268, 270, 272, 331, 346, 421
Swaine, Maj.-Gen. Sir L.V. 319
Switzerland 41, 48, 59, 60, 87, 190, 210
Sykes, Maj.-Gen. Sir F. 51, 62, 165, 203, 204, 234
Syria .. 22, 156, 167, 203, 204, 213, 216, 227, 233-235, 253, 275, 282, 283, 297, 331, 371
Talbot, Lord Edmund 24, 290
tanks .. 24, 25, 81, 82, 94, 141, 154, 159, 162, 191, 199, 340
Tardieu, M. 136, 224, 229, 233-235
Taylor, Colonel W. Pitt 223
Territorial Army 245, 254, 258, 266, 358
Thiepval 375
Third Army 32, 89, 90, 92, 95, 146
Thomas, J. H. 4, 255, 256, 289, 341, 344
Thompson, Graham 104
Thomson, Lord 219
Thomson, Sir Basil 309, 312
Thurles 379
Thwaites, Lt.-Gen. Sir W. 148, 222, 224, 275, 310
Tide (police constable) 56, 135, 147, 190, 361
Times, the .. 4, 50, 51, 53, 100, 109, 115, 131, 139, 239, 259, 271, 356, 370, 380, 396, 397, 403, 404, 417
Tittoni Signor 252
'Tit Willow" (See Sackville-West)
Todmorden 404
Tokio 367, 368
Townshend, General 169
Trade Unions 167
Transcaucasia ... 56, 144, 188, 198, 207, 213, 250, 262, 265, 267
Transport Sub-Committee of Cabinet 268
Trans-Jordania 304, 336
Tudor, Maj.-Gen. Sir H. ... 284, 315, 328
Turkey 9, 13, 22, 153, 158-162, 169, 176-178, 187, 192, 193, 204, 230, 233, 234, 257, 262, 274-276, 279, 280, 292, 295, 299, 335, 339, 345, 347, 349, 352, 353, 356, 357, 372, 374
Udine 25
Ulster 5, 8, 142, 189, 201, 250, 273, 277, 279, 303, 328, 340, 341, 362, 363, 368,

Index

Unionists 296
Unknown Warrior .. 295, 321, 369-371
Valenciennes... 153, 168, 171, 178
Vardar 152
Venice 32, 41
Venizelos, M. ... 46, 177, 219, 229-232, 257, 273, 275, 280, 292-294, 297, 298, 300, 301, 321, 332, 351, 352, 367, 374
Ventry, Lord 338
Verdun 87, 171
Verdun (destroyer) 321
Verona 30-32
Versailles.... 15, 22, 28, 29, 35-37, 40, 41, 43, 47, 50-76, 78, 79, 83, 86, 87, 90-94, 98, 101, 107, 108, 113, 116, 123-125, 127, 128, 133, 136, 138, 142, 148, 155, 158-160, 173, 206, 216, 223, 225, 226, 230, 231, 239, 243, 246, 248, 251, 265, 273, 276, 295, 306, 308, 347, 421
Vesle 123, 141, 144
Vicenza 30, 31, 33, 133
Victoria, Princess (Princess Louis of Battenberg) .. 74, 90, 95, 158, 244, 246-248, 250, 258, 316, 318, 389
Villers-Bretonneux .. 114, 115, 141, 145
Vistula 309
Vladivostok 119, 136
Wake, Col. Hereward . 51, 57, 264, 288, 323, 348, 358, 402
Wales.. 24, 244, 247, 342, 343, 412
War Cabinet .. 3-5, 7, 9, 10, 15, 17, 20-22, 25, 36, 50, 58, 62, 64, 77, 79, 81, 82, 86-90, 94, 96, 97, 99, 100, 102, 105, 106, 112, 119, 127, 369, 372-377, 382-385, 387-391, 393-396, 398-403, 406-408, 417

128, 132, 138, 146-152, 166, 170, 172, 173, 179, 183, 184, 187, 189, 191, 192, 196, 199, 203, 205
War Council . 15, 17, 18, 22, 23, 25, 29, 34, 37, 39-41, 43, 44, 46, 49, 52, 53, 55, 59, 60, 65, 66, 71, 75, 76, 82, 84-87, 101, 102, 115, 117, 131, 133, 135, 137, 138, 150, 163, 177, 178, 217, 248, 268, 270, 272, 331, 346, 421
Warsaw ... 203, 204, 306-308, 311, 329
Washington 68, 102, 132, 163, 190, 258, 366, 367, 369, 370
Waterloo 184, 249
Wemyss, Ad. Lord.... 97, 117, 119, 124, 158, 164, 167, 168, 170, 179, 180, 186, 248
Weser 239-241
Western Front ... 16, 19, 32, 36, 48, 49, 55, 56, 58, 59, 65, 68, 77, 81, 83, 86, 88, 89, 95, 100, 103-105, 116, 123, 132, 134, 139, 143, 144, 146, 151, 153, 155, 156, 164, 167, 169, 171, 195, 420
Westminster Abbey.. 286, 317, 318, 321, 322
White Heather (Wilson's yacht) 302, 360, 373
White Sea 247
Wilson, Lady... 19, 248, 274, 330-332, 360, 361, 402, 404, 415-417
Wilson, President ... 11, 67, 86, 88, 97, 99, 102, 115, 135, 140, 144, 157, 159, 161, 162, 164, 165, 169, 171, 172, 174, 176, 179, 182, 183, 188, 189, 191, 193, 198, 203, 206, 210, 212, 216, 219, 221, 224, 227, 230-

436 *Index*

233, 235, 237-239, 241, 242, 252, 257, 276, 281, 282, 306, 367
Windsor................. 378
Wing, Gen. 99, 166, 298, 361
Wolfe-Murray, Gen. Sir J...... 17
Wolseley, F.-M. Visc..... 416, 418
Worthington-Evans, Sir L. 295, 330, 336, 347, 353, 369, 373, 396
Wrangel, Gen... 305, 307-309, 321
Wroughton, Col. J........... 379
Wytschaete 110, 153
Yeomanry 152, 381, 386
Ypres.... 12, 16, 18, 106, 108, 112, 114, 143, 149, 150
Yudenitch, Gen. 223, 256, 257, 259
Yugo-Slavs 184, 186
Zeebrugge 4, 16, 168, 184

About the Author

Charles Edward Callwell (1859-1928) was a renowned writer on military affairs, as well as a staff officer. Serving as the Director of Military Intelligence for the War Office for most of the Great War, he rose to the rank of Major-General before returning to journalism and writing in October 1918.

www.ingramcontent.com/pod-product-compliance
Lightning Source LLC
Chambersburg PA
CBHW050158240426
43671CB00013B/2169